Advances in Cognition, Education, and Deafness

David S. Martin, Editor

Gallaudet University Press
Washington, D.C.

Gallaudet University Press, Washington, DC 20002
© 1991 by Gallaudet University. All rights reserved
Published 1991
Printed in the United States of America

Library of Congress Cataloging-in-Publication Data

Advances in cognition, education, and deafness / David S. Martin,
    editor.
        p. cm.
    "Second International Symposium on Cognition, Education, and
    Deafness . . . Gallaudet University . . . July 1989"—Foreword.
    Includes bibliographical references and index.
    ISBN 0-930323-79-3
        1. Deaf—Education—Congresses. 2. Cognition—Congresses.
    I. Martin, David S. II. International Symposium on Cognition,
    Education, and Deafness (2nd : 1989 : Gallaudet University)
    HV2430.A38 1991
    371.91'2—dc20   91-10693
                                                                   CIP

The paper used in this publication meets the minimum requirements of American
National Standard for Information Sciences—Permanence of Paper for Printed
Library Materials, ANSI Z39.48-1984.

CONTENTS

9 **Programs for Applied Research**

FOREWORD

In 1984, Gallaudet College (now University) hosted the First International Symposium on Cognition, Education, and Deafness. It is impossible to overstate the importance of this event. Never before had researchers, scholars, and teachers from these three fields come together to share their work, discuss their points of view, and learn from each other. It was a singularly successful conference, accomplishing even more than the organizers had hoped. From the conference came a book, *Cognition, Education, and Deafness*. Publication of this book extended the excitement of the conference to a wider audience and subsequently led to a second conference.

The Second International Symposium on Cognition, Education, and Deafness took place on the Gallaudet University campus in July 1989. Nearly fifty presentations were made, and the symposium attracted more than 250 participants from seventeen different nations. The symposium opened with a keynote address from Dr. Ursula Bellugi of the Salk Institute and closed with another keynote address from Dr. Howard Pollio of the University of Tennessee. Dr. Bellugi has spent much of her career studying the acquisition and use of sign language by deaf people. Dr. Pollio, a psychologist, has studied cognition from many different perspectives, but never before had he focused on the implications of deafness.

Dr. Bellugi, an "insider," began by reminding the participants to look at the *capacities* of deaf individuals, not their *deficiencies*. She then described her twenty years of research on sign language. During the first ten years, she and the others in her lab had found that the properties of signed and spoken languages are very much the same, with similar organizational principles and complexity of grammar. Although they are very different on the surface, at deeper levels the languages appear to be much the same. More recently, Dr. Bellugi and her colleagues have been studying the effect that learning a visual language has on the brain.

Dr. Pollio, an "outsider," ended the conference by giving us the benefit of an outsider's point of view. He was able to observe the issues openly and objectively, without the biases and preconceptions often seen among those of us who spend our lives studying deafness. He cautioned the participants to be careful about how they define deafness, since their definitions will guide their thinking, research, and conclusions about deaf people. I was moved by his conclusion that "researchers in deafness must never lose sight of their phenomenon: the world as lived and experienced by the deaf person."

The symposium was highly stimulating, with a wide variety of viewpoints and perspectives. Papers were presented in the areas of cognitive assessment, cognitive development, cognitive intervention programs, cognitive processes, language and cognition, and neuroscientific issues. In addition, the demonstration sessions enabled participants to see firsthand what is being done in applications in the field. This volume now presents those papers to the scientific and academic community. The publication of this second volume will add a great deal to the field of deafness research. Students of cognition, education, or language will benefit greatly from this collection of some of the best current thinking in the field.

My personal thanks go to Dr. David Martin for his leadership both in the symposia and in the editing of the resulting books. It is through his vision and sheer hard work that such varied points of view can be collected in one text. I was fortunate enough to participate in both the 1984 and 1989 symposia, and I look forward with excitement to the next one.

I. King Jordan
President, Gallaudet University

ACKNOWLEDGMENTS

No undertaking of the scope of this volume is possible by any stretch of the imagination without the indispensable work of many persons. In addition to the obvious debt owed to the hard-working and productive authors of each of these chapters, and the penetrating syntheses carried out by the special chapter writers at the beginning and end of the volume, the analysts who performed careful work in examining the works of authors within each chapter deserve important mention; in each case, they took responsibility for reading, questioning, and then drawing together the threads within each group of papers, as well as providing important directions for future research by raising researchable questions for the coming years.

To Ms. Lena Mitchell and later to Ms. Felicia Jones of the School of Education and Human Services, Dean's Office, a special thanks is owed for their careful preparation of the manuscript in a form that was accessible to the Press and to the editing which followed. To Ms. Tina Amir, Research Assistant at Gallaudet, I owe gratitude for careful follow-up with all authors following the editing process and for the preparation of the index for this volume. I appreciate the tedious and diligent work of Ms. Geraldine Slaughter in the initial preparation of manuscripts. Finally, to Ms. Ivey Pittle Wallace, Managing Editor of Gallaudet Press, I give a special note of appreciation for the critically important work of shepherding a complex manuscript through the various processes leading to publication.

To all, then, I express deep gratitude for bringing this volume to reality.

CONTRIBUTORS

Ms. Dinaz Adenwalla
Department of Education
Gallaudet University
Washington, DC 20002

Dr. Tane Akamatsu
Department of Education
Michigan State University
East Lansing, MI 48824–1034

Dr. Jesus Alegria
Centre Comprendre et Parler
Université Libré de Bruxelles
Brussels, Belgium

Dr. David Alexander
Marie H. Katzenbach School for the Deaf
West Trenton, NJ 08625–0535

Dr. D. Yvonne Aplin
Department of Audiology
University of Manchester
Manchester, U.K. M139PL

Dr. David F. Armstrong
Budget Office
Gallaudet University
Washington, DC 20002–3695

Ms. Cathy Baechle
℅ Ms. Frances R. Croft
School of Preparatory Studies
Gallaudet University
Washington, DC 20012

Dr. Ursula Bellugi
Laboratory for Language and Cognitive
  Studies
The Salk Institute for Biological Studies
San Diego, CA 92138

Ms. Janice Berchin
541 Pelham Road
New Rochelle, NY 10805

Dr. Terry R. Berkeley
Department of Administration and
  Supervision
Gallaudet University
Washington, DC 20002

Dr. Lynne Blennerhassett
Department of Psychology
Gallaudet University
Washington, DC 20002

Dr. Nancy Bonkowski
Department of Education
Michigan State University
East Lansing, MI 48824–1034

Dr. Jeffery P. Braden
School Psychology Program
University of Florida
Gainesville, FL 32605

Dr. Rosemary Calderon
Department of Psychiatry
Children's Hospital
Seattle, WA 98105

Dr. Elizabeth S. Charlson
San Francisco Center on Deafness
University of California
San Francisco, CA 94143

Dr. Kathee M. Christensen
San Diego State University
San Diego, CA 92182–0151

Dr. Jadwiga Cieszyńska
Institute of Psychology
Jagiellonian University
Krakow, Poland

Dr. M. Diane Clark
Department of Psychology
Shippensburg State University
Shippensburg, PA 17257

Dr. Helen B. Craig
The Western Pennsylvania School for the
Deaf
Pittsburgh, PA 15218

Ms. Frances R. Croft
School of Preparatory Studies
Gallaudet University
Washington, DC 20012

Dr. Deborah Dalke
Department of Psychology
Pennsylvania State University
University Park, PA 16802

Dr. Beth Davey
Department of Curriculum and
Instruction
College of Education
University of Maryland
College Park, MD 20742

Dr. Linda Delk
Curriculum and Evaluation
Gallaudet University
Washington, DC 20002-3695

Dr. Asa DeMatteo
Center on Deafness
University of California
San Francisco, CA 94143

Dr. David Deyo
% Dr. Patricia E. Spencer
Center for Studies in Education and
Human Development
Gallaudet University
Washington, DC 20002

Dr. Charles H. Dietz
Model Secondary School for the Deaf
Gallaudet University
Washington, DC 20002

Dr. Kenneth Epstein
School of Preparatory Studies
Gallaudet University
Washington, DC 20012

Dr. Angela Fok
% Dr. Ursula Bellugi
Laboratory for Language and Cognitive
Studies
The Salk Institute for Biological Studies
San Diego, CA 92138

Dr. James Gavelek
Department of Education
Michigan State University
East Lansing, MI 48824-1034

Dr. Maura J. Geisser
The Rhode Island School for the Deaf
Providence, RI 02908

Ms. Jan Gemmill
% Ms. Frances R. Croft
School of Preparatory Studies
Gallaudet University
Washington, DC 20012

Dr. Harold W. Gordon
Western Psychiatric Institute and Clinic
University of Pittsburgh
Pittsburgh, PA 15213

Dr. Mark T. Greenberg
Department of Psychology
University of Washington
Seattle, WA 98195

Dr. Natalie Grindstaff
% Dr. Patricia E. Spencer
Center for Studies in Education and
Human Development
Gallaudet University
Washington, DC 20002

Dr. Carl Grove
% Dr. Michael Rodda
Gallaudet Research Institute
Gallaudet University
Washington, DC 20002

Dr. Catherine Hage
Laboratory of Experimental Psychology
Université Libré de Bruxelles
Brussels, Belgium

Dr. Vicki L. Hanson
% Dr. Diane C. Lillo-Martin
Haskins Laboratories
New Haven, CT 06511–10695

Dr. Eleanor Hillegeist
School of Preparatory Studies
Gallaudet University
Washington, DC 20012

Dr. Karen van Hoek
Laboratory for Language and Cognitive
    Studies
The Salk Institute for Biological Studies
San Diego, CA 92138

Dr. Harry W. Hoemann
Department of Psychology
Bowling Green State University
Bowling Green, OH 43403–0220

Dr. Bruce S. Jonas
6906 Woodstream Lane
Seabrook, MD 20706

Dr. Irmina Kaiser-Grodecka
Institute of Psychology
Jagiellonian University
Krakow, Poland

Ms. Vicki Kemp
Department of Mathematics and
    Computer Science
Gallaudet University
Washington, DC 20002

Dr. Susan King
Department of Curriculum and
    Instruction
College of Education
University of Maryland
College Park, MD 20742

Dr. Edward S. Klima
% Dr. Ursula Bellugi
Laboratory for Language and Cognitive
    Studies
The Salk Institute for Biological Studies
San Diego, CA 92138

Dr. Thomas N. Kluwin
Gallaudet Research Institute
Gallaudet University
Washington, DC 20002

Dr. Anna Knobloch-Gala
Institute of Psychology
Jagiellonian University
Krakow, Poland

Dr. Carol A. Kusché
Department of Psychology
University of Washington
Seattle, WA 98195

Ms. Sanremi LaRue-Atuonah
% Ms. Frances R. Croft
School of Preparatory Studies
Gallaudet University
Washington, DC 20012

Dr. Diane C. Lillo-Martin
Haskins Laboratories
New Haven, CT 06511–10695

Dr. Mimi WheiPing Lou
Center on Deafness
University of California
San Francisco, CA 94143

Dr. Robert H. MacTurk
Center for Studies in Education and
    Human Development
Gallaudet University
Washington, DC 20002

Mr. Bruce Marlowe
1730 U Street, NW
Washington, DC 20009

Dr. David S. Martin
School of Education and Human Services
Gallaudet University
Washington, DC 20002

Mr. Robert E. McDonald
Department of English
Gallaudet University
Washington, DC 20002

Dr. Kathryn P. Meadow-Orlans
Center for Studies in Education and
  Human Development
Gallaudet University
Washington, DC 20002–3695

Dr. Donna M. Mertens
Educational Foundations and Research
Gallaudet University
Washington, DC 20002

Ms. Lorna J. Mittelman
Learning Development Center
Rochester Institute of Technology
Rochester, NY 14623–0887

Dr. Keith E. Nelson
Department of Psychology
Pennsylvania State University
University Park, PA 16802

Dr. Richard C. Nowell
Department of Special Education
Indiana University of Pennsylvania
Indiana, PA 15705

Dr. Angela O'Donnell
Graduate School of Education
Rutgers University
New Brunswick, NJ 08903

Dr. Fatemeh Olia
Department of Educational Technology
Gallaudet University
Washington, DC 20002

Dr. Olivier Perier
Université Libré de Bruxelles
Brussels, Belgium

Dr. Joan S. Pinhas
Department of Speech Pathology
State University of New York
Geneseo, NY 14454

Dr. Howard R. Pollio
Department of Psychology
University of Tennessee
Knoxville, TN 37916

Ms. Marilyn Pollio
Comprehensive Adult and Child Services
Knoxville, TN 37916

Dr. Elizabeth Prinz
Department of Special Education
San Francisco State University
San Francisco, CA 94132

Dr. Philip Prinz
Department of Special Education
San Francisco State University
San Francisco, CA 94132

Dr. Larry K. Quinsland
Office of Faculty Development
National Technical Institute for the Deaf
Rochester, NY 14623–0887

Dr. Michael Rodda
Gallaudet Research Institute
Gallaudet University
Washington, DC 20002

Dr. Pamela Rush
School of Preparatory Studies
Gallaudet University
Washington, DC 20012

Dr. Barbara R. Schirmer
Special Education, Hearing Impaired
Lewis & Clark College
Portland, OR 97219

Dr. Glenda J. Senior
National Technical Institute for the Deaf
Rochester, NY 14623–0887

Dr. Marymargaret Sharp-Pucci
Department of Communicative Disorders
Institute on Deafness
Northern Illinois University
DeKalb, IL 60115–2899

Dr. Suzanne T. Smith
% Dr. Diane C. Lillo-Martin
Haskins Laboratories
New Haven, CT 06511–10695

Dr. Patricia E. Spencer
Center for Studies in Education and
  Human Development
Gallaudet University
Washington, DC 20002

Dr. David A. Stewart
College of Education
Michigan State University
East Lansing, MI 48824–1034

Dr. Michael Strong
Department of Psychiatry
University of California
San Francisco, CA 94143

Dr. M. Virginia Swisher
School of Education
University of Pittsburgh
Pittsburgh, PA 15260

Ms. Victoria Trimm
% Dr. Robert H. MacTurk
Center for Studies in Education and
  Human Development
Gallaudet University
Washington, DC 20002

Dr. Hing Fung Tsui
% Dr. Michael Rodda
Gallaudet Research Institute
Gallaudet University
Washington, DC 20002

Dr. Ryan D. Tweney
Department of Psychology
Bowling Green State University
Bowling Green, OH 43403–0228

Dr. Robert Lee Williams
College of Arts and Sciences
Gallaudet University
Washington, DC 20002–3695

Dr. Louise Wilson
1276 Nursery Hill Lane
Arden Hills, MN 55112

Dr. Laurie Witters-Churchill
Department of Educational
  Administration
Texas A & M University
College Station, TX 77843–4226

Dr. Lee A. Witters
Department of Special Education and
  Communication Disorders
University of Nebraska-Lincoln
Lincoln, NE 68508

Dr. Anthony B. Wolff
Mental Health Research Program
Gallaudet University
Washington, DC 20002–3695

Dr. Abraham Zwiebel
School of Education
Bar-Ilan University
Ramat-Gan 52100, Israel

Advances in Cognition, Education, and Deafness

INTRODUCTION

Introduction

David S. Martin

The Roman god Janus had two faces; he could look both backward and forward. His name is the root word for January, a connection with our impulse to look back on the past and forward to the future when the new year arrives. As we begin the 1990s, it is appropriate that we look back and forward in the same way. We need to see how our views of the deaf learner's cognitive achievement and potential have changed, not over just one year but throughout history, and we need to look at where the field of cognition and deafness may be headed.

Moores (1982), in a review of deafness in history, indicated that the attitudes of persons in the ancient world toward handicapped people were ambivalent. While the ancient Jews showed charity toward deaf people, the book of Leviticus in the Old Testament admonishes against cursing the deaf, suggesting that at least some people were acting negatively toward handicapped persons. We also know that the legal rights of deaf people were limited in some of the same ways as those of helpless and mentally retarded persons.

Because of the high value placed on the spoken word throughout ancient history, little improvement is seen in attempts to educate deaf children when one looks at ancient Egypt, ancient Greece, and then ancient Rome. The Romans appear to have been more harsh and cruel towards deaf people than either the Egyptians or the Greeks (Moores 1982).

The interaction between language and thought has been and continues to be a topic of great interest and debate. In the ancient world, the Greek philosophers believed that spoken words were the necessary means by which a person conceived thought. Aristotle designated the ear as the organ of instruction and believed that

3

hearing was the greatest contributor to intelligence; consequently, he has been accused of keeping the deaf in ignorance for two thousand years (Deland 1931).

A number of important events occurred in Europe more than 350 years ago which, in retrospect, can be considered the start of the first revolution in deafness. Two events in this revolution stand out. First, it was established that in spite of the inability to hear, deaf persons could, depending on the nature of their hearing loss and the application of the appropriate educational technique, learn to articulate and speak with varying degrees of intelligibility. Although we know today that there is no relationship between speech articulation ability and thinking ability, the discovery of this speech articulation potential served to change the attitudes of some hearing people toward deaf persons' intellectual potential.

At the same time, a breakthrough was underway in the recognition and development of the language of signs—communication through movements of the hands and body.

These two developments, pioneered simultaneously in Spain (by Pedro Ponce de Leone and Juan Pablo Bonet), France (by Charles Michel Abbé de l'Epée), Germany (by Samuel Heinicke), Italy (by Girolamo Cardano), and later in England (by George Dalgarno), demonstrated for the first time that deaf people were not retarded and were capable of intelligent thought and communication.

The debate over thought and language was still going on in the nineteenth century. William James (1890) and both Binet and Simon (1910) took the position that thought developed before language in deaf persons; James reported abstract and metaphysical concepts in two deaf persons even when pantomime was the only language used (Moores 1982). On the other hand, Booth (1878) took the position that thought was independent of the mode of expression, and said that thought and language were separate processes, allowing a person to use one or the other alone.

In 1924–1925, the National Research Council reported that deaf subjects were between two and three years "retarded" in comparison to hearing subjects in their responses to the Pintner Non-Language Mental Test (Myklebust & Brutton 1953). Pintner and others reviewed the available information on the intelligence of deaf persons and, in spite of sometimes contradictory results, concluded that deaf children had inferior intelligence (Pintner, Eisenson & Stanton 1941).

The work of Myklebust has been generally cited as another milestone in the history of research in deafness and attitudes toward the deaf population. His studies attributed a "concrete" nature to the intelligence of deaf persons, indicating that deafness restricts the deaf learner to a world of "concrete objects and things" (Myklebust & Brutton 1953). The influence of this attribution has been far-reaching in that educators of deaf children have for many years regarded the deaf learner as less able to work with abstract ideas; fortunately, subsequent research has proven this interpretation to be false. Nonetheless, the work of Myklebust represented at least one step forward in that he regarded the deaf learner as being at least *quantitatively* equal to the hearing learner, although *qualitatively* inferior.

Furth deplored the past centuries during which deaf people were considered to be lacking in normal intelligence because they could not speak; he thus addressed again the age-old question of the relationship between language and intelligence (Furth 1966). Furth (1964) concluded that the poorer performance of deaf persons on some cognitive tests could be explained either by a lack of world experience or by the conditions of those tasks that would favor a background of spoken language. Further, he asserted that "the deaf" can comprehend and can logically apply concepts as well as hearing persons can (1964).

Rosenstein (1961), after a review of a number of studies conducted with deaf learners, found no differences between deaf and hearing persons in regard to conceptual performance when the linguistic elements presented were within the language experience of deaf children; his important conclusion was that abstract thought is *not* closed to deaf persons.

After an exhaustive analysis of many studies, Vernon concluded that deaf youth perform as well in a wide variety of tasks that measure thinking as do other children (1967).

In recent years we have also witnessed a tendency to intervene actively in the cognitive performance of deaf learners in an effort to improve their intellectual functioning. These efforts grow out of the belief that deaf learners have the same range of intellectual potential as the hearing population and can achieve that potential if the environment, instruction, and materials are appropriate.

As we look back at the history of attitudes toward the cognitive potential of deaf persons, we can identify a trend that passes from outright bias and discrimination, through the several phases of comparing deaf and hearing learners on some specific measures but still overgeneralizing or oversimplifying the results, through a period of more systematic analyses that removed the tendency to overgeneralize but still confused the issues of thinking and language. Then the performance of deaf persons began to be analyzed on its own terms and with a better understanding of the particular conditions under which a deaf learner develops, and that phase led in turn to the present, when those more specific analyses continue side by side with active efforts to improve cognitive performance of deaf learners in the firm conviction that such improvement is not only possible but essential.

At this point, it is useful to compare the contents of the First (1984) and Second (1989) International Symposia on Cognition, Education, and Deafness at Gallaudet University. Such an examination helps us to see the immediate past and compare it with the present in this field.

A numerical assessment indicates that, out of the 39 authors presenting papers at the 1989 symposium, 16 were "repeat" authors from the 1984 symposium. From this fact we may conclude that there is some consistency in the themes of research undertaken in this area and that the number of investigators working in the field has increased. Such a combination is encouraging.

An analysis of the titles and content of the 1984 symposium reveals a preponderance of papers on developmental issues, a number of papers on the reading aspects of language and cognition, some separation of education from the cognition and deafness foci, some observable beginning work on proactive classroom intervention strategies designed to enhance the thinking level of hearing-impaired learners, and several overview studies and discussions.

On the other hand, the content of the 1989 symposium is slightly different. A greater emphasis on applications in the educational environment is clear, as is the emergence of an entirely new branch of investigation—the neuro-anatomical dimension of investigating cognition and deafness. In addition, we see a clear emphasis on the relationship between sign languages—especially American Sign Language—and the learning process and cognition. There are more specific topics rather than overviews, and a greater diversity of topics occurs among the corpus of papers, as is reflected in this book. Finally, one sees the beginning of involvement of deaf professionals as members of research teams to a greater degree than in 1984; however, this is but a beginning, and much remains to be done to increase the involvement and leadership of deaf persons in this area.

In looking both backward and forward in the fascinating area of cognition in the hearing-impaired learner, three concepts from the field of futurism are useful. Futurists make a distinction between the *probable* future, the *possible* future, and the *preferable* future. The probable future is one in which, with no specific or proactive initiative, it is possible to predict with high likelihood what the future will hold. The possible future is the scenario that could happen with some unexpected circumstances, although it is not highly likely. And the preferable future is that scenario that will happen only if specific initiatives are taken to ensure it. What, then, would be the probable, possible, and preferable futures in regard to the cognitive development of the hearing-impaired learner?

We can quickly dispose of the possible future that includes certain unlikely events—educators and researchers returning to the old conviction that deaf learners have lower potential than hearing learners, or no further serious investigation being undertaken in regard to cognition and deafness. This possible future is likely only if a complete cut-off of support for research were coupled with a reversion to outmoded attitudes.

A probable future—one in which, with little intervention, certain events will very likely happen—would include the continuation of definite trends that have already begun. For example, it seems highly likely that the new interest in neuro-anatomy as applied to cognition and deafness will expand steadily. In addition, there probably will continue to be a focus on the interaction between language and thought. We can expect that the debate will persist about the primacy of one over the other as well as about their interdependence. It is also probable that the gradual development of improved tools for assessment of the deaf learner's cognition will continue, with an emphasis on broader and fairer approaches to that assessment. And it would appear that the continuing issue of American Sign Language vs. other manually coded systems of communication will be a source of debate, including the roles of these systems in the teaching of language itself and their relationships to the development of higher cognitive processes in the deaf learner.

The preferable future is, of course, less likely without specific planning, initiative, and support (both human and financial). However, the preferable future is one toward which we should all strive. The preferable future would include at least the following in regard to cognition and deafness:

1. Active support for all the elements that were mentioned above under the probable future. In particular, serious investigations into modes

of communication and cognition, neuro-anatomy and cognition, and assessment tools of a broader nature.

2. Incorporation of training in cognitive education within teacher education programs in deaf education.
3. Development and empirical testing of additional varieties of planned interventions in the classroom, and longitudinal studies to accompany them.
4. Greater emphasis and support for early intervention in cognitive development, including the preschool years.
5. Focus on the education of parents (both hearing and deaf) not only in appropriate expectations of their deaf children but also in appropriate interventions that they can use during the preschool years to promote higher-level thinking in their children.
6. Legitimization of other-than-quantitative research methods in deafness research, including even single-subject designs if carefully controlled, as sources of knowledge about deafness and cognition.
7. Production by educational publishers of materials that will provide a greater cognitive challenge to deaf learners than those now available.
8. Systematic education of employers and hearing colleagues of deaf workers in the workplace in maintaining high cognitive expectations (as well as adaptations) that are appropriate for the deaf person.
9. Still wider involvement of deaf researchers in research on deafness.

Although funding is a necessary condition, it is not a sufficient one; the sufficient condition is the continuing conviction, based now on clear evidence, that the deaf learner can indeed achieve the highest levels of cognitive performance, given the appropriate conditions and dedication by professionals. That challenge is the one to which educators and other professionals working with and on behalf of deaf persons must rise now.

The Second International Symposium on Cognition, Education, and Deafness took place at Gallaudet University, July 5–8, 1989. This gathering brought together more than 230 professionals—teachers, researchers, theoreticians, and others interested in the confluence of cognition, education, and deafness. The participants represented 14 different countries (including every continent except Antarctica), and the deliberations focused on the six themes represented in this volume. The purpose of the symposium was to examine the state of the art and its progress since the first symposium in 1984, as well as to establish a research and implementation agenda for the coming years in the field.

The papers in this volume are divided into six thematic sections, and the group of papers in each is followed by a careful analysis of that thematic grouping, including common threads, issues raised, and research questions from that theme which need to be investigated in the near future. The book opens with an important chapter by Ursula Bellugi about the current work on sign languages in the deaf learner and their cognitive implications. A special feature of this volume is a collection of presentations of programs designed to facilitate the learning of deaf subjects in the cognitive realm. This section is intended particularly for practitioners, although the practitioner will also find important implications for practice in most, if not all, of the research papers as well as in chapters 2 through 7. Many challenging and puzzling methodological problems face the researcher interested in deafness, and as a guide to these questions and possible avenues toward their resolution, a special brief chapter (chapter 11) is included after the theme groupings. The closing chapter provides a synthesis of the numerous papers and presentations in this volume, particularly from the viewpoint of a cognitive psychologist from outside the field of deafness; Howard Pollio makes comments that draw together all the individual studies and provides a charge to the field of deafness research in regard to cognition and education.

This book offers the reader the opportunity to assess progress in the field of cognition, education, and deafness since 1984 and to determine avenues of needed investigation. This work is expected to inform serious study in the field in the years to come.

REFERENCES

Binet, A., and Simon, T. 1910. An investigation concerning the value of the oral method. *American Annals of the Deaf* 55:4–33.

Booth, E. 1878. Thinking in words and gestures. *American Annals of the Deaf* 23:223–225.

Deland, F. 1931. *The story of lipreading.* Washington, DC: Volta Bureau.

Furth, H. 1964. *Thinking without language.* New York: Free Press.

———. 1966. *Thinking without language: Psychological implications of deafness.* New York: Free Press.

James, W. 1890. Thought before language: A deaf mute's recollections. *American Annals of the Deaf* 34:135–145.

Moores, D. F. 1982. *Educating the deaf: Psychology, principles, and practices.* 2d ed. Boston: Houghton Mifflin.

Myklebust, H., & Brutton, M. 1953. A study of visual perception in deaf children. *Acta Oto-Laryngologica*, Supplementum, 105.

Pintner, R., Eisenson, J., & Stanton, M. 1941. *The psychology of the physically disabled.* New York: Crofts & Company.

Rosenstein, J. 1961. Perception, cognition and language in deaf children. *Exceptional Children* 27(3):276–284.

Vernon, M. 1967. Relationship of language to the thinking process. *Archives of Genetic Psychiatry* 16(3):325–333.

2

THE LINK BETWEEN HAND AND BRAIN

The Link Between Hand and Brain: Implications from a Visual Language

Ursula Bellugi

T he occasion of the Second International Symposium on Cognition, Education, and Deafness evoked memories of Edward Corbett's keynote address (1985) at Gallaudet's First International Symposium. Dr. Corbett's concerns at that time offer a perspective on how our field has advanced over the last five years.

At that first symposium, Dr. Corbett expressed the need for new directions in research in areas in which the special capacities of deaf people should be revealed. One such area, he asserted, was the visual competence of deaf individuals. He recommended that researchers begin studies of vision and visual language, and that they focus on "the fact that deaf people's cognitive efforts are enhanced by their use of vision, rather than identifying the weaknesses of their auditory mechanisms." He raised several important questions with respect to the contrast between visual and auditory information processing, suggesting that researchers in the field should turn their attention to visually mediated thinking

This research was supported in part by National Institutes of Health grants #DC00146, #DC00201, #HD13249, and #HD266022, as well as National Science Foundation grants #BNS86-09085 and BNS88-20673; the Axe Houghton Foundation grant to The Salk Institute for Biological Studies; and the John D. and Catherine MacArthur Foundation Research Network on 'The Transition to Early Childhood.' We thank David Corina, Karen Emmorey, Angela Fok, Karen van Hoek, Edward S. Klima, Lucinda O'Grady-Batch, and Judy Reilly for their help in these studies. Illustrations copyright Ursula Bellugi, The Salk Institute for Biological Studies.

11

and to investigations of the cerebral cortex with respect to vision in deaf people. Dr. Corbett also pointed out that, unfortunately, many researchers up to that time equated speech with language and vice versa. His directive to the field was to conduct research on visual language and visual processing in order to provide new information to complement our understanding of speech and hearing.

This last decade of the twentieth century is an exciting one for those of us who are involved in sign language research, the study of deafness, and education of deaf children. We stand at a new vantage point now, looking toward future developments that were almost unimaginable only a decade ago. Fundamental and important changes have taken place in our field and in the public's perception of deafness. There is the emerging awareness that American Sign Language is a full-fledged language, as complex and expressive as any spoken language. There is a growing appreciation of Deaf culture in its many manifestations. Additionally, there is a new consciousness of the capabilities of deaf people.

The papers presented in this volume attest to the depth and breadth of the research now being done on the language, cognition, and culture of deaf people. At research centers across the country and around the world, important and far-reaching questions are being addressed. We now see researchers in linguistics, cognitive psychology, and cognitive neurosciences looking to studies of deaf people for important findings about cognition and language and about how language is represented in the brain. Interestingly, that research has taken place in precisely those areas that Dr. Corbett challenged us to address.

The research my colleagues and I have conducted in the Laboratory of Language and Cognitive Studies at The Salk Institute over the past decade, reflect the above-mentioned developments in the field. Initially, we asked questions about the nature of signing: Whether it was a form of pantomime executed face-to-face, whether it was a simple, gestural form of communication, and whether it had any kind of linguistic structure. Over the years, we have worked with more than five hundred deaf people in many different roles, and we have benefited greatly from having several deaf researchers on our laboratory staff, including Lucinda O'Grady-Batch and Freda Norman.

In the past decade we have learned a great deal from the comparison of signed and spoken languages and have made significant discoveries about universal properties that appear in both visual and auditory languages (see, for example, Bellugi, Poizner & Klima 1989; Bellugi & Studdert-Kennedy 1980; Klima & Bellugi 1988). We have found that the basic properties of signed and spoken languages are very much the same. Signed and spoken languages have the same kinds of organizational principles, the same kinds of rule systems, and the same grammatical complexity and expressive power.

We can now define the characteristics of language as it manifests itself in each of the modalities, and can begin to specify precisely which surface aspects of the form language arise from the visual modality compared to the auditory modality. Having established that signed and spoken languages are remarkably similar at the deepest level, we are also interested in determining how differences in transmission modality, between vocal-auditory and manual-visual channels, might affect the surface form of language and also might influence cognitive processing.

Three main points arise from research on signed languages everywhere.

1. The concept of language must now be broadened to include signed as well as spoken languages.
2. Signed languages present an important new alternative to spoken languages and are particularly revealing because they depend so heavily on visual rather than auditory processing.
3. Signed language, like spoken language, is preferentially processed by the left hemisphere, suggesting that the left hemisphere in humans has an innate predisposition for language.

In a number of ways, signed languages provide a new perspective on language and reveal unexpected links between hand and brain.

PROPERTIES OF SPOKEN AND SIGNED LANGUAGES

One of the central issues that we can now address arises from some new discoveries about the nature of language. Until recently, nearly everything we had learned about language had come from the study of spoken languages. But now research into signed languages has revealed that there are primary linguistic systems, passed down from one generation of deaf people to the next, which have become forged into separate languages not derived from spoken languages. Thus for the first time we can examine properties of communication systems that have developed in an alternative transmission system, the *visual-gestural channel*. The existence of such fully expressive systems arising outside the mainstream of spoken languages affords a new vantage point for investigating the biological underpinnings of language and cognition.

The past decade has seen many investigations of language and its formal architecture, as well as its representation in the brain, through the study of languages that have arisen outside the mainstream of spoken languages; that is, the visual-gestural systems developed among deaf people. American Sign Language (ASL) has been forged into an autonomous language with its own internal mechanism for relating visual form to meaning. ASL has evolved linguistic mechanisms that are not derived from those of English (or any spoken language), offering a new perspective on the determinants of language form.

A lively field of research in the structural properties of ASL (e.g., *Sign Language Studies*; Liddell & Johnson 1986; Wilbur 1987; and many others) now exists. In our laboratory at The Salk Institute, we have been specifying the extent to which the modalities involved in the perception and production of languages shape their formal properties. We have found that the modality in which a language develops makes a crucial difference in the form of its grammatical devices.

The complex organizational properties of language have been assumed to be intimately connected with the production and processing of vocally articulated sounds. There is good evidence that human beings have evolved for speech. Spoken languages have been found to manifest certain basic structural principles assumed to result from the fact that language is normally spoken and heard. The existence of signed languages allows us to ask fundamental questions about the determinants of language organization. What would language be like if its transmission were not based on the vocal tract and the ear? How is language processed when its basic lexical units are produced by the hands moving in space and when the signal is organized spatially as well as temporally? What implications does acquiring a visual-spatial language have for the neural substrate for language in the brain? We can now address these issues together and consider their implications for the study of cognition and for the education of deaf children.

What are the differences between spoken and signed languages? That was really our central research question for a long time. What we wanted to do was sift out the properties that are common across all languages and then look at the special properties with respect to sign language on the surface. We are looking at the effect of having a language for the eyes rather than for the ears—a language that is designed and suited specifically for vision.

Signed languages clearly present test cases of communication systems that have developed in alternative transmission systems: in visual-gestural channels. Because American Sign Language is a visual language, it engages different aspects of brain function for its production and perception than does the use of spoken languages. Thus, the study of ASL opens new windows to reveal previously unseen aspects of how the brain is organized to generate and comprehend language. The most striking surface difference between signed and spoken languages is in the reliance on spatial contrasts at all linguistic levels—most evident at the level of syntax. Figure 1 shows ASL grammatical morphology as spatially nested forms and aspects of verb agreement and spatially organized syntax.

SIGN LANGUAGE UNIVERSALS: THE EFFECTS OF MODALITY ON LINGUISTIC FORM

Our research investigates the effects of the change in modality (from ear to eye, from vocal tract to hands) on the form that signed languages take. Our objectives are to determine the underlying properties that all languages have in common and to examine the distinctive properties of signed languages that show the effects of modality on language organization. We are examining the formal devices utilized by Chinese Sign Language (CSL), in contrast to American Sign Language (see Fok, Bellugi & van Hoek, this volume), in order to test our hypotheses regarding the effects of language modality on the form that languages take. We chose to study CSL because it has developed in the context of a completely different spoken language (spoken Chinese) that has essentially no inflectional morphology and a nonalphabetic writing system.

We find that at each level of organization, including phonology, morphology, and syntax, CSL and ASL are remarkably similar in overall surface organization. Signs in both languages are composed of simultaneously articulated layered elements consisting of a small set of handshapes, locations, and movements. Morphological patterning is layered simultaneously with the root. The two languages are similar also in the ways they utilize space and spatial contrasts in the service

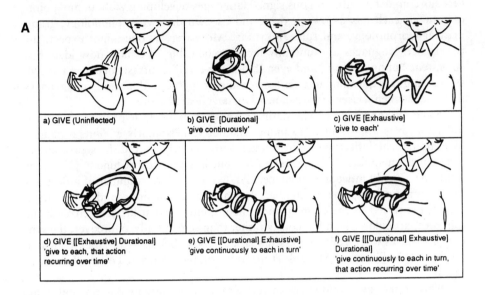

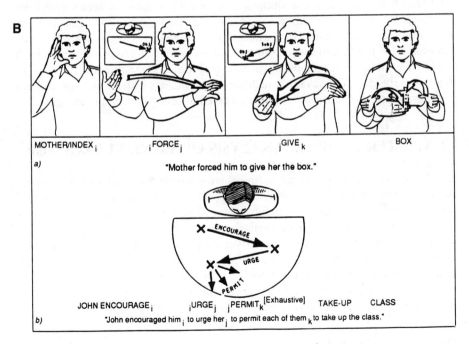

FIGURE 1   ASL-layered morphology and spatially organized syntax.

of syntax. In terms of surface organization, then, CSL and ASL are quite similar, clearly showing the imprint of the modality on language form. But at the same time, as completely autonomous signed languages developing without any points of contact, each has its own lexicon and its own distinctive phonology, grammatical morphology, and rules of syntax. Moreover, as one might expect, the two signed languages are mutually incomprehensible. We have now identified consistent "phonological" and even "phonetic-level" contrasts between the two signed languages, leading to phenomena similar to "accent" in spoken languages that occur when a user of one signed language learns another.

Since spoken Chinese (Mandarin or Cantonese) has little or no grammatical inflection, it is important to examine whether CSL similarly exhibits a paucity of grammatical inflections. Our studies show clearly that CSL is profoundly different from spoken Chinese. Like ASL, but in contrast to Chinese, CSL turns out to be a richly inflecting language. CSL exhibits a large number of inflections for grammatical arguments, number, derivational distinctions, and grammatical aspect, expressed in the form of movement contours that are layered with the sign root, articulated simultaneously rather than sequentially. Moreover, the syntax of CSL, as in ASL, is expressed spatially (Fok, Bellugi, van Hoek & Klima 1988; Fok & Bellugi 1986; Fok et al., this volume; Poizner, Fok & Bellugi, in press).

This course of development in ASL grammar represents one possibility afforded by the visual-spatial modality; whether it is the favored or only possibility for a visual-spatial language is unknown. We are investigating whether principles of linguistic organization (e.g., the spatially organized syntax) will turn out to be more general characteristics of natural signed language systems. We have been examining for the first time the grammatical properties of CSL, focusing on both similarities and differences between ASL and CSL. These studies allow us to determine the detailed ways in which signed languages differ from one another with respect to the most modality-conditioned aspects of signed languages.

COMPUTER GRAPHIC ANALYSIS OF SIGNED LANGUAGE

ASL has developed as a fully autonomous language with complex organizational properties not derived from spoken languages. This fact illuminates the biological determinants of language. ASL exhibits formal structuring at the same levels as spoken language and principles similar to those of spoken language (e.g., constrained systems of features, rules based on underlying forms, and recursive grammatical processes). Yet the surface form of grammatical processes in a visual-spatial language is rooted in the modality in which the language developed. This difference in surface form between signed and spoken languages makes possible new investigations into the perception and production of language.

Dynamic Point-Light Displays

Linguistic analyses and experimental studies of sign language have been linked together, allowing researchers to study the interplay between the perception of language and the perception of motion. Specifically, one can now investigate the nature of perception of movement organized into a linguistic system. To investigate linguistic movement in ASL experimentally, a method was developed to isolate movement of the hands and arms, adapting a technique introduced by Johansson to study the perception of biological motion (Johansson 1975). Small incandescent bulbs were placed at the major joints of the arms and hands, and signing was recorded in a darkened room so that only the patterns of moving lights appeared against a black background (see Figure 2a).

Even with the information reduced to minimal point-light displays, deaf signers identified morphological processes of ASL with a high degree of accuracy, demonstrating that these patterns of dynamic contours of movement form a distinct, isolable layer of structure in ASL.

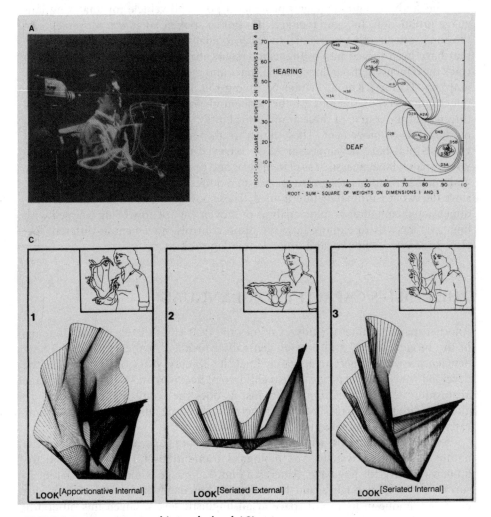

FIGURE 2   Computergraphic analysis of ASL.

The Interplay Between Perceptual and Linguistic Processes

To investigate the relation between basic perceptual and higher-order linguistic processes, the psychological representation of ASL movement by native deaf signers was contrasted with that of hearing nonsigners. Triads of ASL signs were presented as point-light displays, and subjects were asked to judge similarities between movements. Multidimensional scaling and hierarchical clustering of judgments for both groups of subjects revealed that the inflectional movements were perceived in terms of a limited number of underlying dimensions. Furthermore, the psychological representation of movement differs for deaf and hearing subjects, with perception of movement form tied to linguistically relevant dimensions for deaf subjects but not for hearing subjects (see Figure 2b). Thus, the data suggest that acquisition of a visual-gestural language can modify the natural perceptual categories into which linguistically relevant forms fall (Poizner 1983).

The study of sign languages provides a powerful vehicle for analyzing language production. In sign language, but not in spoken language, movements of the hands are directly observable. In order to analyze the structure of movements that have been forged into a linguistic system, methods have been developed to track movements in three-dimensional space and reconstruct them using computer graphics (Poizner, Klima, Bellugi & Livingston 1986). Figure 2c shows three-dimensional reconstructions of the sequential positions of the arm and hand throughout the course of three grammatical inflections expressed in ASL through modulations of movement. These illustrate the essential nature of grammatical contrasts that have developed in ASL, conveyed through dimensions unique to visual-spatial language, such as planar locus and geometric array. Thus, processing grammatical relations in sign language also requires processing of spatial relations, since the two are intimately intertwined. These powerful techniques for the three-dimensional computer graphic analysis of movement are now being coupled with linguistic analysis to explore how the brain controls movement at different levels—*linguistic*, *symbolic*, and *motoric* (see Figure 2).

THE CHILD'S CAPACITY FOR LANGUAGE

Another major avenue of study examines the deaf child's capacity for language in the broader sense, and not (as generally prevailed in the past) cataloguing deficiencies with respect to learning English. Twenty years of research on the development of sign language in deaf children of deaf parents shows that language acquisition in this population occurs just as does the acquisition of spoken language—with the same maturational timetable, the same milestones, and the same capacities for creating complex linguistic systems.

Studies of children's acquisition of spoken language have illuminated the nature of linguistic systems, the biological foundations for language, and the human capacity for language. American Sign Language is markedly different in surface form from English and from spoken languages in general. ASL is, for example, unique in its use of space at all linguistic levels. Given this difference in form, the task that the deaf child faces in learning a sign language may be radically different from that faced by the hearing child learning a spoken language. The change in the transmission system (from the ear to the eye, from the vocal apparatus to the hands) might have a profound influence on the acquisition process. In a language where the articulators are directly observable and manipulable, the language learning situation can take on a different character.

What effects might these special characteristics of a visual language have on the acquisition process? We are investigating the acquisition of spatially organized syntax and the acquisition of its spatial cognitive underpinnings. We have completed studies with more than sixty deaf children of deaf parents, from two to ten years of age, involving tests that tap knowledge of phonological, morphological, and syntactic processes in ASL (Bellugi 1988; Bellugi, van Hoek, Lillo-Martin & O'Grady 1988).

Inflections and Spatial Verb Agreement

The ASL system of verb agreement functions is like that of spoken languages, but the form of verb agreement in ASL requires that the signer mark connections between spatial points. Around the age of two, deaf children begin using uninflected signs, even in imitating their mothers' inflected signs and even where the adult grammar requires marking for person and number. Although they are perceiving complex inflected forms, deaf children begin, as hearing children do, by analyzing the uninflected stems. By the age of three, deaf children have learned the basic aspects of verb morphology in ASL (inflections for person, for temporal aspect, and for number). At this age, they make overgeneralizations to noninflecting verbs, analogous to overgeneralizations like *eated* in the speech of hearing children. Such "errors" reveal the child's analysis of forms across the system. So, despite the difference in the form of spatial marking, the development and the age of mastery of the spatial inflection for verb agreement are the same in ASL as for comparable processes in spoken languages.

Spatially Organized Syntax and Discourse

The integration of the pronominal reference and spatial verb agreement systems in the sentences and discourse of ASL is highly complex. When deaf children first attempt to index verbs to arbitrary locus points in space, they may index all verbs for different referents to a single locus point. In telling stories, for example, three-year-old children characteristically "stack up" referents in space, rather than using arbitrary spatial points to keep referents distinct. By the age of five, however, children give the appropriate spatial index to nearly every nominal and pronoun that requires one, and almost all verbs show the appropriate agreement.

The deaf child, like the hearing child, extracts discrete components of the system. Furthermore, the evidence suggests that even when the modality and the language offer possibilities that seem intuitively obvious or transparent (pointing for pronominal reference, for example), deaf children ignore this directness and analyze the language input as part of a formal linguistic system.

The young deaf child is faced with the dual task in sign language of spatial perception, memory, and spatial transformations on the one hand, and processing grammatical structure on the other, all in one and the same visual event. Our studies of the acquisition process have found that deaf and hearing children show a strikingly similar course of development if exposed to a natural language at the critical time. These data suggest that language, independent of its transmission mechanisms, emerges in the child in a rapid, patterned, and—above all—*linguistically driven* manner.

A Sensitive Period for Learning Language

Current studies of language learning have important implications for education of deaf children and for our understanding of language development. One example is Supalla's research with deaf children of hearing parents whose only language exposure was to Signed English in the classroom and at home (S. Supalla, in press). He elicited the children's use of sign language with specially designed tests that focused on the expression of verbs and verb relations. These studies investigated the children's use of space in sentences, finding that individual children changed the input from Signed English when they signed among themselves by making it more spatial. This finding indicates that language modality, that is, language for the eyes rather than the ears, has a profound effect on language form.

Other research is relevant to a fundamental language issue: "Is there a critical period for language learning?" That is, does language learning have to take place during certain specified periods of early development in order to occur optimally? This point of view has been espoused by researchers such as Lenneberg (1967), who emphasized the maturational and biological aspects of language acquisition. In nonhuman species, there is evidence for critical periods in the acquisition of complex skills. Some species of birds, for example, exhibit a critical period for learning birdsong (Marler 1970).

It has been difficult to obtain clear evidence regarding human spoken language because children usually receive speech input at all stages of their development. However, Newport has conducted a "natural" experiment by studying a group of deaf people who came from the same community, went to the same school for the deaf, and had signed for a minimum of thirty years (Newport 1988). But they had been exposed to sign language at different ages, some early, some later in life. One group of deaf children of deaf parents had been exposed to sign language since birth; another group of deaf children with hearing parents were first exposed to sign language between four and six years of age when they began attending a school for deaf children; a third group were first exposed after the age of twelve.

All subjects were profoundly deaf and used ASL as their primary language. The grammatical processing of these different groups—different only in the age of exposure to sign language—has been studied, and the results suggest that there is indeed a sensitive period for learning language. In other words, language learning in humans is optimized at specific early ages. This is important information, educationally and theoretically.

The Interplay Between Spatial Cognition and Spatial Language

In a series of studies, we are examining the early writing skills of deaf children in Hong Kong who are exposed both to a visual-spatial primary language (Chinese Sign Language) and a visual-spatial script (Chinese kanji or logographs). We have found that deaf children just beginning to learn to write Chinese characters actively seek to discover the internal regularities underlying the architectural forms of the characters, and they make use of such regularities in creating new character forms (Bellugi, Tzeng, Klima & Fok 1989; Fok & Bellugi 1986; Fok et al., this volume). The forms invented by both hearing and deaf children alike are almost always perfectly acceptable character forms following all the implicit rules of character formation. Furthermore, the deaf children bring their own knowledge of sign language to the process of constructing characters. The evidence so far suggests that they actively seek to impose principles of sign construction borrowed from sign language and apply them to the written form of Chinese that they are learning.

In a recent experiment, we investigated the ability of deaf and hearing children who are just beginning to learn to read and write Chinese to analyze Chinese script through movement patterns in space. We used a technique that enabled us to highlight movement patterns as dynamic patterns of light, using a small light-emitting diode attached to the fingertip. We recorded patterns of movement on videotape in a darkened room, resulting in a continuous trace of light as the finger traces a Chinese pseudocharacter. In this way, only the dynamic pattern of movement representing the pseudocharacter is shown on the video screen.

Our subjects were deaf and hearing first-graders living in Hong Kong, who were just beginning to read and write in school. We asked them to watch sixty such continuous movement patterns, and each time, to write down the pseudo-character (involving discrete strokes) that was represented by the continuous flow of motion. The deaf children were significantly better than the hearing children in remembering, analyzing, and decoding spatial displays that involve movement patterns (see Fok et al., this volume). Deaf children exposed to a visual-spatial language appear to bring markedly enhanced spatial abilities to this task.

The Development of Hand Dominance in Signing

Studies of handedness in the past have linked right-hand dominance with left-hemisphere specialization for language. Since ASL uses the hands linguistically, and children begin to sign by their first birthday, testing hand dominance in deaf children who are learning ASL as their native language from their deaf parents represents a unique opportunity to determine degree of hand dominance for language and the implied underlying lateralization at a very early age. We have completed studies of right- and left-handed adult deaf signers (Vaid, Bellugi & Poizner 1989).

A set of cross-sectional linguistic and nonlinguistic studies was given to twenty-six deaf children of deaf parents. The subjects ranged from three to ten years of age. For the linguistic study, we selected a particular set of stimuli—pictures of common objects that were easily labeled with one-handed signs used by young deaf children (e.g., APPLE, BIRD, GIRL). We asked children to produce the signs for these pictured objects, recording which hand was used, and we asked them to produce the signs as rapidly as possible, first with one hand, then with the other, counterbalanced for hand used.

For the nonlinguistic study, we examined reaching for objects presented at midline, as well as performance on the Grooved Pegboard and the Harris Test of Lateral Dominance. Overall, the deaf children showed a hand preference for the nonlinguistic task that is above 50%, equivalent to published norms for age-matched hearing subjects (see Figure 3). However, in the linguistic task (hand dominance for one-handed signing), the children were at 100% dominant hand use, and in tests of speeded signing with the nondominant hand, there were more than 20% intrusions from the dominant hand. The results demonstrated that the subjects in this sample showed strong hand dominance for signs. In the speeded signing tests, the right hand was strongly dominant, even for the youngest children, averaging twice as fast as the left hand.

These findings suggest that hand dominance for linguistic tasks is stronger than hand preference for nonlinguistic tasks in these deaf signing children, and moreover, that hand dominance for linguistic activities is early, reliable, and robust (Bellugi, Klima, Lillo-Martin, O'Grady & Vaid 1986). We obtained convergent evidence by drawing upon our longitudinal study of many deaf children of ages one to three learning ASL as a native language. We scored the one-handed linguistic signs and the nonlinguistic manual behaviors for hand use. The deaf children showed hand preference for nonlinguistic actions generally above 50%, as has been found in hearing children. In contrast, the deaf children showed a stronger hand dominance for signing at levels ranging from 70% to 100%, even from the first signs made at the age of one year. Thus, hand dominance for linguistic activities manifests at an early age and is qualitatively and quantitatively different from that for nonlinguistic activities in young deaf signing children.

Studies of the development of handedness in sign language provide a new

FIGURE 3a   Picture cards used in one-handed signing task.

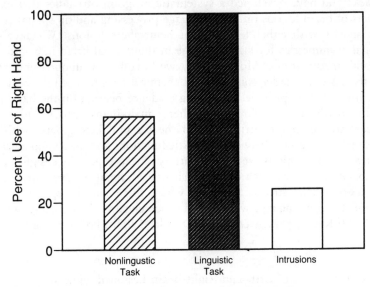

FIGURE 3b   Hand dominance in linguistic tasks and hand preference in nonlinguistic tasks.

perspective on the relationship between hand preference and cerebral specialization, through a language in which the hands are the primary articulators.

BRAIN ORGANIZATION: CLUES FROM A VISUAL-SPATIAL LANGUAGE

Patterns of breakdown of a visual-spatial language in deaf signers may bring a new perspective on the nature of cerebral specialization for language, since in sign language there is interplay between visual-spatial and linguistic relations within the same system. ASL displays the complex linguistic structure found in spoken languages but conveys much of its structure by manipulating spatial relations, thus exhibiting properties for which each of the hemispheres of hearing people shows a different predominant functioning. The study of brain-damaged deaf signers offers a particularly revealing vantage point for understanding the organization of higher cognitive functions in the brain, and how modifiable that organization may be. We address questions such as the following: Is the development of hemispheric specialization dependent upon auditory experience? How is language represented in the brain when it is expressed spatially? Does acquisition of a language with spatially expressed grammatical functions modify cerebral specialization for nonlanguage spatial functions?

We have investigated brain organization for sign language along several parallel tracks and have developed a systematic program of studies that examines the effects of brain lesions on sign language processing and on spatial cognition in deaf signers with either left or right hemisphere lesions. We have studied functional asymmetries for sign language in the normal brain in a series of experimental investigations. Most recently we have had a unique opportunity to extend these studies under conditions of chemical anesthesia to the brain. These lines of investigation provide converging evidence bearing on the basis for specialization of the two cerebral hemispheres in humans. Our broad aim is to investigate the relative contributions of the cerebral hemispheres with special reference to the interplay between linguistic functions and the spatial mechanisms that convey them. Subjects are given a battery of tests especially designed to assess their capacities vis-à-vis each of the levels of ASL linguistic structure. We focus on the levels of the structure of ASL where there may be special processing requirements for a language whose form is perceived visually (Bellugi, Poizner & Klima 1989; Klima, Bellugi & Poizner 1988a, 1988b; Poizner, Klima & Bellugi 1987).

Language Capacities of Left- and Right-Brain-Lesioned Signers

We have worked with many deaf signers who have suffered unilateral brain damage due to lesions. This report concerns three subjects with damage to the left hemisphere and three with damage to the right hemisphere. Our general program includes the following array of probes:

1. Our ASL adaptation of the Boston Diagnostic Aphasia Examination.
2. Linguistic tests we designed to assess the processing of the structural levels of ASL (sublexical, semantic, morphological, and syntactic).
3. An analysis of production of ASL at all linguistic levels.
4. Tests of nonlanguage spatial processing.

The battery of language and nonlanguage tasks was administered to deaf brain-lesioned subjects and to matched deaf controls. The signers with left hemisphere damage showed frank sign language aphasias (as indicated by their results on our aphasia examination) on tests for processing the structural levels of ASL, and on a linguistic analysis of their signing. One left-hemisphere-damaged signer was agrammatical for ASL. Her signing was severely impaired, halting, and effortful, reduced often to single sign utterances, and completely without the syntactic and morphological markings of ASL. Her lesion was typical of those that produce agrammatical aphasia for spoken language.

The other two left-hemisphere-damaged signers had fluent sign aphasias. They differed, however, in the nature of their impairments. One made selection errors in the formational elements of signs, producing the equivalent of phonemic paraphasias in sign language. Her signing, however, was perfectly grammatical, though vague. She often failed to specify to whom or to what she was referring. The third left-hemisphere-damaged signer made many grammatical errors. He made selection errors and additions within ASL morphology and erred in the spatialized syntax and discourse processes of ASL. Thus, differential damage within the left hemisphere produced sign language impairments that were not uniform but cleaved along lines of linguistically relevant components. Figure 4 represents characteristic errors of the three left-lesioned patients.

The signers with right hemisphere damage presented special issues in testing for language impairments because sign language makes linguistic use of space, and these signers showed nonlanguage spatial deficits. Left hemispatial neglect, for example, may introduce particular difficulties in signing, since the addressee must either view signs in the neglected visual field or shift his or her gaze away

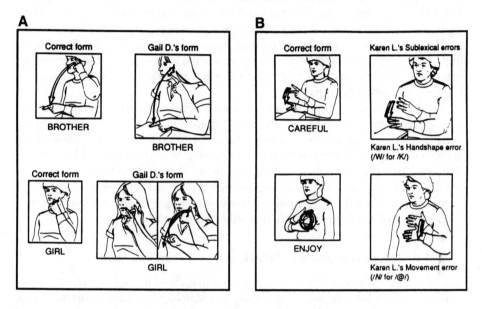

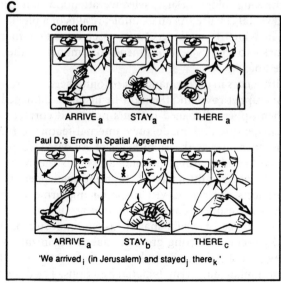

FIGURE 4   **Characteristic errors across patients.**

from the signer. Quite remarkably, the first three signers with right-hemisphere damage whom we examined in depth were not aphasic for sign language. They exhibited fluent, grammatical, virtually error-free signing, with a good range of grammatical forms, no agrammatism, and no signing deficits. Furthermore, only the right-hemisphere-damaged patients were unimpaired in our tests of ASL structures at different linguistic levels.

In one of the tests of ASL linguistic structure, subjects were asked to indicate the two pictures that represented the sign equivalent of *rhyme* in ASL (see Figure 5a). The correct answer in this case would be *apple* and *key* since their associated signs are the same in two of the three major parameters (e.g., they have the same handshape and movement, but differ only in spatial location). On the ASL Rhyming Test and, indeed, across the range of language tests given, the right-hemisphere-damaged signers were not impaired, whereas the left-hemisphere-damaged signers were generally impaired.

This preserved signing existed in the face of marked deficits among the right-hemisphere-damaged signers in processing nonlanguage spatial relations (these deficits are described below). Across a range of tests, these signers showed the classic visual-spatial impairments found in hearing patients with right hemisphere damage. The right-hemisphere-damaged patients, then, had no impairment in the grammatical aspects of their signing, including their spatially organized syntax; they even used the left side of signing space to represent syntactic relations, despite their neglect of the left hemispace in nonlanguage tasks.

Spatial Cognition in Right- and Left-Hemisphere-Damaged Signers

We administered selected tests that are sensitive distinguishers of visual-spatial performance in left- versus right-hemisphere-damaged hearing subjects. These tests included drawing, block design, selective attention, line orientation, facial recognition, and visual closure. As an example, results of a block design test given to deaf signers in which the subjects must assemble either four or nine three-dimensional blocks to match a two-dimensional model of the top surface are shown in Figure 5b.

Clear-cut differences in performance were found between the left-hemisphere-damaged patients (upper row) and the right-hemisphere-damaged patients (lower row). The left-hemisphere-damaged patients produced correct constructions on the simple block designs and made only internal-feature errors on the more complex designs. In contrast, the right-hemisphere-damaged patients produced erratic and incorrect constructions and tended to break the overall configurations of the designs. The general difficulty of the right-hemisphere-damaged patients with this task reflects the classic visual-spatial impairments found in hearing patients with right-hemisphere damage. The two groups of deaf signing patients differed across the range of visual-spatial tasks administered, with right-hemisphere-damaged patients reflecting gross spatial disorganization. These nonlanguage data show that the right hemisphere in deaf signers can develop cerebral specialization for nonlanguage visual-spatial functions. The drawings of the right-hemisphere-damaged patients also tended to show severe spatial disorganization, whereas those of the left-hemisphere-damaged patients did not. The right-hem-

A

Rhyming Test

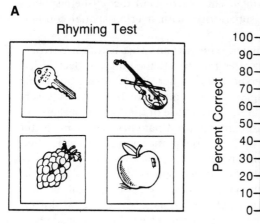

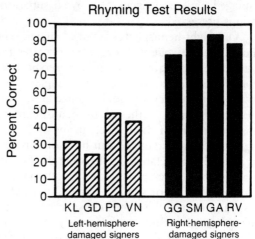

Rhyming Test Results

B

WAIS-R Block Design

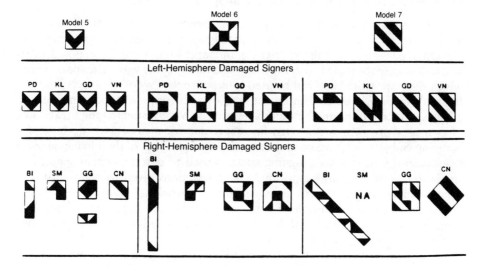

FIGURE 5   The contrast between language and spatial abilities in left- and right-hemisphere-damaged signers.

Note the double dissociation between language abilities (impaired in LHD but spared in RHD) and nonlanguage visuospatial abilities (spared in LHD but impaired in RHD) in these deaf signers.

isphere-damaged patients were not able to indicate perspective; several neglected the left side of space, and one right-hemisphere-damaged patient even added unprompted verbal labels to the drawings. The drawings of the left-hemisphere-damaged patients in general showed superiority, with overlap spatial configurations preserved.

One right-hemisphere-damaged signer, who was an artist before her stroke, showed severe spatial disorganization after the stroke, including neglect of left hemispace and inability to indicate perspective, but her sign language (including spatially expressed syntax) was completely unimpaired. In light of her severe visual-spatial deficit for nonlanguage tasks, correct use of the spatial mechanisms for signed syntax in these right-hemisphere-damaged patients may point to the abstract nature of these mechanisms in ASL. This point shows how little effect right-hemisphere damage can have on language function, even when expressed as a visual-spatial language. In contrast, the left-hemisphere-damaged signer, who was most severely aphasic for sign language (completely agrammatical, without any morphology or syntax), showed normal nonlanguage visual-spatial skills.

In summary, the right-hemisphere-damaged patients generally showed severe left-side neglect and were seriously impaired in nonlanguage visual-spatial capacities, but their signing was still fluent and remarkably unimpaired. They showed virtually no impairments in any of the grammatical aspects of their signing; their impairments, however, were vividly apparent in spatial mapping, which we will consider next.

The Contrast Between Spatial Syntax and Spatial Mapping

Spatial contrasts and spatial manipulations figure structurally at all linguistic levels in ASL. For syntactic functions, spatial loci and relations among these loci are actively manipulated to represent grammatical relations. As opposed to its syntactic use, space in ASL also functions in a topographic way: The space within which signs are articulated can be used to describe the layout of objects in space. In such mapping, spatial relations among signs correspond topographically to actual spatial relations among objects described. We investigated the breakdown of two uses of space within sign language, one for syntax and the other for mapping. Subjects were asked to describe the spatial layout of their living quarters from memory. In this task, signing space is used to describe actual space, and spatial relations are thus significant. The descriptions given by the right-hemisphere-damaged signers were grossly distorted spatially. In contrast, room descriptions of the left-hemisphere-damaged signers were linguistically impaired (matching their linguistic breakdown in other domains) but without spatial distortions.

When space was used in ASL to represent syntactic relations, however, the pattern was reversed. The left-hemisphere-damaged signer who showed consistent failure in his spatially organized syntax was able to describe the layout of his room with some omissions but no spatial distortions. A dissociation was also dramatically displayed in a right-hemisphere-damaged signer. The description she gave of her room showed severe spatial disorganization—furniture was piled in helter-skelter fashion on the right, and the entire left side of the signing space was left bare. However, in her use of the spatial framework for syntax in ASL, she established loci freely throughout the signing space (including on the left) and maintained consistent reference to spatial loci. Thus, even within signing, the use of space to represent syntactic relations and the use of space to represent spatial relations may be differentially affected by brain damage, with the syntactic relations disrupted by left-hemisphere damage and the spatial relations disrupted by right-hemisphere damage (Bellugi, Poizner & Klima 1989).

Lateralization of Facial Signals with Linguistic Function

Investigations of lateralization for sign language have so far focused on manual signs. However, sign language has another structural layer that also can afford a clue to hemispheric specialization, namely nonmanual (facial) signals. For signers of ASL, facial signals can function in two distinct ways, one linguistically, the other to convey affect (Corina 1989; Liddell 1980; Reilly, McIntire & Bellugi 1990, in press). In users of spoken languages, there is by now considerable evidence for right hemisphere involvement in the processing of faces, especially facial affect. Facial signals in ASL thus pose an interesting challenge to strict right-hemisphere processing of facial expression, since certain facial signals in ASL function as part of a tightly constrained linguistic system.

We have new evidence that affective facial signals and linguistic facial signals are differentially lateralized for deaf signers. Parallel lines of investigation in brain-damaged and brain-intact signers are being carried out. In one line of experimentation, linguistic and affective facial signals are presented tachistoscopically to deaf signers without known neurological disorders so that we may infer which cerebral hemisphere is primary in mediating the processing of each type of signal. Figure 6 shows examples of affective and linguistic facial expressions that were used in the delayed matching task. Deaf signers showed greater left-hemisphere mediation of those facial signals that served a linguistic function compared to those with an affective function, while hearing subjects unfamiliar with sign language did not show this difference (Corina 1989).

Two deaf signers, one with a lesion to the right hemisphere and one with a lesion to the left hemisphere, show important dissociations between affective and linguistic facial expression signals. We examined all instances in two stretches of signing (narrative and biographical sketch) of clear sentence contexts in which either affective facial expression would be expected or specifically linguistic facial expression (e.g., adverbial, relative clause, conditional) would be required. Interestingly, the right-lesioned patient was far more likely to produce linguistic facial expression where it was required and showed a clear tendency to omit affective facial expression where it was expected. Thus, linguistic facial expression was relatively spared while affective facial expression was quite impaired in the right-lesioned signer (see Figure 6). In contrast, the left-lesioned signer showed precisely the opposite effect, with full use of affective facial expression present, but linguistic facial expression absent where it would be expected.

These are important findings, since presumably one and the same muscular system is involved. Thus, one cannot account for the findings in terms of weakness of facial musculature, but rather in terms of a dissociation between linguistic and

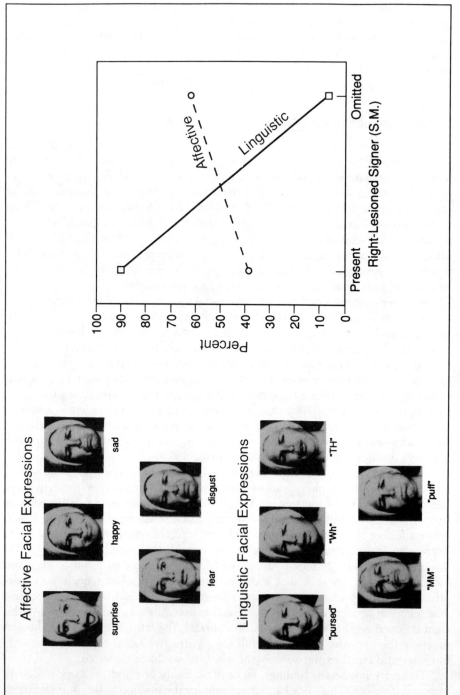

FIGURE 6   Dissociation between linguistic and affective facial signals in a right-lesioned signer.

affective facial expression (Bellugi, Corina, Norman, Klima & Reilly 1989). By examining, in deaf signers, hemispheric specialization for the processing of both affective facial signals and linguistic ones, we can investigate an area in which physical form vs. linguistic function may be finely differentiated as a basis for cerebral dominance.

CONVERGING EVIDENCE REGARDING BRAIN ORGANIZATION FOR SIGN

A recent study analyzed the sign language of a hearing signer proficient in ASL during a left intracarotid injection of sodium amytal (Wada Test), and before and after a right temporal lobectomy for her epilepsy (Damasio, Bellugi, Damasio, Poizner & van Gilder 1986). Neuropsychological and anatomical asymmetries suggested left cerebral dominance for an auditory-based language. Single Photon Emission Tomography revealed lateralized activity of left Broca's and Wernicke's areas for spoken language. The Wada Test, during which all left language areas were rendered inoperative, caused a marked aphasia in both English and ASL. The patient's signing was markedly impaired, with many incorrect sign responses and sign neologisms. Interestingly, since she was hearing and could sign and speak at the same time, it was possible to compare her responses in two languages simultaneously—a unique possibility for languages in different modalities. This comparison revealed frequent mismatches between word and sign, the sign often incorrect both in meaning and in form.

Subsequently, the patient had the anterior portion of her right temporal lobe surgically removed. Analysis of her language after the surgery revealed no impairment of either English or sign language. These findings add further support to the notion that the left cerebral hemisphere subserves language in visual-spatial as well as auditory mode.

Very important converging evidence also comes from a combination of behavioral and neurophysiological studies in deaf signers without lesions (Neville 1988, in press; Neville & Lawson 1987). In Neville's studies, digitized sequences of ASL signs were presented to the left and right visual fields of deaf native signers and hearing nonsigners. The deaf native signers, but not the hearing nonsigners, showed specific left-hemisphere specialization for processing signs of ASL, providing strong evidence for left-hemisphere specialization for sign language in deaf signers without brain lesions. From these converging perspectives, it is becoming clear that the primary specialization of the left hemisphere rests not on the form of the signal, but rather on the linguistic function it subserves.

SUMMARY

We have reviewed some studies that investigate language, its formal architecture, and its representation in the brain, by analyzing visual-spatial languages passed down from one generation of deaf people to the next. Analysis of patterns of breakdown in deaf signers provides new perspectives on the determinants of hemispheric specialization for language. First, the data show that hearing and speech are not necessary for the development of hemispheric specialization: Sound is *not* crucial. Second, it is the left hemisphere that is dominant for sign language. Deaf signers with damage to the left hemisphere show marked sign language deficits but relatively intact capacity for processing nonlanguage visual-spatial relations. Signers with damage to the right hemisphere show the reverse pattern. Thus, not only is there left-hemisphere specialization for language functioning, but there is also a complementary specialization for nonlanguage spatial functioning.

The fact that grammatical information in sign language is conveyed via spatial manipulation does not alter this complementary specialization. Furthermore, components of sign language (lexicon and grammar) can be selectively impaired, reflecting differential breakdown of sign language along linguistically relevant lines. These data suggest that the left hemisphere in humans may have an innate predisposition for language, regardless of the modality. Since sign language involves an interplay between visual-spatial and linguistic relations, the study of sign language breakdown in deaf signers provides a new key to the link between hand and brain.

COGNITION, EDUCATION, AND DEAFNESS: THE FUTURE CHALLENGE

For educators who are committed to the improvement of cognitive functioning of all deaf learners, the data reported here suggest the importance of

1. Continuing experimentation with alternative communication modalities in the classroom;
2. Preparing teachers who are knowledgeable about the application of research results from the general fields of both cognition and language; and
3. Keeping high expectations for deaf learners.

Our data and that of other authors in this volume continue to indicate that deaf learners as a group have the full normal range of intellectual potential, and some aspects of cognition may even show an enhancement. We hope that educators who are familiar with cognition research can devise applications now to help learners reach their full potential.

This is a very exciting time to be thinking about the future of the education of deaf children. As we all know, there has been a rapid increase in awareness of Deaf culture and of its cultural products. Many wonderful expressions of Deaf culture—art, poetry, literature, theater—are occurring now that were not thought of ten or twenty years ago. "The Deaf Way," a celebration of Deaf culture from around the world, took place at Gallaudet University during the summer of 1989. One can now develop an extensive library from excellent videotapes available for teaching sign language and for watching storytelling, poetry, history, and narrative in sign language.

Linda Bove, a deaf actress, is an important figure on *Sesame Street* who provides a role model for deaf children. The television program *Deaf Mosaic*, among many others, is a news magazine that provides news features and interviews with deaf leaders. There are also classics, fairy tales, and stories from different countries on videotape. There are many adult books, children's books, and television programs for teaching different forms of signed language, including Signed English. There are a variety of techniques, including computerized ones, for captioning films and television broadcasts, and even for captioning on-line meetings and classes. There are many books about Deaf culture and history (e.g., Padden & Humphries 1988; Sacks 1989; Lane 1984).

Technologies are becoming available that provide opportunities for education that were undreamed-of ten years ago. For example, Hanson and Padden have developed a laser-disc video interface that allows deaf children to communicate by means of a touch screen and a computer keyboard. In this way, children can go back and forth between English and ASL, touching the screen to see ASL and English at the same time. This is a powerful and highly motivating way to approach English through signs (Hanson & Padden, in press). ASL, now offered for course credit in many colleges and universities across the country, is accepted as a way of fulfilling the foreign language requirement. Deaf children now have access to sign language in a variety of forms, ranging from ASL to Signed English, and some bilingual programs are teaching English through ASL. These teaching methods will have important ramifications in the children's development of language, whether ASL or English.

This is an exciting time for the fields of cognition, deafness, and education. The papers in this volume communicate the current state of these developments and are intended to stimulate the reader to envision the future of deaf education in light of this new work.

REFERENCES

Bellugi, U. 1988. The acquisition of a spatial language. In *The development of language and language researchers, essays in honor of Roger Brown*, ed. F. Kessell, 153–185. Hillsdale, NJ: Lawrence Erlbaum Associates.

Bellugi, U., Corina, D., Norman, F., Klima, E., & Reilly, J. 1989. Differential specialization for linguistic facial expression in left and right lesioned deaf signers. *Academy of Aphasia*, Santa Fe, NM.

Bellugi, U., Klima, E., Lillo-Martin, D., O'Grady, L., & Vaid, J. 1986. *Examining language dominance through hand dominance*. Eleventh Annual Boston University Conference on Child Language Development.

Bellugi, U., Poizner, H., & Klima, E. 1989. Language, modality and the brain. *Trends in Neurosciences* 10:380–388.

Bellugi, U., & Studdert-Kennedy, M., eds. 1980. *Signed and spoken language: Biological constraints on linguistic form*. Deerfield Beach, FL: Verlag Chemie.

Bellugi, U., Tzeng, O.J.L., Klima, E.S., & Fok, A. 1989. Dyslexia: Perspectives from sign and script. In *From reading to neurons*, ed. A.M. Galaburda, 137–172. Cambridge: MIT Press/Bradford Books.

Bellugi, U., van Hoek, K., Lillo-Martin, D., & O'Grady, L. 1988. The acquisition of syntax and space in young deaf signers. In *Language development in exceptional circumstances*, ed. D. Bishop & K. Mogford, 132–149. Edinburgh: Churchill Livingstone.

Corina, D. 1989. Recognition of affective and noncanonical linguistic facial expressions in hearing and deaf subjects. *Brain and Cognition* 9:227–237.

Corbett, E.E. 1985. Cognition, education, and deafness: The challenge. In *Cognition, education, and deafness: Directions for research and instruction*, ed. D.S. Martin, 16–20. Washington, DC: Gallaudet University Press.

Damasio, A., Bellugi, U., Damasio, H., Poizner, H., & van Gilder, J. 1986. Sign language aphasia during left hemisphere amytal injection. *Nature* 322:363–365.

Fok, Y.Y.A., & Bellugi, U. 1986. The acquisition of visual-spatial script. In *Graphonomics: Contemporary research in handwriting*, ed. H. Kao, G. van Galen, & R. Hoosain, 329–355. Amsterdam: North Holland.

Fok, Y.Y.A., Bellugi, U., van Hoek, K., & Klima, E.S. 1988. The formal properties of Chinese languages in space. In *Cognitive aspects of the Chinese language*, ed. M. Kiu, H.C. Chen, & M.J. Chen, 187–205. Hong Kong: Asian Research Service.

Hanson, V.L., & Padden, C. In press. Computers and videodisc technology for bilingual ASL/English instruction of deaf children. In *Cognition, education, and multi-media: Exploring ideas in high technology*, ed. D. Nix & R. Spiro. Hillsdale, NJ: Lawrence Erlbaum Associates.

Johansson, G. 1975. Visual motion perception. *Scientific American*, 232, 76–89.

Klima, E.S., & Bellugi, U. 1979. *The signs of language*. Cambridge: Harvard University Press.

Klima, E.S., Bellugi, U., & Poizner, H. 1988a. Grammar and space in sign aphasiology. *Aphasiology* 2:319–328.

———. 1988b. The neurolinguistic substrate for sign language. In *Language, speech, and mind*, ed. L.M. Hyman & C.N. Li, 138–152. London: Routledge.

Lane, H. 1984. *When the mind hears: A history of the deaf*. New York: Random House.

Lenneberg, E. 1967. *Biological foundations of language*. New York: John Wiley & Sons.

Liddell, S. 1980. *American Sign Language syntax*. The Hague: Mouton.

Liddell, S., & Johnson, R. 1986. American Sign Language compound formation processes, lexicalization, and phonological remnants. *Natural Language and Linguistic Theory* 4:445–513.

Marler, P. 1970. Bird song and speech: Could there be parallels? *American Scientist* 59:669–673.

Neville, H. J. 1988. Cerebral organization for spatial attention. In *Spatial cognition: Brain bases and development*, ed. J. Stiles-Davis, M. Kritchevsky, & U. Bellugi, 327–342. Hillsdale, NJ: Lawrence Erlbaum Associates.

———. In press. Neurobiology of cognitive and language processing: Effects of early experience. In *Brain maturation and behavioral development: Biosocial dimensions*, ed. K. Gibson & A.C. Peterson. New York: Aldine de Gruyter.

Neville, H.J., & Lawson, D. 1987. Attention to central and peripheral visual space in a movement detection task (Parts I-III). *Brain Research* 405:253–294.

Newport, E.S. 1988. Constraints on learning and their role in language acquisition: Studies of the acquisition of American Sign Language. *Language Sciences* 10(1): 147–172.

Padden, C., & Humphries, T. 1988. *Deaf in America: Voices from a culture*. Cambridge: Harvard University Press.

Poizner, H. 1983. Perception of movement in American Sign Language: Effects of linguistic structure and linguistic experience. *Perception and Psychophysics* 33(3):215–231.

Poizner, H., Fok, Y.Y.A., & Bellugi, U. (In press). The interplay between perception of language and perception of motion. *Language Sciences*.

Poizner, H., Klima, E.S., & Bellugi, U. 1987. *What the hands reveal about the brain.* Cambridge: MIT Press/Bradford Books.

Poizner, H., Klima, E.S., Bellugi, U., & Livingston, R. 1986. Motion analysis in a visual gestural language. In *Event cognition,* ed. V. McCabe & G. Balzano, 155–174. Hillsdale, NJ: Lawrence Erlbaum Associates.

Reilly, J., McIntire, M., & Bellugi, U. 1990. Faces: The relationship between language and affect. In *From gesture to language in hearing and deaf children,* ed V. Volterra & C. Erting. New York: Springer-Verlag.

Reilly, J., McIntire, M., & Bellugi, U. In press. Baby face: A new perspective on universals in language acquisition. In *Theoretical issues in sign language research: Psychology,* ed P. Siple & S. Fischer. Chicago: University of Chicago Press.

Sacks, O. 1989. *Seeing voices: A journey into the world of the deaf.* Berkeley: University of California Press.

Sign Language Studies. Linstok Press.

Supalla, S. In press. Manually coded English: The modality question in signed development. In *Theoretical issues in sign language research,* ed. P. Siple & S. Fischer. Chicago: University of Chicago Press.

Vaid, J., Bellugi, U., & Poizner, H. 1989. Hand dominance for signing: Clues to brain lateralization of language. *Neuropsychologia* 27:949–960.

Wilbur, R. 1987. *American Sign Language.* Boston: Little, Brown & Co.

COGNITIVE ASSESSMENT

Identification of Additional Learning Difficulties in Hearing-Impaired Children

D. Yvonne Aplin

Educational psychologists who assess hearing-impaired children are particularly concerned with identifying any learning difficulties, in addition to deafness, that might hinder the child's progress in developing language. Van Uden's suggestion (e.g., Van Uden 1981, 1983) that some deaf children also have dyspraxia is of interest in this context. His concept of dyspraxia differs somewhat from that outlined in the literature on "clumsy" children and involves a number of features that constitute a syndrome. He describes it as a motor handicap that affects fine-finger movements, the development of rhythm, and movements of the speech musculature, so that those who are clumsy with their fingers are also clumsy in their speaking. In addition, he has noted that these dyspraxic children have a strong memory for simultaneously presented visual data (as opposed to memory for successively presented visual data). Eupraxic children (those showing fluent fine-motor and speech movements) have strengths in those areas that dyspraxics find difficult.

The complete version of this paper is available in microfiche or hard-copy from ERIC Document Reproduction Service. Ask for Document No. ED 313 835.

I would like to thank Professor Ian Taylor for his help, advice, and support throughout the duration of the research and subsequent writing. Thanks are also due to Dr. Vijay Das for the audiological and etiological information used, and the Headteachers and staff of the schools concerned for their cooperation in the research, which was supported in part by a grant from the North West Regional Health Authority. Raw data from Van Uden (1983) have been re-analyzed with the permission of the author and Swets and Zeitlinger B.V., Lisse, Holland.

Van Uden reported results of a factor-analytic study that identified a eupraxia/dyspraxia main factor for 83 children aged seven to ten years. Fifteen subtests were used in the test battery. The children all had mean hearing losses in excess of 90 dBHL and a Performance IQ of 90 or above. They all were being educated by oral methods in the primary school department for the "normal deaf" at Holland's Instituut voor Doven in Sint Michielsgestel, and they had no major additional handicaps that would have necessitated placement in a special class.

The analysis showed that tests relating to the fine-motor functions of the fingers and mouth (imitation and memory of finger movements, paper folding, speech rhythms, and words) showed clustered results with positive loadings on the first, main factor. Negative loadings on this factor were found for tests of memory for simultaneously presented visual information (pictures, designs, symbols, and colors), indicating that those who were less fluent on motor tests performed better on such memory tests and vice versa. The importance of the factor increased with age.

Van Uden also reported that a relatively high percentage (more than 30 percent) of deaf children show some dyspraxic features. The children in his research have all attended one particular school for the deaf, and they do not represent the total population of hearing-impaired children. This should therefore be considered when interpreting the research findings. The more severe cases are classified as severely dysphasic and are taught one-handed fingerspelling in addition to speech to assist their development of communication.

The suggestion throughout Van Uden's work is that dyspraxic children can be identified early in their school life by means of his test battery. He has stated that decisions about the need for additional special educational treatment may be made in some cases at the school in Holland when a child is about five and a half years old.

Educational psychologists in Britain and elsewhere are also involved in deciding the appropriate educational placement for young hearing-impaired children. In addition, they frequently see hearing-impaired children at the ages of eight, nine, or even older, who are referred for investigation of specific language-learning difficulties, such as dyspraxia, because they have failed to make the expected linguistic progress.

The idea of identification and early remediation of such learning difficulties in hearing-impaired children is clearly of great interest to psychologists, teachers, and others who work with deaf children. There are also, however, possible dangers inherent in such an approach since it could lead to an educational self-fulfilling prophecy.

Van Uden's work has been influential worldwide through papers read at conferences and courses he has given for educators. Although his work has been familiar to teachers of the deaf in Britain since the early 1970s, no research has been carried out so far to assess whether the profile of dyspraxia can be found in a group of hearing-impaired children there. Internationally, there is a lack of supporting published evidence for his findings.

The relationship between fine-motor movements, speech, and memory proposed by Van Uden is disputable. Do the tests specified by Van Uden cluster together for a different sample of hearing-impaired children? Studies that have linked apraxia of speech with gross- or fine-motor disabilities in hearing children have not always been confirmed in subsequent research (e.g., Williams, Ingham & Rosenthal 1981). It seemed, therefore, that a study was required to investigate the psychometric test profile of dyspraxia in hearing-impaired children. As a member of a team working from the Department of Audiology and Education of the Deaf at Manchester University under the direction of Professor Ian Taylor, the author was in a unique position to carry out this research.

A preliminary report of the work was presented at the sixteenth International Congress on Education of the Deaf (Aplin 1988). A discussion of the statistical techniques used for profile analysis in the study can be found in Aplin (1987a). The social and emotional adjustment of children involved in the research has also been described in Aplin (1985, 1987b).

SUBJECTS

In order to avoid biases in the selection of the study group, a representative sample of children with sensorineural hearing loss was chosen from the total number of children born in the city of Manchester during a ten-year period. All together, 106 school-aged children participated in the study. They were being educated in special schools for the hearing-impaired ($N = 63$) or language disordered ($N = 3$), in units for the hearing-impaired ($N = 5$), or in ordinary schools with support from an itinerant service for the hearing impaired ($N = 35$). There were 54 girls and 52 boys in the sample. Their ages ranged from 7 to 16 years, with a mean (x) of 12.4 years (SD 2.50). Their mean hearing losses in the better ear, averaged over the five frequencies 250Hz, 500Hz, 1kHz, 2kHz, and 4kHz, ranged from 23 to 120 dBHL (x 66.6 dBHL, SD 27.08). Their WISC-R Performance IQs ranged from 45 to 146 (x 98.1, SD16.36). Within the total sample there was a subgroup of 30 children with a mean hearing loss in the better ear of 90 dBHL or more; these children were 7 to 15 years old and had WISC-R Performance IQs ranging from 68 to 129.

Scores reported in Van Uden (1983) for his group of 83 children were used for comparison with those of the Manchester sample. His children were 7 ($N = 20$), 8 ($N = 18$), 9 ($N = 23$), and 10 ($N = 22$) years old. All had mean hearing losses greater than 90 dB (x 108.5, SD 10.3) and WISC-R Performance IQs of 90 or more (x 107.1, SD 11.2).

TESTS ADMINISTERED

All children were assessed individually while wearing their personal hearing aids. Only 12 of Van Uden's 15 suggested subtests (specified in Van Uden 1983) were used in the present study. The tests used were

1. WISC-R (Wechsler 1974) Digit Span (DS): An auditory memory test for digits in forward and reverse order from the WISC-R Verbal Scale.

2. WISC-R Coding (C): A paper-and-pencil digit-symbol test from the WISC-R Performance Scale.
3. Hiskey-Nebraska (Hiskey 1966) Memory for Color (MC): Up to six colors have to be remembered. The use of an internal verbal coding strategy may improve performance on this visual memory test.
4. Hiskey-Nebraska Paper Folding (PF): A visual memory test, where sequences of paper folds have to be remembered. This test assesses memory of successively presented information.
5. Hiskey-Nebraska Visual Attention Span (VAS): Memory of pictures. A sequence of up to seven pictures are presented simultaneously.
6. Successive Pictures (SP): VAS in successive presentation, one at a time instead of all in a row.
7. Berges and Lezine Imitation of Gestures (BL): Imitation of sixteen hand and finger movements.
8. Imitation of Finger Movements (IFM): Van Uden's test of memory for finger-touching sequences.
9. Knox Cube Test (KC): A test of memory for tapped sequences on four blocks. A sequence of up to six taps can be given. This test assesses memory of successively presented information.
10. Rhythm Test (RT): A test of memory for spoken "ba ba" rhythms (e.g., "ba baba" and "baba ba ba"). This test is auditory with a linguistic basis.
11. Benton Visual Retention Test (B): A test of memory of designs shown for ten seconds and then drawn on paper by the child.
12. Number of Words (NW): A test of how many words the child can say in two minutes; a language test.

ANALYSES

Initial R-technique analyses of results from the twelve subtests showed that different factors emerged for the Van Uden and Manchester samples. Q-technique and cluster analyses were also carried out (see also Aplin 1987a).

Only some of the results of the Q-technique factor analyses will be reported here. The Q-technique of factor analysis groups together children (or cases) who show similar scores on certain tests, rather than grouping tests together as in the standard R-technique of factor analysis. Raw test scores are converted to standard scores (in this case T scores with a mean of 50 and standard deviation of 10); the data matrix is then transposed and the factor loadings of the children define the subgroups. Profiles of the particular children isolated in this way can then be investigated for the tests administered and a mean profile of this subgroup can be calculated. Q-analyses were carried out by the PA 2 program (principal factoring with iteration), followed by varimax rotation taken from the *Statistical Package for the Social Sciences* (Nie, Hull, Jenkins, Steinbrenner & Bent 1975). A four-factor solution was derived for the analysis, although only the first factor is presented here. Only those children with a factor loading of .60 or greater were used to arrive at the profiles discussed in this paper.

Re-analysis of Van Uden's own data on the twelve subtests by means of Q-analysis revealed the negative and positive profiles shown in Figure 1. The graph shows the mean score profiles for the children, with negative and positive loadings. From the total group (N = 83), thirteen children showed a negative profile. As predicted from Van Uden's theory, these children showed a "dyspraxic" profile with the lowest scores on tests of fine-finger movements, rhythm, speaking, and successive memory (Digit Span, Paper Folding, Berges and Lezine, Imitation of Finger Movements, Knox Cube, Rhythm Test, and, to a lesser extent, Number of Words). Their strengths were on the simultaneous memory tests: Memory for Color, Visual Attention Span, Benton and Coding (the latter is not a test of memory but of simultaneously presented information). The children with the positive loadings showed the reverse "eupraxic" profile. Factor 1 extracted just over half of the total variance. Very similar profiles were found in the first factor in each age group of Van Uden's sample, when those were analyzed separately.

In order to see if Van Uden's main profiles could be found in the Manchester sample, his mean score profiles for dyspraxia and eupraxia for each of the four age groups were analyzed as dummy cases together with the scores from the Manchester sample separated into three age groups (7 to 10 years, N = 36; 11 to 13 years, N = 33; and 14 to 16 years, N = 37). With the negative version of the profile, the Van Uden study had isolated 13 of the 83 children (15.7%). Only

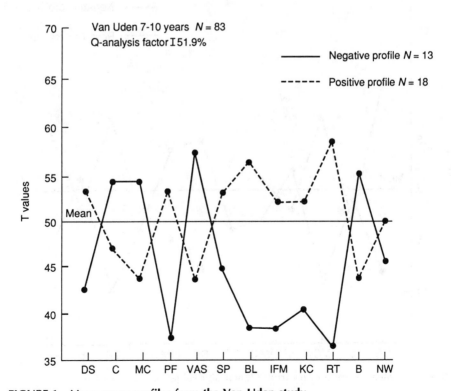

FIGURE 1   Mean score profiles from the Van Uden study.

5 of the 106 Manchester children showed this profile (4.7%)—a very low percentage. Three Manchester children showed his positive eupraxic profile.

Q-analyses carried out on the scores of the Manchester sample alone revealed different mean score profiles compared with those of Van Uden's sample. The Factor 1 profiles extracted for the Manchester sample are shown in Figure 2. Due to limitations of the factor program, only 100 children could be used in this analysis (6 of the oldest children were not included). The first factor extracted 36.5% of the total variance and revealed negative and positive profiles with nine children in each. The negative profile showed low mean scores on Digit Span, Memory for Color, Rhythm Test, and Manchester analyses and seemed to represent the most highly verbal or verbally biased tests within this battery, suggesting a linguistic ability factor. The highest mean scores for the children with the negative profile were on the Paper Folding, Berges and Lezine, Imitation of Finger-Movements, and Benton tests, which are the most nonverbal in the battery. The positive profile showed the reverse of these scores. Q-analysis of the scores of the 30 children with mean hearing losses of 90 dBHL or greater revealed similar mean score profiles and *not* the eupraxic/dyspraxic profile of the Van Uden sample.

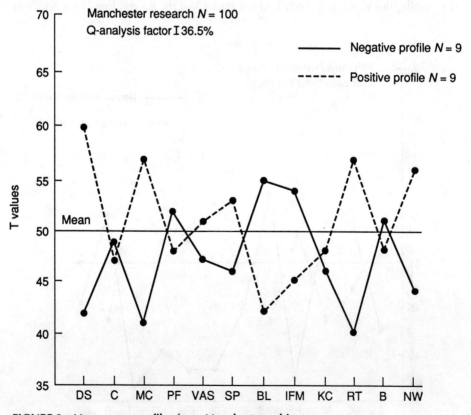

FIGURE 2   **Mean score profiles from Manchester subjects.**

DISCUSSION

The Van Uden data consistently yielded one particular profile that emerged in the first factor of the Q-factor analyses. It was a strong profile which in its positive and negative forms accounted for over half of the variance of the total group. It is consistent with Van Uden's description of dyspraxia (and eupraxia) in deaf children. When the Van Uden profiles were incorporated into the Manchester data, only 5 children emerged with the negative profile, all of whom were attending special schools. If the criteria specified by Van Uden are adhered to— that is, including children with a WISC-R Performance IQ of 90 or above and a hearing loss of more than 90 dBHL—only 2 of the 5 children fit the pattern (1.9% of the total sample, or 6.67% of the 30 children with 90 + dBHL losses).

One of these subjects did indeed have serious problems in developing oral linguistic skills. Her understanding and use of language was extremely limited at approximately a two-year-old level (her chronological age was 8 years 0 months). She was the youngest child of the five, and the only one unable to gain a WISC-R Verbal Scale IQ. She had some fine- and gross-motor coordination difficulties for which she received physiotherapy and had a mean hearing loss of 97 dBHL. Middle-ear problems that had prevented the use of hearing aids at times and an absence from school for a period of some months could have contributed markedly to her poor linguistic progress. As her Performance IQ was below normal limits (68), however, she did not fulfill Van Uden's criterion for nonverbal intelligence.

The only child of the five who fulfilled all of Van Uden's criteria for age (between 7 and 10 years), Performance IQ, and hearing loss was a boy of 10 years 11 months, with a Performance IQ of 129 and mean hearing loss of 96 dBHL. He had been deafened by the rubella virus, in contrast to the other four children, whose deafness was of unknown etiology. He was a restless, fidgety boy, who had particular areas of weakness on four tests from the dyspraxia battery (Knox Cube, Imitation of Finger Movements, Digit Span, and Rhythm Test). However, he gained a Verbal IQ of 73 on the WISC-R and was not thought by his teachers to have additional language-learning problems. After participating in the research, he left a special school to attend a mainstream school with a resource base for hearing-impaired children, where he has been ever since.

The question of the self-fulfilling prophecy is relevant to this case. If this boy had been selected by means of a test battery as having possible dyspraxic difficulties earlier in his life, and if this selection had led to his being educated out of the normal oral system, would he have progressed so well? We can only speculate on the answer.

The three Manchester children who showed Van Uden's positive eupraxic profile ranged in age from 8 years 8 months to 15 years 2 months, with mean hearing losses ranging from 27 to 83 dBHL and WISC-R Performance IQs from 88 to 95. None of the three fulfilled Van Uden's criterion for hearing loss. All were girls for whom the etiology of hearing loss was unknown. One attended a special school, one was in mainstream schooling, and the third was in a unit for hearing-impaired children attached to a mainstream school. They all gained a WISC-R Verbal IQ (range from 74 to 88). However, they were not children showing the greatest linguistic progress in the study, although two had only mild or moderate hearing losses (27 and 43 dB).

Although Van Uden suggested that eupraxic children have facility with oral language, this suggestion was not borne out in the present study. Many other children in the Manchester sample, including some with severe to profound hearing losses, had greater linguistic achievements. (Criterion measures of linguistic ability in the study included an Estimated Expressive Language Age based on scores from some WISC-R Verbal subtests or the Reynell Developmental Language Scales-Revised [Reynell 1977] and a score from the English Picture Vocabulary Test [Brimer & Dunn 1973], which gives a measure of vocabulary comprehension). It is concluded, therefore, that even when children show the association between fluent fine-motor function, speech, and memory, they do not necessarily show a correspondingly high level of oral language ability.

The two groups of nine children identified in the main negative and positive profiles extracted from the Manchester sample were not significantly different in age or Performance IQ (see Figure 2). Those with the positive profile had a significantly lower mean hearing loss, however. In addition to significantly higher mean scores on four dyspraxia tests (Digit Span, Memory for Color, Rhythm Test, and Number of Words) children with the positive profile also had significantly higher mean scores on language and reading measures used in the study (EPVT, Estimated Expressive Language Age, and Best Reading Age) and two other Hiskey-Nebraska tests (Bead Patterns and Memory for Digits), thus emphasizing their linguistic capability and possibly greater use of an internal verbal coding strategy when compared with the children showing the negative profile. The latter children had a significantly higher mean score on the Berges and Lezine test, a finding which is at variance with Van Uden's theory that this test is associated with linguistic ability. Further details about the children in these two groups and about background features affecting their language development can be found in an extended version of this paper that is available through the ERIC system.

CONCLUSIONS

The main profiles emerging from the Van Uden and Manchester samples on the twelve dyspraxia subtests differed. The link between fine-motor, speech, and certain memory tests found for Van Uden's children was not replicated in the Manchester population of children with wider ranges of age and hearing loss. The eupraxic/dyspraxic profile did not emerge for the Manchester children even when those with mean hearing losses of 90 dBHL or greater were investigated. (Further investigations with a smaller population of younger children have now confirmed the present research findings.)

A small percentage of Manchester children showed the dyspraxic profile, but the one child who fulfilled all of Van Uden's specified criteria did not have language-learning difficulties in addition to those expected from his hearing loss. This finding suggests that there may be dangers in the early identification of children by means of a test battery whose validity is uncertain. It also emphasizes the need to verify certain test profiles found in restricted samples of deaf children (such as those attending one particular school) on a wider population of hearing-impaired children. The heterogeneity of samples of hearing-impaired children is well known and well documented. It is perhaps unlikely that a unitary disorder could account for language-learning problems in large numbers of children as heterogeneous as the hearing-impaired (with regard to factors such as etiology, age of diagnosis, use and effectiveness of amplification, specialist support, home and school environments, etc.).

The major profile that emerged for the Manchester sample suggested a verbal/nonverbal dichotomy within the twelve dyspraxia subtests. This profile seems to be meaningful for children with a hearing impairment and suggests that a small number of the subtests in Van Uden's battery may be useful predictors of progress with oral language. Further investigations are being carried out at Manchester to combine these tests with other measures in order to establish a set of best predictors of linguistic ability in hearing-impaired children.

REFERENCES

Aplin, D.Y. 1985. The social and emotional adjustment of hearing-impaired children in special schools. *Journal of the British Association of Teachers of the Deaf* 9(4):84–94.

————. 1987a. Classification of dyspraxia in hearing-impaired children using the Q-technique of factor analysis. *Journal of Child Psychology and Psychiatry* 28(4):581–596.

————. 1987b. Social and emotional adjustment of hearing-impaired children in ordinary and special schools. *Educational Research* 29(1):56–64.

————. 1988. Psychological assessment of hearing-impaired children: The search for meaningful profiles. In *The education of the deaf: Current perspectives* (Vol.IV), ed. I.G. Taylor, 2299–2316. Kent, England: Croom Helm.

Brimer, M.A., & Dunn, L.M. 1973. *Full range English picture vocabulary test manual.* Newnham, England: Educational Evaluation Enterprises.

Hiskey, M.S. 1966. *Hiskey-Nebraska test of learning aptitude manual.* Lincoln: University of Nebraska.

Nie, N.N., Hull, C.H., Jenkins, J.G., Steinbrenner, K., & Bent, D.H. 1975. *Statistical package for the social sciences* (2nd ed.). New York: McGraw-Hill.

Reynell, J.K. 1977. *Manual for the Reynell Developmental Language Scales* (Revised). Windsor, England: National Foundation for Educational Research-Nelson.

Rutter, M. 1967. A children's behavior questionnaire for completion by teachers. *Journal of Child Psychology and Psychiatry* 8:1–11.

Stott, D.H. 1974. The social adjustment of children. *Manual of the Bristol social adjustment guides.* 5th ed. London: University of London Press.

Van Uden, A.M.J. 1981. Early diagnosis of those multiple handicaps in prelingually profoundly deaf children which endanger an education according to the purely oral way. *Journal of the British Association of Teachers of the Deaf* 5(4):112–127.

Van Uden, A.M.J. 1983. *Diagnostic testing of deaf children: The syndrome of dyspraxia.* Lisse, The Netherlands: Swets and Zeitlinger.

Wechsler, D. 1974. *Wechsler Intelligence Scale for Children-Revised Manual.* New York: Psychological Corporation. Anglicized version published by NFER, Windsor, England, 1976.

Williams, R., Ingham, R.J., & Rosenthal, J. 1981. A further analysis for developmental apraxia of speech in children with defective articulation. *Journal of Speech and Hearing Research* 24:496–505.

A Portrait of Children in Transition: Utilizing the Salient Responses of Infants and Toddlers to Evaluate Sensorimotor Change

Terry R. Berkeley

C rossing the boundaries between theory, research, and practice has been an infinitely difficult undertaking in human service disciplines. Bricker (1982) observed that although

> many researchers seem to assume that information flows unilaterally from the laboratory to field applications for the eradication of social ills . . . some writers have questioned whether the unilateral flow from researcher to practitioner provides the greatest positive clinical impact, the most enlightened social policies, or the most effective governmental policies toward social issues. (pp. 1–2)

In the arena of early intervention, Meisels (1985) has suggested that the research to practice dilemma is exacerbated because

---

The complete version of this paper is available in microfiche or hard-copy from ERIC Document Reproduction Service. Ask for Document No. ED 313 836.

I would like to thank Professor Francis M. Duffy, Gallaudet University; Professor Barbara L. Ludlow, West Virginia University; Professor Shelley G. McNamara, Drexel University; Professor John P. Scholz, University of Delaware; Mr. Michael W. Smull, Director of Applied Research and Evaluation Unit, University of Maryland Medical School; and Professor Jeri Traub, San Jose State University for reviewing previous drafts of this work. Their comments and insights were provocative and helpful, and they were always most encouraging. The responsibility for the content of this entire paper, of course, rests with the author.

far too often conclusions are drawn about efficacy without consideration first being given to internal consistency, within and between, of assumptions underlying these programs. Chief among these assumptions are the program's (a) implicit theory of human development, (b) conceptualization of specific interventions, (c) method of measuring developmental change, and (d) strategies for selecting participants. (p. 2)

The intent of this paper is to introduce a model that illustrates the continuities in infant development. The model provides early intervention professionals the opportunity to assess the developmental performance of a very young child and to devise interventions that are understandable to professionals who represent several interrelated disciplines and who use multiple theoretical constructs on which to base their work. Thus, in part, the model can help to resolve the research to practice dilemma.

INTRODUCTION TO THE SALIENT RESPONSES MODEL

Lewis and Starr's (1979) salient responses model is a little-known representation of the progressive states of development interactions with the environment. The model is based on a widely accepted history of theoretical assertions about developmental continuity (Berkeley & Ludlow 1989), as well as on empirical data that support its validity (Lewis & Cherry 1977). This model is especially applicable to infants and toddlers from birth through two years of age.

Lewis and Starr's paradigm offers four principal benefits to early intervention professionals.

1. It is relevant to the major linear, stage, or circular theoretical constructs of human development (e.g., maturational to constructivist to information-processing to behavioral) since its primary attributes are experienced by all children;
2. It assumes that developmental continuities and discontinuities exist, but the discontinuities assist in reorganizing behavior and bringing about developmental change, especially qualitative change;
3. It can be used singularly or as part of a broader protocol for child assessment, as a framework for designing child-centered interventions, and as a frame of reference for evaluating program outcomes; and
4. It can be applied to children at all levels of development: typically developing, atypically developing, or at-risk; or to infants and toddlers who are hearing-impaired.

The salient responses model consists of a set of variables that represent the transitions a child passes through during the process of attaining mastery of conceptual information across all the arbitrarily established separations, or domains of development (e.g., cognition, communication, social-emotional, and motor).

Lewis & Starr (1979) defined salient responses as follows:

Quantity refers to the gross frequency and/or duration with which the behavior is expressed in a given unit of time. In the case of language, for example, this is how much a person speaks. *Quality* refers to the extent the response is effective, efficient, or elaborately differentiated. For example, we can ask whether an infant uses syntactically correct language in a situation. *Speed of acquisition* refers to how quickly a response is acquired. *Utilization* refers to the circumstances in which the behavior is displayed. *Affective tone* refers to the degree of affect associated with use. *Generalizability* refers to the use of the target behavior in place of other responses, while *organizational properties* refers to the relationship of the particular response to others in the individual's repertoire. *Intention* refers to the infant's control of the response and awareness of that control (p. 657).

Berkeley & Ludlow (1989) devised their own definition.

The salient responses of the child can best be seen in the examination of the play of infants . . . As the child develops, play changes with respect to the salient response attributes: the amount of time the child spends engaged in play (quantity); the differentiation of actions the child uses to play with different objects (quality); the length of time it takes the child to learn new play skills (speed of acquisition); the occasions and settings in which the child chooses to play (utilization); the affect displayed by the child during play (affective tone); the inclination of the child to use a play skill in novel settings or with new objects (generalization); the relationship of play behaviors to other responses demonstrated by the child (organization); and, the purpose and meaning the child attaches to play (intention) (p. 16).

THEORETICAL CONCEPTUALIZATIONS OF THE MODEL

The salient attributes of response are traits of development. Lewis (1987) suggested that attributes parallel the concept of traits a child develops in a particular way through its interactions with the environment; he also indicated that changes in development are continuous. Mischel (1968) reported that traits are environmental determinants of behavior. The impact of these traits upon the child's development and the environment must be considered if one finds exceptional outcomes of development, similar to, for example, a psychopathology. Sameroff and Chandler (1975) specified in their transactional model that the environment is "plastic" (p. 235) and adds flexibility to the child's ability to respond and react to its surroundings. Thus, the traits of development are flexible and the "constants in development are . . . the processes by which these traits are maintained in the transactions between organism and environment" (p. 235).

The value of describing developmental performance in this way rests on Lewis and Starr's assumption that the study of development is a study of change in the human organism. Moreover, how changes occur and determining "order" (p. 653) in those changes are part of the ontological pathway upon which development rests. Flavell's (1971) notion of development as progressive steps "leads logically to the paradoxical conclusion that the individual spends virtually all his childhood years 'being' rather than 'becoming'" (p. 426).

INTEGRATED MODELING: HUMAN DEVELOPMENT AS SET THEORY

The salient responses of the child can be seen best in the examination of the play of infants since play, according to Rogers (1982), "is an all-encompassing activity . . . that virtually all areas of . . . development—cognitive, motor, social, emotional, language—can be observed in a child's play" (p. 11). Therefore, play mirrors the integrated quality of a child's development.

In this view, play is similar to set theory. A set, according to Breuer (1958), is a "collection of distinct objects of our perception or of our thought, which are called elements of the set" (p. 4). That is to say, play is a complete "set," and the domains of development (i.e., cognition, motor functioning, social-emotional functioning, and communications) are individual elements comprising the complete set. Once elements of the set are united, an integrated conceptualization of development exists (see Figure 1). Thus, there is no need to arbitrarily separate development into domains. In point of fact, by using play as the mirror of development, every aspect of development can be seen in a child's play, especially the play of infants who are in the midst of the sensorimotor stage, an integrated phase of development.

In itself, the sensorimotor period, although it is the initial phase in Piaget's cognitive scheme, is not just a unidimensional developmental construct. Rather, the sensorimotor stage represents cognition, motor functioning, social-emotional functioning, and communication. Moreover, considering development in any terms other than that of an integrated model seems to limit the understanding of a child's full range of developmental abilities and characteristics. Thus, describing development in domain-specific terms suggests that children's intellectual functioning is separate from their motor, social-emotional, and communications functioning. However, this separation simply is not valid. Another way to conceive of this newer notion is that instead of describing a child's developmental performance as a set of four snapshots, the child's development is thought of as a motion picture of development unfolding.

Thinking of human development as an integrated set is new only because developmental theory is not typically perceived in such terms. Support for such a shift in paradigms is more seminal than one might expect. Bringuier (B) (1980) had the following conversation with Piaget (P) illustrating this point:

B: There's a little of everything in here—insects in glass cases on the wall and plants at the windows. At what level of life does psychology begin, do you think?

P: I am convinced there is no sort of boundary between the living and the mental or between the biological and the psychological. From the moment an organism takes account of a previous experience and adapts to a new situation, that very much resembles psychology.

B: For instance, when sunflowers turn toward the sun, that's psychology?

P: I think, in fact, it is behavior.

B: Isn't there any boundary between sunflowers and us?

Set Theory Notation

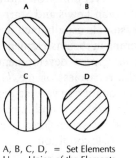

A = Cognition
B = Motor Functioning
C = Communications & Language
D = Social/Emotional Functioning

A, B, C, D, = Set Elements
U = Union of the Elements

Play as Set Theory: An Integrated Notion of Development

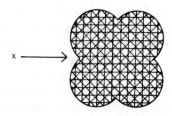

X = Play
X = A U B U C U d

Development as Set Theory: An Integrated Notion of Development

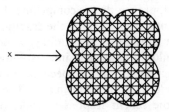

X = Development
X = A U B U C U D

FIGURE 1   Child development as set theory.

P: No. That is the central argument of my book *Biology and Knowledge*, in which I try to show the isomorphisms . . .

B: The analogies?

P: Yes—between organic relations and cognitive processes, the processes of knowledge. There are structures of organisms and structures of intelligence. I try to show that the latter spring from the former and that logic, for example, originates in the general coordination of actions and that the general coordination of actions is based on coordinations of the nervous system, themselves supported by organic coordinations (pp. 2–3).

Evidence about the salient responses model, especially its integrated understanding of development and the way it lends itself to the multiple theoretical approaches to development used by early intervention professionals, suggests that the model has much more practical utility than Lewis and Starr initially thought. Moreover, since early intervention professionals usually included sections on the infant's integrated developmental functioning in their assessment reports, an entire report using this model is a report of *integrated* developmental performance. Also, one must remember that each child, regardless of age, (1) acquires developmental concepts with a certain speed and quality, in varying degrees of quantity, with a specific sense of organization, generalizability, and intention, and with an individual affective tone; and (2) exhibits these salient responses in the presence or absence of a developmental delay or at-risk condition.

CONCLUSION

This discussion is intended to offer evidence that a previously conceptualized model of human development can be utilized by early intervention professionals in their work with infants who are enrolled in programs whose general goal is to stimulate positive developmental change. Further, the intent is to demonstrate that the salient responses model is viable as a foundation for the assessment of infants and for the design of intervention activities. The model also could serve as a framework for the evaluation of early intervention program outcomes.

The salient responses model posited by Lewis and Starr offers early intervention professionals the ability to expand their capacity to discuss their efforts with parents, other professionals, and among themselves by describing developmental performance through a standard approach that is compelling. Further, it is significant that a model of development exists whereby the traditional divisions of development or domains can be considered as a unitary conceptual framework. That is, it is important that children, especially infants whose proportion of development increases at an incredible rate of speed daily, can be thought of in *complete*, rather than *separate* developmental terms. The observation of a child's development through the salient responses model offers a positive view of a child, rather than a deficit-oriented or pathological perspective that is unidimensional in scope.

In relation to deafness, there has been very little specific discussion of the salient responses model in relation to infants who are deaf. It has not been the intent here to overlook the importance of children who happen to exhibit characteristics that represent deafness. Nor has it been the intent here to show disregard for the cultural richness of deaf persons. Rather, it is of the utmost importance for early intervention professionals who conduct screening and assessment procedures or develop programs for deaf children to include those characteristics and an understanding of that cultural richness in their descriptions of and programming for these children, using the salient attributes of response. It will be at that moment in time when early intervention professionals incorporate this understanding about child development into their programs that the notion of "disability" as a "pathology" of children will disappear, and differences among all children will become truly valued.

REFERENCES

Berkeley, T.R., & Ludlow, B.L. 1989. Toward a reconceptualization of the developmental model. *Topics in Early Childhood Special Education* 9(3): 51–66.

Breuer, J. 1958. *Introduction to the theory of sets,* trans. H. Fehr. Englewood Cliffs, NJ: Prentice-Hall.

Bricker, D.D. 1982. Introduction. In *Intervention with at-risk and handicapped infants: From research to application,* ed. D.D. Bricker, 1–2. Baltimore: University Park Press.

Bringuier, J. C. 1980. *Conversations with Piaget,* trans. B.M. Gulait. Chicago: University of Chicago Press.

Feldman, D. 1980. *Beyond universals in cognitive development.* Norwood, NJ: Ablex Publishing Corp.

Flavell, J. 1971. Stage-related properties of cognitive development. *Cognitive Psychology* 2:421–453.

Lewis, M. 1987. Social development in infancy and early childhood. In *Handbook of infant development,* 2d ed., ed. J.D. Osofsky, 419–493. New York: John Wiley & Sons.

Lewis, M., & Cherry, L. 1977. *Development and change in conversation and logic skill.* Unpublished manuscript.

Lewis, M., & Starr, M. 1979. Developmental continuity. In *Handbook of infant development,* ed. J.D. Osofsky, 653–670. New York: John Wiley & Sons.

Meisels, S.J. 1985. The efficacy of early intervention: Why are we still asking this question? *Topics in Early Childhood Special Education* 5(2):1–11.

Mischel, W. 1968. *Personality and assessment.* New York: John Wiley & Sons.

Rogers, S. 1982. Cognitive characteristics of young children's play. In *Developmental and clinical aspects of young children's play,* ed. R. Pelz, 1–14. Monmouth, OR: Western States Technical Assistance Resource, Series Paper #17.

Sameroff, A., & Chandler, M. 1975. Reproductive risk and the continuum of caretaking causality. In *Review of child development research,* Vol. 4, ed. F.D. Horowitz, E.M. Hetherington, S. Scarr-Salapatek, & G.M. Siegel, 187–244. Chicago: University of Chicago Press.

A Meta-Analytic Review of IQ
Research with Deaf Persons

Jeffery P. Braden

T he study of deaf persons' intelligence has long fascinated philosophers
and psychologists because prelingual deafness denies natural acquisition
of spoken language. The ancient Greeks posited that deaf people were
"dumb" (i.e., without reason) because they did not acquire or use language. Since
thought is expressed in speech and deaf persons did not acquire speech, it was
assumed that deaf people lacked the ability to reason. This philosophy was encoded into laws and customs (e.g., inheritance of property was denied to deaf
people), some of which still survive today.

Since the early 1900s, numerous investigations of deaf children's IQs have
been conducted. The focus of this paper is to summarize these investigations
quantitatively using meta-analytic techniques. These techniques provide the means
to combine information across studies, yielding greater statistical power and
understanding of the condition under study than single studies or narrative reviews
of research could provide. The methods employed in this study are followed by
presentation of selected results and a discussion of results in order to define the
scope, nature, and trajectory of research in this area.

The complete version of this paper is available in microfiche or hard copy from ERIC
Document Reproduction Service. Ask for Document No. ED 313 837.

This chapter is based on excerpts from the author's upcoming book, *Deafness, Deprivation, and IQ*. New York: Plenum Press.

Editor's Note: The reader is referred to related papers in this volume by Clark and
Hoemann (chapter 10) and Pollio (chapter 11).

METHOD

Data Sources

Published and unpublished literature describing the results of intelligence tests with deaf subjects were included in the study. Published references were identified by computer searches of *Psychological Abstracts* and *Medline* databases, communication with the manager of the Deafness Collection at the Gallaudet University library, and reviews of reference lists appearing in studies. Unpublished resources were identified through computer searches of *Dissertations Abstracts International* and ERIC databases, communication with the manager of the Deafness Collection at the Gallaudet University library, reviews of reference lists appearing in published and unpublished sources, and personal communication by letter and telephone to researchers in the field. Every attempt was made to capture existing references; sources were excluded only if (a) they did not use a test of intelligence; or (b) they did not report deaf subjects' performance in a manner that allowed comparison with hearing children (e.g., qualitative descriptions were accepted, but distribution-free results, such as correlations, were excluded). A total of 193 unique references, which comprised 285 unique samples, provided 324 reports of IQs.

Subjects and Procedures

Subjects. The samples in the studies ranged from a minimum of 4 to a maximum sample size of 21,307, yielding a cumulative sample size of 171,517 subjects. The most common source of samples was residential schools for the deaf (50% of all samples came from this source). Samples were primarily obtained in North America, although a significant number of subjects (more than 5,000) were from the United Kingdom and Germany. Less than 4% of the studies provided complete information regarding subjects (i.e., age, gender, race, type of school program, degree and onset of hearing loss, parental hearing status, and presence of additional handicaps). Estimates from partial data suggest that the majority of research studies sample children who (a) are school age; (b) are almost balanced with regard to gender (slightly more males); (c) are predominantly white; (d) attend residential schools using sign language instructional methods; (e) are congenitally, severely to profoundly deaf; (f) have hearing parents; and (g) have high incidence rates of additional handicapping conditions. The effect of some of these variables is discussed in the following sections.

Procedures. The majority of children were given performance IQ tests (the Wechsler Performance Scales being the most popular performance test), although verbal and motor-free nonverbal tests (e.g., the Ravens Progressive Matrices) were also used. Administration procedures were most often unstated; of those defining the type of administration, combinations of gestures, signs, and speech were most common, followed by simultaneous presentation of signs and speech. Deaf norms were used in 19 studies, and were only found for the Hiskey-Nebraska

Test of Learning Abilities and the Wechsler Intelligence Scale for Children-Revised (WISC-R) Performance Scale. There was no difference in mean IQ as a function of norm selection.

Data Analysis

Data regarding subjects, test performance, and other comments were gleaned from references and entered into a database. Ratio IQ data were recorded along with the *SD*s reported in the sample (if any). Data from deviation IQ tests which do not follow the Wechsler convention of $M = 100$ and $SD = 15$ were converted to this metric on the basis of normative data (e.g., for the British Ability Scale, $M = 50$, $SD = 10$, $IQ = 60$, was converted to an $IQ = 115$), or on the basis of the mean and standard deviation reported for a hearing population comparison sample if a nonstandard test of intelligence was used.

Study data were analyzed in two ways. First, a bibliometric analysis of the research was attempted using descriptive statistics. This analysis describes the scope, nature, and trends in research investigating the intellectual performance of deaf people. The second analysis manipulated the results of the studies in order to determine what conclusions can be drawn from the research (i.e., How does deafness affect IQ?).

RESULTS

Bibliometric

Modes of Dissemination.   Of the 293 references identified in the literature search, 172 are published, 113 are unpublished, and 8 are unclassified studies. Published references appear in journals that are related to deafness ($N = 118$), psychology ($N = 36$), special education, or other topics ($N = 8$). The primary medium for unpublished studies is books ($N = 35$), followed by ERIC document reports and personally solicited manuscripts ($N = 25$), dissertations ($N = 15$), papers given at conventions ($N = 15$), and newsletters (e.g., newsletters produced by residential schools) ($N = 5$).

Rate of Research.   A common metric of a "healthy" research field is an asymptotic increase in the number of studies over time. The rate of increase in research regarding the intelligence of deaf people is positive and significant ($r = .63, p < .0001$, between frequency of studies and year of publication). However, robust fields of research characteristically double the knowledge base every five to ten years. IQ research in deafness shows a slow rate of growth, with knowledge doubling every fifteen to twenty years.

Effect Sizes

Overall Comparison.   Mean IQs ranged from 56 to 122, with a grand unweighted mean of 97.14, $SD_M = 10.79$. The global average, unweighted for sample size, was well within average limits. The SDs reported within studies ranged from 5.90 to 24.69, with an average of 15.33, $SD_{SD} = 3.38$. It should be noted that global comparisons used some correlated data points (i.e., if a study reported two mean IQs, each was entered as a separate data point in global analyses). Global indices are remarkably similar to normative data from hearing children, although the variation of means among studies is high.

Qualitative descriptions of cognitive performance correspond to the average IQs generated from quantitative descriptions. A total of 52 qualitative descriptions was provided in the literature. Results were assigned to one of six categories based on descriptive categories provided by Wechsler (1974): educable mentally retarded/borderline ($N = 5$), low average ($N = 15$), average ($N = 24$), above average ($N = 3$), superior ($N = 1$), or unclassifiable ($N = 4$). Qualitative descriptions suggest deaf persons' IQs are somewhat lower than average. However, the studies offering qualitative descriptions are typically older studies with poor descriptions of samples and methods (i.e., they appear to lack the rigor associated with quantitative studies).

Results by Intelligence Test Types. Intelligence tests were assigned to one of four categories: (a) performance tests (requiring rapid manipulation of objects), (b) nonverbal tests (nonverbal tasks with no manipulation), (c) verbal tests (verbal content in items), and (d) other tests (not clearly classified or unknown). The type of intelligence test used to obtain levels of intellectual performance affects the corresponding IQ. The mean Performance IQ ($N = 195$, $M_M = 99.95$, $SD_M = 9.54$), with the unknown category ($N = 10$, $M_M = 85.54$, $SD_M = 10.47$) falling between performance and nonverbal means. The differences among these means are statistically significant ($F(3,320) = 21.79$, $p < .0001$).

DISCUSSION

Bibliometric Results

The bibliometric results suggest that research linking intelligence and deafness is moderately active. The positive relationship between the year and the number of studies published suggests that the field is growing, but the rate at which knowledge doubles is about half as fast as that of robust fields of research.

Why is this research field relatively lethargic? On the one hand, researchers in deafness do not often publish outside their own journals, so there is little opportunity to attract the attention of a wide range of scholars. On the other hand, the lack of attention devoted to deafness in the general literature may reflect a publication bias against including deafness-related research. A qualitative review of research methods suggests that deafness researchers may be their own worst enemies. Much of the research appears to be archival (i.e., nonexperimental retrieval of data from school records). Because these data are not linked to a specific experimental question, and because the methods used to collect and analyze data often lack the sophistication and control associated with experimental research, the results may well fail to meet the criteria expected for referred review in nondeafness journals.

Although slow growth of research in the field is a problem, a second problem is the lack of direction among research projects in the field. Few studies are specific extensions of previous work. Many studies unwittingly replicate previous research, and few attempt experimental analysis of widely held beliefs. For example, it has been said that verbal IQ tests are inappropriate for use with deaf children, yet there are no studies using modern methods for detecting test bias.

The bibliometric data lead to three conclusions:

1. There is limited growth of knowledge regarding deaf children and intelligence;
2. The knowledge contained in this field is not disseminated outside deafness-related publications; and
3. There is little theoretical context or direction to the research.

These are sobering conclusions for a field that claims a history spanning at least 300 years.

Effect Sizes

The global effect size is average, suggesting that deaf people as a group have average intellectual abilities. However, this conclusion must be tempered with the subsequent findings that the global effect size obscures important differences between types of tests. In fact, because different methods and tests are used, and because some groups of deaf children are disproportionately represented in the literature, the scatter of the data across studies is unusually high. Therefore, the global effect size does not necessarily represent a homogeneous population statistic for deaf persons.

Educational Considerations

Some results have been omitted from this brief treatment of the meta-analysis. Other factors associated with variation in IQ are hearing loss, presence of an additional handicapping condition, race, gender, parental hearing loss, type of IQ scale, test administration methods, and other factors associated with subjects and experimental methods. These factors, and the evidence reviewing whether IQ tests do, in fact, measure intelligence in deaf populations, are examined elsewhere (Braden in press). The findings clearly show that the selection and administration of tests affects IQ, and that not all nonverbal tests are alike. Therefore, current recommendations to use nonverbal tests with deaf persons should be refined because different results are achieved with motor-free vs. performance nonverbal IQ tests.

A second application of this meta-analysis is that, for the empirical purposes of prediction, verbal IQ tests are likely to be more statistically accurate predictors of achievement than nonverbal IQ tests for deaf persons. This conclusion is due to the fact that the means for verbal IQ tests are similar to those for achievement tests, whereas the mean for nonverbal IQ tests is well above the achievement means for deaf persons (resulting in overprediction). Nonverbal tests are still critical for differentiating deafness from mental retardation, but the exclusion of verbal IQ tests from educational practice and research seems most unfortunate.

This paper has demonstrated the potential value of meta-analytic reviews of research and noted some serious challenges for future research in deafness and cognition. Psychoeducational practitioners might also examine the degree to which practices are based on opinions rather than on sound research.

REFERENCES

Braden, J.P. 1984. The factorial similarity of the WISC-R Performance Scale in deaf and hearing samples. *Journal of Personality and Individual Differences* 5:403–410.

———. 1985a. The structure of nonverbal intelligence in deaf and hearing subjects. *American Annals of the Deaf* 131:496–501.

———. 1985b. WISC-R deaf norms reconsidered. *Journal of School Psychology* 23:375–382.

———. 1987. An explanation of the superior Performance IQs of deaf children of deaf parents. *American Annals of the Deaf* 132:263–266.

———. 1988. Understanding IQ differences between groups: Deaf children as a natural experiment in the nature-nurture debate. In *Individual differences in children and adolescents: International research perspectives*, ed. D. Soklofske & S. Eysenck. London: Hodder & Stoughton.

———. In press. *Deafness, deprivation, and IQ.* New York: Plenum Publishing Corp.

Conrad, R. & Weiskrantz, B.C. 1981. On the cognitive ability of deaf children with deaf parents. *American Annals of the Deaf* 126:995–1003.

Ewing, A.W.G., ed. 1957. *Educational guidance and the deaf child.* Manchester, England: Manchester University Press.

Furth, H.G. 1964. Research with the deaf: Implications for language and cognition. *Psychological Bulletin* 62:251–267.

Kusché, C.A., Greenberg, M.T., & Garfield, T.S. 1983. Nonverbal intelligence and verbal achievement in deaf adolescents: An examination of heredity and environment. *American Annals of the Deaf* 128:458–466.

Moores, D. 1970. An investigation of psycholinguistic functioning of deaf adolescents. *Exceptional Children* 36:377–384.

Pintner, R., & Patterson, D.G. 1915. The Binet Scale and the deaf child. *Journal of Educational Psychology* 6:201–210.

Schildroth, A.N. 1976. *The relationship of nonverbal intelligence test scores to selected characteristics of hearing-impaired students.* Washington, DC: Gallaudet College, Office of Demographic Studies.

———. 1988. Letter to the author, August 17.

Sisco, F.H., & Anderson, R.J. 1980. Deaf children's performance on the WISC-R relative to hearing status of parents and child-rearing practices. *American Annals of the Deaf* 125:923–930.

Summers, E.G. 1986. The information flood in learning disabilities: A bibliometric analysis of the journal literature. *RASE* 7(1):49–60.

Vernon, M. 1967. Relationship of language to the thinking process. *Archives of General Psychology* 16:325–333.

Wechsler, D. 1974. *Wechsler Intelligence Scale for Children-Revised.* New York: Psychological Corporation.

New Methodologies to Evaluate the Memory Strategies of Deaf Individuals

M. Diane Clark

U nderstanding deaf individuals' ability to process visual information is important in investigating their language abilities, since language input is received through this system. Early studies of visual information-processing (Heider 1940; Larr 1956; Myklebust & Brutton 1953; Olson 1967) reported lower levels of performance for deaf subjects when compared to hearing subjects, a deficit attributed to problems in their visual perception. Because English stimuli were used in these studies, the observed deficits may have been the result of a confusion between perceptual and linguistic abilities.

Studies attempting to untangle this confusion (e.g., Blair 1957; Siple, Hatfield & Caccamise 1978; Hartung 1970) have shown some differences between deaf and hearing subjects but have not confirmed the earlier studies' finding of deficiencies in deaf subjects' visual information-processing. When linguistic abilities are equated between deaf and hearing subjects, some researchers have found similar memory performance (Hartung 1970; Morariu & Bruning 1983). In an attempt to control for the discrepancy between visual perceptual skills and linguistic skills, Hartung (1970) manipulated stimulus familiarity in a study utilizing both familiar and unfamiliar linguistic input. He pointed out that English letters,

---

The complete version of this paper is available in microfiche or hard copy from ERIC Document Reproduction Service. Ask for Document No. ED 313 838.

Partial support for this project was received from grant RO1-N20064 awarded to Marc Marschark by the National Institute of Neurological and Communicative Disorders and Stroke.

frequently used in studies of visual information-processing, were linguistic in nature and may not have been as overlearned for deaf subjects as they were for hearing subjects. Hartung found that with English letters (familiar language input), hearing subjects showed a significant advantage. With unfamiliar input (Greek letters), deaf subjects could identify the items as well as hearing subjects, suggesting that prior research had shown linguistic (English) deficits and not perceptual deficits.

Most of the above-mentioned information-processing studies of deaf individuals have evaluated short- and long-term memory, and little investigation has been done on the early stages of information processing or iconic memory in the deaf subject. The aim of the present study was to evaluate the physical parameters of deaf subjects' iconic memory by investigating the duration of that memory. In hearing subjects, iconic memory has a 250 msec "fade" time, while echoic memory has a 1 sec "fade" time. This difference may place constraints on how long visual language information is available for processing. To investigate whether deaf individuals' visual systems have been altered by early feedback in a structure-function type of interaction (see Gottlieb 1976), three interstimulus intervals (ISIs) were included in the study: no delay, 250 msec, and 500 msec, post-stimulus presentation. In order to untangle the earlier discrepancy between perceptual and linguistic abilities, both English letters and ambiguous symbols were presented.

EXPERIMENT 1

Subjects

Eight deaf adults (mean age = 20.5) and eight hearing adults (mean age = 20.6) participated in this experiment. The hearing adults participated for credit in a general psychology course. Six of the deaf subjects attended a local community college, and the other two deaf subjects were residents of the Greensboro, North Carolina, area. All eight of the deaf subjects were prelingually deaf with severe to profound hearing losses (>80 dB in the better ear).

Procedure

The stimuli, eight uppercase English letters and eight ambiguous symbols, were displayed on an IBM computer, which also recorded the data. Each trial consisted of the following sequence:

1. A computer prompt to "press space bar for next trial;"
2. A centered fixation point, one sec in duration;
3. The stimuli, 150 msec in duration, consisting of a circular array of either eight letters or eight symbols (the computer placed these letters and symbols randomly within each circular array; see Figure 1); and
4. An asterisk, one sec in duration, to cue subjects as to which position to recall. The asterisk was located behind the prior position of the cued stimulus, and its placement (i.e., determination of a target) was

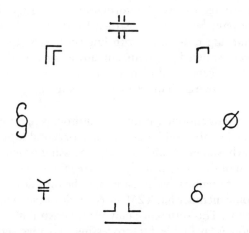

FIGURE 1   Sample stimulus array with symbols as stimuli.

randomly generated by the computer. Depending on the ISI of the specific trial (presented in blocks of 20), the asterisk followed the array either immediately or at an ISI of 250 or 500 msec.

Eight function keys on the IBM computer were programmed to serve as response keys. Overlays of the ambiguous symbols and the English letters were used for the different stimuli sets. The subject's task was to identify which of the stimuli had been at the cued location and to press the appropriate response key.

Each subject was tested individually. Three blocks each of 20 trials were presented—one block at no delay, one at 250 msec ISI, and one at 500 msec ISI. Order of the three blocks was randomly generated by the computer. Order of stimulus presentation (counterbalanced across subjects) was either letters then symbols or symbols then letters. Two series of the three blocks were presented for each stimulus type (120 trials per stimulus type). The first series was a practice series, and the second series was to test recognition.

The study's predictions were that (a) hearing subjects would show an effect of stimulus familiarity with letters having higher recognition scores than symbols, (b) deaf subjects would not show an effect of stimulus familiarity (i.e., equivalent scores between the letters and symbols), (c) recognition scores for symbols would be equivalent between deaf and hearing subjects, and (d) deaf subjects would demonstrate longer iconic memories than hearing subjects (i.e., higher levels of recognition at the 500 msec ISI).

Results and Discussion

The experiment had two between-subject factors (subject group and order of stimulus presentation) and three within-subject factors (series, stimulus type, and delay of cue presentation). A split plot analysis of variance as well as planned comparisons were performed on the recognition scores (i.e., number of correct responses within each block of 20 trials).

Series.   Overall, hearing subjects had significantly higher recognition scores than deaf subjects, $F = 5.00$ ($p < .01$). There was an overall significant practice effect, $F = 17.33$ ($p < .01$), but planned comparisons showed that the only significant increase in performance was between the deaf subjects' two series in the letter condition, $F = 2.50$ ($p < .01$). This practice effect for deaf subjects suggests that both deaf and hearing subjects were capable of comparable performance with English stimuli when the deaf subjects were allowed sufficient practice. Hearing subjects did not show a practice effect, suggesting that English letters were overlearned for this group.

Stimulus Types.   A main effect of stimuli was found, $F = 27.43$ ($p < .01$), with letters being recognized significantly more than symbols. Planned comparisons revealed that hearing subjects had significantly higher recognition scores on the letters than on the symbols. Deaf subjects did not show an overall letter/symbol difference. These results reveal that only the hearing subjects showed an effect of familiarity.

Planned comparisons revealed no significant differences between the recognition scores of deaf and hearing subjects in the symbol condition, thus revealing similar performance with ambiguous symbols for the two groups. Neither group had significant differences between the two series, revealing no practice effects for the symbol stimuli.

Delays of Cue Presentation.   Comparisons of deaf and hearing subjects' responses at all delays revealed no significant differences at any ISI. Contrary to the original hypothesis, this finding suggests that the early stages of deaf and hearing subjects' perceptual processing, or iconic memory, appear to be similar.

Analysis of Position Effects.   In order to reveal possible processing strategies used by deaf and hearing subjects, two split-plot analyses of variance were performed on the number of correct responses at each stimulus position (see Figure 2). A significant hearing status by position interaction occurred in both letter presentations ($F = 2.96$) ($p < .01$), and symbol presentations ($F = 4.48$) ($p < .01$). Newman Keuls analyses revealed that hearing subjects' recognition scores were significantly better at positions 2 and 6, which were on the horizontal. This finding revealed an apparent tendency in the hearing subjects to scan left to right. Deaf subjects showed no significant differences in their scores at the different positions; however, scores were elevated for positions 0, 1, 2, 6, and 7, all located in the top half of the circular array. These different patterns of correct responses may be revealing strategy differences in information-processing styles.

The same general patterns of response occurred in the symbol presentation as had occurred in the letter presentation, in that hearing subjects scored better at positions 2 and 6, while deaf subjects' scores were elevated at positions 0, 1, 2, 6, and 7. This pattern of results suggests that similar recognition scores do not require similar information-processing strategies in deaf and hearing subjects.

In summary, this experiment revealed an effect of familiarity (with English letters) for the hearing subjects only. Deaf and hearing subjects' similar performances with the ambiguous symbols suggest that prior studies had confounded

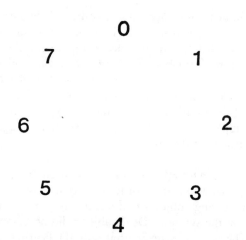

FIGURE 2 Numbering for each stimulus position within the stimulus array.

perceptual and linguistic (English) abilities. Also, contrary to the original hypothesis, deaf and hearing subjects' recognition scores at each of the ISIs were similar, suggesting that the time parameters of their iconic memories were similar. An apparent strategy difference was found between deaf and hearing subjects. The deaf subjects did not appear dependent, as did the hearing subjects, on a left-to-right scan for dealing with visual input but rather appeared to use a strategy of scanning a whole area. These input strategy differences led to questions about whether these differences were related to experiential deficits, as suggested by Furth (1966) and Liben (1978), or to the educational background of the deaf subjects. Experiment 2 was conducted to evaluate these questions by examining whether information-processing strategies used to input visual information into iconic memory are affected by age of sign language acquisition or by different ISIs.

EXPERIMENT 2

Subjects

All twenty-four subjects in Experiment 2 were from Gallaudet University. They included six subjects from oral school backgrounds (mean age = 24.8), six subjects from manual (signing) school backgrounds (mean age = 23.7), six hard-of-hearing subjects (< 65 dB hearing loss; mean age = 26.1), and six hearing staff or faculty who had learned sign language from deaf parents (mean age = 37.6).

Procedure

Materials and procedure were the same as in Experiment 1, with the exception of ISIs of 50, 150, and 250 msec.

Results and Discussion

Analyses were the same as in Experiment 1 in that a split-plot analysis of variance and planned comparisons were performed on the recognition scores.

Series. No effect of oral vs. manual background was revealed. The only significant group difference was in an interaction of educational group by order by interstimulus interval, $F = 2.63$ ($p < .001$). In the letter/symbol condition (i.e., letters followed by symbols), the manual subjects were better at all three ISIs, but this advantage was lost in the symbol/letter condition. This finding suggests that subjects growing up knowing sign language may have some differential advantages that were not detected in this task as a main effect, but further investigation is needed to clarify this point.

Stimulus Types. An effect of familiarity was revealed such that letters had significantly higher scores than did symbols, $F = 25.3$ ($p < .001$). An interaction of stimulus type with order of presentation occurred, $F = 73.6$ ($p < .001$). In the letter/symbol condition there were no significant differences between the stimulus types, but in the symbol/letter condition, letters had significantly higher levels of recognition, suggesting that familiarity effects can be masked, depending on the order of stimulus presentation.

This same pattern of stimulus familiarity was found for hearing subjects in Experiment 1, but not for the deaf students. The major difference between the deaf subjects in the two studies was educational level. If the better or more serious students attended Gallaudet, then the above finding would suggest an experiential deficit. It would appear that better deaf students show performance comparable to hearing students and that past findings of inferior performance on the part of deaf subjects are due to comparisons with groups that have different levels of familiarity with the stimulus information (see Liben & Drury 1977).

Analysis of Position Effects. The three deaf educational groups' recognition scores were compared at the eight different stimulus positions using a multifactor randomized design. A main effect of position occurred ($F = 12.3$) ($p < .01$) where positions 2 and 6 had higher levels of recognition. This pattern is similar to that of the hearing subjects in the first study and appears to be related to a reading strategy by which information is scanned in a left-to-right fashion. It is interesting to note that this pattern was exhibited by the group of deaf subjects attending a four-year university and suggests that some deaf students use a left-right sequential scan in processing English stimuli.

GENERAL DISCUSSION AND CONCLUSION

These two studies suggest that there are differences within the hearing-impaired population in regard to the types of information-processing strategies employed across tasks. Those with well-developed reading skills will use a sequential input strategy in complex tasks, even though they do not use this strategy in more informal tasks. It would seem that deaf subjects are capable of demonstrating equivalent levels of performance even if they utilize different information-processing strategies. Furthermore, when evaluating deaf subjects, it is important to consider their levels of familiarity with the task stimulus. When investigating special populations, one must choose or develop methodologies that take into account the competence-performance distinction and not evaluate all populations as if they were directly comparable to a traditional subject population.

REFERENCES

Blair, F.X. 1957. A study of the visual memory of deaf and hearing children. *American Annals of the Deaf* 102:254–263.

Conrad, R. 1979. *The deaf school child, language, and cognitive function*. London: Harper & Row.

Furth, H.G. 1966. *Thinking without language: Psychological implications of deafness.* New York: Free Press.

Gottlieb, G. 1976. Conceptions of prenatal development: Behavioral embryology. *Psychological Review* 83:215–234.

Hartung, J.E. 1970. Visual perceptual skill, reading ability, and the young deaf child. *Exceptional Children* 36:603–608.

Heider, F.A. 1940. A comparison of the color sorting behavior of deaf and hearing children. *Psychological Monographs* 52:6–22.

Larr, A. 1956. Perceptual and conceptual abilities of residential school children. *Exceptional Children* 23:63–65.

Liben, L. 1978. Developmental perspectives on the experiential deficiencies of deaf children. In *Deaf children: Developmental perspectives*, ed. L. Liben. New York: Academic Press.

Liben, L.S., & Drury, A.M. 1977. Short-term memory in deaf and hearing children in relation to stimulus characteristics. *Journal of Experimental Child Psychology* 27:60–73.

Lichtenstein, E. 1985. Deaf working memory and English language skills. In *Cognition, education, and deafness: Directions for research and instruction*, ed. D. Martin, 111–114. Washington, DC: Gallaudet University Press.

Morariu, J., & Bruning, R. 1985. A contextualist perspective of language processing by prelingually deaf students. In *Cognition, education, and deafness: Directions for research and instruction*, ed. D. Martin, 88–90. Washington, DC: Gallaudet University Press.

Myklebust, H., & Brutten, M. 1953. A study of the visual perception of deaf children. *Acta Otolaryng*, Suppl. 105.

Olson, J.R. 1967. A factor analytic study of the relation between the speed of visual perception and the language abilities of deaf adolescents. *Journal of Speech and Hearing Research* 10:354–360.

Siple, P., Hatfield, N., & Caccamise, F. 1978. The role of visual perceptual abilities in the acquisition and comprehension of sign language. *American Annals of the Deaf* 74:1–29.

Pilot Investigation of Validation of the Modified Learning and Study Strategies Inventory (LASSI) for Hearing-Impaired Preparatory Students at Gallaudet University

Frances R. Croft
Pamela Rush
Sanremi LaRue-Atuonah
Cathy Baechle
Jan Gemmill

In the 1960s, the focus of research in educational psychology shifted from the teacher to the learner, so that the learner came to be viewed as the active processor of information. Wittrock (1974) called this idea the Active Learner Theory.

Research also has shifted from a representational level to an executive level of cognitive psychology. There is a more intense focus in the research literature on strategies, such as conscious sequences of mental operations that manipulate and apply representational knowledge.

Thus the learner becomes the center of learning activities, having both an inner cognitive framework and information-processing strategies. The learner is motivated to use strategies in active construction to relate external information to prior experiences. The power of learning strategies lies in enabling a motivated learner to become active (Miles 1988).

Wittrock's Active Learner Theory (1988) has three components: attention, motivation, and reading comprehension. A fourth component, study processes, should be added because a learner needs to be able to retain and retrieve newly acquired information from storage in long-term memory.

The strategies used in all of the four components of the Active Learner Theory are termed "learning strategies." Mayer defined learning strategies as "behaviors of a learner that are intended to influence how the learner perceives information"

The complete version of this paper is available in microfiche or hard-copy from ERIC Document Reproduction Service. Ask for Document No. ED 313 839.

(1988, p. 11). A "conscious sequence of thoughts" should be added to the behaviors of a learner in order to enhance Mayer's definition. Strategies are conscious and sequential; when strategies become unconscious through automatization, they become skills (Garner 1988).

Metacognition is a recent addition to the Active Learner Model. Metacognition is defined as the self-regulated control of learning strategies, consisting of both cognitive and affective strategies (Zimmerman & Pons 1986). Metacognitive processes are necessary to select and execute a program of the strategies needed for each task, due to the wide range of variables in texts, course requirements, and task assignments. In the 1980s, the definition of learning strategies was broadened to include metacognitive processes (Jacobs & Paris 1987; McKeachie, Pintrich & Yi-Guang 1985; Weinstein & Mayer 1985; Zimmerman & Pons 1986; Weinstein 1987a).

Students need intrinsic motivation in order to learn. Motivation consists of metacognitive, cognitive, and affective processes that influence a learner's tendency to put effort into academic tasks (McCombs 1988).

All the above learning strategies are important for deaf college students with relatively low reading skills. Poor readers especially seem to benefit from developing special learning strategies for reading comprehension. Pressley, Johnson, Symons, McGoldrick, and Kurita (in press) found that specific strategy training helped poor readers make more significant gains in reading than were made by good readers given the same training.

If it is true that poor readers depend more on learning strategies than good readers do, then learning strategies become more important for deaf college students with poor reading skills. First-year deaf students have a particular problem in acquiring new information from reading, which is also true for hearing students at a fourth-grade reading level.

In spite of the subnormal reading achievement of deaf students, their nonverbal performance on the Wechsler Intelligence Scale for Children is in the same range as that of the hearing population (Moores 1987). If deaf students have normal cognitive capacities, then what kind of intervention will ameliorate their developmental lag in reading? One of the answers may be learning strategies training. Several studies of Instrumental Enrichment programs (Feuerstein 1980) demonstrated that deaf high school and college students improve reading comprehension after learning several cognitive strategies (Martin 1985a, 1985b; Rohr-Redding 1985; Jonas & Martin 1985).

In order to understand how a learner actively processes information with cognitive, metacognitive, and motivational strategies, it became necessary to develop an assessment of individual strategies. Individual students need to know their weaknesses and strengths in order to recognize and resolve academic problems themselves. Once they accept their limitations and become more confident in their strengths, they will focus more of their effort into their weak areas and consequently will improve.

Weinstein (1987b) developed the Learning and Study Strategies Inventory (LASSI) to include the metacognitive, affective, and cognitive components of learning strategies in the context of varied situations. The LASSI was given to the deaf preparatory students (first-year students at Gallaudet University) who participated in this study.

DESCRIPTION AND RATIONALE FOR USING LASSI

The Learning and Study Strategies Inventory (LASSI) has five affective scales and five cognitive scales (Weinstein 1987b). The development of the LASSI scales, over nine years, was based on an extensive literature review of cognition, metacognition, motivation, learning, and study strategies. The LASSI went through several pilot tests and revisions before being subjected to a large field test for reliability and validity (Weinstein, Zimmermann & Palmer 1988).

There are two definite advantages of this inventory over other study skills inventories: (a) each of the ten scales is reliable and valid so as to permit individual diagnosis, whereas only a *total* score of the scales of other inventories is reliable and valid; and (b) the inventory includes items to measure metacognition and affective components as well as cognitive strategies.

A computer version of the LASSI makes it easier to administer. Students type in their responses after watching each item presented in American Sign Language (ASL) on videotape.

INVESTIGATION WITH THE ADAPTED LASSI

Purpose

This study was designed to determine the validity and usefulness of the adapted LASSI in conjunction with the ASL videotape for measuring learning strategies among deaf students at the School of Preparatory Studies (SPS) at Gallaudet University (with the assumption that LASSI is as reliable an instrument for deaf students as it is for the hearing population).

An integrated approach using descriptive research correlating LASSI scores with grade point average (GPA) and other performance measures, along with experimental manipulation of the use of the ASL videotape, offered evidence of the validity of the adapted LASSI for prelingually deaf preparatory students. Since learning problems in some students may confound statistical results, two groups of hearing-impaired students—with and without documented learning problems—are compared throughout the study.

Students

In 1988–1989, 260 high school graduates were enrolled in the School of Preparatory Studies at Gallaudet University. Based on the belief that preparatory students generally lack the study skills to earn a GPA of 2.0 or better, all were required to take a Preparatory Academic Survival Skills (PASS) course for one credit. As part of the PASS program they had to take the LASSI.

Procedures

The study population was chosen and defined by specific criteria. The study itself was conducted according to the following steps:

1. *Elimination of students with postlingual onset of deafness and mild hearing losses.* The Audiology Department at SPS provided information on which students to eliminate, based on amount of hearing loss and age at onset of the hearing loss. Through this procedure, 30 students were eliminated from the database.

2. *Classification of students with and without learning problems in addition to their hearing impairments.* The Student Support Services unit at SPS identified 23 students with moderate and severe learning problems that seriously interfered with college learning. Eighteen out of the 23 students were distinguished from the other students as having more serious learning problems.

3. *LASSI administration.* An English teacher whose native language was ASL, along with the school psychologist, developed a videotape using American Sign Language (ASL) translations of the LASSI directions and questionnaire items. The videotape was played on a videocassette recorder next to IBM PC computers running the Electronic LASSI (E-LASSI) software program. In the fall semester of 1988, 78 preparatory students took the LASSI with the ASL videotape. On some days, when the ASL videotape was not provided, 81 students had to read the inventory items in English on the computer monitor itself. This process provided a comparison between the ASL-with-English and the English-only versions of the LASSI.

4. *Performance measures.* GPAs were compiled, calculated, and correlated with average LASSI scores and with each of the subscale scores on the LASSI scales, along with reading comprehension test results.

5. *Analysis of ASL and English version of LASSI.* An English teacher with expertise in both ASL and English analyzed the LASSI items and the ASL translations and found no cultural bias toward deaf students.

6. *Comparison of poor, average, and good reader groups on other measures.* The reading comprehension scores from the Degrees of Reading Power (DRP) test taken in August were used to distinguish good readers from poor readers. The students were placed into five levels based on standard deviation of DRP scores. The reading levels of these groups were compared with the LASSI scores, GPA, and other reading comprehension measures. They were used to predict GPAs along with certain LASSI scores.

7. *Degree of comprehension of ASL and English version of LASSI compared with communication preferences and reading levels.* Fifty-eight students were asked to fill out the questionnaire after taking the LASSI to discover their communication preferences and their understanding of the computer and videotape versions of the LASSI.

8. *Use of LASSI as a predictor of GPA to be compared with actual GPA in May, for ten new students.* In January of 1989, 10 new students

took the LASSI, along with the Scholastic Aptitude Test, Hearing-Impaired adaptation (SAT-HI), upon admission. Their GPA was compiled in May and compared with the predicted GPA based on the LASSI and May DRP scores.

RESULTS AND DISCUSSION

The LASSI raw subscale scores, GPA, and other reading comprehension scores of 186 students were analyzed using the SPSS T-test, ANOVA, Multiple Regression, and Pearson-product moment correlation coefficient procedures. The percentile equivalent scores of the LASSI raw subscale scores were noted for comparison purposes.

The average score of the 78 deaf students (without learning problems) in the experimental group who took the inventory with the ASL videotape was at the 57.31st percentile, as compared with the norm of 50th percentile for hearing students in a large southern university. The average scores of the 81 students in the control group who took the inventory without the videotape was at the 50.27th percentile. The former showed a higher score, with significant difference from the latter group ($t = 2.83$, $p < .005$), indicating that the videotape seemed to help students understand more than those students who were not exposed to the videotape (Table 2). Table 2 provides average scores on the LASSI and GPAs for the four groups. There was an interaction effect between videotape experiment and LASSI average scores and Degrees of Reading Power test taken in August (Table 5).

Four subscales showed significant differences favoring the experimental group over the control group: attitude ($t = 2.91$, $p < .004$), motivation ($t = 3.25$, $p < .001$), selecting main ideas ($t = 2.22$, $p < .028$), and self-testing ($t = 2.52$, $p < .01$). Two subscales showed strong similarities between the experimental and control group: anxiety ($t = -.01$, $p = .996$) and test-taking ($t = .36$, $p = .712$) (see Table 1).

The lowest scale was in the test-taking strategies, on the 31.82nd percentile, compared with the highest scale, the 78.78th percentile in self-testing strategies. Students seemed to know how to review for tests, but they did not know how to take certain types of tests. Two low affective scales were in attitude and anxiety, the 43.26th percentile and the 45.01st percentile respectively. Deaf students as a group were also low on selecting main ideas, in the 49.11th percentile (see Table 1). Correlation of the average LASSI subscales both with and without the videotape with the fall semester GPA were positively and significantly correlated at the .01 probability level (.26 and .36 respectively). Four subscales were significantly correlated with GPA for both groups: motivation (.19 and .35), time management (.26 and .30), study aids (.19 and .21), and self-reviewing techniques (.28 and .31) (see Table 4).

The lower, although insignificant, correlation of the adapted LASSI scores (using the ASL videotape) with GPA can be attributed to better understanding of items, independent of reading levels that were correlated with GPAs. These

TABLE 1   LASSI Raw Scores for Regular SPS Deaf Students (with percentile ranks in parentheses)

Variable	$\bar{X}$	Mean (in percentile)	SD	t value	p value
		T-tests of LASSI Scores between Experimental and Control Groups			
Affective					
Group A	n = 78	(56.61)	Experimental (with videotape)		
Group B	n = 81	(48.56)	Control		
ATT-Group A	30.36	(43.26)	3.92		
Group B	28.41	(29.93)	4.49	2.91	.004*
MOT-Group A	32.28	(59.66)	4.45		
Group B	29.88	(45.78)	4.85	3.25	.001*
TMT-Group A	27.59	(70.27)	5.11		
Group B	26.38	(64.30)	4.75	1.54	.124
ANX-Group A	24.54	(45.01)	5.90		
Group B	24.57	(42.90)	5.50	-.01	.996
CON-Group A	27.81	(64.84)	5.01		
Group B	26.89	(59.90)	5.33	1.12	.265
Cognitive					
Group A		(58.01)	Experimental		
Group B		(51.98)	Control		
INP-Group A	29.39	(65.96)	4.29		
Group B	28.01	(62.48)	6.43	1.58	.117
SMI-Group A	17.47	(49.11)	2.98		
Group B	16.38	(36.29)	3.21	2.22	.028*
STA-Group A	27.19	(64.40)	5.23		
Group B	25.80	(58.60)	5.88	1.57	.118
SFT-Group A	30.94	(78.78)	4.93		
Group B	28.75	(70.43)	5.93	2.52	.010*
TST-Group A	26.22	(31.82)	4.36		
Group B	25.93	(32.10)	5.71	.36	.712

* Significant differences below the $p < .05$ level.

results suggested that the students were not as dependent upon their reading skills when the ASL videotape was shown, as opposed to the students who were not shown the videotape and relied on reading. This area needs to be investigated further with deaf students.

Some of the LASSI subscale scores of regular deaf students (with no serious learning problems) correlated with the other reading comprehension measures

TABLE 2   LASSI Averages and Grade Point Averages

T-Tests: LASSI Averages & GPAs between Experimental and Control Groups

Variable	$\bar{X}$	Mean (in percentile)	SD	t value	p value
TOTAL LASSI AVERAGE (Affective and Cognitive)					
Group A	27.38	(57.31)	2.83		
Group B	26.10	(50.27)	2.87	2.83	.005*
Grade point averages for students with no learning problems					
FALL					
Group A	2.67		.74		
Group B	2.47		.72	1.70	.090
SPRING					
Group A	2.69		.72		
Group B	2.47		.62	1.60	.110
Grade point averages for experimental group (ASL videotape)					
FALL					
Group C	2.67				
Group D	2.03			2.28	.025*
SPRING					
Group C	2.69				
Group D	1.89			2.51	.015*

Note: Group A—Experimental group using LASSI with videotape ($n = 78$). Group B—Control group using LASSI without videotape ($n = 81$). Group C—Regular students with no learning problems ($n = 53$). Group D—Students with learning problems ($n = 6$).
  * Significant differences below the $p < .05$ level.

(see Table 4). The analysis of LASSI subscale scores with the reading comprehension measures should be continued in order to discern why only certain subscales show correlation to GPAs and to certain reading comprehension measures.

Through multiple regression statistical procedures, average LASSI scale score, attitude, time management, and self-testing subscale scores with August DRP scores did predict individual Fall GPAs (Multiple $R = .47$; variance $= .22$). May DRP scores and the above LASSI scores predicted May GPAs. The new group of students had a higher predictive value, closer to significance (Multiple $R = .91$, variance $= .82$, $F = 4.50/p = .087$). Certain parts of the LASSI did show some validity through the ability to predict some of the grade point averages (see Table 6).

Students with learning problems seemed to confound the results of the ASL videotape experiment; students with *no* learning problems had higher correlations of most LASSI subscale scores with grade point averages than did either the experimental or the control group (see Table 4). This finding indicated that the LASSI results of both the experimental and control groups were confounded by the inclusion of a few students with learning problems.

Students with serious learning problems also showed significant effects on GPA, but not on LASSI subscales (see Table 5), and they scored better on LASSI

TABLE 3   LASSI Raw Scores for SPS Deaf Students with Learning Problems (with percentile ranks in parentheses)

Variable	$\bar{x}$	Mean (in percentile)	SD	t value	p value
Affective					
Group A	n = 8	(49.75)	Experimental (with videotape)		
Group B	n = 8	(46.50)	Control (without videotape)		
ATT-Group A		(25.75)			
Group B		(25.62)			
MOT-Group A		(60.00)			
Group B		(46.88)			
TMT-Group A		(58.75)			
Group B		(68.12)			
ANX-Group A		(38.75)			
Group B		(37.50)			
CON-Group A		(65.50)			
Group B		(54.38)			
Cognitive					
Group A		(59.54)	Experimental		
Group B		(73.21)	Control		
INP-Group A		(57.50)			
Group B		(73.00)			
SMI-Group A		(28.87)			
Group B		(48.75)*			
STA-Group A		(69.38)			
Group B		(78.75)			
SFT-Group A		(68.75)			
Group B		(85.50)			
TST-Group A		(23.50)			
Group B		(25.63)			
AVG-Group A		(49.68)			
Group B		(54.41)			

Note: T-Tests of LASSI Scores between Experimental and Control Groups

* Significant differences below the $p < .05$ level.

without the ASL videotape (see Table 3). This finding needs to be investigated further to find out whether it was the small sample size, the distraction of the ASL videotape, the close spacing of keyboard responses, or a combination of these factors that confounded the results.

TABLE 4 Pearson Correlation Coefficients for LASSI Scores with Grade Point Averages for Experimental and Control Groups and for Regular Students

Variables LASSI subscales	Fall GPA	Spring GPA	Aug DRP	Dec DRP	May DRP	Aug EPR	Dec EPR	May EPR
ATT-Group A	.01*							
Group B	.21							
Group C	.44	.30			.33			
MOT-Group A	.19*							
Group B	.35**							
Group C	.34	.30	.35	.46		.31	.43	
TMT-Group A	.26**							
Group B	.30**							
Group C	.38	.34						.33
ANX-Group A	.10							
Group B	.11							
Group C								.32
CON-Group A	.11							
Group B	.15							
Group C	.41	.46						.41
INP-Group A	.14							
Group B	.23*							
Group C	.64**	.37	.48*	.58*				
SMI-Group A	.11							
Group B	.13							
Group C			.41	.40	.31	.36		
STA-Group A	.19*							
Group B	.21*							
Group C	.36	.31						
SFT-Group A	.28*							
Group B	.31**							
Group C	.53*							
TST-Group A	.01							
Group B	.07							
AVG-Group A	.26*							
Group B	.36**							
Group C	.53*	.39						

Note: Group A: Experimental group using the LASSI with videotape (*n* = 90). Group B: Control group using the LASSI without videotape (*n* = 104). Group C: Students with no learning problems. 1-tailed significance: * *p* < .01. ** *p* < .001.

CONCLUSION

The results suggested that the adapted Learning and Study Strategies Inventory with an ASL videotape predicted achievement in GPA and in the Degrees of Reading Power test scores. The results suggested the validity of the adapted LASSI

TABLE 5   Interaction Effects of DRP, Learning Problem, and Video on GPAs and LASSI Scores (ANOVA)

Variables	F value	Probability of F
GPA average		
Main	5.992	.000
Aug DRP levels	1.586	.185
Lprob	21.880	.000
Video	.751	.388
Fall GPA		
Main	5.263	.000
Aug DRP levels	2.478	.048
Lprob	15.929	.000
Video	.751	.388
Spring GPA		
Main	4.032	.001
May DRP levels	1.225	.305
Lprob	14.339	.000
Video	1.795	.184
LASSI average		
Main	2.873	.012
Aug DRP levels	3.411	.012
Lprob	.008	.931
Video	4.022	.047

F value = 4.50.
Probability of F = .087.

as an appropriate instrument for measuring the learning strategies repertoire of preparatory students at Gallaudet University. The LASSI scores provided an interesting conceptualization of the students as a group, while their communication preferences needed to be investigated further. The preparatory students seemed to have problems with test-taking strategies, selecting important ideas, feelings of anxiety, and attitude. The PASS program and the preparatory curriculum need to focus on training the students to develop strategies in these areas.

Regarding the special groups of deaf college students with learning problems and below-average reading skills, the adapted LASSI scores could predict poor readers who will need special intervention, such as reading tutorial services that include learning-strategies training. Further investigation is needed for students who have serious learning problems. Therefore, further validation of the LASSI is suggested for hearing-impaired freshmen at the college and university levels. Research can then proceed and face new challenges in the development of learning and study strategies for students with hearing impairments.

TABLE 6   Prediction of GPAs for Students with No Learning Problems

Variables	B (Slope)	Multiple R	Variance
Fall GPA			
LASSI Average	.39	.47	.22
August DRP levels	.02		
Attitude (LASSI)	.33		
Time Management	.02		
Self-Testing	.03		
Spring GPA			
Lassi Average		.33	.11
May DRP levels			
Attitude (LASSI)			
Time Management			
Self-testing			
Spring GPA for 10 new students			
LASSI average	.06	.91	.82
May DRP levels	.07		
Attitude (LASSI)	.68		
Time Management	.06		
Self-Testing	.05		

REFERENCES

Anderson, T.H. 1979. Study skills and learning strategies. In *Cognitive and effective learning strategies*, ed. F.O. Neil, Jr., & C.D. Speilberger, 77–108. New York: Academic Press.

Anderson, T.H., & Armbruster, B.B. 1985. Studying strategies and their implications for textbook design. *Designing usable texts*, 159–177. New York: Academic Press.

Chall, J.S. 1983. *Stages of reading development*. New York: McGraw-Hill.

Dansereau, D.F. 1985. Learning strategy research. In *Thinking and learning skills, volume I: Relating instruction to research*, ed. J. Segal, S. Chapman, & R. Glaser. Hillsdale, NJ: Lawrence Erlbaum Associates.

Dansereau, D.F., Collins, K.W., McDonald, B.A., Holley, C.D., Garland, J., Diekoff, G., & Evans, S.H. 1979a. A development and evaluation of a learning strategy training program. *Journal of Educational Psychology* 71(1):64–73.

Dansereau, D.F., McDonald, B.A., Collins, K.W., Garland, J., Holley, C.D., Diekoff, G.M., & Evans, S.H. 1979b. Evaluation of a learning strategy system. In *Cognitive and affective learning strategies*, ed. F.O. O'Neil, Jr., & C.D. Speilberger, 3–43. New York: Academic Press.

Feuerstein, R. 1980. *Instrumental enrichment: An instructional program for cognitive modifiability*. Baltimore: University Park Press.

Garner, R. 1988. *Metacognition and reading comprehension*. Norwood, NJ: Ablex Publishing Corp.

Goodstein, A. 1988. *Fall 1988 admissions/enrollment summary*. Washington DC: Gallaudet University. Report.

Gray, W.S. 1925. A modern program of reading instruction for the grade and high school. In *Report of the national committee on reading*, ed. G. M. Whipple, 21–74. 24th yearbook of the National Society for the Study of Education, Part I. Bloomington, IL: Public School Publishing Co.

Guthrie, J.T. 1988. Locating information in documents: Examination of a cognitive model. *Reading Research Quarterly* 23(2):178–199.

Harris, A.J., & Sipay, E.R. 1986. *How to increase reading ability.* 8th ed. White Plains, NY: Longman, Inc.

Jacobs, J.E., & Paris, S.G. 1987. Children's metacognitions about reading issues on definition, measurement, and instruction. *Educational Psychologist* 22(3,4):255–278.

Jonas, B.S., & Martin, D.S. 1985. Cognitive improvement of hearing-impaired high school students through instruction in Instrumental Enrichment. In *Cognition, education, and deafness: Directions for research and instruction,* ed. D. S. Martin, 172–175. Washington, DC: Gallaudet University Press.

LaSasso, C., & Davey, B. 1983. An investigation of the criterion-related validity of the SAT-HI reading comprehension subtest for deaf students. *Directions* 3:66–69.

Martin, D. S. 1985a. Enhancing cognitive performance in the hearing-impaired college student: a pilot study. In *Cognition, education, and deafness: Directions for research and instruction,* ed. D. S. Martin, 176–179. Washington, DC: Gallaudet University Press.

———. 1985b. Introduction. In *Cognition, education, and deafness: Directions for research and instruction,* ed. D. S. Martin, 2–13. Washington, DC: Gallaudet University Press.

Mayer, R.E. 1988. Learning strategies: an overview. In *Learning and study strategies: Issues in assessment, instruction, and evaluation,* ed. C.E. Weinstein, E.T. Getz, & P.A. Alexander, 11–22. New York: Academic Press.

McCombs, B.L. 1988. Motivational skills training. In *Learning and study strategies: Issues in assessment, instruction, and evaluation,* ed. C.E. Weinstein, E.T. Getz, & P.A. Alexander, 141–167. New York: Academic Press.

McKeachie, W. J. 1988. The need for study strategy training. In *Learning and study strategies: Issues in assessment, instruction, and evaluation,* ed. C. E. Weinstein, E. T. Getz, & P. A. Alexander, 3–9. New York: Academic Press.

McKeachie, W.J., Pintrich, P.R., & Yi-Guang, L. 1985. Teaching learning strategies. *Educational Psychologist* 20(3):153–160.

Meadow, K.P. 1980. *Deafness and child development.* Los Angeles: University of California Press.

Mealey, D.L. 1988. Test review: Learning and study strategies inventory (LASSI). *Journal of Reading* 31(4):382–385.

Miles, C. 1988. Cognitive learning strategies: implications for college practice. In *Learning and study strategies: Issues in assessment, instruction, and evaluation,* ed. C.E. Weinstein, E.T. Getz, & P.A. Alexander, 333–347. New York: Academic Press.

Moores, D.F. 1985. Reactions from the researcher's point of view. In *Cognition, education, and deafness: Directions for research and instruction,* ed. D.S. Martin, 224–228. Washington, DC: Gallaudet University Press.

———. 1987. *Educating the deaf: Psychology, principles, and practices.* 3rd ed. Boston: Houghton Mifflin.

O'Malley, J.M., Russo, R.P., Chamot, A.U., & Stewner-Manzanares, G. 1988. Applications of learning strategies by students learning English as a second language. In *Learning and study strategies: Issues in assessment, instruction, and evaluation,* ed. C.E. Weinstein, E.T. Getz, & P.A. Alexander, 215–231. New York: Academic Press.

Per-Lee, M. 1986. *Admissions statistics.* Washington, DC: Gallaudet University. Memorandum.

Pressley, M., Johnson, C.J., Symons, S., McGoldrick, J.A., & Kurita, J.A., In press. Strategies that improve children's memory and comprehension of what is read. *The Elementary School Journal.*

Rohr-Redding, C. 1985. Can thinking skills be incorporated into a curriculum? In *Cognition, education, and deafness: Directions for research and instruction,* ed. D.S. Martin, 168–171. Washington, DC: Gallaudet University Press.

Rohwer, W.D., Jr. 1984. An invitation to an educational psychology of studying. *Educational Psychologist* 19:1–14.

Rothkopf, E.Z. 1988. Perspectives on study skills training in a realistic instructional economy. In *Learning and study strategies: Issues in assessment, instruction, and evaluation,* ed. C.E. Weinstein, E.T. Getz, & P.A. Alexander, 275–286. New York: Academic Press.

Spring, C. 1985. Comprehension and study strategies reported by university freshmen who are good and poor readers. *Instructional Science* 14:157–167.

Trybus, R.J., & Karchmer, M.A. 1977. School achievement scores of hearing impaired children: National data on achievement status and growth patterns. *American Annals of the Deaf: Directory of Programs and Services* 22:62–69.

Weinstein, C.E. 1982. Training students to use elaboration learning strategies. *Contemporary Educational Psychology* 7:301–311.

Weinstein, C.E. 1987a. Fostering autonomy through use of learning strategies. *Journal of Reading* 30(7):590–595.

———. 1987b. *LASSI user's manual.* Clearwater, FL: H & H Publishing Company.

Weinstein, C.E., & MacDonald, J.D. 1986. Why does a school psychologist need to know about learning strategies? *Journal of School Psychology* 24:257–265.

Weinstein, C.E., & Mayer, R.E. 1985. The teaching of learning strategies. In *Handbook of teaching.* 3rd ed., ed. M. C. Whittrock. New York: Macmillan.

Weinstein, C.E., Underwood, V.I., Wicher, F.W., & Cubberly, W.E. 1979. Cognitive learning strategies: verbal and imagined elaboration. In *Cognitive and effective learning strategies,* ed. F.O. O'Neil, Jr., & C.B. Speilberger. New York: Academic Press.

Weinstein, C.E., Zimmermann, S.A., & Palmer, D.H. 1988. Assessing learning strategies: The design and development of the LASSI. In *Learning and study strategies: Issues in assessment, instruction, and evaluation,* ed. C.E. Weinstein, E.T. Getz, & P.A. Alexander, 25–39. New York: Academic Press.

Wittrock, M.C. 1974. Learning is a generative process. *Educational Psychologist* 11(2):87–95.

———. 1978. The cognitive movement in instruction. *Educational Psychologist* 13:15–29.

———. 1988. Review of learning strategies research. In *Learning and study strategies: Issues in assessment, instruction, and evaluation,* ed. C.E. Weinstein, E.T. Getz, & P.A. Alexander, 287–297. New York: Academic Press.

Wolk, S. 1985. A macroanalysis of the research on deafness and cognition. In *Cognition, education, and deafness: Directions for research and instruction,* ed. D.S. Martin, 202–208. Washington, DC: Gallaudet University Press.

Zimmerman, B.J., & Pons, M.M. 1986. Development of structured interview for assessing student use of self-regulated learning strategies. *American Educational Resources Journal* 23(4):614–628.

WAIS-R Verbal and Performance Profiles of Deaf Adolescents Referred for Atypical Learning Styles

Pamela Rush
Lynne Blennerhassett
Kenneth Epstein
David Alexander

It is estimated that 6% to 8.6% of hearing-impaired children and youth experience specific learning disabilities not attributed to mental retardation, emotional/behavioral problems, or other sensory/health impairments (Center for Assessment and Demographic Studies 1988; Craig & Craig 1987). In one survey, 23% of a sample of over 7,500 hearing-impaired students were identified as learning disabled (Elliot, Powers & Funderburg 1988).

Although these atypical learners represent the largest segment of multihandicapped hearing-impaired students, there are no specific definitions or agreed-upon criteria to identify this special population. However, practitioners experienced with this population report the presence of atypical learning characteristics, including problems with memory, sequencing, sensory integration, fine/gross motor coordination, visual/tactile/kinesthetic processing, attention, and acquisition of nonverbal and verbal language, all differing from those of hearing-impaired peers (Funderburg 1982; Rowell 1987). In a national survey of programs that served 11,057 hearing-impaired students, atypical deaf learners were differentiated from nonreferral students on nine criteria: memory difficulties; attentional problems; perceptual problems; discrepancy between achievement and potential; language problems; unique learning styles; poor organizational skills; secondary

---

The complete version of this paper is available in microfiche or hard copy from ERIC Document Reproduction Service. Ask for Document No. ED 313 840.

behavior problems; and inconsistent performance (Powers, Elliot & Funderburg 1987). In another national survey, Elliot and his colleagues (1988) identified five criteria unique to this population: processing problems; memory problems; atypical language problems; discrepancy between IQ and achievement; and behavioral problems.

Identification of learning-disabled hearing-impaired (LDHI) students is difficult due to the low incidence of such students and to ambiguities in defining learning disabilities among the general school-age population. Nevertheless, identification of LDHI students may be necessary to secure appropriate support services (Laughton 1989). Identification of LDHI students is also difficult due to lack of instrumentation and variability in rater judgments (Powers, Elliot, Fairbank & Monaghan 1988). Kachman and Rush (1988) recommend a multidisciplinary team approach, stressing that school psychologists, teachers, language/communication specialists, and audiologists pool data from their collective observations and formal/informal assessments. They stress the need for evaluators who are familiar with the effects of hearing impairment on language acquisition and achievement in order to discriminate atypical hearing-impaired learning styles.

For hearing students, the Verbal and Performance Scales of the Wechsler Intelligence Tests have been identified as tools that aid in the discrimination of atypical learners. Kaufman (1979) identified the Freedom from Distractibility cluster (made up of the Arithmetic, Digit Span, and Coding subtests) as low-score groupings for hearing students with attentional and learning problems. Several studies report that the Distractibility cluster discriminates learning-disabled hearing students from their nondisabled peers (Lombard 1978; Stedman, Cortner, Lawles & Achterberg 1978; Petersen & Hart 1979). Groff and Hubble (1982) found the Distractibility factor was found to be somewhat inconsistent across the ages of 6 to 16 years, with the Picture Arrangement subtest loading along with Arithmetic, Digit Span, and Coding (Van Hagen & Kaufman 1975).

With hearing-impaired students, the Wechsler Performance Scales are the most frequently used tests of intelligence—the WISC-R administered to children between the ages of 6–16 years; the WAIS-R administered to students above 16 years of age (Blennerhassett 1985; Gibbins 1989; Levine 1974; Spragins & Gibbins 1982). Studies suggest that the WAIS-R Performance Scale IQs of deaf adolescents are higher than those of hearing adolescents, with mean Performance IQs of 107 to 109 (Balow & Brill 1975; Blennerhassett, Moores, Hannah & Woolard 1988). Mean Verbal IQ scores of deaf adolescents, considered measures of achievement rather than intelligence, ranged from 82 to 91, with Arithmetic subtest scores typically higher than scores on the other Verbal Scale subtests (Blennerhassett 1987; Blennerhassett et al. 1988; Geers & Moog 1987; Hine 1970; Kohoutek, Pulda & Zemanova 1971).

The purpose of the present study was to investigate the degree to which WAIS-R Verbal and Performance Scale profiles of atypical deaf learners differ from those reported for nonreferral deaf peers, and the degree to which the test profiles of atypical deaf students resemble those reported for atypical hearing students.

METHOD

Subjects

The sample consisted of 28 hearing-impaired students between the ages of 18 and 23 years, enrolled at Gallaudet University. Twenty-six of the students were enrolled as preparatory (or pre-freshman) students; two were freshmen. All students in the sample were referred by teachers and/or academic advisors because of atypical learning problems, specifically math and science, communication, and/or English. All referring teachers and academic advisors were experienced with hearing-impaired students and familiar with the effects of deafness on achievement and language. Mixed etiologies were represented in the sample, but none of the participants had additional health or sensory handicaps. The peer group from which the sample was referred had the following characteristics:

1. Preparatory Students
   a. Mean reading comprehension at 5.3–5.7 grade level,
   b. 73% attended residential high schools, 25% attended mainstream high schools.
2. Freshman Students
   a. Mean reading comprehension at 10.0–10.4 grade level,
   b. 47% attended residential high schools, 48% attended mainstream programs.

Procedure

School psychologists trained in working with deaf students administered the Verbal and Performance Scales of the WAIS-R to all the subjects. They administered all the subtests according to the procedures established in the WAIS-R manual, using a form of Pidgin Sign English (PSE). Raw scores on the six Verbal Scale subtests and five Performance Scales subtests were converted to standard scores using WAIS-R norms for same-age peers. Similarly, Verbal IQ and Performance IQ scores were derived by converting raw scores to standard scores using norms for same-age peers.

The referral sample was then compared to nonreferral deaf scores available from previously reported research (Blennerhassett et al. 1988). Although the most appropriate comparison sample would have been nonreferral Gallaudet peers matched on reading level, previous school placement, and other salient personal variables, such a control group was not available to the authors. Rather, data reported in previous research using the WAIS-R with older deaf adolescents was identified as the most appropriate comparison base available. That nonreferral deaf sample consisted of 72 hearing-impaired adolescents between 16 and 18 years of age who were administered the WAIS-R Verbal and Performance Scales in Pidgin Sign English. Mixed etiologies were reported, but the sample excluded students with learning problems or additional handicapping conditions. All students were from residential schools. Mean reading achievement was at 6.0 grade level.

Scores were analyzed using discriminant analysis (Norusis 1986) to determine which subtests were most important in distinguishing between referral and non-referral samples. Univariate tests of IQ and subtest means revealed significant differences among several measures.

RESULTS

Table 1 presents comparisons of WAIS-R Verbal and Performance scores obtained from the sample of hearing-impaired referral students with scores reported in previous research on nonreferral deaf students.

The mean intelligence of deaf referral students, as measured by the Performance IQ, was 97.75. Like their hearing peers who are referred for specific learning disabilities, these hearing-impaired students scored in the average range of intelligence. The subtest cluster of Arithmetic, Digit Span, and Digit Symbol that typifies hearing learning-disabled students did not emerge as a distinct, low-score profile for the deaf referral sample. However, scores on the Arithmetic subtest, along with Picture Arrangement, Picture Completion, and Block Design, were significantly lower for the referral deaf sample than for their nonreferred deaf peers.

The mean Arithmetic score for nonreferred deaf students was 8.12, which represented the area of highest subtest performance on the Verbal Scale. For referral deaf students, the Arithmetic subtest was the only Verbal Scale subtest to differentiate between the two deaf groups, with the mean score of 6.17 for

TABLE 1   WAIS-R Verbal and Performance Scale Differences Between the Referral Deaf Sample and Nonreferral Deaf Peers

	Referral Deaf		Nonreferral Deaf			
	Mean	SD	Mean	SD	F Value	p
Verbal IQ	77.46	5.83	82.20	10.36	5.20	.0247
Performance IQ	97.75	13.09	109.95	15.46	13.62	.0004
Verbal Subtests						
Information	6.46	1.89	6.97	2.66	0.84	.3601
Digit Span	6.10	2.33	6.91	2.61	2.05	.1549
Vocabulary	4.96	1.20	5.81	1.71	5.83	.0176
Arithmetic	6.17	1.80	8.12	2.84	11.27	.0011
Comprehension	6.25	1.75	7.34	2.20	5.56	.0203
Similarities	6.60	2.16	7.62	2.47	3.64	.0592
Performance Subtests						
Picture Comprehension	9.46	2.23	11.11	2.28	10.63	.0015
Picture Arrangement	9.57	2.39	11.73	3.00	11.62	.0009
Block Design	10.17	2.45	12.00	3.17	7.46	.0075
Object Assembly	10.46	2.57	11.77	2.98	4.20	.0431
Digit Symbol	9.67	2.45	10.50	2.48	2.22	.1393

deaf referral sample significantly lower ($p <.01$). Significant differences between the deaf referral sample and the nonreferral norms were noted on four Performance scale measures. The mean Performance IQ of 97.75 for the deaf referral sample was significantly lower ($p <.01$) than the mean IQ of 109.95 for the nonreferral deaf sample. Similarly, the referral deaf sample scored significantly lower on Picture Arrangement (mean = 9.57), Picture Completion (mean = 9.46), and Block Design (mean = 10.17) than the nonreferral deaf group who earned mean scores of 11.73 on Picture Arrangement, 11.11 on Picture Completion, and 12.00 on Block Design.

DISCUSSION

The WAIS-R profile of scores obtained by hearing-impaired adolescents referred for atypical learning styles differed from the scores reported in previous research with a nonreferral deaf sample. Specifically, Performance Scale IQs of deaf referral students, although average, were found to be significantly lower than those reported in previous research. In addition, deaf referral students performed significantly lower on Arithmetic—the Verbal Scale subtest upon which deaf students typically perform best. Significantly lower scores were also noted for deaf referral students on three Performance Scale subtests: Picture Arrangement, Picture Completion, and Block Design.

Low scores on the Picture Arrangement and Picture Completion subtest cluster have been identified as tapping a shared weakness in "visual organization without essential motor activity" (Kaufman 1979, p. 175). These two Performance Scale subtests also require "distinguishing essential from non-essential details" (ibid., p. 176). Low scores on Block Design have been attributed to difficulties in planning and organization of novel abstract stimuli under timed conditions (Jacobson & Kovalinsky 1976). Further research is needed on a larger sample to determine whether LDHI students are weaker than their peers in these cognitive abilities.

The present research has implications for both assessment and remediation. Although the Wechsler Verbal Scales are not generally administered to deaf populations, except for research purposes, it may be useful to standardize and include the Arithmetic subtest (or some similar measure) within diagnostic batteries. Further research is needed to determine whether or not the Arithmetic, Picture Arrangement, Picture Completion, and Block Design cluster proves useful in identifying and discriminating atypical deaf learners throughout the developmental years. Assessing the relative importance of these variables will require further research and analysis.

For practitioners, low scores on subtests that measure visual organization, planning, and distinguishing essential from nonessential information may prove useful in designing remediation strategies for students who exhibit this profile. Incorporating essential motor activities into coursework and projects may provide a strategy for enhancing the learning of such students. This point may be especially important for older students, for whom coursework is typically weighted with reading, lectures, and other activities which are void of essential motor strategies. Further research would be needed to determine the feasibility and effectiveness of such educational modifications on achievement.

REFERENCES

Balow, I.H., & Brill, R.G. 1975. An evaluation of reading and academic achievement levels of 16 graduating classes of the California School for the Deaf, Riverside. *Volta Review* 77(4):255–266.

Blennerhassett, L. 1985. Report of an on-site survey of current psychoeducational and linguistic assessment practices. (Available from L. Blennerhassett, Gallaudet University, Washington, DC).

———. 1987. Experimental use of the WISC-R and WAIS-R Verbal Scales with hearing impaired adolescents. Paper presented at the National Association of School Psychologists, March, New Orleans, LA.

Blennerhassett, L., Moores, D.F., Hannah, J., & Woolard, L. 1988. The impact of parental deafness on WISC-R and WAIS-R Verbal and Performance Scores of deaf adolescents. Paper presented at the National Association of School Psychologists, April, Chicago, IL.

Center for Assessment and Demographic Studies. 1988. *Annual survey of hearing impaired children and youth, 1986–1987.* Washington, DC: Gallaudet University.

Craig, W.N., & Craig, H.B. 1987. Programs and services for the deaf in the United States. *American Annals of the Deaf* 132(2).

Elliot, R., Powers, E., & Funderburg, R. 1988. Learning disabled hearing impaired students: Teacher survey. *Volta Review* 90:277–286.

Funderburg, R. 1982. The role of the classroom teacher in the assessment of the learning disabled child. In *The multihandicapped hearing impaired: Identification and instruction*, ed. D.Tweedie & E. H. Shroyer, 61–74. Washington, DC: Gallaudet University Press.

Geers, A.E., & Moog, J.S. 1987. *Factors predictive of the development of reading and writing skills in the congenitally deaf: Report of the oral sample.* Washington, DC: National Institute of Neurological and Communicative Disorders and Stroke. Report No. NIH-NINCDS-83–19.

Gibbins, S. 1989. The provision of school psychological assessment services for the hearing impaired: A national survey. *Volta Review* 91:95–103.

Groff, M., & Hubble, L. 1982. WISC-R factor structures of younger and older youth with low IQs. *Journal of Consulting and Clinical Psychology* 50(3):148–149.

Hine, W.D. 1970. The abilities of partially hearing children. *British Journal of Educational Psychology* 40(2):171–178.

Jacobson, S., & Kovalinsky, T. 1976. *Educational interpretation of the Wechsler intelligence scale for children-revised (WISC-R).* Linden, NJ: Remediation Associates, Inc.

Kachman, W., & Rush, P. 1988. Learning disabilities among the deaf population: Evaluation and interpretation. Paper presented at the National Association of School Psychologists, April, Chicago, IL.

Kaufman, A.S. 1970. *Intelligent testing with the WISC-R.* New York: John Wiley & Sons.

Kohoutek, R., Pulda, M., & Zemanova, A. 1971. A contribution to the problem of intellectual achievement in the deaf. *Psychologia A Patopaychologia Dietata* 6(2):147–154.

Laughton, J. 1989. The learning disabled hearing impaired student: Reality, myth, or overextension? *Topics in Language Disorders* 9(40):70–79.

Levine, E.S. 1974. Psychological tests and practices with the deaf: A survey of the state of the art. *Volta Review* 76:298–319.

Lombard, T.J., & Riedel, R.G. 1978. An analysis of the factor structure of the WISC-R and the effect of color on the Coding subtest. *Psychology in the Schools* 5(2):176–179.

Norusis, M.J. 1986. *SPSS PC+: Advanced statistics*. Chicago: SPSS Inc.

Peterson, C.R., & Hart, D.H. 1979. Factor structure of the WISC-R for a clinic-referred population and specific subgroups. *Journal of Consulting and Clinical Psychology* 47(3):643–645.

Powers, A., Elliot, R., Fairbank, D., & Monaghan, C. 1988. The dilemma of identifying learning disabled hearing impaired students. *Volta Review* 90(4):209–218.

Powers, A., Elliot, R., & Funderburg, R. 1987. Learning disabled hearing impaired students: Are they being identified? *Volta Review* 89(2):99–105.

Rowell, E.G. 1986. Learning disabilities assessment. In *Mental health assessment of deaf clients*, ed. H. Elliot, L. Glass, & J.W. Evans. San Diego: College-Hill Press.

Spragins, A., & Gibbins, S. 1982. Interaction effect: School psychology and deafness in training and practice. Paper presented at the National Association of School Psychologists, March, Toronto, Ontario.

Stedman, J.M., Cortner, R.H., Lawles, G.F., & Achterberg, G. 1978. Relationships between WISC-R factors, Wide Range Achievement Test scores, and visual-motor maturation in children referred for psychological evaluation. *Journal of Counseling and Clinical Psychology* 46(5):869–872.

Wechsler, D. 1974. *Manual for the Wechsler Intelligence Scale for Children-Revised*. New York: Psychological Corporation.

———. 1981. *Manual for the Wechsler Adult Intelligence Scale-Revised*. New York: Psychological Corporation.

Auditory Sensitivity and Performance on Measures of Mental Status in Elderly Nursing Home Residents

Marymargaret Sharp-Pucci

T he elderly nursing home resident typically presents problems that cross physical, cognitive, and psychologic domains. Since these problems often interact, the analytic and logistic difficulties in assessment can increase exponentially. It follows that assessment of the elderly patient must be approached with emphasis on a characteristic feature of aging—overlap of system pathology. The National Nursing Home Survey indicates that the majority of institutionalized individuals have a primary diagnosis of organic brain syndrome (U.S. Vital and Health Statistics 1977). Bingea, Raffin, Aune, Baye, and Shea (1982) estimated the prevalence of significant hearing impairment to be close to 90% of the nursing home population. The interaction of these two states (cognitive impairment and hearing impairment) can obscure the art and science of assessment.

Assessment of cognitive functioning is often based on mental status exams designed to tap an individual's level of orientation. Since hearing loss denies exposure to external stimuli necessary to maintain level of orientation (e.g., interpersonal communication, radio, television), a hearing-impaired person may be unable to offer valid answers to questions related to this index of functioning.

A causal relationship has not yet been demonstrated between auditory sensitivity and mental-status test performance, but it has been suggested that this reduced sensory acuity may limit the amount of information available to the elderly person and therefore interfere with the ability to respond appropriately on these measures. This study investigated the relationship between auditory sensitivity and cognitive test performance among institutionalized elderly persons, with a particular emphasis on the role of information supplied through auditory means.

METHODS AND PROCEDURES

Mental Status Questionnaire (MSQ) and Short Portable Mental State Questionnaire (SP-MSQ)

The MSQ of Kahn, Goldfarb, Pollack, and Peck (1960) and the SP-MSQ of Duke University (1978) were both administered to 77 subjects. Both are ten-item instruments designed to provide gross screening for organic brain syndrome (OBS) in the elderly. Both instruments assess orientation to surroundings as well as recent and remote recall. The SP-MSQ also taps the capacity to perform serial mathematical tasks. The MSQ and SP-MSQ are two of the most widely used brief assessment instruments for determination of mental status in the elderly. Total score reflects the severity of cognitive dysfunction, with lower scores representing more severe impairment.

Mental Status Assessment

Each subject was administered the MSQ and SP-MSQ in random order through individual interview. Test items were presented individually in an aural and visual format that included a clear, slow speech pattern and large print.

Auditory Assessment

The subjects' acuity for pure tones was assessed at several frequencies, including 500 Hz, 1000 Hz, 3000 Hz, 4000 Hz, 6000 Hz, and 8000 Hz. Determination of individuals' levels of auditory acuity was based on a three-frequency pure-tone average (PTA) within the speech range (500, 1000, 2000 Hz) in the better ear. Subjects' hearing losses were categorized as normal-mild, moderate, or severe-profound based on these results.

Assessment of Information Exposure

The activities directors of all facilities were asked the following question as it pertains to each individual item of both mental status questionnaires: "During the course of an average week, are the residents at this facility exposed to this information through staff contact, conversation, announcements, orientation sessions, therapeutic sessions, or facility activities?" Based on the responses, individual test items were categorized as either exposure or nonexposure. This question replicates the procedure that Ohta, Carlin, and Harmon (1981) used in their investigation of mental status performance and cognitive testing.

RESULTS

Characteristics of the Sample

Fifty-seven residents, including 31 males and 26 females from four skilled-nursing facilities, served as subjects. The mean age of this sample was 78.09 years

(*SD* = 8.68). The sample's mean three-frequency PTA was 50.79 (*SD* = 14.72). These figures are comparable to those reported in the literature for elderly populations (Corbin, Reed, Nobbs, Eastwood & Eastwood 1984; Ventry & Weinstein 1982).

MSQ and SP-MSQ Total Score Analysis

The results indicate a high correlation (*r* = .88) between the two equivalent measures of cognitive status, the MSQ and the SP-MSQ. A mean MSQ total score of 6.33 (*SD* = 3.24) and SP-MSQ score of 6.79 (*SD* = 3.02) (both indicative of mild-moderate impairment) was obtained.

A one-way analysis of variance (ANOVA) performed on total MSQ scores indicated significant differences between auditory categories (*p* ≤ .0001). Post hoc analysis indicated significant MSQ score differences (*p* ≤ .05) between mildly impaired versus moderately and severely impaired groups, and significant differences (*p* ≤ .05) in moderately vs. severely impaired groups. Equivalent results were obtained in an analysis of SP-MSQ total scores. These results demonstrate that those elderly persons with marked decrements in auditory acuity score significantly lower than those with better auditory abilities on the MSQ and SP-MSQ tests of mental status.

Item Analysis

An item analysis was conducted for each measure using a 2 x 3 chi square test. Individual MSQ test items and percentages of correct responses by auditory level are presented in Table 1. This table also indicates whether nursing home residents had auditory exposure to the requested information, as reported by activity directors of the facilities. SP-MSQ data are not shown but the results are similar to those obtained through the MSQ.

The chi square analysis investigated differences between correct and incorrect individual items and total responses among the three levels of auditory abilities for the MSQ and SP-MSQ. Both exposure and nonexposure questions indicated significant differences among auditory abilities for the MSQ and the SP-MSQ. These data illustrate that significant differences do exist in the ability of elderly persons to score correct responses, dependent on auditory ability, but that auditory access to the necessary information does not appear to be a factor in this relationship.

DISCUSSION

This investigation initially sought to establish level of auditory sensitivity as a factor in the outcome of mental status scores as measured by the MSQ and SP-MSQ. Results confirmed this contention, demonstrating that elderly persons with marked decrements in auditory ability score significantly lower than those with

TABLE 1   Activity Directors' Responses to the Question Regarding Daily Opportunity to Hear Information Requested by the MSQ

Item	Adequate Auditory Exposure to Information	Percentage of Correct Responses			Statistical Significance
		Mild	Moderate	Severe	
1. What is the name of this place?	Yes	94	55	25	$p \leq .001$
2. Where is this place located?	Yes (2 sites) No (2 sites)	72	41	08	$p \leq .01$
3. What day in the month is it today?	Yes	89	48	08	$p \leq .001$
4. What day of the week is it today?	Yes	82	55	17	$p \leq .01$
5. What year is it?	Yes	100	74	33	$p \leq .001$
6. How old are you?	Yes	89	89	75	
7. When is your birthday?	No	89	78	33	$p \leq .01$
8. In what year were you born?	No	83	78	67	
9. What is the name of the president?	Yes	72	59	25	$p \leq .05$
10. Who was the president before this one?	No	83	59	08	$p \leq .001$

better auditory abilities. A strong inverse relationship between degree of hearing loss and degree of success on cognitive measures is not surprising. Such findings are similar to those reported by other investigators (Eisdorfer 1960; Granick, Kleban & Weiss 1976; Ohta, Carlin & Harmon 1981; O'Neil & Calhoun 1975; and Schaie, Baltes & Strother 1964). The relationship is apparent; greater decrements in auditory sensitivity are associated with lower scores on cognitive measures. The *nature* of this association, however, is not apparent.

Three hypotheses may define the relationship between hearing loss and cognitive status. O'Neil and Calhoun (1975) offered two hypotheses, a central one and a peripheral one. They concluded that senile manifestations are related to overall sensory loss and note that such manifestations may be interpreted in two ways: (a) by viewing sensory deficits and cognitive deterioration as concomitants of a central change process (central hypothesis); or (b) by assuming some degree of causality within the sensory loss, meaning that increased peripheral sensory thresholds may lead to cognitive deterioration (peripheral hypothesis).

The third hypothesis is that informational supply is blocked by a sensory deficit, leaving the information needed to succeed on measures of mental status inaccessible to the subject (informational hypothesis). This investigation sought to gather data in support of this informational hypothesis. However, no evidence exists within this study that would implicate a lack of informational accessibility through auditory means as a factor in the outcome of MSQ and SP-MSQ cognitive test scores. Because significant differences exist among scores obtained by mildly, moderately, and severely hearing-impaired subjects, regardless of auditory exposure to the information, the postulation of a blocked informational supply does not appear tenable. If informational supply were a factor in score outcome, it would be reasonable to expect that individual item responses involving auditory exposure would result in significant differences among the three auditory levels (e.g., What is the name of this place?). At the same time, questions that do not involve auditory reception of information would result in no significant differences among auditory abilities (e.g., What is your mother's maiden name?). Thus, it is reasonable to examine alternative hypotheses, most importantly the central interpretation.

The suspicion of a co-morbid process between cognitive decline and central presbycusic hearing loss is accepted. Support is gained at the cellular level, with replacement of dead or defective cells being either limited or nonexistent in the older patient. Noticeably diminished organic and functional abilities result. A decreased brain weight and decline in neuronal cell density in the cerebral cortex and peripheral nervous system clearly indicate a cumulative cellular loss (Boone, Bayles & Koopman 1982). While the implications of these alterations in the etiology of OBS have been realized for some time, it is only more recently that such changes are being related to age-dependent central-mediated hearing loss (Marshall 1981).

This relationship may be significant in view of the results obtained in the present study. A significant association between a diagnosis of OBS as measured by either the MSQ and SP-MSQ and degree of hearing impairment was established. Subjects categorized as having severe auditory deficits comprised 27% of the age group 60–69 and 29% of the 70– to 79–year-old group, yet they comprised only 7% of the 80– to 89–year-olds and 14% of the >90 group. These percentages represent significant differences between the combined younger and older age groups. It must be noted, however, that the results obtained in this study are not consistent with those previously reported in the literature (Katsarkas & Ayukawa 1986), where frequency of severe impairment is shown to increase proportionally with age. Of significant import, however, is that the majority of studies investigating auditory acuity among the aged use subjects in the community rather than institutionalized samples. Further, those studying an institutionalized sample often exclude residents with a diagnosis of OBS due to difficulties inherent in the testing procedure with this patient group.

The percentage of severe hearing impairment is not consistent throughout the age span in this sample. Instead it declines with age. Questions arise as to why this diminished representation of severely hearing-impaired persons exists in the more advanced age group; auditory sensitivity is not known to improve with age. One may suspect attrition of this group as a result of (a) death (which is correlated to a diagnosis of OBS) or (b) an inability to participate in the study due to a severe lack of functional capacity (also correlated to a diagnosis of OBS). Bergman, Kay, and Foster (1971) and Kay (1962) have demonstrated a high correlation between short-term memory disturbances (as are measured by the MSQ and SP-MSQ) and subsequent mortality. The death rate among patients with acute and chronic brain syndromes has been shown to be consistently higher than among the general age-related population (Kay 1962).

As hearing impairment in and of itself is not known as a prognostic indicator of mortality, a functional decline in auditory sensitivity alone cannot explain a diminished representation of severely hearing-impaired persons in advanced years. However, because OBS is considered to be a predictor of mortality, consideration of a co-morbid process between auditory and cognitive decline can provide plausible interpretation of this study's demonstrated significant decline in the percentage of severe hearing impairment with age. This finding would indicate a decline in the percentages of severely hearing-impaired subjects as a result of higher death rates, possibly mediated through a co-morbid auditory and cognitive decline process. While the present investigation did not set out to study this issue, its occurrence can be considered suggestive in nature and indicates that further investigation in this area may be justified.

Discussion at the Second International Symposium on Cognition, Education, and Deafness centered on the methodological difficulties in separating peripheral components from central ones. These difficulties indeed exist. As more sophisticated assessment procedures measuring both auditory and cognitive functioning are refined, the distinction between peripheral and central processes can become more clear.

CONCLUSIONS

The results of this study support the hypothesis that degree of auditory sensitivity is a factor in performance on measures of mental status. It is reasonable to consider that cognitive decline and auditory decline coexist in a notable proportion of institutionalized elderly patients. The pathological mechanisms which lead to this coexistence are not clear. Further investigation with larger samples may provide a more definitive answer to this question.

REFERENCES

Bergman, K., Kay, D.W., & Foster, E.M. 1971. Follow-up study of randomly selected community residents to assess the effects of chronic brain syndrome and cerebral vascular disease. *Proceedings of the 5th World Congress of Psychiatry.* Mexico City: Excerpta Medica International Congress Series No. 274.

Bingea, R.L., Raffin, J.J., Aune, K.J., Baye, L., & Shea, S.L. 1982. Incidence of hearing loss among geriatric nursing home residents. *The Journal of Auditory Research* 22:275– 283.

Boone, D.R., Bayles, K.A., & Koopman, C.F. 1982. Communicative aspects of aging. *The Otolaryngology Clinics of North America* 15(2):313–327.

Corbin, S., Reed, M., Nobbs, H., Eastwood, K., & Eastwood, M.R. 1984. Hearing assessment in homes for the aged: A comparison of audiometric and self-report methods. *Journal of the American Geriatrics Society* 32(5):396–400.

Duke University. 1978. Multidimensional functional assessment: The OARS methodology. Durham, NC: Duke University Press.

Eisdorfer, C. 1960. Developmental level and sensory impairment in the aged. *Journal of Projective Techniques* 24:129–132.

Granick, S., Kleban, M.H., & Weiss, A.D. 1976. Relationships between hearing loss and cognition in normally hearing aged persons. *Journal of Gerontology* 31(4):434–440.

Kahn, R.L., Goldfarb, A.I., Pollack, M., & Peck, A. 1960. Brief objective measures for the determination of mental status in the aged. *American Journal of Psychiatry* 117:326–328.

Katsarkas, L., & Ayukawa, H. 1986. Hearing loss due to aging (presbycusis). *Journal of Otolaryngology* 15(4):239–244.

Kay, D.W. 1962. Outcome and cause of death in mental disorders of old age: Long-term follow-up of functional and organic psychoses. *Acta Psychiatrica Scandinavia* 38:249–252.

Marshall, L. 1981. Auditory processing in aging listeners. *Journal of Speech-Hearing Disorders* 46(3):226–240.

Ohta, R.J., Carlin, M.F., & Harmon, B.M. 1981. Auditory acuity and performance on the mental status questionnaire in the elderly. *Journal of American Geriatrics Society* 29(10):476–478.

O'Neil, P.M., & Calhoun, K.S. 1975. Sensory deficits and behavioral deterioration in senescence. *Journal of Abnormal Psychology* 84(5):579–582.

Schaie, K.W., Baltes, P., & Strother, C.R. 1964. A study of auditory sensitivity in advanced age. *Journal of Gerontology* 19:453–457

U.S. Vital and Health Statistics. 1977. The national nursing home survey: 1977 summary for the United States. DHEW Publication No. PHS 79–1794, Series 13, No. 43. Washington, DC: U.S. Government Printing Office.

Ventry, I.M., & Weinstein, B.E. 1982. The hearing handicap inventory for the elderly: A new tool. *Ear and Hearing* 3(3):128–134.

Analysis

Linda Delk

E ducators of deaf children frequently ask, "Are available tests valid for use with deaf students?" Recent developments in psychometric theory and in the political and social arenas have stimulated renewed interest in this question. As more deaf students are being educated in public school programs, concerns relate to decisions about appropriate placement as well as about the use of minimum competency testing by states to certify students for high school graduation. Issues relating to the assessment of handicapped populations have arisen in response to the requirement for fair testing practices imposed in P.L. 94–142 and in Section 504 of the Rehabilitation Act.

At the same time, test validity is receiving renewed attention in the general testing community. The reconceptualization of test validity as a unified construct grows out of the need for clearer understanding of tested constructs, the interpretation of test results, and the consequences of their use. The three-part classification of validity into content, criterion, and construct has given way to the notion of test validation as a continuous process. It is no longer sufficient to think of validity as a property of a test that can be established once and for all by a correlation coefficient. Construct validity has become the central focus and a means of linking test concepts, evidence, social and personal consequences, and values (Cronbach 1988). This unified conception of validity involves "an integrative evaluative judgment of the degree to which empirical evidence and theoretical rationales support the *adequacy* and *appropriateness* of *inferences* and *actions* based on test scores or other modes of assessment" (Messick 1989).

This unified concept of validity provides a useful framework for examining the papers in this chapter. Berkeley explores the need for an integrated, qualitative approach to assessment of infants and toddlers and discusses assessment in light of its many possible uses and consequences. Aplin examines the adequacy and appropriateness of using a battery of tests to diagnose learning difficulties among deaf students and presents empirical evidence to challenge Van Uden's construct of dyspraxia. Croft et al. examine the utility of a test of study skills for predicting the academic success of deaf college students. Braden focuses on the theoretical limitations of existing research for improving understanding of the construct of intelligence as it applies to deaf persons. At a different level, Rush explores the IQ test profiles of atypical deaf learners. Clark explores the different strategies that deaf and hearing adults may use in visual information-processing tasks. And Sharp-Pucci examines evidence to support selection of a causal theory to explain the simultaneous decline of hearing and cognitive functioning among elderly persons.

Berkeley describes a theoretical framework for observing and documenting the dimensions, or salient attributes, of children's responses to the environment. Application of the salient-responses approach may ensure that behaviors at any level of complexity are observed in context, especially when the salient attributes such as utilization and generalization are specified. The reader is left to assume, however, that the choice of theoretical orientation to development will guide the sampling of behaviors to be assessed using the salient attributes of responses framework. While an integrated view of development is desirable, especially for young children, the very nature of the salient-responses approach seems to require that some behavior at some level, such as play, communication, or walking, must be specified. The act of choosing some behaviors to observe necessitates paying less attention to others. If more than one behavior is observed using salient responses, one of the tasks of assessment still remains—that of integrating information across behaviors. Berkeley could help bridge the gap between theory and practice by providing more examples of how the salient-attributes approach could be applied to assessment, intervention, and program evaluation.

Aplin's study of the identification of learning difficulties in deaf children begins by questioning Van Uden's assertion that dyspraxia can be identified using a particular battery of tests and that this identification should be used to recommend the type of educational program which deaf children should receive. By using a large, heterogeneous sample of deaf students in public school programs and combining factor analysis with qualitative methods of profile analysis, Aplin concluded that Van Uden's dyspraxia test battery is not adequate for identifying young deaf children for purposes of placement. Aplin's caution speaks to the social and personal consequences of test use. More studies like Aplin's are needed to improve decisions, not only about how tests should be used, but also about whether or not empirical evidence supports their use, given other alternative assessment methods. Her study also emphasizes the importance of the continuous process of test validation with different groups under different circumstances.

Clark's investigation of memory strategies used by deaf and hearing subjects is another case in which current research reexamines assessment questions using refined methodology. The result is a better understanding of *why* deaf subjects perform less well on sequential memory tasks than do hearing subjects. The studies provide evidence counter to the medical or deficit model of deafness by illustrating that deaf and hearing subjects can attain similar visual-processing scores through application of different strategies.

Braden criticizes research on intelligence by arguing that researchers are not asking appropriate questions and are not advancing the field by moving beyond traditional normative research. His meta-analysis is a take-all study, incorporating all known studies of intelligence scores of deaf persons. Given his observation that not all IQ tests are created equal, inclusion of verbal, nonverbal, and performance tests in the analysis may be considered a first step preceding a more in-depth look at different kinds of intelligence assessments. In addition to differences in administration procedures, it may be assumed that tests in different formats may be constructed from somewhat different conceptions of intelligence. It may be useful to focus meta-analyses on more delimited sets of IQ studies in order to capitalize on what Braden terms a natural experiment. Readers would be able to evaluate his conclusions if selected subsets of the studies were summarized in tabular form, such as results of studies using verbal vs. nonverbal tests. Braden also asserts that deafness and its impact on IQ test results are similar to the effects found among minority groups, such as African-Americans, reflecting more than lack of language. Having drawn that conclusion, Braden could pursue the possible causes of lower reported IQ scores among minority groups, including the important possibility of cultural bias.

Clark describes a series of experiments aimed at examining the parameters of deaf and hearing persons' visual processing abilities, separate from linguistic abilities. She describes previous research and a series of new experiments, questioning old assumptions about memory deficits among deaf persons. Clark's experimental procedures are described in precise detail, providing the possibility that other researchers may replicate or develop refinements of her methodology. The description of subjects is incomplete, however. The sample characteristics may have influenced the outcomes of these experiments and be important in explaining conflicting results between the first and second groups. College students are a very select group. It can be assumed that they do at least as much reading as other portions of the population. Therefore, overlearning of English letters may be assumed. Alternative explanations might be found in information about the number of hours per week spent in reading and about their current preferred mode(s) of communication instead of communication history. Familiarity with other testing dimensions could be determined, such as subjects' prior experience with computers or psychology students' familiarity with experiments of this kind, as compared to students with other majors.

Croft et al. present preliminary results of an investigation of the validity of using a study skills assessment to predict the academic success of deaf college students, as measured by GPA. The intention is to be able to diagnose students' strengths and weaknesses in study strategies and then design appropriate interventions. The study examines the validity of the LASSI within the rich context of the instructional program in which it is to be used. More detailed delineation of the research questions of this exploratory study would be helpful, however, including the rationale for the variety of measures used, how they contribute to the establishment of validity, and how they fit the model of the active learner. While the preliminary results are encouraging, the study could be strengthened by using random assignment of students to testing conditions and raw scores instead of percentiles for statistical analyses.

The obtained correlations between the LASSI and GPA, while significant, are of small magnitude. While the LASSI provides some explanatory power about future success, other unspecified factors clearly contribute to the variance in GPA. The finding of higher correlations between the English-only version of the LASSI and GPA suggests that the contribution of reading ability should be included in the equation predicting college success. The researchers may find it valuable to utilize more integrated, multivariate analyses to better understand the contribution of LASSI scores in combination with other variables, such as reading ability, for predicting GPA.

In contrast to Braden's global look at IQ tests, Rush et al. initiated an in-depth investigation of student profiles on the WISC. They present an important piece of work in the area of cognitive assessment that goes beyond the use of IQ tests for establishing overall levels of functioning, by investigating the use of subtest profiles for differential diagnosis of students with atypical learning patterns. They discuss the potential for using this information for tailoring instruction to meet the needs of students with atypical learning styles. It is interesting that while the verbal subtests of the WISC have been seen as mainly measures of English proficiency, the identification of a cluster of subtests which includes a verbal subtest calls for a reexamination of what IQ tests measure in different modalities.

Sharp-Pucci presents a well-designed study that illuminates the processes underlying the relationship between the decline of hearing and cognitive functioning among elderly persons. The study goes beyond establishing the existence of a relationship all the way to examining evidence to test causal theories that may explain that relationship. This reasoned approach could also benefit the assessment of processes that underlie cognitive functioning levels in children.

These papers examined cognitive assessment from a range of theoretical and practical perspectives, focusing on age groups from infancy to old age. They provide evidence that professionals who focus on the cognitive assessment of deaf individuals are concerned not only with the properties of tests, but also with assessment in context—be it theoretical context or the context of test use. By engaging in research that addresses the need for information about test meaning, use, interpretation, and consequences, they affirm that test validity applies as much to the test user as to the test itself. In addition, they advance the understanding of human cognition, as Glaser (1988) has so aptly expressed it,

> [enabling] us to focus more precisely . . . on the complex processes that underlie . . . achievement—a focus that emphasizes the structure and coherence of knowledge and its accessibility in problem solving and reasoning. . . . The impact of tests in the service of learning is evident particularly when a test result becomes more than a tool for placing students in a category. A test result's function should not end with a classification that precludes judgment by the teacher and student about paths of action. Measurement, as in other fields . . . results in an action.

REFERENCES

Cronbach, L.J. 1988. Five perspectives on validity argument. In *Test validity*, ed. H. Wainer & H.I. Braun. Hillsdale, NJ: Lawrence Erlbaum Associates.

Glaser, R. 1988. Cognitive and environmental perspectives on assessing achievement. In *Assessment in the service of learning: Proceedings of the 1987 ETS Invitational Conference*. Princeton, NJ: Educational Testing Service.

Messick, S. 1989. Meaning and values in test validation: The science and ethics of assessment. *Educational Researcher* 18:5–11.

RESEARCH QUESTIONS

1. How could the salient-attributes-of-responses approach be applied to the assessment of deaf children?
2. How can we use tests in conjunction with other means of assessment to identify more effectively the cognitive abilities and potential of deaf persons?
3. What alternative approaches to assessment are needed to improve the cognitive assessment of deaf persons?
4. From what implicit theories of development and cognition do service providers operate in their day-to-day decision making?
5. Is the pattern of cognitive functioning of deaf persons different from that of hearing persons? If so, how? What are the implications for cognitive assessment?
6. How can educators of deaf persons use test results to forge closer connections between cognitive assessment and intervention strategies?
7. Do deaf and hearing persons respond similarly or differently to dynamic and static visual displays? Do they use similar or different information-processing strategies for the different displays?
8. What is the repertoire of information-processing strategies from which deaf and hearing persons choose? What information-processing functions relate to linguistic abilities?
9. What is the range of cognitive processes that underlies similar profiles of achievement and abilities? How can such information be used to serve instructional design and individualization for students?
10. How do hearing ability and cognitive functioning interact throughout the entire span of a person's life? How does the relationship change as life progresses?
11. What kinds of research into underlying processes will help us choose among competing theories of cognitive functioning?

4

LANGUAGE AND COGNITION

Deaf Readers' Acquisition of Word Meanings from Context

Beth Davey
Susan King

A great deal of recent research has focused on the question of how readers acquire elaborated word meanings from context during reading, although this research has primarily concentrated on hearing individuals. We have little information about how deaf readers acquire word meanings from written contexts. We suggest that this is an important issue both for researchers involved in studying the impact of cognitive processes on the educational outcomes of deaf learners and for practitioners engaged in enhancing deaf learners' reading skills. For example, ample research over the years has shown vocabulary size to be a strong and consistent predictor of success in a variety of reading comprehension and verbal processing tasks (Anderson & Freebody 1981; Davis 1968; LaSasso & Davey 1987; Mezynski 1983). Research has also documented that deaf readers' vocabularies are substantially lower than those of their hearing peers (DiFrancesca 1972; Walter 1978). Gaining an understanding of how deaf learners acquire word knowledge while reading should be particularly informative for educators committed to developing the size of deaf readers' vocabularies.

Although readers can acquire meanings of new words in numerous ways (Jenkins & Dixon 1983), perhaps the most important is through exposure to new words in written context. A growing number of researchers (Daneman 1988; Elshout-Mohr & van Daalen-Kapteijns 1987; Nagy, Anderson & Herman 1987; Sternberg & Powell 1983) suggest that most word learning by older hearing students can be attributed to rich contextual exposures through reading rather than to direct vocabulary instruction or to morphological analysis. Sternberg's (1987) assertion that "most vocabulary is learned from context" (p. 59) seems to have strong research backing and is a particularly important notion for those involved in the education of hearing-impaired students.

Several cognitive processes appear to be involved in deriving the meaning of unknown words from context. Sternberg and Powell (1983), for example, have described three central processes in their model of knowledge acquisition from written contexts. Successful word learners separate relevant from irrelevant information; they integrate and combine relevant cues to develop plausible definitions; and they then compare this new learned information with information they have previously learned about the concept. Although they basically agree with Sternberg and Powell, Daneman and associates (Daneman 1988; Daneman & Carpenter 1983; Daneman & Green 1986) have proposed, as have Nagy, Anderson, and Herman (1987), that the key cognitive component undergirding contextual learning of word meanings is one of integration skill. To derive meaning from context, readers must be able to connect or relate bits of information signalled by features of written contexts. The research by Daneman et al. provides strong evidence of this process and also demonstrates how individual differences in working memory processes affect the efficient use of integration skills.

Only a limited number of investigations are relevant to contextual processing characteristics in deaf readers. Previous studies such as those by McGill-Franzen and Gormley (1980) and by Nolen and Wilbur (1985) provide support for use of context by deaf readers, although there is conflicting evidence with regard to actual differences between hearing and deaf readers' abilities to use context. Using cloze procedures, several researchers have found that deaf subjects make quantitatively more errors than do hearing subjects (Davey, LaSasso & Macready 1983; Moores 1970; Marshall 1970; Odom, Blanton & Nunnally 1967). However, Odom et al. (1967) found that when the number of words between cloze blanks increased, deaf readers' scores improved to a higher degree than did hearing readers' scores. This finding suggests that under certain conditions, deaf readers may actually be *better* able to utilize contextual information to develop appropriate word replacements for cloze blanks. Also of interest, Fischler (1983) concluded that deaf and hearing subjects may not differ in terms of processes used, but rather in terms of the specific linguistic and semantic knowledge sources needed for sentence-completion tasks.

This issue of potential process differences between deaf and hearing readers' use of context was recently explored by Strassman, Kretschmer, and Bilsky (1987). In two studies conducted with deaf high school students, Strassman et al. found that these subjects were able to use sentence contexts when directed to do so, but that they did not *spontaneously* generate or instantiate specific meanings for general terms as suggested by the sentence contexts. Also, there was a recall advantage for sentence contexts when critical relationships were explicitly stated rather than implied. It was concluded that such behavior may be due to "impoverished semantic representations," or to problems with integrative processes, or, perhaps, to inadequate educational experiences with "constructive and inferential processes when reading" (p. 3). Thus there appear to be a number of factors that can affect the degree to which deaf readers successfully use context to derive meanings for new words.

Against this background, we assessed the processes by which deaf readers acquire elaborated word meanings from sentence contexts (Davey & King 1989). We were particularly interested in differences between successful (high-vocabulary scoring) and less successful (low-vocabulary scoring) deaf readers in the processes they use to derive contextual meanings. It is assumed that individuals with high scores on a vocabulary test have been more successful in the past at deriving word meanings from context than have been individuals with low vocabulary scores (Anderson & Freebody 1981; Nagy, Anderson & Herman 1987; Sternberg 1987). Therefore, it was our view that any observed differences between these two groups could shed light on factors and processing strategies that account for successful context use by deaf readers.

We asked fourteen moderately to profoundly deaf college students to figure out the meanings of three new words. These low-frequency words were selected from dictionaries of rare words (Byrne 1974; Dickson 1982) and met two criteria: they represented concepts that were deemed familiar to this population, and they had definitions that consisted of three meaning specifications. Four sentences were constructed for each target word. The first sentence was intended to present the reader with a superordinate model for the word meaning. Each of the remaining sentences was intended to provide the reader with a further specification of the overall meaning of the word. The sentence sets differed in terms of how explicitly the meaning units were signalled. All sentence sets were evaluated for syntactic complexity and found to be comparable.

For each target word, the successful and less successful reader groups read one sentence at a time, "thinking aloud" about possible meanings for the new word. Each sentence was presented on a separate page, and subjects were directed to write possible meanings for the target word based on sentence information. The subjects were not permitted to look back to preceding pages. When they finished reading each of the four sentences, they were asked to provide a complete and precise definition of the target word based on all the sentences. Subjects' protocols were analyzed in terms of the number of appropriate meaning units generated after each sentence presentation, the final definition accuracy (the number of correct meaning specifications included in the definition), and the processing strategies utilized.

We observed three processing strategies used consistently by our deaf readers as they attempted to construct an overall and compete meaning for each new word based on specific sentence information. The *refinement* strategy occurred when the reader adjusted an initial hypothesis about the target word's meaning based on new sentence information. In this case, readers were observed to integrate bits of information across sentences. With the *replacement* strategy, readers were observed to abandon a previously hypothesized meaning for the new word and to replace it with an entirely new meaning model. Finally, the *retention* strategy was evident when readers maintained their hypothesized meanings for the new words; they did not attempt to adjust or replace their meaning models based on new sentence information.

Results indicated that high- and low-vocabulary deaf readers generated comparable numbers of meaning units and utilized similar processing strategies when the material explicitly and unambiguously signalled the central meaning units. However, with the less explicit sentence sets, the high vocabulary group exceeded the low group in generating acceptable meaning units. (Note the similar findings from Strassman et al. 1987.)

Perhaps most important were the group differences noted when the sentences taxed schema utilization and integration processes. In this case, low vocabulary deaf readers appeared to revert to a sentence-based processing approach, with heavier use of a replacement strategy. In addition, they committed substantially more errors of syntactic processing and exhibited more strategies of simple sentence reconstruction and simple visual matching than did high vocabulary readers.

Also of note were group differences in self-reported use of strategies. When asked, "What do you do when you're reading a book and you come to a word that you don't know the meaning of?", 86% of the high-vocabulary subjects indicated use of a contextually based strategy first, then, if unsuccessful, use of a dictionary. On the other hand, only 14% of the low-vocabulary subjects indicated use of a contextually based strategy, whereas 57% indicated use of a dictionary.

From this study and the related research and theory, we can draw several implications for research and practice. First, we need more systematic investigation of the many text, task, and reader factors that may influence the effectiveness by which deaf learners utilize written contexts to derive word meanings. Ultimately, this research may assist practitioners in making critical decisions concerning which words to teach directly and which can be acquired from reading alone. For example, one exposure to a word during reading may be sufficient for learning new words *if* word meanings are explicitly cued by sentence contexts, and *if* learners can apply effective context-based strategies for deriving meanings for new words.

Second, we need careful studies of critical differences between hearing and deaf readers' meaning acquisitions. For example, the work of van Daalen-Kapteijns and Elshout-Mohr (1981) suggests that hearing readers may not be as influenced in their processing strategies by features of the sentence texts as are deaf readers. Daneman's research concerning the importance of working memory processes in the integration skill underlying contextual learning might also be a fruitful starting point for investigations of important group differences.

Finally, based on the conclusions of Strassman et al. (1987) and the self-reported strategy behaviors of our subjects, it appears that low-vocabulary deaf readers need training in self-monitoring and contextually based strategies for figuring out the meanings of unknown words. Sternberg (1987) and Jenkins, Matlock, and Slocum (1988) have begun to consider the role that direct instruction in the use of context may play in word-acquisition processes. Their studies suggest that training in *how* to use context can be particularly effective for low-verbal readers. This area appears to be a particularly important line of inquiry for researchers of deaf learners, with potential implications for instructional design.

Of course, our results can only be generalized within the limits of the particular text and task features we employed. Specifically, we did not assess how deaf readers use context spontaneously; our "think-aloud" task required subjects to generate possible meanings based upon sentence presentations. It is not known whether the processing strategies we observed would hold for tasks in which incidental learning of word meanings is assessed. Also, our task required subjects to hold previous sentence information in memory (they were not permitted to look back to earlier sentences). This task feature placed particular demands on working-memory processes. Future studies are needed to assess processing strategies and outcomes under more naturalistic reading situations, such as situations in which readers are allowed to reinspect texts.

We have attempted to describe some aspects of deaf readers' use of context to derive meanings for new words. While the research to date is meager concerning deaf learners' acquisitions of meaning, it is anticipated that the growing base of research and theory regarding hearing readers will result in several important studies of deaf readers in the future.

REFERENCES

Anderson, R. C., & Freebody, P. 1981. Vocabulary knowledge. In *Comprehension and teaching: Research reviews*, ed. J. Guthrie, 71–117. Newark, DE: International Reading Association.

Byrne, J. H. 1974. *Mrs. Byrne's dictionary of unusual, obscure, and preposterous words.* Secaucus, NJ: Citadel Press.

Daneman, M. 1988. Word knowledge and reading skill. In *Reading research: Advances in theory and practice*, ed. M. Daneman, G. E. MacKinnon, & T.G. Waller, 145–176. New York: Academic Press.

Daneman, M., & Carpenter, P. 1983. Individual differences in integrating information between and within sentences. *Journal of Experimental Psychology: Learning, Memory, and Cognition* 9:561–583.

Daneman, M., & Green, I. 1986. Individual differences in comprehending and producing words in context. *Journal of Memory and Language* 25:1–18.

Davey, B., & King, S. 1989. *Meaning acquisitions from context by deaf readers.* Manuscript submitted for publication.

Davey, B., LaSasso, C., & Macready, G. 1983. A comparison of reading comprehension task performance for deaf and hearing subjects. *Journal of Speech and Hearing Research* 26:622–628.

Davis, F. 1968. Research in comprehension in reading. *Reading Research Quarterly* 3:499–545.

Dickson, P. 1982. *Words.* New York: Delacorte Press.

DiFrancesca, S. 1972. *Academic achievement test results of a national testing program for hearing-impaired students.* Washington, DC: Gallaudet College, Office of Demographic Studies.

Elshout-Mohr, M., & van Daalen-Kapteijns, M.M. 1987. Cognitive processes in learning word meanings. In *The nature of vocabulary acquisition*, ed. M. McKeown and M. Curtis, 53–71. Hillsdale, NJ: Lawrence Erlbaum Associates.

Fischler, I. 1983. Contextual constraint and comprehension of written sentences by deaf college students. *American Annals of the Deaf* 128:418–424.

Jenkins, J. R., & Dixon, R. 1983. Vocabulary learning. *Contemporary Educational Psychology* 8:237–260.

Jenkins, J. R., Matlock, B., & Slocum, T. A. 1988. *Effects of specific vocabulary instruction and instruction in deriving word meaning from context.* Paper presented at the annual meeting of the American Educational Research Association, New Orleans, LA.

LaSasso, C., & Davey, B. 1987. The relationship between lexical knowledge and reading comprehension for prelingually profoundly hearing-impaired students. *Volta Review* 89:211–220.

Marshall, W. A. 1970. Contextual constraint on deaf and hearing children. *American Annals of the Deaf* 115:682–689.

McGill-Franzen, A., & Gormley, K. 1980. The influence of context on deaf readers' understanding of passive sentences. *American Annals of the Deaf* 125:937–942.

Mezynski, K. 1983. Issues concerning the acquisition of knowledge: Effects of vocabulary training on reading comprehension. *Review of Educational Research* 53:253–279.

Moores, D. F. 1970. An investigation of the psycholinguistic functioning of deaf adolescents. *Exceptional Children* 36:645–652.

Nagy, W. E., Anderson, R. C., & Herman, P. A. 1987. Learning word meanings from context during normal reading. *American Educational Research Journal* 24:237–270.

Nolan, S., & Wilbur, R. 1985. The effects of context on deaf students' comprehension of difficult sentences. *American Annals of the Deaf* 130:231–235.

Odom, P. B., Blanton, R. L., & Nunnally, J. C. 1967. Some cloze technique studies of language capability in the deaf. *Journal of Speech and Hearing Research* 10:816–827.

Sternberg, R. J. 1987. Most vocabulary is learned from context. In *The nature of vocabulary acquisition*, ed. M. McKeown & M. Curtis, 89–105. Hillsdale, NJ: Lawrence Erlbaum Associates.

Sternberg, R. J., & Powell, J. S. 1983. Comprehending verbal comprehension. *American Psychologist* 38:878–893.

Strassman, B., Kretschmer, R., & Bilsky, L. 1987. The instantiation of general terms by deaf adolescents/adults. *Journal of Communication Disorders* 20:1–13.

van Daalens-Kapteijns, M. M., & Elshout-Mohr, M. 1981. The acquisition of word meanings as a cognitive learning process. *Journal of Verbal Learning and Verbal Behavior* 20:386–399.

Walter, G. 1978. Lexical abilities of hearing and hearing-impaired children. *American Annals of the Deaf* 123:976–982.

Input/Output Modalities and Deaf Children's Psycholinguistic Abilities

Harry W. Hoemann
Ryan D. Tweney

T he research described in this report explores the psycholinguistic properties of American Sign Language (ASL) and the psycholinguistic abilities
of deaf children. Two related questions are addressed. First, are ASL and
English equally suitable for deaf children's linguistic, cognitive, and communicative needs? Or is it possible, as some have suggested (Fusfeld 1958; Myklebust
1964), that ASL is too iconic or ideographic to support deaf children's intellectual
development? Second, do deaf and hearing children use the same cognitive processes and develop the same psycholinguistic abilities at about the same time and
in the same sequence, regardless of the modality of the language they are learning
to use? Or is it possible, as some have suggested (Levine 1960; Lewis 1968;
Myklebust 1964), that deaf children's linguistic deficiency in English limits their
ability to engage in certain kinds of abstract thinking and their development of
cognitive and psycholinguistic abilities?

Our review is selective; we focus on work in which we have participated.
Readers interested in related research are directed to the relevant selections of
Bellugi and Studdert-Kennedy (1980), Friedman (1977), Furth (1966), Kavanaugh
and Cutting (1975), Klima and Bellugi (1979), and Wilbur (1987). Our data come
from five different research areas: translation science, the grammatical structure
of ASL, word/sign associations, organization of a subjective lexicon, and categorical coding in short-term memory.

The preparation of this manuscript was supported by the Department of Psychology,
Bowling Green State University, and by the Bowling Green Press, Inc.

TRANSLATION SCIENCE

Many observers have been struck by the fact that the lexicon of ASL is relatively iconic: Some signs look like what they mean. Does this feature limit ASL's ability to function as a fully abstract language system? We think not. Only a small percentage of the ASL lexicon is transparent, and many ASL signs in no way resemble their referents (Hoemann 1975). Moreover, metaphoric uses of many signs (HUNGRY and WISH, ERASE and FORGIVE, CLEAN and NICE, TERRIBLE and AWESOME) indicate that the underlying imagery of signs does not impose strict limits on their meanings. We doubt that deaf people are even aware of the imagery that hearing people tend to see in many signs. This area may be worthy of investigation.

We are even more reluctant to believe that ASL cannot communicate abstract ideas. If this point were true, propositions involving abstract concepts expressed in English could not be translated into ASL as a target language. However, two back-translation studies, in which English originals were translated into ASL and then back into English by different translators, support the opposite conclusion (Hoemann & Tweney 1973; Tweney & Hoemann 1973a).

A comparison of the English original versions with the back-translated versions revealed that the meaning of the original was preserved even when the surface structure was not. This finding is important; if the surface structure had been preserved along with the meaning, one could argue (as did Lewis 1968) that sign languages are effective only when they draw on a spoken language for their structure. The fact that the surface structure could be changed while the meaning was preserved supports the view that ASL has strategies for coding abstract meaning that are different from English.

GRAMMATICAL STRUCTURE

Several varied studies have confirmed the general point that ASL, like any spoken language, possesses complex grammatical, morphological, and phonemic structure (Klima & Bellugi 1979; Liddell 1980; Stokoe 1960, 1972; Wilbur 1987). More to the point, such structure is functionally available to the deaf user as a carrier of abstract semantic content.

Thus, Tweney, Heiman, and Hoemann (1977) demonstrated that ASL grammatical structure serves to offset "noise" in the visual channel just as English grammatical structure serves to offset noise in the acoustic channel. In other words, both ASL and English possess inter-item redundancy in the informational sense. Tweney and Heiman (1977) and Hoemann and Florian (1976) found similar effects in memory: ASL structure, like English structure, can serve as an automatically encodable basis for the enhancement of memory performance. Tweney, Liddell, and Bellugi (1983) showed that sophisticated nonmanual embedding processes in ASL sentences served to structure the perception and memory of complex ASL sentences. Poizner, Bellugi, and Tweney (1980) have shown that formational parameters of ASL (handshape, location, and movement) function in short-term memory in a way that is exactly analogous to the way phonemic characters function in hearing children.

WORD/SIGN ASSOCIATIONS

Studies using the word association technique have demonstrated that preschool children are prone to give a response that belongs to a different grammatical class than the stimulus; that is, a *syntagmatic* response (e.g., *dog-bark*). Older children are more likely to give a response that is in the same grammatical form class as the stimulus; that is a *paradigmatic* response (e.g., *dog-cat*). This shift from syntagmatic to paradigmatic responding occurs in hearing children at about age six (Entwisle 1966), and it is probably related to changes in children's cognitive and linguistic behavior that occur about the same time.

Previous word association tests administered to deaf children using English words have yielded conflicting, ambiguous, or uninterpretable results (Kline 1945; Koplin, Odom, Blanton & Nunnally 1967; Nunnally & Blanton 1966). We designed a word/sign association test including nouns, verbs, and adjectives that could be administered to deaf subjects (Tweney & Hoemann 1973b). The task was administered individually to prelingually deaf children and to a group of hearing subjects in the same age range.

There was a significant tendency on the part of both deaf and hearing subjects to make more paradigmatic responses with increasing age. The syntagmatic-paradigmatic shift was as consistent and as regular for deaf children as it has previously been shown to be for hearing children. Although hearing children produced *quantitatively* a greater proportion of paradigmatic responses, the deaf and hearing groups' performances were *qualitatively* similar. These results suggest that the course of linguistic and conceptual development of deaf children using a visual language parallels the development of hearing children using a spoken language.

ORGANIZATION OF THE SUBJECTIVE LEXICON

Free sorting tasks offer subjects an opportunity to classify stimuli into categories of their own choosing. We used free-sorting tasks to examine the semantic structures of a group of deaf adolescents and a group of hearing adolescents (Tweney, Hoemann & Andrews 1973). Miller (1969) and Anglin (1970) had demonstrated that abstract conceptual relations are reflected in the subjective organization in a person's lexicon. Miller showed that the presence or absence of abstract relations can be detected by means of hierarchical cluster analysis, a technique developed further and described by Fillenbaum & Rapoport (1971). To detect hierarchical structure, two different variants of the same algorithm are executed. When the two procedures yield identical solutions, it can be concluded that the data are hierarchical. Nonhierarchical structure or inconsistencies among the subjects produce differences between the solutions. Hence, the degree of overlap can serve as an index of the amount of hierarchical structure present, ranging from 1.00 for identical solutions to 0.00 for solutions with no common clusters.

Two studies were conducted. The first used decks of cards showing pictures of common objects, the English words that could serve as names for the objects, and words referring to sounds (a control condition for experiential differences between the groups). The second study used decks of cards with high-imagery words, low-imagery words, and the nouns used in the first study. Adolescent deaf and hearing subjects were given one deck at a time and were instructed to place the cards in piles that went together. They could make as many piles as they wished, and they could put as many cards in each pile as they wished, as long as the cards in each pile went together.

Overlap coefficients for the deaf and hearing subjects, respectively, in the first study were .706 and .653 for pictures, .627 and .539 for the noun words, and .328 and .449 for the words referring to sounds; and, in the second study, .50 and .50 for high-imagery words, .611 and .666 for low-imagery words, and .644 and .689 for the noun words.

It is apparent from these results that deaf and hearing subjects manifest similar degrees of hierarchical structure in their subjective lexicon except, as expected, for words referring to sounds. The deaf adolescents, when sorting words or pictures of common objects, attached meanings to them that were similar to those for the hearing adolescents, and they related them to other objects in the same way that hearing adolescents related them to each other. Both deaf and hearing adolescents thus possess the abstract thinking skills required to develop and use semantic categories.

Differences in hierarchical structure associated with high- and low-imagery words could be seen in both deaf and hearing subjects. This finding contradicts the assumption that deaf persons are able to deal adequately with concrete items but not with abstract items. Moreover, the deaf subjects were not adversely affected by the absence of "acoustic mediators." The central cognitive processes and the psycholinguistic abilities required to produce a hierarchical solution did not depend on mediators that shared the input/output channels of the subjects' respective language modalities. The central linguistic and symbolic processes of deaf persons are, in the full sense of the word, abstract.

CATEGORICAL CODING IN SHORT-TERM MEMORY

Studies of proactive interference have demonstrated that humans code information in short-term memory in terms of semantic categories (Wickens, Born & Allen 1963), even when the subjects in the experiment are not consciously aware of the semantic category to which stimulus elements belong. The evidence for categorical coding is derived from procedures in which trigrams from the same semantic category (e.g., *dog, cow, goat; pig, horse, cat*) are presented in repeated trials along with an interpolated task (e.g., counting backwards by threes) to prevent rehearsal. When this is done, proactive interference builds up rapidly, and performance decrements occur on the second and third trials. However, if subjects are shifted to a different semantic category on the last trial (e.g., *lamp, chair, table*), there is an immediate recovery from interference. Control subjects who are not switched to the new category continue to make many errors.

The application of these procedures to deaf subjects provides a way to explore their short-term memory functions as well as to test the hypothesis that they are deficient in the abstract thinking required to construct semantic categories. If deaf subjects lack such abstract thinking ability, they should experience no proactive interference and, of course, no release from interference when switched to a different semantic category.

Thirty-seven deaf children, aged 8 to 12, were recruited from a state residential school for the deaf and administered a series of trials with stimuli from a single category, animals (Hoemann, Andrews & DeRosa 1974). Half the subjects were switched to stimuli from the category of common objects on the fifth trial. Hearing children from a public school in northwest Ohio were tested similarly except that they responded in English instead of Sign.

There were no differences between the deaf subjects and the hearing subjects. Both groups showed a significant decline in performance across trials one to four, reflecting a build-up of proactive interference. Only the experimental subjects showed a significant improvement on the last trial, reflecting a release from interference. These results suggest that the short-term memory functions of deaf persons are essentially normal. Deaf children and adults code categorically in short-term memory; consequently, they experience both proactive interference and a release from interference when switched to a different semantic category.

A series of studies was subsequently conducted involving linguistic stimuli (Hoemann 1978). Subjects were drawn from the student body of Gallaudet University and from a residential school for the deaf. Stimuli were handshapes or line drawings of the Manual Alphabet and letters from the English alphabet as well as ASL signs and English words. When the Manual Alphabet was presented with live handshapes and English letters were presented on paper, there was a build-up of interference and a symmetrical release from interference on the part of both experimental groups—those switched from the Manual Alphabet to English and vice versa. When signs and English words were used as stimuli and when the Manual Alphabet characters were presented as line drawings, there was evidence of proactive interference, but the release was not symmetrical. There was a release from signs to words and from Manual Alphabet characters to English letters, but not vice versa, perhaps because of covert translating.

These results support Kolers' (1963) hypothesis that different languages have different memory stores. The data also reveal that the handshapes of the Manual Alphabet are not processed by deaf persons as a code for English but derive their status as an integral aspect of ASL.

CONCLUSION

We have described procedures that verify that ASL is able to code abstract meaning embodied in an original English text. When translators not familiar with the

English original translated the ASL version back into English, the surface structure was often changed, but the semantic content was preserved intact. These results confirm that the input/output modality of ASL does not affect its ability to code semantic content. Whether ASL is or is not iconic is irrelevant as a criterion for judging its ability to translate English prose.

Our research indicates that the sources of structure that are found at the phonological, morphological, and syntactic levels in ASL are functionally available to the perceptual and memory systems of deaf children and adults. We have also described research showing that deaf children older than six tend to make paradigmatic responses in a sign/word association test, that deaf adolescents manifest a hierarchical organization of their subjective lexicon that is similar to that of hearing adolescents, and that deaf children code information categorically in short-term memory.

We see no evidence that deaf children's psycholinguistic abilities are qualitatively different from those of hearing children when they acquire ASL spontaneously from a natural linguistic environment and are allowed to demonstrate their abilities in ASL rather than in English. The input/output modality of ASL is different from English, but the central cognitive processes involved in the acquisition and use of language are the same for deaf and hearing persons, and they function independently of the channel properties of the language.

REFERENCES

Anglin, J. M. 1970. *The growth of word meaning.* Cambridge: MIT Press.

Bellugi, U., & Studdert-Kennedy, M., eds. 1980. *Signed and spoken language: Biological constraints on language form.* Deerfield Beach, FL: Verlag Chemie.

Entwisle, D. R. 1966. *Word associations and young children.* Baltimore: Johns Hopkins University Press.

Fillenbaum, S., & Rapoport, A. 1971. *Structures in the subjective lexicon.* New York: Academic Press.

Friedman, L. A., ed. 1977. *On the other hand: New perspectives on American Sign Language.* New York: Academic Press.

Furth, H. G. 1966. *Thinking without language: Psychological implications of deafness.* New York: Free Press.

Fusfeld, I. S. 1958. How the deaf communicate: Manual language. *American Annals of the Deaf* 103:264–282.

Hoemann, H. W. 1975. The transparency of meaning of Sign Language gestures. *Sign Language Studies* 7:151–161.

———. 1978. Categorical coding of Sign and English in short-term memory by deaf and hearing subjects. In *Understanding language through sign language research*, ed. P. Siple, 289–305. New York: Academic Press.

Hoemann, H. W., Andrews, C. D., & DeRosa, D. V. 1974. Categorical coding in short-term memory by deaf and hearing children. *Journal of Speech and Hearing Research* 17:426–431.

Hoemann, H. W., & Florian, V. 1976. Order constraints in American Sign Language: The effects of structure on judgments of meaningfulness and on immediate recall of anomalous sign sequences. *Sign Language Studies* 11:121–132.

Hoemann, H. W., & Tweney, R. D. 1973. Is the sign language of the deaf an adequate linguistic channel? *Proceedings of the 81st Convention of the American Psychological Association* 2:801–802.

Kavanaugh, J. F., & Cutting, J. E., eds. 1975. *The role of speech in language.* Cambridge: MIT Press.

Klima, E. S., & Bellugi, U. 1979. *The signs of language.* Cambridge: Harvard University Press.

Kline, T. K. 1945. A study of the free association test with deaf children. *American Annals of the Deaf* 90:237–257.

Kolers, P. A. 1963. Interlingual word associations. *Journal of Verbal Learning and Verbal Behavior* 2:291–300.

Koplin, J. H., Odom, P. B., Blanton, R. L., & Nunnally, J. C. 1967. Word association test performance of deaf subjects. *Journal of Speech and Hearing Research* 10:126–132.

Levine, E. S. 1960. *The psychology of deafness.* New York: Columbia University Press.

Lewis, M. M., ed. 1968. *The education of deaf children: The possible place of finger spelling and signing.* London: Her Majesty's Stationery Office.

Liddell, S. K. 1980. *American Sign Language syntax.* The Hague: Mouton.

Miller, G. A. 1969. A psychological method to investigate verbal concepts. *Journal of Mathematical Psychology* 6:169–191.

Myklebust, H. 1964. *The psychology of deafness: Sensory deprivation, learning, and adjustment.* 2d ed. New York: Grune & Stratton.

Nunnally, J. C., & Blanton, R. L. 1966. Patterns of word associations in the deaf. *Psychological Reports* 18:87–92.

Poizner, H., Bellugi, U., & Tweney, R. D. 1980. Processing of formational, semantic, and iconic information in American Sign Language. *Journal of Experimental Psychology: Human Perception and Performance* 7:1146–1159.

Siple, P., ed. 1978. *Understanding language through sign language research.* New York: Academic Press.

Stokoe, W. C. 1960. *Sign language structure: An outline of the visual communication system of the American deaf.* Studies in Linguistics, Occasional Papers, No. 8. Buffalo, NY: University of Buffalo.

Stokoe, W. C. 1972. *Semiotics and human sign languages.* The Hague: Mouton.

Tweney, R. D., & Heiman, G. W. 1977. The effect of sign language grammatical structure on recall. *Bulletin of the Psychonomic Society* 10:331–334.

Tweney, R. D., Heiman, G. W., & Hoemann, H. W. 1977. Psychological processing of sign language: Effects of visual disruption on sign intelligibility. *Journal of Experimental Psychology: General* 106:255–268.

Tweney, R. D., & Hoemann, H. W. 1973a. Back translation: A method for the analysis of manual languages. *Sign Language Studies* 2:51–72.

———. 1973b. The development of semantic associations in profoundly deaf children. *Journal of Speech and Hearing Research* 16:309–318.

Tweney, R. D., Hoemann, H. W., & Andrews, C. E. 1973. Semantic organization in deaf and hearing subjects. *Journal of Psycholinguistic Research* 4:61–73.

Tweney, R. D., Liddell, S. K., & Bellugi, U. 1983. The perception of grammatical boundaries in sign language. *Discourse Processes* 6:295–304.

Wickens, D. D., Born, D. G., & Allen, C. K. 1963. Proactive inhibition and item similarity in short-term memory. *Journal of Verbal Learning and Verbal Behavior* 2:440–445.

Wilbur, R. B. 1987. *American Sign Language: Linguistic and applied dimensions.* 2d rev. ed. Boston: College-Hill Press.

The Relationship of Educational Background to Cognitive and Language Development Among Deaf Adolescents

Mimi WheiPing Lou
Michael Strong
Asa DeMatteo

T he research discussed in this paper describes linkages between the cognitive, educational, and linguistic development of deaf children by examining comprehensive longitudinal data on 39 deaf individuals who were followed from the time they first entered preschool until they graduated from high school. These data were originally gathered as part of a longitudinal study begun in 1969 of 40 deaf toddlers of hearing parents (Schlesinger & Meadow 1972, 1976). When the original study began, the children ranged from 2.5 to 4 years old; were profoundly prelingually deaf with a hearing loss of at least 80 dB in the better ear; had no other major diagnosed handicap; were living with both parents, who were white, English-speaking, and hearing; were enrolled in a preschool program for the deaf in the San Francisco Bay Area; were judged by their teachers not to be retarded or unusually slow; and did not have a twin. The data for the present study are drawn from the fifth testing sequence.

The 39 participating subjects included 22 girls and 17 boys, ranging from 15 to 17 years old, in grade levels ranging from 7th grade to 11th grade. While a majority still lived in California (in the San Francisco Bay Area), the remainder were scattered around the country, and one subject traveled from Venezuela to participate. In the first round of this study, four toddlers were in Total Com-

This research was funded by NIDRR Grant #G008300146 to the University of California, San Francisco, Center on Deafness. The authors also thank Hilde Schlesinger, M.D., without whose foresight and years of work the data on which this research is based would not exist.

munication (TC) preschool programs, the remaining 36 were in oral preschool programs. By the fifth round, 13 subjects were enrolled in oral programs (9 mainstreamed in public schools, 4 in private schools); 12 were in public day programs holding a TC philosophy; and 14 were enrolled in public residential programs with exposure to American Sign Language (ASL).

To capture the issues of mainstreamed deaf education versus special programs or schools, as well as TC versus oral approaches, we considered the assessment data with two sets of questions in mind:

1. Is type of schooling related to cognitive development, reading achievement, and communicative competence?
2. Is language style related to cognitive development, reading achievement, and communicative competence?

"Type of schooling" and "language style" were determined by student history rather than current placement. Table 1 lists the assessment measures we examined.

Verbal Intelligence—WISC-R Information, Similarities, and Comprehension Subtests. These tests were administered in the language variety of the subject's choice.

Nonverbal Intelligence—WISC-R Performance Scale and Mazes Subtest. These tests were also administered in the language of the subject's choice, and were used as measures of cognitive functioning independent of language modality.

Reasoning—Piaget's Pendulum Problem. The level of reasoning of each subject was assessed using Piaget's pendulum problem (Inhelder & Piaget 1958; see Lou 1987 for task description and issues in scoring). This task was chosen as a measure of cognitive development because 1) information about reasoning does not depend on task success, 2) subjects can demonstrate reasoning through either explanation (i.e., verbally) or demonstration (i.e., nonverbally), and 3) the problem draws on subjects' real-world problem-solving abilities.

TABLE 1 Variable Measures

Predictor Variable Measures	
Percentage of Time Mainstreamed	Language Style—Strict English, Mixed Language Mode—Oral, Sign

Outcome Variable Measures	
WISC-R Information subtest	Reading Level (SAT Reading Comprehension)
WISC-R Similarities subtest	Written Syntax Task
WISC-R Comprehension subtest	Story Recall
WISC-R Mazes subtest	Linguistic Competence Rating
WISC-R Performance IQ	Communicative Competence Rating
Piagetian Pendulum Task	Organization of Conversation Rating

Language Measure—Linguistic Competence, Communicative Competence. These measures were ratings of a 45-minute conversation covering familiar topics conducted in any language variety or combination which the subject chose. The conversation was rated for linguistic competence, communicative competence, and organizational skill. A rater-reliability check on ten subjects resulted in coefficients of inter-rater agreement ranging from .83 to .97.

Reading Grade Level. Reading level was derived from the reading comprehension subtest scores of the Stanford Achievement Test (SAT) by calculating the difference between test grade level score and actual grade level placement.

Written Syntax. Subjects were presented sentences one at a time from a story (based on Forman & Albertini 1981) and asked to recall and write down the sentence as accurately as they could remember. Scores reflected recall errors of target grammatical constructions. Spelling and nontarget errors did not affect subjects' scores.

Story Recall. Subjects were presented with videotaped well-structured stories (Mandler & Johnson 1977) in one of the following language varieties (chosen by the subject): oral English, SEE, Signed English, or ASL. They were then asked to recall as much of the story as possible, retelling it in whatever language variety they preferred. Scores were the number of story propositions recalled.

School Type—Mainstream, Special Program, Residential. Educational history was obtained from interviews with the students and parents. We then determined the proportion of school time spent in different kinds of programs: mainstream, residential, and special class.

Language Style—Strict English/Mixed; Oral/Sign. Two dimensions of language style were identified:

1. The conversation described above was rated for proximity to ASL or English, and two groups were identified—those who used strictly English (either spoken or signed), and those who used something other than strict English.
2. Language style, either signed or oral, was determined by reviewing educational history and current language preference.

DATA ANALYSIS

There was a strong relationship between the percentage of time spent in various programs (i.e., mainstreamed, special program, residential) and both language preference and educational history (i.e., TC and oral): Canonical analysis resulted in a Canonical $R = .81$, $p < .0001$, suggesting that there was little reason to maintain them as separate predictor variables. We further found that subjects with a history of TC tended to use other than strict English, while those with primarily an oral education tended to prefer strict English (Table 2). For this reason, we chose to eliminate the nonmatching dimensions, that is, those subjects who used mixed language but who had primarily an oral education ($n = 1$) and those who used strict English but had primarily a TC education ($n = 3$). This procedure left 35 subjects distributed as Mixed Language Preference/TC Education ($n = 20$) vs. Reading Levels, Strict English Preference/Oral Education ($n = 15$), where the dimensions of language preference and educational history are inextricably confounded.

We then subjected the data to Multiple Analysis of Variance (MANOVA) in order to examine for systematic differences between these two groups on all outcome variables simultaneously. A significant Wilk's Lambda score (.355, $df = 12,22$, $p < .01$) allowed examination of individual dependent variables. Results (Table 3) show that the Oral/English adolescents performed significantly better than the Sign/Mixed Language adolescents on WISC-R Similarities and Comprehension subtests, and had higher superior Written Syntax performance,

TABLE 2   Group Membership: Educational History by Language Preference

	Educational History	
Language Preference	Oral	Total Communication
Strict English	15	1
Mixed Language	3	20

Chi square = 21.59, $p < .0001$.

TABLE 3   Univariate Tests ($df = 1.33$)

Dependent Measure	Means		F-Ratio	p
	Oral/English	Sign/Mixed Language		
WISC-R Information subtest	7.9	5.8	3.24	
WISC-R Similarities subtest	10.0	7.1	9.29	<.01
WISC-R Comprehension sub-test	10.1	6.6	5.69	<.05
WISC-R Mazes subtest	10.7	10.3	.17	
WISC-R Performance IQ	108.2	104.9	.72	
Piagetian Pendulum Task	4.8	3.1	10.73	<.01
Reading Level	−1.1	−4.4	13.28	<.01
Written Syntax Task	96.3	71.6	13.60	<.01
Story Recall	28.3	21.8	4.59	<.05
Linguistic Competence Rating	3.1	3.2	.05	
Communicative Competence Rating	3.4	3.4	.09	
Organization of Conversation Rating	2.6	2.4	.54	

better Story Recall, and more advanced reasoning on the Pendulum Problem. There was also a trend ($.05 < p < .08$) toward difference on the WISC-R Information Subtest. Subjects did not, however, differ substantially on conversational ratings (Linguistic and Communicative Competence, Organization of Conversation) or on nonverbal intelligence (WISC-R Mazes, WISC-R Performance IQ).

It was clear that there was a high degree of intercorrelation between certain subsets of the dependent variables (Table 4). Cluster analysis of the intercorrelations revealed two major conversational ratings (communicative competence, linguistic competence), and a third rating that included all of the WISC-R verbal IQ measures—Reading Level, Written Syntax, Story Recall, and the Pendulum Problem (i.e., all the variables on which the two groups differed significantly) along with the Conversational Organization rating. Table 5 presents a hierarchical clustering of these same variables.

DISCUSSION

In general, these data suggest that the children who have had primarily a TC education and use other than strict English are similar in their nonverbal intelligence and communicative competence to the children who have had primarily an oral education and use strict English. We found differences in these particular children, however, in verbal abilities, reasoning, and memory for verbal material. It is not surprising that the oral/strict English children should excel in WISC-R Verbal IQ measures, reading level, and English syntactic skill: It is typical to understand such differences as reflections of incidental linguistic differences, specifically that mastery of English is a necessary condition for adequate performance in English-based reading, writing, and verbal IQ tests.

It is less clear why these children should excel in memory for stories and on the Pendulum Problem. Stories were presented in the child's language of choice, suggesting that English mastery ought not to be necessary. Also, the Pendulum Problem could be solved by verbal explanation or physical demonstration, that is, without language at all. It is also remarkable that Story Recall and the Pendulum Problem clustered with the English reading and writing measures and verbal IQ, but not with nonverbal IQ. We suggest four possible interpretations for these findings.

The first possibility is that the Piagetian Pendulum Problem and the memory task actually measure English ability. For those who preferred some variety of English, story recall might be enhanced by superior skills in that language. However, for those who selected ASL, it is difficult to conclude that English ability was relevant to performance on the two tests. Nor is a satisfactory explanation provided for the Pendulum Problem, which allowed physical experimentation and demonstration for solution rather than language.

The second possible explanation is that a selection factor determines both who ends up with better verbal, reading, and reasoning ability, and who continues in an oral education or mainstreamed setting. For example, there may be some

TABLE 4 Intercorrelations of Outcome Variables

	WISC-R Infor-mation	WISC-R Similar-ities	WISC-R Com-prehen-sion	WISC-R Maze	WISC-R Picture	Pendulum Problem	Reading Level	Written Syntax	Story Recall	Linguistic Compe-tence	Communication Competence
WISC-R Similarities	.78[d]										
WISC-R Comprehension	.83[d]	.83[d]									
WISC-R Maze											
WISC-R Picture				.47[b]							
Pendulum Problem	.54[c]	.67[d]	.63[d]								
Reading Level	.75[d]	.80[d]	.80[d]			.63[d]					
Written Syntax	.73[d]	.75[d]	.70[d]			.48[b]	.75[d]				
Story Recall	.66[d]	.67[d]	.61[d]			.54[c]	.65[d]	.76[d]			
Linguistic Competence		.37[a]	.37[a]								
Communication Competence		.34[a]	.33[a]					.36[a]	.38[a]	.78[d]	
Conversational Organization	.44[b]	.61[d]	.64[d]			.41[b]	.47[b]	.56[c]	.55[c]	.49[b]	.58[c]

[a] $p < .05$.
[b] $p < .01$.
[c] $p < .001$.
[d] $p < .0001$.

TABLE 5   Hierarchical Clustering of Outcome Variables

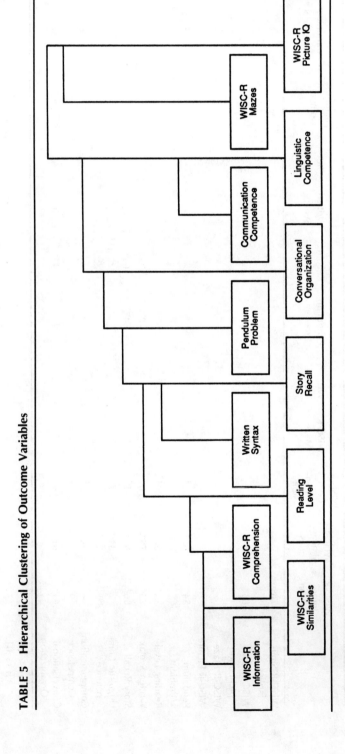

parental motivation factor or early communication factor. Indeed, Schlesinger (1988) suggests that particular sorts of parent-child dialogues (e.g., those that mirror and expand on what the child says, involve information rather than yes/no questions, etc.) are related to later reading ability. Alternatively, certain parents may support and motivate their children more effectively in both English and academic tasks.

A third possibility is that more general cognitive ability may play a role. Specifically, the same "g" factor that operates in nonverbal intelligence may be operating in the verbal cognition factor. Although WAIS-R Verbal and Performance IQ do not seem to correlate in our sample ($r = .15$, $p > .36$), this failure is almost entirely accounted for by four outliers who manifested quite high verbal scores but unexpectedly low performance IQ. Remove these outliers and the correlation rises dramatically ($r = .56$, $p < .0001$). It may seem that it is not appropriate to remove troublesome data. Consider, however, the expected relationship between verbal and performance IQ for both hearing and deaf students: For hearing students the expectation is for positive covariance. For deaf students, a low performance score should predict a low verbal score; however, a high performance score should not necessarily predict anything about the verbal score. Conversely, a high verbal score for deaf students should predict a high performance score while a low verbal score should not necessarily predict anything about the performance score. If these relationships do not hold (viz., there is a high Verbal, low Performance score combination for a deaf subject), then the data take on clinical significance and must be explained by factors other than "g." We expect there is some clinical explanation for these four high verbal/low performance outliers. In any case, it may be that intelligence scores alone or in large part select who will perform better on reading, reasoning, and verbal tasks as well as who will continue in oral programs, experience more mainstreaming, or both.

It may be that the ecology of oral or hearing educational environments is substantively different from that provided in TC or otherwise signing environments. For example, more time might be devoted to general knowledge, reasoning, and academics in regular classrooms where students are mainstreamed as opposed to special programs for hearing-impaired students only. It is possible that students with more capabilities move up to more general, "normalized" instruction while educational standards in the deaf education classrooms are set to match the "lowest common denominator" of the remaining students. In any case, it is as important to determine what factors hold the TC/mixed language students back in reading and problem-solving as it is to determine what facilitates the performance of the oral education/strict English students.

A final possibility is that those students who have remained in oral education the longest have been exposed to more consistent, comprehensible input (in this instance, in English) than those students in the programs where the teachers use simultaneous communication. In fact, Strong and Charlson (1987) found that the signed component of teachers' simultaneous communication was neither complete nor consistent. Perhaps consistent, comprehensible language alone is sufficient to improve academic and cognitive functioning. If this conclusion is correct,

English is not the crucial element; it should be possible to substitute any language (e.g., ASL) in a systematic fashion and achieve the same results.

IMPLICATIONS

These findings should not be taken as a recommendation for any particular educational approach. First, our data set is too small for one to generalize with confidence. Secondly, one cannot determine causality in the relationships delineated above. Finally, the full range of approaches to deaf education is not sampled in this study. Thus, these findings must be interpreted and, more importantly, used with great caution. They do, however, raise important questions: Clearly there is a relationship between language input and reasoning, but what gives rise to this relationship, and what ramifications does it have for decisions regarding the linguistic aspects of deaf education? If there are selection factors which determine that some hearing-impaired students will be more successful in school, then how can students not sharing those factors compensate sufficiently to be successful as well? If there are features of the ecology of deaf education that hold students back, then how can these features be identified and alternative methods developed? Not all students will be appropriate for mainstreamed environments, but all students should receive a rich academic experience appropriate to their potential. Finally, it is important to evaluate the contribution of consistent linguistic input in facilitating academic achievement and to determine whether such consistency can be achieved with sign systems of English or ASL, thus preserving the cultural values of the deaf community without compromising educational goals.

REFERENCES

Forman, J., & Albertini, J. 1981. *Documentation for syntax specific test (SST): Visual dictation scoring procedure.* Rochester, NY: National Technical Institute for the Deaf.

Inhelder, B., & Piaget, J. [1955] 1958. *The growth of logical thinking: From childhood to adolescence.* Trans. A. Parsons and S. Milgram. New York: Basic Books.

Lou, M. W. 1987. Cognitive structural diagnosis: A spiral course of advancement. *Human Development* 29:315–327.

Mandler, J. M., & Johnson, N. S. 1977. Remembrance of things parsed: Story structure and recall. *Cognitive Psychology* 9:111–151.

Schlesinger, H. S. 1988. Questions and answers in the development of deaf children. In *Language learning and deafness*, ed. M. Strong, 261–291. Cambridge, England: Cambridge University Press.

Schlesinger, H. S., & Meadow, K. P. 1972. *Sound and sign: Childhood deafness and mental health.* Berkeley: University of California Press.

———. 1976. *Studies of family interaction.* San Francisco: University of California, Langley Porter Neuropsychiatric Institute.

Strong, M., & Charlson, E. S. 1987. Simultaneous communication: Are teachers attempting an impossible task? *American Annals of the Deaf* 132:376–382.

The Interplay Between Visuospatial Language and Visuospatial Script

Angela Fok
Karen van Hoek
Edward S. Klima
Ursula Bellugi

T he diversity of writing systems across languages provides excellent opportunities for investigators of human cognition to examine how children,
hearing or deaf, adjust to meet various task demands imposed by different
orthographies. Among the writing systems existing in the world today, Chinese
characters are perhaps the most radically different from the English alphabetic
system. In this paper we report on a study of deaf and hearing children in the
beginning stages of learning to write in two very different languages: English and
Chinese. We may glean clues to the effects of the orthographic organization on
the learning process by examining the approaches taken by four different groups
of children: hearing children who are acquiring spoken English or Chinese as a
first language, and deaf children who are acquiring American Sign Language
(ASL) or Chinese Sign Language (CSL) as a native language. We also examine
the interplay between visual language, visuospatial processing, and processing of
script.

This study is one of a series in which we have examined the effects of different

This work was supported in part by National Institutes of Health Grants DC00146,
DC00201, P50–NS 22343, HD 13249, and by National Science Foundation Grant
BNS8820673 to the Salk Institute for Biological Studies. We would like to thank the
faculty and staff as well as the students and their families at the California School for the
Deaf in Fremont, the Canossa School for the Deaf in Hong Kong, and the Hong Kong
School for the Deaf for their participation in these studies. Illustrations copyright Ursula
Bellugi, The Salk Institute.

native-language modalities—spoken and signed—and different orthographic systems in deaf and hearing children (Bellugi 1988; Fok & Bellugi 1986; Fok, Bellugi, et al. 1988). The deaf children in our studies have little or no access to the phonological forms of the spoken language, while they do have native competency in signed languages whose surface patterning, having developed in the visuospatial mode, is very different from that of spoken languages. How does a deaf child approach the task of learning a written representation of a spoken language he or she has never heard? We investigate the young deaf child's beginning approach to writing with respect to different scripts, examining the interplay between primary language modality (auditory or visuospatial) and orthographic structure (alphabetic or logographic).

ALPHABETIC AND LOGOGRAPHIC ORTHOGRAPHIES

English and Chinese were selected as the target written languages because they represent two very different types of orthographic systems. The English writing system is largely based on the principle of letter-for-sound correspondence. Letters representing phonemes are arranged in a linear order that indicates the temporal sequencing of the phonemes. The Chinese system, in contrast, is opaque with respect to the speech/script relationship, and is emphatically spatial in the layout of every logographic symbol. Each character or logograph represents one morpheme, rather than a phoneme. Characters are internally composed of units arranged according to a *spatial architecture* (Tzeng & Wang 1984; Tzeng in press). The internal components of characters may be placed side by side, one above the other, in quadrants, or in one of a number of other configurations. Learning to write Chinese therefore depends on learning complex spatial relationships and arrays entirely unlike anything confronting the child learning English. These two very different orthographies can be expected to present different problems for learners, and in particular, may present very different tasks to those learners who do not know the spoken languages—deaf children whose native languages are signed languages.

AMERICAN AND CHINESE SIGNED LANGUAGES

A large number of studies have demonstrated that American Sign Language is a full-fledged language, completely separate and independent from English, with its own grammatical mechanisms (Klima & Bellugi 1979; Bellugi, Poizner & Klima 1989). The grammar of ASL is essentially spatialized, making pervasive use of spatial contrasts for signaling morphological and syntactic information. Our studies of Chinese Sign Language (CSL) show that it too is an independent language, not derived from spoken or written Chinese (although there are occasional borrowings from written characters). As Figure 1 shows, CSL has its own principles of word formation, of morphology, and of syntax, which are similar to principles of ASL in their use of space, but which differ in language-

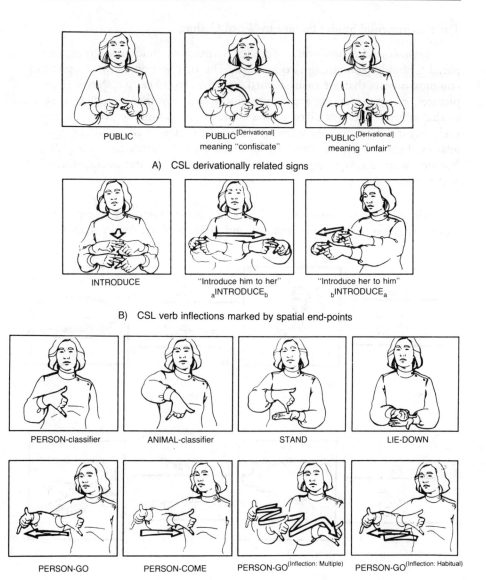

A)   CSL derivationally related signs

B)   CSL verb inflections marked by spatial end-points

C)   CSL classifiers and related forms

FIGURE 1   Chinese Sign Language grammatical structure.

specific ways as well (Fok, Bellugi, van Hoek & Klima 1988; van Hoek, Bellugi & Fok 1988). Deaf children in both America and Hong Kong bring with them the knowledge of a visuospatial signed language as they approach the task of script acquisition. In the following experiment, we examine the ways in which young deaf and hearing children approach the entry into script and examine the relationships between sign, speech, and script.

The Experimental Study: Picture-to-Word Coding

Methods and Procedures.   To elicit samples of children's writing, we prepared a booklet containing two sections. The first section shows 35 pictures of common objects that are easily named, and the second section shows 10 pairs of pictures, one representing a concrete object and the other an action in relation to that object. The task given to the children was simply to write the name of each picture. The children were encouraged to guess if they did not know the answer. Figure 2 shows some of the items on the picture-to-word coding test booklet, with sample responses from American and Chinese deaf children in the first grade.

Subjects.   Sixty American and sixty Chinese children participated in the study. They were all in the first, second, and third grades in school. The 30

FIGURE 2   Sample responses from deaf Chinese and American first grade children on the writing test.

American hearing subjects were students at a public school in Southern California. The language of instruction in the school was English. The 30 American deaf subjects were students at a school for the deaf in California. They were all fluent signers of ASL. The language of instruction was Signed English. The 30 Chinese hearing subjects were students at a normal hearing school in Hong Kong. The language of instruction was Cantonese. The 30 Chinese deaf subjects were from two different schools for the deaf in Hong Kong; all were fluent signers of CSL. The language of instruction at the school for the deaf was auditory/oral.

We present first the number correct for each subject group, and then the breakdown of error responses, organized according to the bases of the errors: phonological, visual, and sign-language-based. Table 1 gives the percent correct in the responses from the deaf and hearing Chinese and American subjects, by grade. Interestingly, the group with the lowest percent correct overall was not either of the deaf groups, but rather the hearing American first grade children, apparently because the American hearing children are initially impeded by a tendency to focus almost exclusively on sound-symbol mapping. As we examine the nature of the errors across subject groups and across scripts, we focus on differences between deaf and hearing children's approaches to the entry into script, as well as differences due to the properties of the two scripts.

Analysis of Types of Error Patterns

Phonologically Based Errors.   English script is phonemically based. The task confronting an aspiring reader/writer of English is in part a problem of discovering the mapping principles connecting phonological form with visual representation (Gleitman 1985). A child who fails to make the connection between the written forms and the appropriate level of linguistic structure (for English, the phonemic level) has failed to comprehend the fundamental principles underlying the script system. Understanding Chinese script, in contrast, requires very little knowledge of the phonological system; this is attested to by the fact that speakers of distinct mutually unintelligible Chinese dialects are able to use the same set of logograms to write their language. The task confronting a beginning learner of written Chinese is therefore substantially different from that facing the child acquiring written English.

In our study of the entry into script, we first addressed the issue of the extent to which the members of each subject group based their responses on phonological representations. We did so by examining the error patterns presented by the different groups, to determine the extent to which errors showed interference

TABLE 1 Percentage Correct Responses by Subject Group

Grade	American Deaf	American Hearing	Chinese Deaf	Chinese Hearing
First	35.7%	3.7%	15.0%	37.5%
Second	37.1%	38.3%	34.9%	51.7%
Third	50.2%	40.3%	47.2%	63.4%

from phonological form or other evidence that the written form was partially determined by phonological form. We will first present the results from the two American groups, learning a script that is largely (though not entirely) organized according to the phonological structure of English. We will then present the results from the Chinese children, learning a script that is largely independent from considerations of phonological form.

American Hearing and Deaf. In the American study, we found the hearing group taking a sound-based approach to script that the deaf did not take. To determine the extent to which the children in the American deaf and hearing groups were taking a phonological approach to spelling, we counted the number of responses that captured the phonological form of the target, but in a nonconventional way—i.e., which represented invented spellings corresponding to pronunciation.

The results from our American hearing subjects confirmed the findings of Mann, Tobin, and Wilson (1986); Read (1971); and others, in that 16%-44% of the hearing children's responses were nonconventional representations of phonological form. The first-grade hearing children tended to write only one letter, corresponding to the first phoneme, or else they produced responses composed largely or entirely of consonants, which seemed to represent syllables: e.g., *ndn* for 'Indian,' *pno* for 'piano'; of all three grades, they seemed to be the most dependent on phonological analysis, resulting in high numbers of errors. In contrast, only 4%-6% of the responses from the deaf children could be classed as nonconventional representations of phonological form. Moreover, in almost all instances, these errors could also be analyzed as based on *visual* representation. For example, the deaf children's responses to the picture of a chair often began with *ch*, making them partial phonological representations but also partial visual representations as well. The hearing children tended to begin their responses to that item with *j* or *g*, letters that bear no visual resemblance to the target but are reasonable attempts to represent the first phoneme (Read 1971).

Table 2 gives the percentage of such phonologically based errors for both deaf and hearing American groups, as well as the percentage of phonologically based errors in Chinese (the basis for those errors will be discussed below).

TABLE 2 Phonologically Based Errors in Chinese and English

	Chinese	American
Hearing		
Grade 1	1.4%	16.0%
Grade 2	1.1%	44.8%
Grade 3	1.1%	30.9%
Deaf		
Grade 1	0	6.0%
Grade 2	0	4.8%
Grade 3	0	4.8%

Chinese Hearing and Deaf. Since Chinese script is not based upon representation of individual phonemes, the nature of the errors that we term 'phonologically-based' will be different from those in English. The phonological errors in Chinese consisted of substitutions of homophones for the target characters. For example, the character pronounced /ge/ meaning 'neck' was written instead of the target word /ge/ meaning 'glass,' and the character pronounced /si/ meaning 'time' was written instead of the target word /si/ meaning 'key.'

Table 3 gives the percentage of responses that were actually-occurring characters homophonous to the target characters. Note that the deaf children made no such errors. We can see from these numbers that spoken Cantonese plays a small role in character retrieval for the hearing subjects, but not at all for the deaf subjects. Figure 3 presents some of these phonologically based errors from the Chinese hearing children.

The results from all the groups indicate first that the hearing children—but not the deaf—are in fact drawing on spoken-language representations to guide their attempts at writing, although there are significant differences—due to the differences in the orthographies—in the ways in which the hearing children can do so. We turn now to an examination of the extent to which the deaf and hearing groups' responses were based upon purely visual representations of the written forms.

VISUALLY BASED ERRORS

The different organizational principles underlying English and Chinese orthography may lead learners to take very different approaches to their respective scripts. Here we examined the responses from the American and Chinese groups,

TABLE 3 American Deaf Children's Visually Based Responses

	Target	Response
First Grade	gum	gun
	gum	pan
	pie	pim
	pig	gig
	ball	bod
	duck	dutn
	knife	kifei
Second Grade	girl	gid
	pie	piz
	dog	doy
	knife	knike
Third Grade	knife	kinfe
	earring	eagging
	fork	tork
	chain	cair

FIGURE 3   Phonologically based errors of Chinese hearing children.

focusing on the visuospatial relationships between the children's responses and the targets.

American Hearing and Deaf.   We found some responses from the American deaf children that strongly implicated visual, and explicitly not phonological, representations of the words. The nature of the English alphabetic script is such that it is difficult to separate responses based on phonological representations from those based on visual representations; nevertheless, we found that the deaf children made errors involving substitution of letters that were *visually* similar to the target letters, but that failed to preserve the phonological form. (We note that these responses were all written by the children in lower-case letters.) Table 3 gives some selected examples of the visually-based errors found in the deaf children's responses. We see that the overall shape of the word, particularly the distribution of ascending and descending letters, is generally preserved, though not with the correct letters—e.g., *p* and *y* substitute for *g*, and vice versa. Importantly, the incorrectly inserted letters, which do succeed in preserving much of the visual form of the word, cannot plausibly be considered representations of pronunciation.

In order to partially quantify the rates of visually-based responses from the deaf and hearing American groups, we devised a system for scoring a subset of the items from a visual perspective. We did this by examining the number of 'silent' letters in the children's responses. A letter was counted as 'silent' if it did not represent a phonological segment. For example, both the *k* and the *e* in *knife* were counted as silent letters. For the word *apple*, children were given credit for one silent letter if they included both *p*'s. There were 16 items with silent letters, for a total of 18 possible silent letters per subject. We determined the percentage of silent letters in terms of the total number possible (Table 4). The results indicate that the hearing children omit more silent letters than the deaf children, suggesting that the deaf were attentive to purely visual properties of the written word, more so than the hearing children who, as we saw, were biased towards representing the phonological forms.

Chinese Hearing and Deaf.   We now turn to Chinese, a script that may offer a good opportunity for deaf children to take a purely visuospatial approach to the script acquisition task. The Chinese script system is, as previously explained, based on complex principles of spatial architecture governing the combination of components within the internal structure of characters. These spatial regularities of patterning do not derive from properties of the spoken language, and may therefore be accessible to deaf children who do not have knowledge of spoken Chinese. We examined the Chinese error responses that were invented (i.e., non-existent) characters, focusing on the possible visual bases for the errors. We found that a large proportion (over 90%) of the invented characters of hearing and deaf children in this category were well-formed characters that conformed to the structural rules of existing Chinese characters, demonstrating that both groups of subjects had extracted regularities about the formal properties of Chinese characters. For example, the error word that was written instead of the character meaning *medical* (Figure 4) resembles the target in spatial layout, and the internal components resemble the components of the target.

We find, then, that the deaf and hearing children alike showed sensitivity to visual-spatial aspects of character formation: the architecture, the components, their arrangements, and their spatial layout, and even configurational aspects in which the subcomponents tended to be orthographically legal and in allowable spatial positions. We thus find that the deaf Chinese children are sensitive to the implicit principles governing the spatial architecture of Chinese characters, even without benefit of knowledge of the spoken language, and are able to use them creatively. We next examine a class of errors made by the Chinese children that show a special sensitivity to internal regularities within Chinese script.

TABLE 4   Percentage of Silent Letters in English Responses

	Deaf	Hearing
Grade 1	52.8%	8.9%
Grade 2	59.1%	57.8%
Grade 3	92.7%	65.9%

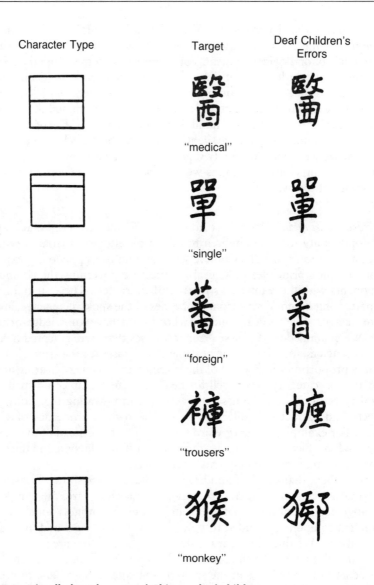

FIGURE 4   **Visually based errors of Chinese deaf children.**

RESPONSES BASED ON SEMANTIC REGULARITIES IN CHINESE SCRIPT

The architecture of Chinese script includes relationships between meaning and written form that are not represented in English script. Chinese characters are internally decomposable into a number of distinct components. Most characters that contain more than one component include a phonic component, which gives a clue to the pronunciation, and a semantic radical, which is found in many characters that share certain semantic properties.

A number of the errors made by the deaf Chinese subjects could be described as both semantic and "morphological" in nature. These were error responses that contained the same semantic radical as the target. For example, some of the deaf children responded to the picture of a chair with the character meaning *table*. The characters meaning *chair* and *table* in Chinese have in common the presence of a semantic component meaning *wood* in the left half of the character. A large class of characters in Chinese that refer to things made of wood or connected to wood contain this component. Deaf children also produced the character for *chicken* in response to the picture of a duck (both characters have the *bird* radical), the character for *cat* for the picture of a pig and the character *lion* for the picture of a monkey (targets and errors share a radical used for reference to animals), and so forth (Figure 5).

We scored some of the deaf and hearing Chinese children's error responses to determine whether there was a bias toward representing either semantic or phonic components. We examined the responses to the thirteen items on the test that had both a phonic component and a semantic component, and counted the number of correct components in the responses. Among the 30 hearing subjects, there was almost an equal number of phonic and semantic components correct, but there was a slight bias toward having the phonic components correct (there were 18 responses with the semantic component correct, compared with 26 responses with the phonic component correct). The deaf children showed a significantly higher number of errors with only the semantic component correct (there were 32 such errors) than errors with only the phonic component correct (there were 7 such errors).

The responses from the Chinese deaf subjects suggest that they may be constructing their internal lexicon of Chinese characters on the basis of component shapes that represent semantic cues, using these cues as a partial basis for an organizational or retrieval strategy. Such a strategy could be considered to resemble one of the morphological subsystems in CSL, by which classifiers (handshapes that refer to semantic classes, e.g., *animal, person, vehicle, round object,* etc.) can be combined into morphologically complex forms. The deaf children may be extracting certain of the semantic radicals (Figure 5) in the Chinese characters and using them to reference semantic classes. Thus they are extracting the implicit rules of spatial architecture and semantic correspondence—but they are doing this without showing any evidence of mediation through spoken Cantonese. In the next section, we discuss other clues to the representations the deaf children may be drawing on, both in America and in Hong Kong, as they learn to write.

DEAF CHILDREN'S ATTEMPTS TO CONNECT SIGN WITH SCRIPT

The results of our studies have so far indicated that the deaf children in both countries largely ignore the correlations between phonological forms and written forms, taking a primarily visual approach instead. This finding naturally leads

FIGURE 5   **Errors by Chinese deaf children based on semantic radicals.**

us to ask whether the deaf children in either group attempt to master script as an isolated system, or whether they attempt to relate it to their primary language— either ASL or CSL. The different properties of the two script systems, English and Chinese, might afford different opportunities, and impose different limitations, for deaf children attempting to base their written language on their primary signed language. In this section we present evidence that both deaf groups did in fact make an effort to base their written responses on principles of their respective sign languages—with very different results.

American Deaf Children's "Borrowing" from ASL Principles.   Aspects of the Interaction between ASL and other linguistic systems in the deaf child's environment (signing, fingerspelling, and script) in preschool deaf children of deaf parents have previously been examined in the literature (O'Grady, van Hoek & Bellugi 1990; Padden in press; Padden & LeMaster 1984). O'Grady, van Hoek & Bellugi (1990) report on a study that included deaf American preschool children. It was found that many of the children at age three produced scribbles rather than letters, and only at the age of four could most of the deaf children write English letters. However, some of the scribbles of the youngest children proved insightful in terms of their attempts to make connections across linguistic systems. One child volunteered that what he had scribbled for the picture of a duck and for the picture of a pie were in fact based on the forms of the corresponding ASL signs (Figure 6a). He made the ASL sign DUCK, pointed to the handshape and then to the "writing," indicating that the two were intended to be the same. For *pie*, the child first drew a square and then showed that he was illustrating the first handshape of the sign. He then made another drawing and indicated that he was illustrating one hand moving across the other. Thus his written responses (or more appropriately, his graphic representations) involved invented forms for representing the handshape and/or movement of the ASL sign, providing explicit evidence that he was attempting to connect the written language with his native language, ASL.

Although there are only very tenuous points of contact between ASL signs and English words, we did find instances in the present study in which school-age deaf children attempted to connect writing to their primary language, ASL. As an example, many of the incorrect written responses of the young deaf children to *Indian* began with the letter *f*, whereas the most common first letter in the incorrect responses to *motorcycle* was the letter *s*. Children explained their responses by showing the ASL signs INDIAN and MOTORCYCLE, which are made with the ASL handshapes also used for *f* and *s* in fingerspelling (Figure 6b). Many of the responses for the picture of a nurse began with an *h*. The handshape used in the ASL sign NURSE is the same as the fingerspelled *h*. These results taken together suggest that deaf children who do not have access to the phonological forms of the spoken language nonetheless attempt to bring to bear a visual approach to the entry into writing English, and even at times make attempts to connect the opaque orthographic system to their native language, American Sign Language.

Chinese Deaf Children's "Borrowing" from CSL Principles.   The visuospatial organization of Chinese script may offer particular opportunities for deaf children attempting to bring their knowledge of a visuospatial primary language to bear on the task of writing. Our studies of CSL have found that there are classes of signs and of grammatical operations on signs that are indigenous to CSL, not borrowed from the surrounding spoken or written languages; moreover, CSL has arisen independently of any other signed language and is mutually incomprehensible with ASL. CSL has its own grammatical regularities forming lexical items, for compounding (not derived from compounding in Chinese), for classifiers (not related to classifiers in Chinese), and for morphological processes.

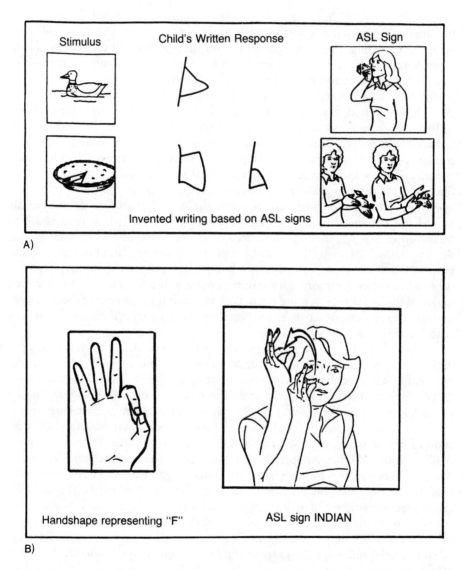

FIGURE 6 American deaf children's 'borrowing' from ASL principles.

Some of the nonexistent character errors that deaf children created appeared to be based on such sign language principles.

Figure 7 shows three examples of such borrowing from sign language. One pair of pictures (7a) depicts a door and a girl opening a door. A deaf subject wrote the correct character for the picture of a door. But for the picture showing a girl opening a door, the subject wrote down the semantic radical for *person* next to the character for *door*, producing a composite form that was similar to the kind of compilation of classifier forms he might have used in his sign language.

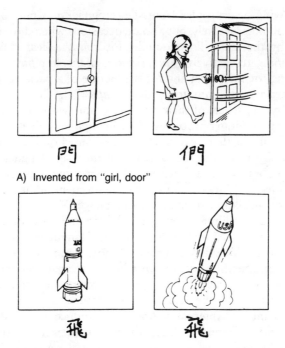

A) Invented from "girl, door"

B) The character "rocket" with movement squiggle added

C) Invented script forms using size and shape specifiers

FIGURE 7   Deaf children's 'borrowing' from Chinese Sign Language principles.

In another example (7b), the deaf subject wrote a character meaning *airplane* for the picture of a rocket; for the rocket taking off, the deaf subject added two additional upward squiggles, perhaps to denote movement of action! This clearly violates the rules of character formation in Chinese, but interestingly, conforms very well to principles of sign formation which distinguish the sign ROCKET and its associated verb form meaning "rocket taking off" by the addition of an upward movement.

Such borrowing of principles from sign language not only occurred at the lexical and morphological levels, but also on occasions when the names of objects were invented by the child. For example, for *chair*, a deaf child wrote three characters, meaning respectively, *four, square, shape*; for *pie*, a child wrote a response meaning *round, shape*; and for the picture of a package of gum, a child wrote three characters meaning *four, long, shape* (7c). This strategy of naming objects by specifying aspects of their size and shape is very common in CSL, as one of several compounding processes (Fok, Bellugi, van Hoek & Klima 1988). These examples suggest that deaf children's responses on the writing task may also be mediated by aspects of the structure of their sign language.

We find that both deaf and hearing children show appreciation of orthographic regularities in Chinese character formation; in addition, deaf children show evidence of mediation through sign language. We thus find evidence for the position that deaf children learning either written English or written Chinese will attempt to draw on their knowledge of a signed language in producing written forms. The extent to which they can succeed, however, is severely limited by the nature of the script. Neither English nor Chinese script is designed to represent sign language, but the Chinese script appears to offer a particular affordance for the deaf child's efforts, as the visual-spatial architecture of the script and the availability of meaningful internal components produce a great deal more similarity between written Chinese and CSL than exists between written English and ASL.

The Interplay Between Spatial Language and Spatial Cognition

We designed a separate series of studies to investigate the interplay between sign language, script, and visuospatial processing. To examine the spatial abilities that deaf and hearing children bring to bear in learning a visuospatial script, we designed an experiment to assess the ability of young deaf and hearing children to analyze Chinese script presented as moving patterns of light in space. We presented pseudocharacters—nonexistent but possible Chinese characters—written in the air in a darkened room with a light-emitting diode on the fingertip. The resulting video displays present dynamic patterns of moving point-lights. We tested deaf and hearing children from four schools in Hong Kong, asking them to watch each point-light display and write down the character underlying the continuous flow of movement. Figure 8 shows responses from hearing and deaf Chinese first-graders to one item, as well as results comparing deaf and hearing children across grade levels. (A target pseudocharacter is presented on the lower right, along with a tracing of the movement pattern the children saw on the videoscreen.) The results showed dramatic differences between deaf and hearing children. Deaf Chinese children, even in first grade, were significantly better than their hearing counterparts, and this difference held across grade levels. It is evident that this spatial cognitive task taps special abilities for spatial analysis of movement on the part of deaf children. Our results suggest that deaf children exposed to a visuospatial language appear to bring enhanced spatial abilities to this task (Bellugi, Tzeng, Klima & Fok 1989; Bellugi, O'Grady, Lillo-Martin, van Hoek

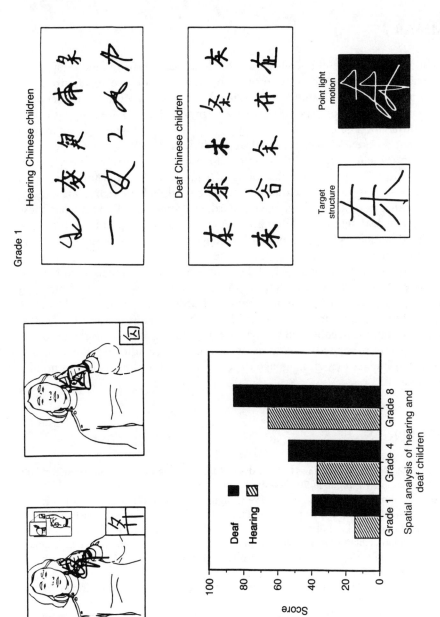

FIGURE 8   Spatial analysis of dynamic point-light displays.

& Corina in press). In these studies, we investigate visuospatial language and visuospatial script, and some aspects of the interplay between them.

SUMMARY

Deaf children who have not acquired a spoken language bring a new perspective to the early stages of the acquisition of script. Whereas for hearing children, the task of script acquisition can be characterized as a problem of mapping between spoken language and corresponding visual form, for deaf children the task may be quite different. The nature of the script—alphabetic or logographic—may in itself present different challenges for deaf children in the early stages of learning script. Our evidence suggests that both Chinese and American deaf children approach script through a nonphonological route. Their errors underscore an essentially visual approach to either logographic or alphabetic representations of spoken languages that they have never heard. An important finding from these studies is that deaf signing children attempt to extract principles from their primary signed languages (American Sign Language or Chinese Sign Language) and map them to the process of learning to write.

We also find that the fundamental differences between the English and Chinese script systems have far-reaching effects on the approaches taken by both deaf and hearing children. We have found that the visuospatial architecture of Chinese script exhibits certain parallels to visuospatial signed languages, and that deaf Chinese children bring enhanced visuospatial processing abilities to the decoding of Chinese script presented as patterns of movement, providing an illustration of the potential impact of sign language experience on other linguistic and nonlinguistic domains.

REFERENCES

Bellugi, U., & Newkirk, D. 1981. Formal devices for creating new signs in American Sign Language. *Sign Language Studies* 30: 1–35.

Bellugi, U., Klima, E.S., & Poizner, H. 1988. Sign language and the brain. In *Language, communication, and the brain*, ed. F. Plum, 39–56. New York: Raven Press.

Bellugi, U., O'Grady, L., Lillo-Martin, D., O'Grady, M., van Hoek, K., & Corina, D. 1990. Enhancement of spatial cognition in deaf children. In *From gesture to language in hearing and deaf children*, ed. V. Volterra and C. Erting, 278–298. New York: Springer-Verlag.

Bellugi, U., Poizner, H., & Klima, E.S. 1989. Language, modality and the brain. *Trends in Neurosciences* 10:380–388.

Bellugi, U., Tzeng, O.J.L., Klima, E.S., & Fok, A. 1989. Dyslexia: Perspectives from sign and script. In *From reading to neurons*, ed. A.M. Galaburda, 137–172. Cambridge, MA: MIT Press/Bradford Books.

Fok, Y.Y.A., Bellugi, U., van Hoek, K., & Klima, E.S. 1988. The formal properties of Chinese languages in space. In *Cognitive aspects of the Chinese language*, ed. M. Liu, H.C. Chen, and M.J. Chen, 187–205. Hong Kong: Asian Research Service.

Gleitman, L. 1985. Orthographic resources affect reading acquisition—if they are used. *Remedial and Special Education* 6(6):24–36.

Klima, E.S. & Bellugi, U. 1979. *The signs of language*. Cambridge, MA: Harvard University Press.

Mann, V.A., Tobin, P. & Wilson, R. 1986. Measuring phonological awareness through the invented spellings of kindergarten children. Irvine: University of California, Irvine. Typescript.

Newport, E. & Meier, R. 1986. The acquisition of American Sign Language. In *The crosslinguistic study of language acquisition*, ed. D.I. Slobin. Hillsdale, NJ: Lawrence Erlbaum Associates.

O'Grady, L., van Hoek, K., & Bellugi, U. 1990. The intersection of signing, spelling, and script. In *SLR 1987: Papers from the fourth international symposium on sign language research*, ed. F. Karlsson, 224–234. Hamburg, Germany: SIGNUM-Verlag Press.

Padden, C. In press. The acquisition of fingerspelling in deaf children. In *Theoretical issues in sign language research*, ed. P. Siple and S. Fischer. Chicago: University of Chicago Press.

Padden, C.A., & LeMaster, B. 1984, April. An alphabet on hand: The acquisition of fingerspelling in deaf children. *Sign Language Studies* 47(2): 161–172.

Read, C. 1971. Pre-school children's knowledge of English phonology. *Harvard Educational Review* 41.

Tzeng, O.J.L. In press. Brain organization for language functions. In *Oxford International Encyclopedia of Linguistics*, ed. W. Bright.

Tzeng, O.J.L., & Wang, W. S-Y. 1984. In search for a common neuro-cognitive mechanism for language and movement. *American Journal of Regulatory, Integrative, and Comparative Physiology* 246:R904–R911.

van Hoek, K., Bellugi, U., & Fok, Y.Y.A. 1988. *Sign language universals: Evidence from Chinese Sign Language*. San Diego, CA: The Salk Institute.

Deaf Readers' Comprehension of Complex Syntactic Structure

Diane C. Lillo-Martin
Vicki L. Hanson
Suzanne T. Smith

W hat differentiates adult deaf readers who are proficient at reading English from those who are less proficient? Are there aspects of English grammar that the good reader understands but the poor reader does not? Is there some cognitive factor in the process of reading that good readers are better at? In this paper we address these questions by examining good and poor deaf readers' understanding of some aspects of English grammar. In particular, we examine comprehension of one complex syntactic structure—relative clauses—using tests of the comprehension of relative clauses in written English, signed English, and American Sign Language (ASL). We also investigate how good and poor deaf readers' use of phonological coding in short-term working memory contributes to reading differences (Conrad 1979; Hanson 1982; Lichtenstein 1985).

Studies with good and poor hearing readers have indicated that poor readers exhibit a variety of language-related impairments, including phonological segmentation difficulties, naming difficulties, working-memory deficits, and impaired performance on tests of the comprehension of complex syntax (for review see Liberman & Shankweiler 1987). However, despite these seemingly disparate im-

---

This work was supported in part by National Institutes of Health NIDCD Grant #DC00183 (formerly NINCDS #NS18010) to Diane Lillo-Martin at Haskins Laboratories. We would like to thank Deborah Kuglitsch for running the subjects; Mike Karchmer, Ken Epstein, and Gallaudet University for assistance in gathering subjects; and the subjects who participated.

146

pairments, a unified account of poor readers' difficulties can be given by locating the source of reading impairment in the phonologically based working-memory system (Shankweiler & Crain 1986). Under this account, poor hearing readers have trouble using phonologically based coding in working memory, and this difficulty underlies their apparent lexical and syntactic problems.

What makes phonological coding in working memory so important? In reading and listening, individual words of a sentence must be retained while the grammatical relations among words are determined. Evidence suggests that working memory is most efficient for verbal material (including written material) when the processing involves phonological coding. For readers suffering from impaired phonological coding in working memory, processing individual words and putting these words together into phrases and sentences can be computationally over-loading, impairing overall reading performance.

Is it even possible for deaf readers to use phonological coding in the absence of auditory input? We note that, despite common assumptions that a phonological code must be auditory, this assumption is not supportable. Phonological units relate not specifically to sounds, but rather to articulatory gestures and, as such, could also have motor and visual components (see Hanson 1989 for a discussion). Studies of good and poor deaf readers have indicated that use of a phonologically based working-memory code is characteristic of good deaf readers (Conrad 1979; Hanson, Liberman & Shankweiler 1984; Lichtenstein 1985). Thus it is possible that poor deaf readers, like their hearing counterparts, suffer from difficulties in using a phonologically based code. It is interesting to note, however, that tests of short-term memory for American Sign Language stimuli show evidence that deaf readers use a sign-based code (Bellugi, Klima & Siple 1975; Krakow & Hanson 1985; Poizner, Bellugi & Tweeney 1981).

Since hearing children are exposed to spoken language in sufficient quantity for normal language acquisition to occur, it is perhaps not surprising that most hearing children with reading difficulties do not have a specifically syntactic deficit. However, for deaf readers, since much of the input for English syntax comes from written material, it is reasonable to ask whether syntactic deficits might remain, possibly in addition to deficits in phonologically based working-memory processes.

Evidence for a processing deficit over a syntactic deficit in deaf readers takes the following form: In tests of syntactic processing, subjects (adults and children, good and poor readers) will always make some errors, and certain sentence types might be more taxing than others. If good readers have syntactic competence, which poor readers lack, then poor readers should have an overall depressed level of performance on syntactic tasks, and we do not predict a particular pattern of errors across sentence types. However, if poor readers have the same syntactic competence as good readers but are suffering from a processing impairment of the type suggested by the unified-processing-deficit hypothesis, then we would expect to find a similar pattern of errors across sentence types for the two groups. That is, sentence types that are especially taxing for good readers will be similarly taxing for poor readers, while the sentence types producing the highest performance for good readers will also produce the highest performance for poor readers.

Given this background, this study was designed to follow up on reports of deaf students' syntactic difficulties (e.g., Quigley, Smith & Wilbur 1974), with a test battery designed to differentiate the hypothesis that deaf adult students have a specific syntactic deficit in written English from the hypothesis that a processing deficit might underlie syntactic difficulties. We began with a study examining comprehension of relative clauses in order to be able to examine a variety of sentence types and to be able to make comparisons with studies of hearing readers (e.g., Smith 1987).

We tested the two hypotheses using a battery of tests for the comprehension of relative clauses in English and ASL, and a serial-memory test that should indicate whether phonologically based coding was being used (for details, see Lillo-Martin, Hanson & Smith n.d.). The subjects who participated in this study included twenty-six students at Gallaudet University, all of whom were in their preparatory or freshman year, were severely or profoundly deaf, and came from deaf families who used ASL as the primary means of communication. On the basis of a paragraph-reading comprehension test administered in this study, subjects were divided into two groups of thirteen each: good readers and poor readers. These two groups form the basis for the comparisons in the syntactic tests.

TEST BATTERY

The test battery included the following tests:

1. The Raven's Progressive Matrices (1965) ten-item screening test, a nonverbal measure used to ensure that the two groups were equivalent in intelligence scores;
2. The Gates-MacGinitie Reading Test (1978)-Comprehension Subtest, a multiple-choice test using questions based on short paragraphs, providing grade-equivalent scores used to divide the subjects into good and poor reader groups;
3. The Test of Syntactic Abilities (Quigley, Steinkamp, Power & Jones 1978)—Relativization 1: Comprehension subtest (selected items), an assessment test used to provide a measure of the subjects' comprehension of relative clause structures based on a standardized reading test normed on deaf children and adults;
4. American Sign Language relative clause comprehension tests—picture choice and figure manipulation, used to assess subjects' comprehension of relative clause structures in ASL, following Smith (1987) in design, with some modifications for the signed presentation;
5. Signed English relative clause comprehension test—picture choice and figure manipulation, used to assess subjects' comprehension of relative clause structures in Pidgin Sign English, similarly following Smith (1987); and
6. A serial recall test, following Hanson (1982), used to measure phonological coding in working memory by comparing memory for rhyming versus nonrhyming lists of words.

RESULTS

The groups were different in reading ability by four grade levels (good readers grade level, 9.34; poor readers grade level, 5.08), although their intelligence scores did not differ significantly. Thus, the groups were appropriate for comparison. On the written English relative clause test and all the signed tests, the groups were not significantly different in their percentage of correct responses, although the poor-reader group was consistently lower overall than the good-reader group. Furthermore, in all five of these tests, the groups performed exactly parallel across sentence types, as evidenced by a significant effect of sentence type, but no group-by-sentence-type interaction was found. This result is entirely predicted by the unified-processing deficit hypothesis. Unexpectedly, there was no evidence for phonological coding in the serial recall test for either the good-reader group or the poor-reader group.

DISCUSSION

Although these groups were significantly different in their reading scores, with a difference of four grade levels, we found no significant difference in the syntactic comprehension ability for complex sentences with relative clauses. Whether given in written English, Pidgin Sign English, or ASL, relative clause structures were comprehended by the subjects in both of these groups. In fact, an analysis of the (few) errors that were made shows that the pattern was exactly parallel. The distribution of correct responses across sentence types, and the type of erroneous responses given, were parallel across the two groups (as evidenced by an effect of sentence type without a group effect or interaction). Furthermore, the errors on the tests were parallel to the error patterns found in a similar study by Smith (1987) with hearing subjects. Thus, across the signed tests, and comparing signed tests with spoken tests administered to hearing subjects, a parallel pattern of results was found.

The results of the tests discussed here support the hypothesis that syntactic knowledge (in particular, knowledge of relative clause structures) is not deficient in poor deaf readers. However, there were some important differences between subjects' performance on the signed tests and on the written English test. First, the average score on the written test was below the average on all the signed tests. Second, the error pattern was not parallel across the signed and written tests. This result was unexpected, given the results found in many relative clause studies with hearing children and adults, both good and poor readers. However, we suggest that this finding can be accounted for by considering the differences in test and stimuli design between the two test types. In particular, the signed tests took into account pragmatic factors that have been found to make an important difference in studies of relative clause comprehension by hearing children (Hamburger & Crain 1982; Goodluck & Tavakolian 1982). The standardized written test did not take these factors into account.

There was one unexpected result in this test battery. Given the results of previous studies of working memory in deaf college students (e.g., Hanson 1982; Lichtenstein 1985), we fully expected to find that the good readers, at least, would show evidence of phonological coding. However, such phonological effects were not apparent in the present study, and we do not know whether this was due to inadequate testing procedures or to the failure of these subjects to use phonological coding. Given the evidence from previous studies, the possibility of phonological processing differences distinguishing between good and poor deaf readers must still be considered.

Even without the expected phonological coding difference, the results from the syntactic tests suggest that grammatical knowledge is equivalent in both reader groups, at least with respect to relative clauses. Given this result and the previous literature cited above, we suggest that the differences in reading ability between the groups of deaf readers that we tested are likely to be based on processing differences rather than on differences in grammatical knowledge. An underlying processing difference would account for the slightly lower performance by the poor reader group, along with parallel error-type performance by the two groups. Any hypothesis claiming that these poor readers have deficient structural knowledge compared to the good readers is not supported by these findings. Thus, the cognitive basis for reading in relation to the processing function merits continued investigation by researchers in deafness. Our further work is investigating additional sentence types, as well as various techniques for examining memory coding.

REFERENCES

Bellugi, U., Klima, E., & Siple, P. 1975. Remembering in signs. *Cognition* 3:92–125.
Conrad, R. 1979. *The deaf school child*. London: Harper & Row.
Gates-MacGinitie Reading Tests. 2d ed. 1978. Boston: Houghton Mifflin.
Goodluck, H., & Tavakolian, S. 1982. Competence and processing in children's grammar of relative clauses. *Cognition* 11:1–27.
Hamburger, H., & Crain, S. 1982. Relative acquisition. In *Language development, volume 1: Syntax and semantics*, ed S. Kuczaj, 245–274. Hillsdale, NJ: Lawrence Erlbaum Associates.
Hanson, V. 1982. Short-term recall by deaf signers of American Sign Language: Implications for order recall. *Journal of Experimental Psychology: Learning, Memory, and Cognition* 8:572–583.
———. 1989. Phonology and reading: Evidence from profoundly deaf readers. In *Phonology and reading disability: Solving the reading puzzle*, ed. D. Shankweiler and I. Y. Liberman, 69–89. Ann Arbor: University of Michigan Press. International Academy of Research on Learning Disabilities Monograph Series.
Hanson, V., & Fowler, C. 1987. Phonological coding in word reading: Evidence from hearing and deaf readers. *Memory and Cognition* 15:199–207.
Hanson, V., Liberman, I., & Shankweiler, D. 1984. Linguistic coding by deaf children in relation to beginning reading success. *Journal of Experimental Child Psychology* 37:378–393.
Krakow, R., & Hanson, V. 1985. Deaf signers and serial recall in the visual modality: Memory for signs, fingerspelling, and print. *Memory and Cognition* 13:265–272.
Liberman, I., & Shankweiler, D. 1987. Phonology and the problems of learning to read

and write. *Memory and Learning Disabilities: Advances in Learning and Behavioral Disabilities* Suppl. 2, 203–224.

Lichtenstein, E. 1985. Deaf working memory processes and English language skills. In *Cognition, education, and deafness: Directions for research and instruction*, ed. D. Martin, 111–114. Washington, DC: Gallaudet University Press.

Lillo-Martin, D., Hanson, V., & Smith, S. n.d. Deaf readers' comprehension of relative clause structures.

Poizner, H., Bellugi, U., & Tweeney, R. 1981. Processing of formational, semantic, and iconic information in American Sign Language. *Journal of Experimental Psychology: Human Perception and Performance* 7:1146–1159.

Quigley, S., Smith, N., & Wilbur, R. 1974. Comprehension of relativized sentences by deaf students. *Journal of Speech and Hearing Research* 17:325–341.

Quigley, S., Steinkamp, M., Power, D., & Jones, B. 1978. *Test of syntactic abilities.* Beaverton, OR: Dormac.

Raven, J. 1985. *Advanced progressive matrices.* New York: Psychological Corporation.

Shankweiler, D., & Crain, S. 1986. Language mechanisms and reading disorder: A modular approach. *Cognition* 24:139–168.

Smith, S. 1987. Syntactic comprehension in reading-disabled children. Ph.D. Diss., University of Connecticut.

A Paradigm for Teaching Written English to Deaf Students: A Cognitive Fluency Assessment Model

Lorna J. Mittelman
Larry K. Quinsland

Historically, teachers of deaf students have been centrally concerned with techniques for facilitating the development of literacy. For many years this concern was manifest in the development of spoken English literacy. During the past three decades, the focus evolved into a concern for the development of sign communication literacy (in its many forms) and a concern for the development of reading and writing skills in English. Numerous assessment tools, technological innovations and instructional strategies have been developed. In spite of these efforts, there are still many deaf people whose lives are economically or socially constrained by an inability to use written English effectively. For this reason, it is important that professionals who work with deaf students continue to search for ways to improve opportunities for deaf people to attain written English fluency. The authors propose a paradigm shift for teachers of deaf students and describe an approach that includes consideration of indicators of how students think as they pursue written English fluency.

The process described here is based on the assumption that written, spoken, signed, and typed communication, as well as other observable behaviors, provide clues to cognitive functioning. By observing these behaviors in varying contexts, patterns of cognitive functioning emerge. A cognitive fluency assessment model is described in which deaf students are categorized in terms of observable characteristics. Assumptions underlying this assessment process are described, and benefits and limitations of experimenting with this model are outlined.

It is critical for anyone in the position of facilitating learning to have a conceptual foundation (a model) upon which to test ideas and base planning of learning activities. In this context, it is important for teachers to be able to justify their actions and articulate their goals (Quinsland & Van Ginkel 1984). Readers without a conceptual base are encouraged to search for models that best fit both their own personality and the individuals they teach. Those who have a model with which they feel comfortable and familiar tend to benefit by examining other models as a way of maintaining flexibility and currency.

FROM THE LANGUAGE OF DEFICIENCY TO A POSITIVE PARADIGM

The literature in deaf education is replete with research studies, assessment designs, and instructional strategies that show a marked discrepancy of apparent functioning abilities between deaf and hearing students. Indeed, the field seems to express itself in a framework based on the medical deficit model (Sacks 1988), which regards deafness as a profound handicap rather than a sensory difference. Much useful information has been collected based on this model, but it has some serious limitations in its implications for teaching.

Education systems for deaf students can, regardless of positive intent, create and reinforce some of the very "problems" they seek to understand and remedy. Teachers who function within a deficit model of deafness often subconsciously limit the development of deaf students. It is the experience of these authors that many young deaf adults have learned to feel less intelligent than hearing people with respect to the ability to express themselves in written English. Many state that they (or "other deaf") are more childish and less adequate socially than hearing people (Tucker 1988). Such negative self-imaging leads many neither to recognize nor to strive to develop the native powers that could be used to help meet the challenges that deafness creates in a hearing world.

Instead of regarding deafness as a profound handicap, the authors propose a paradigm shift, encouraging other teachers to reconsider how they look at deaf students. As opposed to viewing English writing as *the problem*, it is proposed that teachers assume the perspective of accepting the unique knowledge base and writing skills of each student as a point of departure. This paradigm suggests a neutral acceptance of the cognitive fluency abilities that exist, combined with a positive view that all students can change. It is postulated that, by basing action on a positive theoretical model, the resulting purposeful interactions with students will ultimately lead to shifts in cognitive fluency by deaf students. The positive attitude that a teacher assumes while working with students is a prerequisite for successful application of the cognitive fluency assessment process.

PATTERNS OF COGNITIVE FLUENCY

Students succeed or fail in college for many different reasons. Quinsland and Templeton (1989) have identified and classified the greatest barriers to success in college for deaf students. Three of the four areas (teaching/learning preferences, adaptation skills, and affective considerations) are thought to be factors for both hearing and deaf students. The fourth area, cognitive fluency in English, has proven to be a more significant barrier to success for deaf students.

In any given class, particularly introductory courses, individuals may differ greatly in English cognitive fluency as well as in fluency in other languages. Each language has its own cognitive framework and its way of classifying and describing reality. This point is not only true for auditory-based languages such as Chinese and English, but it is also true for American Sign Language, which is visual and image-based in nature.

For many years the authors have taught and observed deaf students at the college level in a variety of classes in English composition, academic content, and tutorials. As we became more skilled at observing, consistent patterns of cognitive and language functioning emerged. When students were grouped according to apparent Hearing-world knowledge, Deaf-world knowledge, apparent English fluency and ASL (visual-based) fluency, and written English proficiency, ten categories emerged. These categories are described below and illustrated in Table 1.

The terms invented to identify the cognitive fluency types are in no way to be interpreted in a pejorative sense. The process in creating these terms was an attempt to select designations that would be readily comprehended and retained by experienced teachers of deaf students. It is also important to note that the use of the term "ASL fluency" is used in a general sense to indicate a visual "image-based" type of cognitive perception and processing (as opposed to an English language-based type of perception and processing). "ASL fluency" is not intended to indicate ASL expressive or receptive proficiency. A student might view the world in a visual image-based manner but, through lack of exposure, might be unable to communicate well using American Sign Language.

In applying the cognitive fluency model, information is collected in several ways. Students are required to produce a wide variety of prepared and spontaneous writing, including writing samples, private dialogue journals, formal papers on familiar and unfamiliar topics, group writing projects, and individual papers. Other factors such as handwriting, typing, and face-to-face communication (signed and spoken) are noted in the contexts and interactions in which they occur. The primary objective of this process is to observe students carefully and begin to recognize cognitive fluency clues early in a course. Student language samples are analyzed using a cognitive "networking" technique that gives visual clues to the types of thinking the students are doing. These clues also provide some guidance in the selection of appropriate instructional strategies. Observations continue throughout the course to monitor changes in written English cognitive fluency and related progress on the cognitive fluency scale.

Students in the first four groups shown in Table 1 have generally grown up in English language environments, have hearing families, and have attended mainstreamed programs. They may have learned some form of Pidgin Sign English, but they usually have not been exposed to ASL before attending college. Their thinking has developed primarily within an English framework, and students in these groups usually identify themselves as hearing-impaired. The writing by students in these groups preserves the general order of ideas and sequences expected in English. Students in the first three groups differ primarily in amount of knowledge and extent of fluency. The fourth group is quite different and often

TABLE 1 Indicators of Cognitive Fluency in Deaf College Students

Number	Title	Hearing World Knowledge	Deaf World Knowledge	ASL/Visual-Based Thinking	English Thinking	English Writing
1	Advanced Unicognitive English	High College level and beyond	Late, limited	None or limited	Fluent	Error-free Articulate
2	Unicognitive English	Undergraduate level	Late, limited	None or limited	Almost fluent Freshman level	Minor errors Occasional awkwardness
3	Neo-unicognitive English	Undergraduate level	Late, limited	None or limited	Beginning integration	Many errors Awkwardness
4	Pseudo-hearing	Junior high High school level	Limited or none	None	Word chains	High complexity Low meaning
5	True Bicognitive	High college level or beyond	Early	Fluent	Fluent	Error-free or Almost articulate
6	Bicognitive	Limited	Early	Fluent	At fluency threshold	Some suffix errors Some order errors
7	Neo-Bicognitive	Limited	Early	Fluent	Approaching Fluency Threshold	Many suffix errors Many order errors
8	English-Fragmented Bicognitive	Very limited	Early	Fluent	Very Fragmented	Serious omissions Errors of order and syntax
9	Seriously Fragmented	Very limited	Early or limited	Limited	Very limited	Frequently incomprehensible
10	Unique	No identifiable patterns or trends within the group. Do not fit in other groups.				

puzzles many professionals, due to a marked discrepancy between spoken and written English proficiency. Although these students appear to be quite fluent in English, due to excellent speech skills and mastery of many colloquialisms, an analysis of their spoken and written English reveals that these students have not developed the cognitive activity that forms the basis of meaningful communication. There is a similarity between this student and the hearing student who has grown up in a language-deprived environment. The first four categories and examples are as follows (all language samples are verbatim).

1. *Advanced Unicognitive English*: "The book was outstandingly written because it also explains the frustrations regarding body building. He gives information to bodybuilders who are married, have children, have important jobs or are in college. He helps those people with major responsibilities by telling them that bodybuilding is a part of life and that there will always be frustrations and barriers."
2. *Unicognitive English*: "Miss Smith is also great at helping others. One day I was so upset and frustrated that I ran outside and hid my face against a tree. She told me to come back with her and we talked. Later on, Miss Smith wrote a letter of recommendation for a high school program at a local college. The letter was so great I was accepted into the program."
3. *Neo-cognitive English*: "In the past 10 years, there has been a big increase in the number of drunk driving especially teenagers. Every year shows the increase of automobile accidents, death by accidents, and drunk driving and ended up in going to jail and loses their car licence mostly be teenagers. Teenagers think they are all grown up and do what as they pleased and ended up into a big trouble for when they do that, they start to drink and drive and ended up in a car accident. It would hurt the teenagers and other people on the road."
4. *Pseudo-hearing*: "The first reason of this proposal is about why the students may be required to spend one year working on the full time job. This is about the students who can learn about the jobs which is related to his/her major. In fact, the majors which can be depended on by the students who are required to take the co-op as if it is necessary to take it."

Students in groups five through eight generally have good to excellent ASL communication skills and are developing fluency in thinking in English. Students range from fully fluent in both languages in group five to fluent in ASL but not yet fluent in English in group eight. They have usually attended residential school programs for much, if not all, of their lives; may have deaf parents; and usually have had exposure to deaf communities as children. In general, they are serious, hard-working students who regard learning to use English effectively as extremely important in their professional lives but do not regard English as a fundamental component of their cultural or personal identity. Most students in the developing groups understand the need to learn English thinking skills and continue to work through months and years of frustrating apparent "lack of improvement" (Patino

1982). They work toward a threshold or struggle with breaking through to what one student calls "idea control," the ability to establish idea categories and relations and put them together in a way that will "flow" (Miller 1988). The next four categories are as follows:

    5. *True Bicognitive*: "During my years of competitive figure skating. I was performing on the ice in front of a thousand eyes of spectators. My music was heard around the arena, and I was sure that they were not aware of my hearing loss. Whenever they found out, they always asked: how did my timing with music go so well without hearing it? I always gave a long involved answer but until last week I did not have a term that fit well. Now I have a clearer answer; "inner dialogue" is the way to describe what I do."

    6. *Bicognitive*: "Secondly, a child should be in deaf residential instead of mainstreamed. The reason is because the deaf residential students have a lot of opportunity to participate in any sports or organization as they wish. Any deaf residential students can participate in different groups like athletes or political as they feel comfortable. Also, deaf students can communicate to anyone in deaf residential. In mainstreamed, there is very limited for deaf students. They couldn't participate to anything due to lack of communicate. They are more passive in this situation."

    7. *Neo-bicognitive*: "The Deaf communities are so important for hearing impaired people to get involvement and services. They offer us the various workshops, conferences, Language sign classes, picnic and recreation. This is the most important of reason why more cities and towns should have the Deaf communities. It help the Deaf society to get the better fellowship. Even, they can make more Deaf friends from the apart towns and share together about the experience of their lives."

    8. *English-fragmented Bicognitive*: "I read this clearly easy to understand. This are okay main points. Feeling show for an introduction is great to help me reader more motivation as curiously. It's action story what happened between deaf and hearing students."

Students in the last two groups have unique ways of processing language and thought. Students in the "seriously fragmented" group have no well-developed native language and tend to be faced with serious barriers to intellectual and social growth. Students in the "unique" category can be the most intriguing and challenging. They do not fit into other categories because their cognitive or learning styles vary so much from those of other people. Some students are in this group because they have conditions other than deafness that have an effect on their learning or thought processes. These conditions might include visual impairments, true learning disabilities, various neurological organic impairments, and covert emotional disturbances. While most student do not think about, nor even comprehend, how they process information and communicate it, sometimes "unique" students will attempt to hide a condition, thereby presenting the teacher with another challenge. The last categories are as follows:

9. *Seriously Fragmented*: "A lot of noisome things are existed today gave us aversion from TV news program. Fading away our affection everyday we should rid a biased view of bigots, a tangled party and hostility which an expansion of nuclear armament is increasing the United States and Russia."

10. *Unique*: "What are my persenal success in the past? I have been some good things in my good experience, which those experiencie helped me to be a good persen. Here is three reasans how I have learned to be successful persenal in the past."

Assuming that members of a class display diverse cognitive fluency, learning occurs most effectively when the teacher has a large number of individual and group strategies available to interact with each student for optimum growth. Most teaching strategies are not new, nor are they magic. The authors have identified many alternative teaching strategies and have matched strategies with cognitive fluency type. It is the conscious attempt to match a teaching strategy to the perceived cognitive level of the student that makes the strategy effective. For example, one student's thinking may have reached the point of needing a specific grammatical structure to express his thoughts accurately. Another student may know the appropriate structure but needs to practice more precise editing skills. A third student not yet fluent in English may benefit from a group assignment far more than from any instruction the teacher could provide.

TEACHING WITHIN A POSITIVE PARADIGM

The cognitive fluency model described above is one attempt to create a positive framework for instruction. It assumes that each student has within him or her the resources or powers needed lo learn English effectively. It assumes that each student is capable of marshaling the resources needed to learn, regardless of how formidable the task might appear. It further assumes that a person's "whole being" is involved in learning and that effective learning occurs when the strategies engage the whole student and involve the center or motivation where the person forms meaning and direction for oneself (Dilts, Grinder, Bandler & DeLozier 1980). The more internally motivated a student is, the more energy and time the student tends to spend on task.

In spite of the fact that courses are generally constructed to measure the quality of products, this approach to teaching allows the teacher to focus on the process of language development as well as the products. In this model, the products are considered signs or symbols of internal processes and are used as a vehicle for providing feedback to a student. Only when the process is completely finished to the satisfaction of the student is it measured as a product in relation to the required standards of the course. The intent then becomes the ability to function effectively in English and thus produce fluent English prose rather than simply to produce correct and accurate prose. The goal for the student becomes one of *proving* thoughts and new learning in English through the development of prose that is increasingly more detailed, accurate, and sequenced according to the expectations of the English reader.

TEACHER/LEARNER OUTCOMES

It is important to discuss the apparent benefits to both teachers and students in utilizing the cognitive fluency assessment process. For a teacher, use of the assessment process can take a lot of the guesswork out of interactions with students. By working to comprehend some of the more salient student characteristics, some of the mystery of why some students write the way they do is resolved.

The use of this model (or any model) provides a sophisticated basis for discussion among professional colleagues. The model also offers a partial solution to the time crunch that most teachers report. For example, by identifying cognitive fluency levels that respond well to peer-tutoring strategies and forming the requisite groups, the teacher frees up time to spend with students whose cognitive fluency levels respond best to intensive one-on-one interaction. The resulting increase in "quality time" spent with students tends to reduce teacher stress. Probably the greatest professional benefit for teachers is the attitude shift, described by some as "liberating," that occurs when students are truly perceived as individuals with unique cognitive abilities.

In terms of benefits to students, utilization of the assessment process can increase student self-knowledge and can lead to empowerment. Heath (1978) describes empowerment as an essential condition for individuals to be able to grow and to develop the characteristics our society has determined as qualities of adult effectiveness. The skilled teacher can help a student become more aware of how he or she thinks and expresses that thought in writing. Increased awareness of self, in a positive environment that reinforces change, can and does produce powerful results. It is important to note that for some students, initially, the "reality check" of becoming aware of current capabilities can be unpleasant. For example, college students who have been passed on by teacher after teacher in a mainstreamed environment can be in for a shock when confronted with a true reflection of their written English capabilities. The teacher who can accurately and sensitively focus on actual cognitive fluency abilities can help students, through their writing, to develop a healthy awareness of how they perceive their world. When this increased self-knowledge is combined with the establishment of written English fluency goals, the student becomes empowered to believe in the ability to make changes and develops a greater intrinsic motivation to improve written English fluency (Ryan, Connell & Grolnick in press).

SOME LIMITATIONS

The reader must recognize that the cognitive fluency assessment process described here has conditions that can maximize effectiveness. At the outset it is important to realize that, for this process to be truly generalizable, it must be applied by many skilled teachers of writing with many deaf students. Writing sample records must be kept of changes that occur in student cognitive fluency levels. The true test will be whether the teacher notices improvements when the assessment process is compared with methods utilized earlier. Readers are encouraged to share their experiences with the authors.

For assessments to be valid and for the process to be applied successfully, a teacher must have adequate Pidgin Sign English, American Sign Language, and speech comprehension skills to be able to assess accurately the cognitive fluency levels of students in all ten categories. Observations and assessments should be ongoing throughout the course if they are to be reliable, so that proper instructional strategies can be matched to the cognitive fluency level. In this way, an atmosphere of acceptance and positive encouragement of change is created for both the student and the teacher.

It should be noted that teaching writing by assessing written English fluency primarily in terms of grammar and structure is not enough. When grammar and structure clues are combined with an assessment of *content* and *expression* clues, a much more accurate picture of cognitive fluency is achieved. Then other clues gained through dialogue (oral and/or manual) with the student are added to this assessment. It is a gestalt of these factors that produces a judgment concerning the cognitive fluency level of a given student.

Finally, the use of this assessment/teaching paradigm has occurred most successfully when assignments are perceived to be of high interest, have strong emotional (affective) appeal, and/or are enjoyable to do. The writing that gives the most accurate clues to cognitive fluency levels occurs naturally under conditions that encourage the best thinking.

Student response to this approach has been consistently positive, and many students have developed English skills more rapidly than they had in the past. Research is under way to assess the validity of the initial ten categories, identify their usefulness to other teachers in a variety of classrooms, and identify teaching strategies that maximize student progress relative to a given cognitive fluency category. In this context, readers who experiment with the model are encouraged to share their experiences with the authors. Research within this paradigm also needs to be conducted to discover and facilitate not the weaknesses that deaf students demonstrate with respect to hearing students, but the strengths that they develop as a result of being deaf and that they bring to the challenges of functioning in a hearing world.

REFERENCES

Annual trainer's course presented by NLP International I London. 1985.

Dilts, R., Grinder, J., Bandler, R., & DeLozier, J. 1980. *Neuro-linguistic programming: Volume I: The study of the structure of subjective experience.* Cupertino, CA: Meta.

Greenberg, E. 1978. The community as a learning resource. *Journal of Experiential Education* 1(3):22–25.

Heath, D. 1978. Teaching for adult effectiveness. *Journal of Experiential Education* 1(3):8–13.

Miller, S. 1988. Personal communication.

Patino, P. 1982. Personal communication.

Quinsland, L., & Van Ginkel, A. 1984. How to process experience. *Journal of Experiential Education.* 7(2).

Quinsland, L., & Templeton, D. 1989. *The deaf student in college: A student success model.* Rochester, NY: National Technical Institute for the Deaf.

Ryan, R., Connell, J., & Grolnick, W. In press. When achievement is *not* intrinsically motivated: A theory of internalization and self-regulation in school. In *Achievement and motivation: A social-developmental perspective*, ed. A. Boggiano & T. Pittman.

Sacks, O. 1988. The revolution of the deaf. *The New York Review of Books*, June 2, 23.

Tucker, J. October 22, 1988. *Hey listen!* Panel discussion moderated by Jackie Schertz. WUHF, Rochester, New York.

SUGGESTED READING

Bandler, R., & Grinder, J. 1979. *Frogs into princes: Neuro-linguistic programming*. Moab, UT: Real People Press.

————. 1982. *Reframing*. Moab, UT: Real People Press.

Cundy, L. 1988. Stop apologizing for your child's deafness. *NAD Broadcaster*, November, 19.

Deloz, L. 1986. *Effective teaching and mentoring*. San Francisco: Jossey-Bass.

Ferguson, M. 1980. *The Aquarian conspiracy*. Los Angeles: J.P. Tarcher, Inc.

Gardner, H. 1983. *Frames of mind: The theory of multiple intelligences*. New York: Basic Books.

Kazmierski, P. 1985. *Simplified model of thinking and learning*. Rochester, NY: Rochester Institute of Technology. Typescript.

Osguthorpe, R. 1980. *Tutoring special students*. Provo, UT: Brigham Young University. Typescript.

Pragmagraphics and belief systems. 1985. Santa Cruz, CA: Dynamic Learning Center.

Quinsland, L., & Long, G. 1986. Experiential learning vs. lecture learning: A comparative study with postsecondary hearing-impaired learners. Paper presented at the Convention of the American Educational Research Association.

Sacks, O. 1985. *The man who mistook his wife for a hat and other clinical tales*. New York: Summit Books.

Spradley, J.P. 1979. *The ethnographic interview*. New York: Holt, Rinehart & Winston.

Springer, S., & Deutsch, G. 1985. *Left brain, right brain*. New York: W. H. Freeman.

Wlodkowski, R.J. 1978. *Motivation and teaching: A practical guide*. Washington, DC: National Education Association Press.

Processes for Text and Language Acquisition in the Context of Microcomputer-Videodisc Instruction for Deaf and Multihandicapped Deaf Children

Keith E. Nelson
Philip M. Prinz
Elizabeth A. Prinz
Deborah Dalke

Traditionally, children using classroom computers have been given few opportunities to initiate language. Moreover, there have been very few instructional software programs available that have truly interactive characteristics (Arcanin & Kawolkow 1980; Behrman 1984; Rose & Waldron 1983; Schwartz 1984; Ward & Rostron 1983). The present report concerns reading and writing instruction through a highly interactive program for Apple IIe and IIgs microcomputers. The program has been employed for more than six years with deaf and multihandicapped deaf children in a project termed the ALPHA Microcomputer-Videodisc Project for Interactive Reading, Writing, and Communication. In the present research the children utilized text communication from the outset, relying on a special keyboard that displays words rather than letters and a system that permits exploratory learning. On this system, a child can easily and rapidly create new sentences and trigger lively graphics and video images by selecting words that make up messages such as "The clown chases the monkey and the horse" or "The horse eats the popcorn." Another novel (and crucial) component of this project is the reliance on sign language to ensure that the text activities are meaningful and productive for the signing deaf child. The software

---

This research was supported by two Technology Effectiveness Research Grants (Nos. G008302959 and G008430079) from the U.S. Department of Education (Office of Special Education and Rehabilitative Services), a gift from the Hasbro Children's Foundation, and National Science Foundation Grant No. INT8722794. The authors thank Keith Freeman and Cathy Fuller for their assistance in developing the lessons.

provides signs from American Sign Language (ASL) on the TV screen through the videodisc. Moreover, sign language exchanges occur between the teacher and the child as part of the interactive instructional sessions.

In the ALPHA project, children receive computer-assisted instruction (CAI) in reading and writing one to three times weekly. In contrast to the regular classroom text instruction, the ALPHA program provides important new activities and opportunities for new ways of processing text and related information. There are six key aspects of ALPHA's alternative approach.

1. Drill and practice is replaced by highly interactive activities. Most children are strongly motivated by the chance to initiate messages that are displayed through printed text, picture and sign animations, and video images. The child and the teacher are then free to comment on, clarify, and expand these messages. Thus the CAI structures and content are meaningfully and immediately connected to knowledge and experience that the child has already accumulated (cf. "recasting" in first language learning, Baker & Nelson 1984; Nelson 1977, 1980, 1988; "recasting" in sign language, Prinz & Masin 1985).

2. The child learns both sentence structure and vocabulary in a program mode called "Create Sentences." The child selects word keys and tells the computer and the videodisc what to do by creating (writing) a complete text sentence. For example, if the child selects special word keys to write onto the TV the sentence "The squirrel bumps the ball," the child can then in rapid order read the sentence on the TV and see the sentence acted out through pictorial animation. One more quick key selection will then display the ASL signs that convey the same message as the newly-created sentence.

3. The activity sequence described above takes advantage of special CAI presentation capacities that are usually absent in the child's encounters with text in books, handouts, exercises, notes, and so forth (cf. Lepper & Malone 1986; Sheie 1985). The microcomputer and videodisc can display the child's own text message and then rapidly follow with lively, colorful animations, video images, and sequences that show the meanings of the text. Seeing parallel meanings in a short time period in text, picture, and sign (and optional synthesized voice) may aid the child in connecting these modes and in working out a new understanding of the text material.

   In information-processing terms, the child needs to evaluate in working memory how already-known structures for ASL and events compare with the structures to be learned—the printed English sentences (Baddely 1984; Bonvillian, Nelson & Charrow 1976; Conlin & Paivio 1975; Nelson 1980, 1987, 1988; Shand 1982; Siple, Caccamise & Brewer 1982). These well-structured multimedia sequences in ALPHA allow the child to put into working memory within 20 seconds or less the following forms of representation: the text, the CAI animations that show the precise meaning of the text (not true for most books children read), the ASL signs from CAI, any ASL signs used in the side conversations with the teacher, and images and signs and text examples retrieved from long-term memory. These parallel meanings from different sources should allow the child to "crack the code" of text. The special processing opportunities in this ALPHA system that assist text learning thus combine these important properties: rapid access, precisely parallel meanings, and several redundant channels of meaning.

4. Another aspect of the alternative learning activities provided in ALPHA is that the children are not pressured to demonstrate knowledge of how sign language and English structures are related. Instead, the children are freed to explore sentence after sentence and to discover how their newly created English text sentences map to the English-order ASL on the computer and to the sign language structures they use with their teachers. Matches and mismatches in word order for sign and for English can be observed. Moreover, the teacher and the child are encouraged to discuss these structural variations between English and sign. For both modes of language, the explicit pictorial meanings from CAI animations anchor the search for understanding.

5. Using the ALPHA materials does not burden the teacher with additional paperwork; the computer provides assessment and record keeping.

6. In preparation for using written messages at school, at home, and in future job settings, the child must learn to deal with text as a "formal code" (Olson 1977; Olson & Nickerson 1978; Moores 1982; Cole & Scribner 1974) that has a precise meaning. Often that meaning will be imaginative and unrealistic rather than literal and realistic. So, in ALPHA instruction the children are expected to create and to comprehend both realistic and fanciful sentences.

In this chapter, gains are reported for two samples of deaf children. Rapid selection of individualized ALPHA lessons through the software allowed the teachers to use the same basic system with children whose ages, reading levels, and language skills varied widely.

METHODOLOGY: STUDY 1

The subjects in Study 1 included 63 deaf children between the ages of 3 years 4 months and 11 years 8 months at pretest. Most of these children had a severe to profound hearing impairment, but three had a moderate hearing impairment. Children worked with Level I ALPHA materials.

METHODOLOGY: STUDY 2

In Study 2, 16 deaf students between the ages of 5 years 11 months and 20 years 3 months participated. For these subjects, the ALPHA material from the Apple

IIe microcomputer used in Study 1 was supplemented with videodisc still and action sequences. In addition to the Level I ALPHA used in Study 1, many subjects in Study 2 also used Level II ALPHA, which incorporates longer and more grammatically complex sentences.

Subjects in both studies were selected to participate in the study only if they had average or better intelligence, beginning reading skills, and at least preschool language levels. Subjects also had to be unable to read the majority of the vocabulary in the ALPHA lesson set.

EQUIPMENT AND SOFTWARE: STUDY 1 AND STUDY 2

Each subject worked with an Apple IIe microcomputer system (+ 64 K bytes), which was set up with a special, large interface keyboard (Keyport 717 by Polytel Corporation or Power Pad by Dunamis, Inc.) with interchangeable overlays that allowed more flexibility than a regular computer keyboard. Each overlay corresponds to one of the different lessons in Level I or Level II of the ALPHA Interactive Language Software. After the child selected words (one key per word) on the interface keyboard overlay, the text was printed and displayed on a large color monitor along with corresponding graphics in pictures or signs.

RESULTS AND DISCUSSION

In both studies the deaf children achieved high levels of mastery on the ALPHA text materials. After each lesson was explored, sentence tests were presented, and the children averaged between 82% and 91% correct. Table 1 shows how well the deaf children in Study 2 performed when given videodisc-assisted ALPHA lessons. This same table also highlights a 19% pre-post gain in print vocabulary.

By pretesting and posttesting children on a general reading battery before and after ALPHA instruction, in Study 1 it was possible to estimate generalization

TABLE 1   ALPHA Videodisc Supplement: Percentage Scores on Computer-generated Sentence Tests and Reading Vocabulary

N	Number of Sessions	Ages	Pretest Score	Posttest Score	Percentage Gain
		ALPHA LEVEL I			
13	22	5;11−20;3	.71	.82	.11
		LEVEL II			
6	24	6;10−17;0	.70	.82	.12
		READING VOCABULARY			
16	23	5;11−20;3	.54	.73	.19

or carryover from the interactive computer lessons to broader skill gains in the text area (see Nelson, Prinz & Dalke, in press). Three groups of children were compared, all matched on pretest levels of reading and language—high, medium, and minimal frequency of ALPHA microcomputer instruction. Generalized gains in reading were indicated by much stronger average pretest-to-posttest advance for the medium (+ 15.9%) and high (+ 20.1%) ALPHA instructional groups than for the minimal comparison group (+ 8.5%) children who rarely or never worked with the ALPHA system.

From Study 2 another important finding emerged—children did equally well on realistic-probable and fanciful-improbable sentence tests. They generated sentences correctly on 87% of trials. The skilled child in this testing context observed a pictorial action sequence on the TV and then proceeded to generate the appropriate text from the ALPHA keyboard, showing equal facility for contrasting sentence types such as "The dog chases the car" and "The barn hides behind the farmer."

These outcomes need to be viewed in relation to the ALPHA instructional activities. During exploratory learning the children are richly supported by context. Whether a child generates an unrealistic sentence or a realistic one, the CAI context shows precisely what that sentence means. The context includes computer graphic animation of the sentence's precise meaning plus sign language by the computer and by the teacher. This richly supportive context allows the child to successfully abstract the text structures so that they then pass the context-free sentence testing; whatever events are shown in the CAI test, realistic or not, the children typically generate a referential text message that precisely describes the events.

Results of the present studies match but also extend previous findings (Prinz & Nelson 1985; Prinz, Nelson & Stedt 1982; Prinz, Pemberton & Nelson 1985), which demonstrate that through ALPHA instruction deaf children as young as 3 to 5 years of age can acquire reading and writing skills. We see the present positive outcomes as illustrations that reading and writing can be beneficially integrated within a system of exchange of information between teachers and children (Stokes & Branigan 1984). In addition, computer-generated "writing" (through word key presses on the special student keyboard) may serve as a catalyst for more active information processing and thus further facilitate reading processes (Maxwell 1983; Prinz 1982; Prinz, Pemberton & Nelson 1985).

Moreover, the CAI writing activities by the child are interrelated with teacher-child conversation about CAI events. In this context, the teacher's elaborations and recasts present new language structures in reply to prior comments by the children. Such conversational events probably aid the ALPHA children's learning, just as these adult reply strategies aid first language learning (Baker & Nelson 1984; Nelson 1977, 1980, 1987, 1988; Prinz & Masin 1985). Thus, the ALPHA activities provide the deaf child with rapid access to multiple channels of English text, sign, and pictures that provide rich opportunities for learning to process and use text appropriately.

Results of the ALPHA Interactive Language studies have cognitive educational implications for the development of literacy skills in deaf and multihandicapped children. Four metacognitive variables—text, task, strategies, and learner characteristics—identified by Brown, Campione, and Day (1981) appear to be essential to the development of reading and writing skills using microcomputer and videodisc technology. The child has one or more purposes, tasks, or goals to accomplish in reading and writing to learn. There appear to be individual differences between deaf learners in their awareness of the processing and retrieval demands of the tasks as well as in their ability to adapt literacy skills to meet these requirements. The most important task in learning from reading and writing is comprehension, the derivation of meaning from the text (Ewoldt 1981; Just & Carpenter 1987). The computer graphics and videodisc images incorporated in the ALPHA Program appear to aid deaf learners (shown by present results) and multihandicapped deaf learners (shown by research in progress) in comprehending the meaning of the text.

In addition, the ALPHA Program facilitates the metacognitive strategies of knowing what to do to remedy comprehension errors or failures (cf. Flavell 1978). In the ALPHA Program, children are provided with positive feedback in terms of lively sentence animations only after they produce a grammatically correct sentence.

Finally, another major aspect of metacognition is the deaf and multihandicapped deaf child's awareness of his or her own learning style and characteristics (e.g., knowledge, interest, skills, and deficiencies) and how reading and writing behaviors should be monitored to satisfy the demands of the text. The ALPHA program aids in the development of metacognitive awareness and metacognitive use of relevant prior knowledge. The child has maximum control over the reading and writing process and the activation of computer graphics and videodisc images.

In summary, the results of the present research suggest enhanced processing of text in ALPHA's CAI learner-controlled system through rapid activation of parallel channels of text, picture, and sign meaning. Deaf children were shown to master unrealistic and realistic English sentences equally. Built-in dialogue between the teacher and the student seems to facilitate the use of metacognitive processes by drawing attention to ways in which the student can modify strategies for unknown vs. familiar content and for particular types of text and sign structure. The child's interrelated activities with the computer and the teacher help the student develop control of learning by elucidating the interaction of the metacognitive factors and the importance of assuming an active role in regulating the interaction.

REFERENCES

Arcanin, J., & Kawolkow, G. 1980. Microcomputers in the service of students and teachers—Computer assisted instruction at the California School for the Deaf: An update. *American Annals of the Deaf* 125:807–813.

Baddely, A. 1984. Reading and working memory. In *Proceedings of the conference on visible language*, ed. P. A. Kolers, M. E. Wrolstad, & H. Bpouina, 311–322. New York: Plenum Publishing Corp.

Baker, N., & Nelson, K. 1984. Recasting and related conversational techniques for triggering syntactic advances by young children. *First Language* 5:3–22.

Behrman, M., ed. 1984. *Handbook of microcomputers in special education.* San Diego, CA: College-Hill Press.

Bellugi, U., Klima, E., & Siple, P. 1975. Remembering in signs. *Cognition* 3:93–125.

Bonvillian, J., Nelson, K., & Charrow, W. 1976. Language and language-related skills in deaf and hearing children. *Sign Language Studies* 12:211–250.

Brown, A. 1980. Metacognitive development and reading. In *Theoretical issues in reading comprehension,* ed. R. J. Spiro, B. C. Bruce & N. F. Brewer. Hillsdale, NJ: Lawrence Erlbaum Associates.

Brown, A., Campione, J., & Day, J. 1981. On training students to learn from texts. *Educational Researcher* 10:4–21.

Cole, M., & Scribner, S. 1974. *Culture and thought.* New York: John Wiley & Sons.

Conlin, D., & Paivio, A. 1975. The associative learning of the deaf: The effects of word imagery and signability. *Memory and Cognition* 3:335–340.

Ewoldt, C. 1981. Factors which enable deaf readers to get meaning from print. In *Learning to read in different languages,* ed. S. Hudelson. Washington, DC: Center for Applied Linguistics.

Flavell, J. 1978. Metacognitive development. In *Structural process theories of complex human behavior,* ed. J. M. Scandura & C. J. Brainerd. Alphen a.d. Rign, The Netherlands: Sijthoff and Noordhoff.

Hamilton, H. 1985. Linguistic encoding and adult-child communication. In *Cognition, education, and deafness: Directions for research and instruction,* ed. D.S. Martin, 91–93. Washington, DC: Gallaudet University Press.

Hanson, V. 1985. Cognitive processes in reading: Where deaf readers succeed and where they have difficulty. In *Cognition, education and deafness: Directions for research and instruction,* ed. D.S. Martin, 108–110. Washington, DC: Gallaudet University Press.

Just, M., & Carpenter, P. 1987. *The psychology of reading and language comprehension.* Newton, MA: Allyn and Bacon.

Lepper, M., & Malone, T. 1986. Intrinsic motivation and instructional effectiveness in computer-based education. In *Aptitude, learning, and instruction: III,* ed. R. E. Snow & M. J. Farr. Hillsdale, NJ: Lawrence Erlbaum Associates.

Maxwell, M. 1983. Language acquisition in a deaf child of deaf parents: Speech, sign variations and print variations. In *Children's language,* Volume 4, ed. K. E. Nelson, 283–314. Hillsdale, NJ: Lawrence Erlbaum Associates.

Moores, D. 1982. *Educating the deaf: psychology, principles, and practices.* 2d ed. Boston: Houghton Mifflin.

Nelson, K. 1977. Facilitating children's syntax acquisition. *Developmental Psychology* 13:101–107.

———. 1980. Theories of the child's acquisition of syntax: A look at rare events and at necessary, catalytic, and irrelevant components of mother-child conversation. *Annals of the New York Academy of Sciences* 345:45–67.

———. 1987. Some observations from the perspective of the rare event cognitive comparison theory of language acquisition. In *Children's language,* Volume 6, ed. K. E. Nelson & A. van Kleeck, 289–331. Hillsdale, NJ: Lawrence Erlbaum Associates.

———. 1988. Strategies in first language teaching. In *The teachability of language,* ed. M. Rice & R. Schiefelbusch, 263–310. Baltimore: Paul H. Brookes.

Nelson, K., Heimann, H., Abuelhaija, L., & Wroblewski, R. 1989. Implications for language acquisition models of children's and parents' variations in imitation. In *The many faces of imitation in language learning,* ed. G. E. Speidel & K. E. Nelson, 305–324. New York: Springer-Verlag.

Nelson, K., Prinz, P., & Dalke, D. In press. Transitions from sign language to text via an interactive microcomputer system. In *Language development and sign language*, ed. J. Kyle & B. Well. Cambridge, England: Cambridge University Press.

Prinz, P. 1982. "Requesting" in normal and language-disordered children. In *Children's language*, Volume 3, ed. K. E. Nelson, 139–203. Hillsdale, NJ: Lawrence Erlbaum Associates.

Prinz, P., & Masin, L. 1985. Lending a helping hand: Linguistic input and sign language acquisition in deaf children. *Applied Psycholinguistics* 6:357–370.

Prinz, P., & Nelson, K. 1985. Alligator eats cookie: Acquisition of writing and reading skills by deaf children using the microcomputer. *Applied Psycholinguistics* 2:283–306.

Prinz, P., Nelson, K., & Stedt, J. 1982. Early reading in young deaf children using microcomputer technology. *American Annals of the Deaf* 127:529–535.

Prinz, P., Pemberton, E., & Nelson, K. 1985. ALPHA interactive microcomputer system for teaching reading, writing, and communication skills to hearing-impaired children. *American Annals of the Deaf* 13:444–461.

Rose, S., & Waldron, M. 1983. Microcomputer use in programs for hearing-impaired children: A national survey. *American Annals of the Deaf* 129:338–342.

Schwartz, A., ed. 1984. *Handbook of microcomputer applications in communication disorders*. San Diego, CA: College-Hill Press.

Shand, M. 1982. Sign-based short-term coding of American Sign Language signs and printed English words by congenitally deaf signers. *Cognitive Psychology* 14:1–12.

Sheie, T. 1985. Integration and implementation: A four-point mainstream model. *American Annals of the Deaf* 130:397–401.

Siple, P., Caccamise, F., & Brewer, L. 1982. Signs as pictures and signs as words: Effect of language knowledge on memory for new vocabulary. *Journal of Experimental Psychology: Learning, Memory and Cognition* 8:619–625.

Stokes, W., & Branigan, G. 1984. Operating principles in the acquisition of literacy. Paper presented at the Third International Congress for the Study of Child Language, Austin, Texas.

Ward, R., & Rostron, A. 1983. Computer assisted learning for the hearing-impaired: An interactive written language environment. *Volta Review* 85:346–352.

Visual Reception of Sign Language in Young Deaf Children: Is Peripheral Vision Functional for Receiving Linguistic Information?

M. Virginia Swisher

The amount of information available to a deaf child in a given communication situation is limited in two ways: First, the child has only one primary input channel, vision, to use for gaining both environmental and linguistic information, and second, that channel is directional as opposed to global in reception. The child does not have access to information—whether environmental or linguistic—from behind, and typically, of course, the range of vision is provided by a very small portion of the retina (1 to 2 degrees of arc), constraining us to turn and focus on things if we are to see them clearly. Peripheral vision is generally considered inadequate for detailed form perception, apart from limited identification of letters just beyond the point of fixation in reading.

Although peripheral vision is not useful for situations in which high acuity is required, there is reason to ask whether it might be functional for the perception of signs. Signs are comparatively large visual stimuli, and they involve motion, to which peripheral vision is comparatively sensitive. In fact, signs are perceived peripherally under normal circumstances, in the sense that the addressee in a signed conversation focuses on the signer's face rather than the hands (Siple 1978).

My sincere thanks to Dr. Helen Craig and the staff and students at the Western Pennsylvania School for the Deaf, without whom this study would not have been possible. My thanks also to Karen Christie and Sandra L. Miller for their assistance in working out the design and carrying out the study. Finally, my thanks to our many kind advisors, in particular Dr. H. N. Reynolds, who provided guidance and expertise from the project's inception, and Carol Baker, who performed the statistical analyses.

The question here is whether signs can be identified farther into the periphery, in situations where the addressee is not looking directly at the signer.

One reason to think such identification might be possible is that the steepest drop in acuity occurs just outside the fovea, and it could be that the further decrease in acuity between the area where signs are normally perceived and the extreme periphery would not significantly affect perception, particularly not of familiar visual stimuli such as signs. In addition, deaf students have some visual skills that might be useful for the perception of signs in degraded conditions. For example, they tend to do best on visual tests that call for global pattern recognition, such as block design and pattern matching, as well as on tests of visual closure, where they perform better than hearing people (Parasnis 1983; Siple, Hatfield & Caccamise 1978). Visual closure, in particular, might facilitate the recognition of signs in conditions of poor acuity.

The question of how far into the periphery the perception of signs is possible (the extent of deaf children's functional visual field) is educationally relevant in three ways. First, for many deaf children, vision is the primary avenue for language acquisition. The overall amount of data reaching the children and the completeness of the data are two factors that are likely to contribute to the success or failure of the children's acquisition of English via signed input, and both depend on what the child sees. If the child does not need to be focusing on the signer in order to take in signed information, then more input would be potentially available (ignoring for the moment more complex issues of how visual and cognitive attention intersect). Second, if deaf children were more sensitive than hearing children to peripheral visual information, and particularly if they could receive linguistic information peripherally, they might be more vulnerable to visual distraction than are hearing students. Third, the extent of deaf children's functional visual field may have implications for the presentation of visual information in the classroom, and for the positioning of educational interpreters, particularly where the teacher is performing a demonstration and talking about it at the same time.

SUBJECTS

The present study, investigating the abilities of deaf students between 8 and 12 years of age, is the second in a series of studies of deaf students' ability to read signs in peripheral vision. In the first study, reported in Swisher, Christie, and Miller (1989), procedures were developed and students between 15 and 18 years of age were tested.

In both studies, live signers presented signs in isolation, with the goal of establishing whether students could identify signs seen in the periphery and, if so, with what level of performance. The seven students in the present study were all congenitally profoundly deaf, with hearing losses of 90dB (BEA) (mean 103.6, SD 10), and they ranged in age from 7 years 11 months (to turn 8 within a day or two of testing) to 11 years 8 months. All were students in a residential school for the deaf. The number of years of signing ranged from "two to three" to ten, with an average of 4.8. Five of the children were girls and two were boys.

PROCEDURES

The children were tested in the evening (in order not to interfere with their school programs) in a classroom at the school for the deaf. The children sat facing a video camera seven feet away. The signers sat on either side of the subject, facing him or her, four and a half feet away in two different positions. In the easier of the two conditions, which was always presented first to ensure some success and comfort with the task, the signing space (approximately the width of the signer's chair) was at an angle of 45–61 degrees (midpoint 53 degrees) from the subject's line of sight. In the more difficult condition, the signing space was at an angle of 61–77 degrees (mid-point 69 degrees) from the line of sight. The classroom was brightly illuminated by fluorescent lights suspended from the ceiling. Medium blue sheets were draped behind the two signers, both to equalize the background against which the signers would be seen and to increase contrast, which is important for peripheral perception. The signers, who were similar in build and coloring, wore black so as to increase contrast and make the signs easier to see.

Two sets of 24 common signs were used, presented in different random orders for each subject and in different random sequences of left-right alternation, cued by an assistant standing behind the subject. Random alternation was used in order to test the subjects' ability to identify the signs even when they did not know on which side they would appear, thus approximating a real-life situation. Three types of signs were used: Signs occurring at the face, one-handed signs occurring on the body or in neutral space, and two-handed signs on the body or in actual space. This factor was of interest in that signs occurring below the neck are seen comparatively farther into the periphery under normal conditions (compared to face signs), and it was hypothesized that there might be fewer errors for those signs because they might be formationally adapted for peripheral perception.

The instructions were given in American Sign Language by a deaf signer. The children were told to look at the camera lens and not to move their eyes, that signs would be presented off to the side in a nonregular sequence of left-right alternation, and that they should sign back to the camera what they thought they saw. They were instructed to guess if they were not sure what they had seen. Where necessary, the procedure was demonstrated, with the experimenters and/or another child as a model. Three practice trials were given before each condition, using common signs of the three types. After the third item, the research assistant reinstructed the children, if necessary, about the need to maintain fixation on the camera lens, and reminded them not to look at her for confirmation after they had answered.

The subjects' responses, as well as eye movements, if any, were recorded by the video camera. In 6 instances (out of a possible 336) a child's eye movement coincided with the presentation of the sign, and the child's response was counted wrong. In a reliability procedure in which only the subject's eyes were visible on tape, a rater was required to make a forced choice decision whether each sign had been presented to the right or left; since in the great majority of cases the children's eyes did not move, the rater's decision was purely arbitrary. There was 55% agreement between the judgments and the actual side of presentation: i.e., agreement was approximately at chance.

RESULTS AND DISCUSSION

The children's mean performance was 70% correct in the easier condition (*SD* 7) and 56.6% correct in the more difficult one (*SD* 11.7). As with the older subjects, the children were clearly able to do the task, and variability within the group was not high. Performance, while good, was not quite as high as that of the older students in the first study, whose performance was at 79.7% in the easier condition and 68.3% in the more difficult one. (It should be noted that the probability of a student correctly identifying a sign purely by chance is very small.)

In order to look at the relationships between the two variables in the first study, namely angle of presentation and type of sign, and the effect of age, the data from the younger children were added to those of the older group; a three-way analysis of variance was performed, with angle of presentation and type of sign as within-subjects factors, and age as a between-subjects factor. The analysis found that the main effect of age was significant ($p = .005$), i.e., the results for the younger children were stably lower than those for the older group. (It is of interest that such an effect was found even with a relatively small number of subjects.) There was a large main effect for angle of presentation ($p = .002$). With the addition of the younger children, there was a main effect for sign type ($p = .005$) and an interaction of the effect of type of sign and age group ($p = .04$). Whereas the older subjects had not been significantly different in their performance on the three types of signs, inspection of the data showed that the younger children made a larger number of errors on face signs, coinciding with the original hypothesis that these signs would be more difficult.

It is particularly impressive that the younger subjects performed as well as they did, considering that the group included two children who had not been signing for more than two or three years, and it is interesting that the variability in performance was so small in spite of the range of sign experience.

The errors of the younger group were not notably different from those of the older subjects; the distribution of categories of errors in the younger children followed the same rank order as for the older subjects. For both groups, handshape was the most difficult feature of a sign to identify correctly. In the younger group, errors of handshape alone (e.g., HARD as a response for NAME) constituted the largest category, followed by handshape plus movement (NOW for FINISH); these two categories alone accounted for more than half the errors. However, the younger students made more errors of place alone and more of place plus movement than the older subjects. For the younger group approximately 80% of the errors included an error of handshape, compared with 95% of the errors for the older group.

It was apparent from the students' performance that the task had both meaning-based and phonetic components. Students were often making closure based on meaning rather than simply copying accurately without actually recognizing the sign, as indicated by the fact that many of the subjects mouthed verbal labels as they signed their responses. On the other hand, the fact that students sometimes produced nonsense signs or distortions of real signs indicates that at times they were simply trying to copy what they saw.

What are the implications of the findings? The study tells us on a literal level that profoundly deaf children aged 8 through 12 in a residential program have the capacity to identify with a high degree of accuracy single signs that occur well out into the periphery, when the target for fixation is a simple shape (the camera lens) and when there is little or no competition for the children's cognitive attention. In other words, within these limits it is clear that the answer to the question posed in the title is yes, and that deaf children have the perceptual and cognitive abilities necessary to identify signs peripherally. Peripheral vision does have sufficient resolution for visual patterns to allow students to identify signs, given constraining information such as predictability derived from the use of common signs as stimuli, and in some cases the use of more readily perceived information (such as type of movement and place of the sign) to help narrow the field and zero in on the correct sign (among candidates with different handshapes). Considering that correct identification of signs was so high even when signs were presented in isolation, one must imagine that if context were supplied, accuracy would probably be very high indeed.

It is interesting to note that while the younger children performed well, they did not do as well as the older subjects. This finding is consistent with the literature on other types of peripheral vision tasks with hearing subjects, which show some developmental changes over time (Holmes, Cohen, Haith & Morrison 1977). Recent work has also found significant decreases between eight-year-olds, eleven-year-olds, and college students in the time needed to redirect cognitive attention to the peripheral field (Pearson & Lane 1989), and it seems likely that the speed with which a child could orient cognitively to the periphery would affect the ability to identify a sign correctly.

Having answered the basic question about the students' "raw ability" to read signs peripherally, how should we approach the question of how they might use this ability in real life? It is clear that we cannot extrapolate directly from performance on the experimental task, because the use of peripheral vision in real life will typically be complicated by competing demands for cognitive attention and varying degrees of complexity and predictability in the information to be attended to. The most important unknown is whether the students can attend to two things at once, and if so, what the limits of this ability are.

In short, much more research is needed in this area, and we should not assume from the data that students will necessarily learn signed information that they are not looking at directly. After all, visual and cognitive attention go together under most circumstances. On the other hand, the present results do suggest that, at a minimum, peripherally-seen signs have a potential for distraction in the classroom because of their meaning for the students.

REFERENCES

Holmes, D.L., Cohen, K., Haith, M.M., & Morrison, F.J. 1977. Peripheral visual processing. *Perception and Psychophysics* 22:571–577.

Parasnis, I. 1983. Visual perceptual skills and deafness: A research review. *Journal of the Academy of Rehabilitative Audiology* 16:161–181.

Pearson, D.A., & Lane, D.M. 1989. Visual attention movements: A developmental study. Paper presented at the biennial meeting of the Society for Research in Child Development, April, Kansas City, MO.

Siple, P. 1978. Visual constraints for sign language communication. *Sign Language Studies* 19:95–110.

Siple, P., Hatfield, N., & Caccamise, F. 1978. The role of visual perceptual abilities in the acquisition and comprehension of sign language. *American Annals of the Deaf* 123:852–856.

Swisher, M.V., Christie, K., & Miller, S.L. 1989. The reception of signs in peripheral vision by deaf persons. *Sign Language Studies* 63:99–125.

Analysis

David F. Armstrong

I n 1985 I had the opportunity to write a similar analysis of papers from the First International Symposium on Cognition, Education, and Deafness. At that time, there was an identifiable underlying theme in the papers that reflected a positive direction in research in this area. That theme was an increasing attention to the importance of context in the study of language development and in the teaching of language. It is encouraging that this trend appears to be continuing, at least in the set of papers in this chapter. Several other questions that were raised in the 1985 analysis have also now been taken up in these papers: The effects on learning to write of the use of nonalphabetic scripts, further investigation of brain organization in deaf signers, and the effect of mixed linguistic modes (i.e., simultaneous speech and signing) on educational achievement. Also evident is a shift away from a "deafness as deficit" paradigm to an explicit interest in identifying educational approaches that maximize the perceptual and cognitive *strengths* of deaf students.

It is especially noteworthy that the current research represented by these papers has moved beyond simple questions concerning the linguistic status of American Sign Language and other signed languages of the deaf, to more detailed questions concerning manageable strategies to enhance the learning and educational environments of deaf students. The range of these questions is impressive, from questions concerning the use of the entire visual-perceptual field, to questions regarding the effects of various forms of writing, to questions concerning appropriate use of various linguistic modes. It is also evident that increasingly sophisticated technologies and methodologies are being applied to these questions.

The paper by Swisher represents several of the points outlined above. The specific intent here is to identify how much of the visual field is available for decoding linguistic (signed) information. This question is particularly critical for educators of the deaf, because vision, unlike hearing, requires physically directed attention. A normal expectation would be that signs could be decoded only if received by foveal vision. Therefore, it is important for parents, teachers, and others to know if sign detection is possible in the peripheral vision. That is an important finding, with possible consequences for the design of educational settings for deaf students.

The diverse set of research questions considered among this group of papers suggests the need for individual consideration to be given to each of them; let us commence with the paper by Davey and King. This paper examines the effect of context on deaf students' ability semantically to decode unknown written words. An important finding is that training in the use of context to extract meaning might be beneficial for at least some deaf readers. This result again is indicative of a trend noted in 1985, toward more holistically based approaches to assessing the reading competence of deaf students. Explicit attention to the knowledge base of students can then be recommended as an integral part of curriculum in the education of deaf students.

Hoemann and Tweney provide a retrospective analysis of nearly two decades of work on the linguistic strengths of deaf students. Again, we need to be cognizant of the importance of moving away from a deficit model in deaf education, toward models that seek to take advantage of deaf students' strengths. Hoemann and Tweney present evidence concerning the extent to which processing strategies in ASL and English are similar, but it is also important to consider ways in which they may be different; just such a study is summarized by Fok, Klima, van Hoek, and Bellugi.

In 1985 we raised the question of whether deaf children might differ from hearing children in their ability to use various kinds of scripts, and Fok et al. present evidence that this varied use is indeed the case. Here we have evidence of differences in processing strategies that may actually give deaf students an advantage over hearing students in one aspect of written language learning. An additional point that we should now consider is whether there might be any advantage in introducing more complex scripts into the teaching of American students, given this information concerning the abilities of Chinese deaf students.

Lou, Strong, and DeMatteo consider the challenging and controversial question of whether simultaneous use of speech and sign in educational environments may have detrimental effects on general cognitive functioning. This question represents a direct challenge to the Total Communication philosophy that has dominated the education of the deaf for the past two decades in the United States. The reader should be cautioned against uncritical acceptance of the conclusions in this paper, because they are based on an extremely small sample. Nevertheless, it is possible to conclude that much more objective research is needed on the effects on educational achievement of various pedagogical strategies.

Lillo-Martin et al. explore the question of whether problems with reading for deaf students have to do primarily with syntactic problems (as is commonly assumed) or with lower-level processing difficulties. They find no evidence for syntactic deficits in the particular reading problem they investigate. However, the reader should keep in mind that these authors are considering a model that assumes universal grammatical features, and a problem with syntax for a deaf reader might be a problem in handling a particular construction in English, even if the student can handle the same logical construction in ASL. The authors recognize that there needs to be considerably more research in order to determine whether the measured reading deficits in poor deaf readers are, in fact, due to problems with phonological processing or instead with processing deficits at some other level.

Mittelman and Quinsland, and Nelson et al. take the alternative approach, not of looking at the factors that contribute to poor reading, but at new approaches that might lead to increased fluency in written English. Quinsland and Mittelman specifically underline the importance of taking greater advantage of the individual strengths of students who exhibit particular "cognitive styles." This idea seems admirable, but we will need considerable evaluation of the methods proposed and some consideration of the types of teachers who might be most likely to succeed in applying them. An extension of this idea would be to view the writing of deaf students more naturalistically and less critically. It might be worthwhile to develop a more systematic understanding of the particular constructions used by deaf students, not as errors, but as learned linguistic features. The path to moving the deaf writer closer to standard English might then be easier, as Quinsland and Mittelman suggest.

Nelson et al. advocate the increased application of interactive microcomputer technology to solving the problems of deaf readers and writers. In this approach, the interaction is with words and images stored in the microcomputer. This approach can be contrasted with interactive microcomputer approaches, such as the Electronic Networks for Interaction (ENFI) model developed at Gallaudet, in which the interaction is *through* the microcomputer and *with* people in real time at other microcomputer workstations. Given the ubiquitousness of the machinery, these approaches to the teaching of reading and writing deserve increasing attention. In fact, the ENFI method represents the rare application of a teaching methodology developed for use with deaf students teaching hearing second-language students and others having difficulty with the standard written language.

The papers in this section touch on many of the most important issues confronting those interested in the relationship between language development and the development of facility with written language in deaf children. This area continues to be very challenging, and one in which there are large areas of disagreement and equally large areas of almost completely uncharted territory. Perhaps the largest question that goes unexplored here is how best to teach written language skills to young deaf students with varying degrees of deafness and ages of onset. A plethora of methods and numerous claims abound, but there continues to be very little systematic, concrete evidence. As a result of this dearth of reliable research, parents, teachers, and deaf people themselves frequently have little to depend on when confronting a choice of fundamental importance in the education of the deaf child.

The methodological controversy has recently been reopened by three members of the Gallaudet University Department of Linguistics (Johnson, Liddell & Erting 1989). Their work represents a direct attack on the method of simultaneous communication involving concurrent speaking and signing in the education of deaf children. This work and the debate it has engendered point out once again how little is known about the ways in which deaf children actually learn and about what methods might be optimal to achieve various pedagogical goals.

In addition to the absence of clear and objective research results on pedagogical efficacy, there continues to be an absence of clearly defined and explicit goals at most levels of deaf education. These goals must extend beyond vague statements about increasing reading levels or rates of literacy. We need to adopt global goals that call for language *mastery* by deaf students. These goals should recognize that deaf students should be working toward mastery in *two* distinct language systems: written and/or spoken English and American Sign Language.

The route to mastery of the first system is very much open to debate and should be a primary focus of research during the final decade of the 20th century. There are several competing models, including those models based on current total communication/simultaneous communication approaches; bilingual approaches separating speech and American Sign Language, and literacy development through the use of ASL; and, finally, traditional oral-only approaches. All of these methods need objective evaluation with students who have various degrees of hearing loss and ages of onset. It is reasonably safe to say that as of the end of the ninth decade of the twentieth century, none has yet been reliably and credibly evaluated.

Development of mastery in ASL must clearly involve increasing participation in the educational process by educated deaf adults, and the success of the overall educational process should no longer be judged solely on the basis of literacy in English. It needs to be explicitly recognized that development of mastery of a language system is one of the primary goals of education, whether that language is English or ASL.

The outlines of a research program for the near future designed to assess the success of various approaches is relatively easy to delineate. The most fundamental observation is that a large-scale longitudinal approach will be essential. Execution of such a research program will require the cooperation of institutions and schools that have not hitherto always, or even usually, seen eye to eye. Problems of credibility remain. This problem was recently made clear by an exchange carried in the popular weekly publication *Science News*, in which the reliability of work carried out by researchers associated with the oralist method was questioned by a leading researcher at Gallaudet (Moores 1988). As the field becomes further fractionated into oralist, Total Communication, and bilingual camps, we can expect this sort of divisiveness at the research level to intensify.

There is a solution to this credibility problem, and it involves the introduction of experts in methodology from outside the field of deafness research, to adjudicate questions involving the reliability of research findings. It is the contention of this writer that any attempt to mount a large-scale longitudinal study of the sort outlined above must include outside adjudicators whose objectivity cannot be questioned. A further and final requirement is that any assumptions and any questions of moral and cultural values must be made explicit at the outset of such studies, and that deaf adults and parents of deaf children should have a major part in posing these questions.

REFERENCES

Johnson, R.E., Liddell, S.K., & Erting, C.J. 1989. *Unlocking the curriculum: Principles for achieving access in deaf education.* Gallaudet Research Institute Working Paper 89–3. Washington, DC: Gallaudet University.

Moores, D.F. 1988. Letter to the editor. *Science News*, October 15, 134(16):243.

RESEARCH QUESTIONS

1. How can we optimize the relationship between pedagogical goals and instructional methodology?
2. How can we balance ethical and cultural values in education against traditional notions of educational efficacy?
3. Which educational strategies optimize visual input?
4. Are there scripts or writing systems other than alphabetic ones that might prove advantageous for teaching literacy skills to young deaf students? Could alternative writing systems serve as steps toward the acquisition of alphabetic systems?
5. What is the proper role of computer-based technological innovations in the education of deaf children and in their acquisition of language skills?

5

COGNITIVE DEVELOPMENT

Education and the Social Construction of Mind: Vygotskian Perspectives on the Cognitive Development of Deaf Children

Nancy Bonkowski
James Gavelek
Tane Akamatsu

In his role as respondent from a researcher's perspective to the 1984 International Symposium on Cognition, Education, and Deafness, Donald Moores wrote that "probably the biggest discrepancy in relation to theory and its applications was the rare reference to the work of Vygotsky" (1985, p. 225). To this observation we can only say "Amen!" Though it has been more than a half a century since his death, no individual spoke more cogently of the relationship between education, cognition, and development, and none addressed more the central role of language in this relationship than did Vygotsky (Vygotsky 1985; Wertsch 1985b). We believe the implications of applying Vygotsky's sociohistorical theory to understanding cognitive development in deaf children to be as far-reaching as they are profound. Such an approach provides insights into understanding the cognitive difficulties that deaf children may experience while at the same time empowering the parents, teachers, and others who share in the responsibility for fostering development in deaf children. Sampson (1985) argued that much of cognitive psychology (i.e., information-processing and Piagetian) may be criticized for its individualistic bias, evidenced by the pervasive tendency of cognitive psychologists to look to the individual in explaining the origins of thought. Social factors are assumed to fulfill a facilitative, as opposed to formative, function in bringing out qualities that already reside within the individual. At issue here is what is, or ought to be, the fundamental unit of analysis in understanding the origins and processes of transformation of higher-order cognitive functions—the individual or the social? As a result of this bias, education (a fundamentally social process) is relegated to a facilitative role in the development of mind, rather than the formative role that it more properly deserves. And language, the primary vehicle by which education takes place, is treated as a formalistic system of signs, removed from its cultural-historical origins and from the social contexts in which it is practiced.

Vygotsky assumed that the communicative use of language in both formal and informal educational contexts is essential to cognitive development. Thus, unless extraordinary measures are taken, deaf children are likely not only to experience difficulty in acquiring communicative use of language, but also, by implication, difficulty in their cognitive development.

In what follows we first examine the essentials of a Vygotskian perspective of the cognitive development of both hearing children and deaf children. Then we discuss some of the implications of this perspective for conceptualizing educational research with deaf children.

ESSENTIALS OF VYGOTSKY'S THEORY

Three major, interrelated, themes characterize Vygotsky's conception of cognition: The importance of developmental analysis, the social origins of mind, and the sign-mediated nature of thinking (Wertsch 1985b; Kozulin 1986). Each of these themes holds the promise of providing insights that will help in conceptualizing the development of thinking in deaf individuals.

Developmental Analysis

Vygotsky maintained that to understand any psychological process, one must understand its origins and the mechanisms by which it changes (Vygotsky 1985). He distinguished among four levels of developmental analysis: (1) phylogenesis, (2) cultural history, (3) ontogenesis, and (4) microgenesis (Wertsch 1985b).

An analysis of *phylogeny*, the development of the species, enables us to understand what distinguishes humans from other animals. Bruner reminds us that a major transformation in our development as a species was our increasing ability to engage in deliberate teaching and learning, and more generally, the growth of culture (Bruner 1986). Indeed, it is this evolution of educability that has enabled us to create and pass on to our progeny uniquely human higher psychological functions.

For Vygotsky, the distinction between our elementary and higher psychological functions is of critical importance. Elementary psychological functions refer to those basic processes (e.g., involuntary attention or memory) that characterize humans, biologically, as a species. These processes are environmentally driven and beyond the control of the individual. In contrast, higher psychological functions are made possible by historically evolved, culturally shaped, and socially mediated tools and signs. Higher functions enable individuals to control and regulate their own behavior. Vygotsky believed that the transformation of processes such as those associated with memory from elementary to higher psychological functions is made possible through individuals' communicative acquisition of various sign systems, most notably language. In this context, *sign* and *sign systems* refer to arbitrary or conventional sets of symbols, utterances, or gestures used to express or convey an idea. Therefore, a sign system can be oral, manual, written, mathematical, etc. Misconceptions concerning deaf individuals as intellectually inferior or limited to concrete forms of thinking may result from a failure to understand the extent to which the development of higher psychological processes results from the communicative use of language (Pintner & Patterson 1917; Myklebust 1964; Lane 1988).

Cultural history refers to the sort of transformations that take place in an individual's thinking as a result of historical change and cultural variability in a society's institutions, tools, and practices. Vygotsky believed that understanding institutions (e.g., the family, the school, deaf communities) and their associated practices is important in understanding the nature of thinking of the people in that society. Thus the advent of schooling, with its emphasis on deliberate, taught learning of a literate kind, could be expected to significantly influence not only *what* we think but *how* we think.

Vygotsky suggested that the study of a society's artifacts or tools and how they are actually used is essential to understanding the people's thinking and development. He further distinguished between the sort of material tools that we typically associate with the term and what he referred to as psychological tools, most notably sign systems such as language and mathematics. This distinction is important in understanding Vygotsky's conception of cognitive development because he believed that while material tools such as the printing press or the hearing aid could bring about marked changes in our environment and thus in our thinking, it was through our appropriation and use of sign systems that we came to control and regulate our behavior with respect to that environment (Wertsch 1983). It is with respect to the development of manual sign systems (i.e., psychological tools) and their associated practices in communication both with and among deaf children that one finds that cultural-historical transformations have taken place. For example, manual sign systems have changed over time. They also present cultural variability at any given point in time. The extent to which these changes occur (over time and across cultures) has implications for how deaf peoples' thinking can change both over time and across cultures, and even within a culture.

Linguistic analyses of both spoken and signed languages have revealed that the same principles govern both kinds of languages, although one is perceived auditorily and the other visually (Siple 1978; Wilbur 1987; Klima & Bellugi 1979). However, the shift from an oral to a manual system of language representation may have brought a corresponding transformation in how deaf individuals are able to think. Thus, Bellugi and her colleagues suggested that there is a new sort of linguistic space created through the use of sign that has no analogue in oral language. They argue that this "space" enables individuals who communicate in sign to express and understand nuances not available to nonsigners (Bellugi et al. 1990).

Ontogenesis refers to the development of individuals over the course of their lifetimes. It is this level of analysis that we most often associate with the term *development*. Such development is assumed to result from the joint interaction of natural (i.e., biological) and cultural-historical factors. Indeed, Vygotsky assumed that the natural and cultural lines of development combine, resulting in the emergence of higher psychological functions (e.g., sign systems) that are not predicted by either alone. Thus qualitative transformations brought about by a person's use of cultural-historical tools characterize ontogenetic development.

Finally, *microgenesis* refers to the transformations in a psychological process that are observed to take place over relatively short periods of time (e.g., a single instructional episode). Thus, the intensive observation of events leading up to, during, and after Helen Keller's initial understanding of the concept *water* would be an example of microgenetic analysis. Vygotsky maintained that these "thick" analyses enable us to understand the origins of a process or a budding conceptual distinction before it becomes "fossilized." Microgenesis is a particularly important lens for studying the cognitive development of deaf children. The fine-grained analysis of adult-child interactions, with particular attention paid to the function of language and the role of dialogue, can contribute greatly to our understanding of higher psychological processes.

THE SOCIAL ORIGINS OF MIND

Vygotsky believed that one must look beyond the individual to the society in order to understand the development of higher psychological processes within the individual (Vygotsky 1985; Wertsch 1985b). This seemingly paradoxical conclusion is based on the assumption that higher psychological processes (e.g., language) only emerge in the interaction among individuals. Thus, Vygotsky distinguished between two different levels of social analysis, one the cultural-historical level discussed above, the other the more localized, face-to-face interactions that take place between members of a particular society.

This latter form of social influence is expressed well in Vygotsky's general genetic law of cultural development. He maintained that all higher psychological functions occur at two levels, first at the interpsychological level or between individuals and later at the intrapsychological level or within individuals. Thus, the road to independent problem solving, intentional memory, language, indeed consciousness itself, is to be found first in our interactions with others. It is through such interactions that individuals eventually appropriate and are able to independently use culturally shaped and historically evolved tools (e.g., sign systems). There are two dimensions to the process by which higher psychological functions are eventually internalized by the individual. The first is represented by the transition from social to individual control over these functions; the second refers to a movement from the public to the increasingly private (and thus unobservable) use of these processes.

An important and increasingly studied construct that follows from Vygotsky's general law of cultural development is the zone of proximal development (ZPD) (Rogoff & Wertsch 1984). Vygotsky distinguished between the ZPD and an individual's level of actual development. The ZPD refers to those functions that require the assistance of another for successful task completion. The level of development refers to those psychological processes that an individual has already internalized and consequently can carry out without assistance.

An understanding of the ZPD concept is especially important in conceptualizing issues related to the instruction and assessment of deaf children. Vygotsky maintained that all good instruction occurs in a child's zone of proximal development. Note that the zone concept does not simply represent another individual difference variable, but rather speaks to a child's ability to perform successfully within a particular cognitive task domain. As such, the zone represents a dynamically organized and changing area of instructability, mutually constituted by the individual as knower and the domain as known.

For the purposes of assessing deaf children, the ZPD cautions against oversimplified, able/disabled dichotomies. A child who is unable to perform successfully when presented with items on a conventional standardized, unassisted test format might be in the process of transformation and might perform successfully with assistance.

SEMIOTIC MEDIATION

It is informative to reiterate the role that Vygotsky attributed to social interaction in understanding the concept of semiotic mediation, for it is by means of interindividual communication through signs that individuals eventually become able to use those signs in the regulation of their own behavior. The major semiotic issue for Vygotsky was how sign systems, especially speech, control human activity. (Vygotsky used the term *speech* to refer to how language is actually practiced in discourse, to differentiate it from more formal approaches to studying language. In this paper, *speech* and other terms that refer to participants in interactive communication [e.g., speaker, listener] may be taken to mean either manual or oral language used in communicative discourse.) Vygotsky believed that it was essential to distinguish between language as a system of abstract signs and the ways that such signs were actually used for communication between individuals. We must look to language in action, that is, the actual discourse that takes place between individuals, if we are to understand the nature of thinking within the individual.

Dialogue

Vygotsky repeatedly emphasized the interrelationship of social, egocentric, and inner speech (1980). He believed that inner speech was dialogic in nature and argued that dialogue, rather than monologue, should be the starting point in the analysis of speech. Therefore, to understand the influence of social interaction on inner language it is necessary to analyze dialogic interactions (i.e., social speech) between adult and child. Dialogue provides a rich opportunity for participants to reflect upon and revise thoughts within temporarily shared realities. Wertsch (1980, 1985a) noted that dialogue allows for "selecting, foregrounding, and creating perspectives on reality ... dialogue permits a unique form of collaboration with others, provides children with an initial point of entry into many of the concepts and strategies found in a culture" (p. 112). Thus, dialogue is a powerful semiotic tool used in developing psychological processes in all children.

In order to study the nature of thinking in deaf children, it is necessary to analyze their dialogic use of language in interactions with other individuals—both hearing and deaf. Often deaf children have much less dialogic interaction with other deaf children than with hearing children. Adults may not have sufficient communication skills to sustain lengthy and complex interactions with deaf children, and these children may not have an adequately developed language system. These communication factors may help to explain research showing that hearing parents of deaf children use more direct imperatives and negative verbal responses, and ask fewer questions, than do parents of hearing children (Matey & Kretschmer 1985; Schlesinger 1988).

The resulting problems highlight the need for increased social interactions consisting of rich, sustained dialogue with many opportunities to practice language skills. Meaningful dialogic activity leads to the establishment of intersubjectivity and ultimately to the internalization of thought and language processes by the child.

Intersubjectivity

Intersubjectivity exists when two individuals are able to agree on the definition of a given task and are aware that they do so (Rommetveit 1985; Wertsch 1984). Participation in interaction leading to intersubjectivity requires that the listener (or signee) attend to the speaker's (or signer's) communicative act and engage in dialogue with the speaker. This point presupposes both a recognition on the part of the listener that what a speaker says may make sense, and an ability to use all available linguistic and extra-linguistic (i.e., contextual) cues to infer the meaning. These participatory factors are contingent upon contextually appropriate specification and elaboration of meaning by the speaker. The directive role of adults in establishing intersubjectivity is critical. Wertsch (1979) differentiates between successive levels of intersubjectivity that reflect a child's increasing ability to assume responsibility in a communicative dialogue. Initially, a child's definition of the task may be so different from that of the adult that little communication may be taking place. Intermediate levels of intersubjectivity are likely to be characterized by a child's enhanced ability to understand the nature of goal-directed action and to make the kinds of inferences needed to interpret the adult's directives even when they are implicit. Eventually the child is able to assume complete responsibility for carrying out a goal-directed task.

A lack of intersubjectivity indicates a failure to create a temporarily shared social reality through semiotic mediation. Unless deaf children have adequate access to a rich communicative environment, they will experience even greater difficulties than hearing children in entering into intersubjectivity (Stewart, Akamatsu & Bonkowski 1988). This case particularly applies when attempting to interact with deaf children in decontextualized situations (i.e., situations that refer to events removed in space and/or time). When word meaning is limited and when adequate syntactical structures allowing for conceptual flexibility and manipulation have not yet been developed in the deaf child, it is difficult to move beyond concrete and highly contextual settings.

The processes that enable intersubjectivity to be established are interactive. Consequently, an additional breakdown in the process of establishing and maintaining intersubjectivity may be the result of adults' inadequate communication skills. This situation is especially likely when there is a poor match between hearing, but nonsigning, adults (particularly parents and teachers) and the prelingually deaf children with whom they attempt to communicate (Quigley & Paul 1984; King & Quigley 1985; Bochner & Albertini 1988).

In a review of the literature on social interactions, Antia (1982) found that deaf children with severe language problems engage in shorter dialogues, interact less frequently with peers, and are more dependent on teachers than are their hearing peers and their linguistically more competent hearing-impaired peers. The degree to which the child becomes self-regulated greatly depends on the adult's ability to communicate and establish intersubjectivity. If there is poor communication between adult and child, this self-regulation may be limited to very concrete, contextual tasks that can be transferred visually.

IMPLICATIONS FOR EDUCATIONAL RESEARCH

For this book, whose primary theme is the conjunction of cognition, education, and deafness, the message from a Vygotskian perspective is as straightforward as it is powerful. More than simply playing a facilitative role, Vygotsky assumed education to be formative in the cognitive development of the individual, such that there emerge cognitive capabilities that result from formal and informal instruction and are not likely to occur in its absence. El'konin (1967) suggested that Vygotsky believed "instruction and cognitive development are organically connected." Vygotsky rejected the theory that mental development was a process of maturation and that it was determined from within.

Thus, while it is certainly true that not all teaching leads to learning, and not all learning occurs as the result of teaching, it is nevertheless also true that there are forms of knowledge that are likely to result only from the conjunction of the two. By means of learning what is taught, individuals become able to make conceptual distinctions and acquire ways of knowing (i.e., cognitive and metacognitive processes) that they would be far less likely to do if they were left to discover these cultural artifacts on their own.

It is to educational discourse in both its formal (e.g., school) and informal (e.g., family) contexts that we must direct our attention if we are to understand cognitive development in deaf children. We have seen that it is the nature of signs, the manner in which they are organized into systems, and the ways in which the signs are used in discourse between individuals that ultimately determine what gets internalized and how it is that individuals are able to think.

In these sign-mediated interactions with others, the child comes to appropriate historically evolved and culturally situated purposes as well as the mediational means by which these purposes are to be achieved. Because of the importance that Vygotsky placed upon the communicative use of language, his theory holds special relevance in our understanding of the relationship between education and cognition in deaf children.

A major precept of Vygotsky's theory is that learning is a transactional process, with the child representing only one half of an interacting partnership (White 1987). The other half is the more knowledgeable "other" (i.e., parent, teacher, or peer). Arguing from a Vygotskian perspective, White maintained that all children need a highly individualized and interactive setting as a basis for learning language. She further suggested that children with hearing losses are likely to experience a good deal of irregularity during their language-learning years, especially if the people in their environment are limited to using oral languages with reliance on acoustic signals. Schein and Delk (1974) reported that 90% of all prelingually deaf children come from hearing families, not from deaf families. Moreover, 85% of the teachers of deaf children are hearing females.

As a result of the irregular socialization interactions these children are likely to experience, the linguistic marking of everyday experience can become problematic for a deaf child. In school, teachers may misunderstand student questions and answer inappropriately, leaving students mystified by the explanation. Moreover, teachers may use communication strategies appropriate to hearing situations and may be inconsistent between what they sign and what they say.

What becomes apparent from a Vygotskian perspective is that the disposition to learn is inextricably bound to problems of meaning. How do deaf children eventually come to understand the meanings of concepts when the semiotic markers associated with those concepts seem arbitrarily applied? What are the respective responsibilities of teacher and child in achieving these meanings?

Many of the uniquely human purposes and means for achieving these purposes have evolved historically, vary culturally, and are appropriated by the individual as a result of social interaction. It cannot be assumed, however, that a child will automatically "own" these purposes and their associated means. Thus, while children are assumed to be active contributors to their own learning, questions remain as to what the object of this learning is to be and why. Whose purpose is it? The problem of mediating the motivation to learn is especially acute in deaf children because of the difficulties of establishing intersubjectivity. Why, for example, should a deaf child adopt the societal strategies and goals necessary to be literate if the child lacks even a rudimentary understanding of what literacy is?

To act is to behave purposively. And yet as we have seen, the purposes of social acts may not be shared by the deaf child, since these purposes are more often than not mediated through an inaccessible modality (e.g., oral language). Vygotsky believed that mastery of sign systems transforms an individual's existing (i.e., natural) forms of mental functioning into higher psychological processes. From such a perspective, the origin of cognitive and metacognitive strategies is to be found in an individual's interactions with knowledgeable others, within the contexts of sign-mediated, goal-oriented activity. It is as a result of such sign-mediated communication, in which one's behavior is being directed and controlled by others, that individuals eventually come to regulate their own behavior. Given the importance of social mediation in children's acquisition of cognitive and metacognitive strategies, it is no surprise that deaf students tend to be "strategy poor." A greater understanding is needed of conditions that foster the acquisition of strategic behaviors in deaf children as well as of those factors that may hinder such behaviors.

CONCLUSION

Vygotsky's sociohistorical theory enables us to understand and study both the difficulties observed in deaf children who do not have early access to communication and the normal functions observed in deaf children who have access to a rich language environment. It is a conception that potentially empowers those who are in a position to socially mediate the cognitive development of deaf children (i.e., parents, teachers, and peers), and in so doing, one that ultimately empowers deaf children themselves.

REFERENCES

Antia, S. 1982. Social interaction of partially mainstreamed hearing impaired children. *American Annals of the Deaf* 127:18–25.

Bellugi, U., O'Grady, L., Lillo-Martin, D., O'Grady, M., van Hoek, K., & Corina, D. 1990. Enhancement of spatial cognition in hearing and deaf children. In *From gesture to language in hearing and deaf children*, ed V. Volterra & C. Erting. New York: Spring-Verlag.

Bochner, J.H., & Albertini, J.A. 1988. Language varieties in the deaf population and their acquisition by children and adults. In *Language learning and deafness*, ed. M. Strong, 3–48. Cambridge, England: Cambridge University Press.

Bruner, J. 1986. *Actual minds, possible worlds.* Cambridge, MA: Harvard University Press.

El'konin, D.B. 1967. The problem of instruction and development in the works of L. S. Vygotsky. *Soviet Psychology* 5:34–41.

King, C.M., & Quigley, S.P. 1985. *Reading and deafness.* San Diego: College-Hill Press.

Klima, E., & Bellugi, U. 1979. *The signs of language.* Cambridge, MA: Harvard University Press.

Kozulin, A. 1986. The concept of activity in Soviet psychology: Vygotsky, his disciples and critics. *American Psychologist* 41: 264–274.

Lane, H. 1988. Paternalism and deaf people: An open letter to Mme. Umuvyeyi. *Sign Language Studies* 60:251–270.

Matey, C., & Kretschmer, R. 1985. A comparison of mother speech to Down's Syndrome, hearing-impaired, and normal-hearing children. *Volta Review* 87:205–213.

McAnnaly, P., Rose, S., & Quigley, S. 1988. *Language learning practices with deaf children.* Boston: College-Hill Press.

Moores, D.F. 1985. Reactions from the researcher's point of view. In *Cognition, education, and deafness: Directions for research and instruction*, ed. D.S. Martin, 224–228. Washington, DC: Gallaudet University Press.

Myklebust, H. 1964. *The psychology of deafness.* New York: Grune & Stratton.

Pintner, R., & Patterson, D. 1917. A comparison of deaf and hearing children in visual memory span for digits. *Journal of Experimental Psychology* 2:76–88.

Quigley, S.P., & Paul, P. 1984. *Language and deafness.* San Diego: College-Hill Press.

Rogoff, B., & Wertsch, J.V., eds. 1984. *Children's learning in the zone of proximal development.* San Francisco: Jossey-Bass.

Rommetveit, R. 1985. Language acquisition as increasing linguistic structuring of experience and symbolic behavior control. In *Culture, communication, and cognition: Vygotskian perspectives*, ed. J. V. Wertsch, 183–204. New York: Cambridge University Press.

Sampson, E.E. 1981. Cognitive psychology as ideology. *American Psychologist* 36:730–743.

Schein, J.D., & Delk, M.T., Jr. 1974. *The deaf population of the United States.* Silver Spring, MD: The National Association of the Deaf.

Schlesinger, H. 1988. Questions and answers in the development of deaf children. In *Language learning and deafness*, ed. M. Strong, 261–291. Cambridge, England: Cambridge University Press.

Siple, P., ed. 1978. *Understanding language through sign language research.* New York: Academic Press.

Stewart, D.A., Akamatsu, C.T., & Bonkowski, N. 1988. Factors influencing simultaneous communication behaviors in teachers. *The ACEHI Journal* 14:43–58.

Vygotsky, L.S. 1985. *Thought and language.* Cambridge, MA: Harvard University Press.

Wertsch, J.V. 1979. From social interaction to higher psychological processes: A clarification and application of Vygotsky's theory. *Human Development* 22:1–22.

———. 1980. The significance of dialogue in Vygotsky's account of social, egocentric, and inner speech. *Contemporary Educational Psychology* 5:150–162.

———. 1983. The role of semiosis in L.S. Vygotsky's theory of human cognition. In *The sociogenesis of language and human conduct*, ed. B.Bain, 17–31. New York: Plenum Publishing Corp.

———. 1984. The zone of proximal development: Some conceptual issues. *Children's learning in the zone of proximal development*, 7–18. San Francisco: Jossey-Bass.

———. 1985a. Adult-child interaction as a source of self-regulation in children. *The growth of reflection in children*, 69–97. New York: Academic Press.

———. 1985b. *Vygotsky and the social formation of mind.* Cambridge, MA: Harvard University Press.

Wilbur, R. 1987. *American Sign Language: Linguistic and applied dimensions.* 2d ed. Boston: Little, Brown & Co.

White, S.J. 1987. Lost for words: A Vygotskian perspective on the developing use of words by hearing-impaired children. *The Quarterly Newsletter of the Laboratory of Comparative Human Cognition* 9:111–115.

The Influence of Family Coping on the Cognitive and Social Skills of Deaf Children

Rosemary Calderon
Mark T. Greenberg
Carol A. Kusché

T he ability of hearing families to adapt to having a deaf child has been understudied. Those studies that have explored the dynamic between hearing parents and their deaf children have generally used a univariate model with a stress-pathology paradigm (Calderon 1988). This study uses a multivariate model to explore the varying levels of adaptation in these families.

This project used a family stress and coping model to conceptualize and assess the adjustment of deaf children and their hearing families. This model attempts to examine how the current adjustment of the parent and the child are affected by different types of intrapersonal and interpersonal family resources (e.g., social-cognitive strategies, personal beliefs, social support systems, utilitarian resources) as well as by demographic and historical factors regarding the child and hearing loss.

The presence of a deaf child in a hearing family is continuously felt as a source of potential stress. The parents' ability to cope with this chronic stressor is likely to affect both the family and the deaf child. A comprehensive model for examining and predicting adjustment by the child and by the family as a whole would require an assessment and analysis of coping resources to determine their effect on family and child outcomes. Folkman, Lazarus, and Schaeffer (1979) have developed an integrative model for conceptualizing how both the individual's appraisal of stress and his or her coping resources can predict adjustment. In the present study we apply this model to studying deaf children and their families.

Folkman et al. (1979) delineated five types of coping resources that moderate the adverse effects of stress. They have categorized the five domains of coping resources as: (1) problem-solving skills; (2) social networks; (3) utilitarian resources; (4) general and specific beliefs; and (5) health/energy/morale. Brief descriptions of these five domains of coping resources follow.

Problem-solving skills include the abilities to search out and analyze information, to generate alternatives, and to consider the consequences of the alternatives to challenging life situations. *Social networks* are defined as potentially supportive relationships (e.g., spouse, friends, extended family) that may facilitate positive adaptation, especially during crises. Social networks are assessed by examining the quantity and, more important, the quality of satisfaction with these networks. *Utilitarian resources* include such factors as income, outside intervention and professional services, and education. Several utilitarian resources specific to deafness are available to hearing-impaired children and their families, including sign language classes, parent support groups, early intervention programs, and contact with deaf adults in the community. *General and specific beliefs* include feelings of self-efficacy, locus of control, and religiosity or spirituality. Parents' attitudes, expectations, and beliefs about their deaf child's potential might also be considered under this coping resource. *Health/energy/morale* is the level of physical and emotional well-being both before and during the period of stress. This factor was not assessed in the present study.

These five coping resources are not mutually exclusive. They show some significant overlap (e.g., self-efficacy and parental depression; early intervention and social support). Although they have been divided into five domains for heuristic purposes, their interrelatedness is an important consideration when attempting to understand and explain outcome as a function of the individual's coping resources.

In summary, family and child adjustment can be viewed as a function of the coping resources available to the family and the moderating impact that these resources have on the perceived stress associated with the presence of a deaf child. The purpose of the present study was to apply this coping-based model to families of deaf children in an attempt to more fully understand differential adjustment outcome.

METHOD

Subjects

Thirty-six families were recruited from four school districts in northeastern Washington State. Of the participating families, 85% were white and 15% were of other ethnicities. The deaf child in each case lived at home and attended self-contained classrooms in public schools. The classes used a Total Communication approach.

Two parents were present in 66% of the families. Mean ages were 35 for mothers and 40 for fathers. Families were at a middle to lower middle socioeconomic level, and most parents reported having at least 12 years of education.

Twenty-seven girls and 9 boys comprised the sample, with a mean age of 10 years 2 months. Their mean unaided hearing loss was a 93 decibel loss (profound), and their mean aided loss was a 62 db loss (severe). Forty-four percent were first-born children.

Procedure

Parents were asked to complete several questionnaires and to participate in a home interview. The questionnaires were designed to assess four of the five domains of coping resources and to measure (1) the parents' current level of adjustment to having a deaf child, (2) the current level of personal and family life adjustment, and (3) the negative impact of current life experiences. To gain a better understanding of past stressors, concerns, and history with their deaf children, home interviews with both parents (when fathers were available) were conducted by two trained interviewers. Relationships with the school and other professional contacts regarding the child were also explored. Observed behaviors were rated by the interviewer after completion of the home visit. A standardized oral problem-solving task was also administered.

The parents were then assessed using a number of adjustment scales. Parents were asked to rate their adjustment to having a deaf child on a scale of 1 to 5 (1 = "very well," 5 = "it has always been difficult"). Their deaf children were assessed with an extensive battery of coping, academic-cognitive, social-cognitive, and neuropsychological measures. The measures used were as follows.

A. Parent Coping Resources and Outcome Measures

1. *Parent Problem Solving Assessment Task* (PPSAT) (Doyle 1985)
2. *Questionnaire on Social Support* (QSS) (Crnic, Greenberg, Ragozin, Robinson & Basham 1983)
3. *Marital Adjustment Scale* (MAS) (Locke & Wallace 1959)
4. Socioeconomic Status
5. *Structured Home Interview* (SHI) (Greenberg 1980; Greenberg, Kusché & Calderon 1984)
6. *Religiosity Measure* (RM) (Friedrich 1979)
7. *Parental Locus of Control Regrading Child's Handicap* (PLC) (DeVellis et al., in press)
8. *Life Events Survey* (LES) (Sarason, Johnson & Siegel 1978)
9. Life Satisfaction Rating from the QSS
10. Relationship Dimension, *Family Environment Scale* (Moos 1974)
11. Quality and Harmony of Home Atmosphere subscale from the *Home Quality Rating Scale* (Nahira, Meyers & Mink 1980)
12. *Questionnaire on Resources and Stress-Revised* (QRS-R) (Friedrich, Greenberg, & Crnic 1983)
13. *Parenting Experiences (Daily Hassles)* (PE) (Crnic & Greenberg 1985)

B. Child Outcome Measures

1. *Wechsler Intelligence Scale for Children-Revised*, Performance Scale (Wechsler 1974) (mazes subscale only)

2. Color Form Test and Trail Making Test for Children, *Reitan-Indiana Neuropsychological Test* battery (Boll 1981)
3. Reading Section of the Special Edition for Hearing-Impaired Students of the *Stanford Achievement Test* (Madden, Gardner, Rudman, Karlsen & Merwin 1972)
4. *Social Problem Situation Analysis Measure*-revised (SPSAM) (Elias, Larcen, Zlotlow & Chinsky 1978)
5. *Matching Familiar Figures Test* (MFF) (Kagan, Rosman, Day, Albert & Phillips 1964)
6. *Kusché Emotional Inventory* (KEI) (Kusché 1984)

Data Reduction of Coping Resources and Outcome Variables

The data collected on each subject was extensive and had to be reduced in a manner that would reflect and distinguish the four coping resources and parent and child outcomes. Both rational and empirical approaches were used to determine the resulting variables.

Parent and child outcome variables were divided into sets of outcomes for mothers and children. There were two maternal outcomes. The first focused on current feelings about overall personal life and family relationships. The second consisted of those feelings and attitudes specifically related to their adjustment to their deaf child. The child's outcome was assessed using performance on measures of cognitive and social-cognitive abilities.

RESULTS

This study primarily examined the relationship between (1) parent-coping resources and child adjustment, and (2) parent adjustment and child adjustment in families with a deaf child.

Maternal Coping Resources and Child Outcomes

Findings for the relationship between parent-coping resources and child outcomes suggest that maternal problem-solving ability was positively related to the child's emotional understanding and to cognitive and interpersonal problem solving. Furthermore, a high maternal belief in chance was negatively related to the child's cognitive and interpersonal problem-solving skills. Utilitarian resources (socioeconomic status, sophistication of child's education, and communication needs) were positively correlated with child's reading achievement.

Interestingly, the findings also showed that maternal life stress, social support, and religiosity (all coping resources) did not appear to be meaningfully related to the child-outcome measures.

Maternal Outcomes and Child Outcomes

Positive adjustment by the mother to her child was related to lower child impulsivity (MFF), greater cognitive flexibility (Color Form Trail), and higher social understanding (SPSAM).

Maternal assessment of her own general personal adjustment was not strongly related to the various child outcomes.

CONCLUSIONS

Maternal thoughts and beliefs specific to her deaf child appear to have greater impact on the child than do maternal perceptions of her own general adjustment or lifestyle (e.g., reported life stress and satisfaction with social support). This contrast in contributing factors is similar to findings reported by Calderon (1988) in examining parent coping resources and socioemotional adjustment in hearing families with deaf children.

Thus, although the presence of a hearing impairment is different from many other stressors because of its chronicity, the application of Folkman et al.'s (1979) stress and coping model to the broader social system of the family shows promise as a first step toward a better understanding and explanation of differential outcome in families with a hearing-impaired child.

The findings of the present study provide insights into the needs and concerns of deaf children and their parents. The findings indicate that parenting classes that provide improved communication skills and appropriate understanding regarding deafness, and that teach parents alternative solutions for problem situations, would probably be of great benefit to the family and to the child.

The present adaptation of a stress and coping model suggests possible guidelines for synthesizing the disparate variables examined in previous studies examining the effect of deafness. The model also suggests that "buffering" effects may exist between perceived stress and outcome, which is in direct contrast to the "main-effect" approach previously advanced. It also encourages the consideration of coping resources in the larger ecological contexts of the individual, the family, peer groups, and societal institutions. In summary, the stress and coping model provides a valuable tool for conceptualizing family and child adjustment to deafness.

REFERENCES

Boll, T.J. 1981. Halstead-Reitan Neuropsychological Battery. In *Handbook of clinical neuropsychology*, ed. S.B. Filskov and T.J. Boll, 577–607. New York: John Wiley & Sons.

Calderon, R. 1988. Stress and coping in hearing families with deaf children: A model of factors affecting adjustment. Ph.D. diss., University of Washington.

Crnic, K.A., & Greenberg, M.T. 1985. Parenting daily hassles: Relationship among minor stresses, family functioning, and child development in risk and normal five year olds.

Paper presented at the biennial meeting of the Society for Research in Child Development, April, Toronto.

Crnic, K.A., Greenberg, M.T., Ragozin, A.S., Robinson, N.M., & Basham, R.B. 1983. Effects of stress and social support on mothers and premature and full-term infants. *Child Development* 54:209–217.

DeVellis, R.F., DeVellis, B.M., Revicki, D.A., Lurie, S.J., Runyan, D.K., & Bristol, M. In press. Development and validation of the child improvement locus of control (CILC) scales. *Journal of Social and Clinical Psychology.*

Doyle, P. 1985. The effects of a problem-solving training program for mothers of developmentally delayed children. Ph.D. diss., University of Washington.

Elias, M., Larcen, S.W., Zlotlow, S.P., & Chinsky, J.H. 1978. An innovative measure of children's cognitions in problematic interpersonal situations. Paper presented at the American Psychological Association, Toronto.

Folkman, S., Schaeffer, C., & Lazarus, R. 1979. Cognitive processes as mediators of stress and coping. In *Human stress and cognition,* ed. V. Hamilton and D.W. Warburton. New York: John Wiley & Sons.

Friedrich, W.N. 1979. Predictors of the coping behavior of mothers of handicapped children. *Journal of Consulting and Clinical Psychology* 47:1140–1141.

Friedrich, W.N., Greenberg, M.T., & Crnic, K.A. 1983. A short form of the questionnaire on resources and stress. *American Journal of Mental Deficiency* 88(1):41–48.

Greenberg, M.T. 1980. Hearing families with deaf children: Stress and functioning as related to communication method. *American Annals of the Deaf* 125:1063–1071.

Greenberg, M.T., Calderon, R., & Kusché, C.A. 1985. Early intervention using simultaneous communication with deaf infants: The effects on communicative development. *Child Development* 55:607–616.

Hollingshead, A.B. 1975. *Four-factor index of social status.* New Haven, CT: Yale University.

Kusché, C.A. 1984. The understanding of emotion concepts by deaf children: An assessment of an affective education curriculum. Ph.D. diss., University of Washington.

Locke, H.J., & Wallace, K.M. 1959. Short marital-adjustment and prediction tests: Their reliability and validity. *Marriage and Family Living* 21:251–255.

Madden, R., Gardner, E.F., Rudman, H.C., Karlsen, B., & Merwin, J.C. 1972. *Stanford Achievement Test: Special edition for hearing impaired students.* New York: Harcourt Brace Jovanovich.

Meyers, E.C., Mink, I.T., & Nihira, K. 1981. *Home Quality Rating Scale Manual.* Los Angeles: University of California at Los Angeles.

Moos, R.H. 1974. *Preliminary Manual for Family Environment Scale.* Palo Alto, CA: Consulting Psychologists Press.

Sarason, I.G., Johnson, J.H., & Siegel, J.M. 1978. Assessing the impact of life changes: Development of Life Experience Survey. *Journal of Consulting and Clinical Psychology* 45:932–946.

Wechsler, D. 1974. *Manual for the Wechsler Intelligence Scale for Children-Revised.* New York: The Psychological Corp.

The Understanding of Time
by Deaf Pupils

Irmina Kaiser-Grodecka
Jadwiga Cieszyńska

In psychology, the issue of time focuses upon the experience of past, present, future, simultaneity, and duration. It is also possible to divide the question of time into two complementary concepts: (1) time as an order of events or as relation of the type *now, earlier, later,* and (2) time as duration or as the experience of the measure of time.

Orientation to time and mastery of the fundamentals of the time system are acquired through education. Educators claim that a child needs about twelve years to grasp time concepts and how our fundamental time system works, but the child will not master its details completely. Even children who can hear and speak have difficulty in understanding the relationships between time and velocity, or the inclusion of one duration time in another. It is also difficult for them to overcome the tendency to present the time sequence of phenomena so that it agrees with the order of spatial sequence. In the course of development, however, children surmount the barriers and start to use historical and prehistorical time; when they get older, they comprehend sidereal time, and finally a moment comes in their education when time is explained to pupils in terms of relativity theory.

However, in a special school for the deaf, both the younger pupils and the older ones ask questions and behave in ways that indicate that their understanding of time and related concepts is inadequate, incomplete, and often virtually non-existent. This fact not only seriously complicates the teaching process, but also disturbs the children's social functioning.

In their everyday experience, teachers observe deaf children's inability to abandon in their thoughts the "here and now" for the sake of different time, even time that refers to important events in childhood. The deaf child's time is viewed to be oriented toward the present.

However, the lack of grammatical tenses in the natural sign language used by Polish deaf children does not reflect a lack of time awareness. Even in cultures in which no clear conceptualization of time may be encountered, the awareness of time does exist (Whitrow 1979). Consequently, we should pose the question, What kind of intuition lies behind the time concepts created by deaf children?

For the understanding of distance and time relationships, historical events, and causal connections, it is necessary to create a sense of historical time. It is not actually experienced time, but an abstract category whose creation necessitates understanding of time experienced here and now. Thus, the time being experienced is primary to historical time, which is secondary. Secondary time cannot appear in the child's mind before primary time is crystallized. Observing mistakes in understanding of primary time leads to the conclusion that the deaf child has little sense of historical time or that the created concepts are inadequate.

In the adopted two-level model of time, the primary level consists of the following categories:

1. Understanding and feeling of the cyclic flow of time that evolves culturally (e.g., the division of a day according to meals or other fixed activities, division of the year into school and holidays, etc.).
2. The feeling of time flowing in accordance with measurable time units, such as those used in a clock or a calendar.
3. Ability to move from the "here and now" to the past and to the future.
4. Understanding the inclusion of one duration of time with another (e.g., older-younger relationships and grasping generation connections in a family).

Although the first two categories are based mainly on learning and memory, the remaining categories are intuitively shaped in the child's mind and are marked by high individualism.

The first stage of our investigations reported in this paper consisted of the evaluation of Polish deaf pupils' understanding of those temporal concepts that function within the third category of primary time.

Twelve-year-old deaf and hearing children and 15-year-old deaf children were studied. In the first experiment they had to answer 13 questions (given in writing and translated into sign language) about some remote events from both the past and the future. Both 12-year-olds and older deaf children experienced serious difficulty in correctly using simple time concepts. We graded answers flexibly (the children could answer either in sign language or in writing, and we tolerated grammatical mistakes), yet we were surprised by the large proportion of incorrect answers and by the fact that correct answers were scant and schematic. Even the children who chose to answer in sign language did not demonstrate any originality, fantasy, or imagination. Their statements were also brief and frequently incorrect. We were then faced with the question of whether or not these responses were caused by the children's limited language skills or by other factors.

In order to reduce as much as possible the role of language in revealing the students' ability to shift from the present to the past and the future, we used the following graphic form:

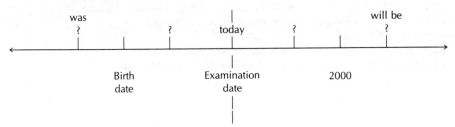

The task, assigning some concrete facts to the points marked on the time scale, turned out to be very difficult for the deaf children regarding both the past and the future. We were particularly surprised by the fact that they could remember hardly anything from their own lives. One may explain this finding by the fact that hearing children remember events from their childhood because parents or other adults relate family events over and over again ("When you were little . . ."). Deaf children of hearing parents cannot remember events from their past with the parents until the age of six because of the language barrier, and when they go to residential schools (as a large majority of them do), they cannot discuss their past with the people they live with because they do not know each other's past.

Imagining the future caused particular difficulty for the deaf children. They could not present their plans and dreams either orally or in sign language, unlike the hearing children, who presented surprisingly ingenious and colorful descriptions. This inability could be the result of limitations in imagination, which seems to be indirectly influenced by language and which normally flourishes when stimulated by children's literature, by listening to fairy tales, or by describing one's own dreams and fantasies.

In Poland, most parents of deaf children, whether hearing or deaf, want their children to have an oral education. It would therefore be interesting to perform the same tests with deaf children who had grown up with a rich environment of sign language from an early age—it is quite possible that these findings would be quite different for such deaf children.

The investigations confirm the conclusion that deaf 12-year-olds, as well as 14- and 15-year-olds, make a number of essential mistakes in the application of time concepts. They have serious difficulties in verbal descriptions of time phenomena. Investigators should remember that language, in addition to individual experience and intuition, is a strong factor in shaping time understanding. However, inappropriate and ill-functioning time concepts among deaf children do not result only from language deficits. We should bear in mind that time experience consists also of ordering events in a sequence, and other studies conducted at the Institute of Psychology of the Jagiellonian University demonstrate that the development of the sequential ordering processes in deaf children is seriously retarded, and this retardation may also have a disturbing influence on their understanding of time phenomena. Further investigation seems to be warranted, possibly in collaboration with other universities.

REFERENCES

Hall, E.T. 1987. *Bezglosny jezyk (The silent language)*. Warsaw, Poland.
Piaget, J. 1977. *Psychologia i epistemologia*. Warsaw, Poland.
Whitrow, J. 1979. *Time and sciences*. UNESCO.
Zajackowski, A., ed. 1988. *Czas w kulturze*. Warsaw, Poland.
Zwart, P.J. 1976. *About time*. New York: Elsevier North-Holland.

Language and Cognitive Development of Deaf and Hearing Twin Sisters

Barbara R. Schirmer

T he child's ability to symbolize is manifested in the emergence of language and imaginative play during the second year of life. As aspects of the child's developing semiotic function (Piaget 1962), both language and play require that the child be able to represent reality in thought.

Evidence for a developmental sequence in imaginative play that corresponds with early language development comes primarily from studies of normally developing children (Fein 1981; McCune-Nicolich 1981; Rubin & Pepler 1982; Westby 1980). Studies of handicapped children have confirmed the existence of relationships between imaginative play and language development (Casby & Ruder 1983; Lombardino & Sproul 1984; Owings & Workman 1983; Terrell, Schwartz, Prelock & Messick 1984). Investigations into the play of hearing-impaired children have shown that delays in one system correspond to delays in the other (Casby & McCormack 1985; Higginbotham & Baker 1981; Mann 1984).

The relationship between language and cognitive development is of central concern to educators of hearing-impaired youngsters. The purpose of the present study was to investigate this relationship within the special environment of twins, one deaf and one hearing. The specific research questions were: (1) What is the pattern of sameness or difference in their language and cognitive development, and (2) What aspects of their interaction enhance or impede language and cognitive development?

SUBJECTS AND PROCEDURE

The subjects were one pair of identical twin sisters who were 4 years 5 months old. Dena had normal hearing. Jill had a profound sensorineural hearing loss

205

that had been diagnosed at 18 months of age. She had no other handicapping condition.

Two 60-minute sessions were used to observe the twins. The first session took place in a clinical setting in which Jill interacted individually with the investigator. The second session took place in the children's home 13 days later. The materials were designed to elicit spontaneous, representative, expressive language and to encourage imaginative play. Included were a picture book of *The Three Bears* with no written words and three sets of Fisher-Price toys (doll house, farm, and garage) with miniature people.

SEMANTIC AND SYNTACTIC LANGUAGE ANALYSIS

Brown (1973) defined five stages of child language development that he considered to be central to the child's acquisition of meanings and forms. Within each stage he postulated the development of a major language process that accounted for much of the power within language and whose development in child language it had been possible to chart.

Jill produced 92 utterances in the individual session. Her mean length of utterance (MLU) was calculated to be 1.49, which placed her in Brown's Stage I language (1.00–1.99). Of the total corpus, 58.7% were single-morpheme utterances and 40% were two-morpheme utterances. She used six of the eight two-term semantic relations identified by Brown as indicative of Stage I language. She also demonstrated use of several Stage II grammatical morphemes. Of the Stage III modalities of the simple sentence, she used eight yes/no questions (use of voice intonation only without sentence transformation) but no wh-questions (questions requiring that a constituent be specified), no negatives, and no imperatives. She used no Stage IV embedding of one sentence within another and one Stage V coordination of a simple sentence with the conjunction *but*.

Jill's eighteen utterances in the joint session with Dena demonstrated considerably less language than she had produced in the individual session. Of this total, 77.8% were single-morpheme utterances and 22.2% were two-morpheme utterances. She used one of the Stage I 2-term semantic relations and no Stage III grammatical morphemes. She used no features from the other three stages. Her MLU in this session was 1.33.

Dena produced 276 utterances in the joint session. Her MLU was 6.01, which placed her well beyond Stage V language (3.75 +). She demonstrated the use of all the Stage III modalities. She also used the three types of embedded sentences from Stage IV, including object-noun phrase complements, embedded wh-questions, and relative clauses. Of the Stage V coordinators, Dena used *and*, *because*, *but*, and *so*.

ANALYSIS OF FUNCTIONAL LANGUAGE USE

Halliday (1975) considered the learning of language to be essentially the learning of a semantic system. He found that this content-expression system is well under way before the child has any words or structures at all. Halliday related this system of meanings to linguistic function—the functions that language serves for the child. He found that the developing child used six functions—instrumental, regulatory, interactional, personal, heuristic, and imaginative. He found that the seventh function, the informative, did not emerge until considerably after the others and is dominant in the language of adults.

Of Halliday's seven categories of language functions, Jill used five in the individual session. The largest percentage of these were interactional (70.7%). She also used the imaginative (22.7%), heuristic (9.3%), personal (9.3%), and instrumental (8%). These functional categories overlap so that one utterance can serve more than one function. Analysis of the functions Jill used in the joint session revealed her ability to use language differently within a different environment. Although the majority of her utterances were still interactional (61.1%), she used the regulatory function in this setting (33%), which she had not used at all in the individual session. She also used the instrumental (11.1%) and the personal (5.6%) functions.

Dena's language was largely informative (70.7%). In addition, she used the heuristic (21.3%), imaginative (21.3%), interactional (10.7%), personal (4%), regulatory (2.7%), and instrumental (1.3%) functions.

ANALYSIS OF INTERACTION

Interaction patterns were analyzed using Savic and Jocic's (1975) description of five dialogue patterns observed between twins. It was found that Jill and Dena engaged in only one of the patterns—quarreling. In approximately 50% of their dialogue, they quarreled either verbally or nonverbally. During the remainder of their interaction, they requested and demanded things of each other or identified play objects. They did not use the other four patterns indicative of twins' interaction—joint statements, mutual correction, verbal games, or repeating. Within the one-hour session, Jill predominantly used oral and sign language to communicate. She also used some gestures.

Within the joint session, her oral language was largely babbling (which she had not used at all in the individual session). She used few signs and many gestures. She used the picture book and pictures to demonstrate concepts rather than expressing them through language. When she interacted with Dena, she frequently pointed in order to express herself. Dena used few signs when interacting with Jill and simplified her language and exaggerated her speech when talking directly to her twin.

ANALYSIS OF IMAGINATIVE PLAY

Imaginative play was analyzed using Westby's (1980) cognitive play scale. In the individual session, Jill demonstrated one type of imaginative play behavior representative of children at Stage V. She was able to represent daily experiences with symbolic play. She also demonstrated one type of Stage VIII play—the ability to play imaginatively with Fisher-Price toys which, as miniatures, are considered less realistic in nature. In the joint session, Jill demonstrated no imaginative play behaviors.

Dena demonstrated Stage X symbolic play behaviors. She played an equivalent amount of time with toys more representative of daily experiences (e.g., the house) as with toys less representative of daily experiences (e.g., the barn). She developed a number of different scenarios or story lines for her imaginative play with all the toys. She engaged in dialogue with the toys and used planned pretend (i.e., she talked about anticipated or planned play).

DISCUSSION

Language analysis revealed that the twins were at very different stages of language development. The hearing twin, Dena, expressed her semantic intentions in a range of complex syntactic forms. Her functional uses of language were very similar to the adult's. The deaf twin, Jill, used the semantic relations found in the language of children at the early stages of development. The grammatical morphemes she used were those that Brown observed to be the first in the order of acquisition by normally developing children. Her language functions were indicative of what Halliday called a transitional phase between a simple content-expression system (with no vocabulary and no grammar) and the ability to use language to express all social meaning.

Analysis of interaction indicated that the twins communicated with each other largely to identify common play objects and to argue about them. Jill used considerably less language with her sister than she used with the investigator, and the language she did use was grammatically simpler. Dena also simplified her language when communicating with her twin as compared to the language she directed at the investigator. The girls did not appear to have developed any special twin language that was idiosyncratic of their interactions with each other.

Analysis of their imaginative play demonstrated that both girls were able to engage in symbolic play behaviors, although at different levels of development.

Language and imaginative play both require that the child be able to symbolize. This capacity for symbolic functioning was found in both the deaf and hearing twin sisters. The pattern of differences in their language and imaginative play levels provides evidence that there is a relationship between the development of language and the development of imaginative play in the child's cognitive system.

Given an environment offering considerable opportunity to play with a same-age, genetically identical sister, it is unclear why the deaf and hearing twins were unable to *enhance* each other's linguistic and cognitive development. The major implication is that merely bringing young children of similar ages together does not necessarily create an environment of effective communication and interaction that will concomitantly stimulate language and cognitive development. By understanding the interrelationship of the symbolic processes in cognition and the effects of the environment on the development of these processes, educators can actively help young children to stimulate each other through language and play.

REFERENCES

Brown, R.A. 1973. *A first langua͜ e early stages.* Cambridge, MA: Harvard University Press.

Casby, M.W., & McCormack, S.M. 1985. Symbolic play and early communication development in hearing impaired children. *Journal of Communication Disorders* 18:67–78.

Casby, M.W., & Ruder, K.F. 1983. Symbolic play and early language development in normal and mentally retarded children. *Journal of Speech and Hearing Research* 26:404–411.

Fein, G.G. 1981. Pretend play in childhood: An integrative review. *Child Development* 52:1095–1118.

Halliday, M.A. 1975. *Learning how to mean.* New York: Elsevier North-Holland.

Higginbotham, D., & Baker, B. 1981. Social participation and cognitive play differences in hearing impaired and normally hearing preschoolers. *Volta Review* 83:135–149.

Lombardino, L.J., & Sproul, C.J. 1984. Patterns of correspondence and non-correspondence between play and language in developmentally delayed preschoolers. *Education and Training of the Mentally Retarded* 19:5–14.

Mann, L.F. 1984. Play behaviors of deaf and hearing children. Paper presented at the International Symposium on Cognition, Education, and Deafness, June, Washington, DC. (Available as ERIC Document Reproduction Service No. 247 722)

McCune-Nicolich, L. 1981. Toward symbolic functioning: Structure of early pretend games and potential parallels with language. *Child Development* 52:785–797.

Owings, N., & Workman, S. 1983. Assessing the representational behaviors of play, language, and drawings in normal and language-delayed children. Paper presented at the Annual Montana Symposium on Early Education and the Exceptional Child, April, Billings, MT. (Available as ERIC Document Reproduction Service No. 242 178)

Piaget, J. 1962. *Play, dreams, and imitation.* New York: W.W. Norton & Co.

Rubin, K.H., & Pepler, D.J. 1982. Children's play: Piaget's views reconsidered. *Contemporary Educational Psychology* 7:289–299.

Savic, S., & Jocic, M. 1975. Some features of dialogue between twins. *Linguistics* 153:33–52.

Terrell, B.Y., Schwartz, R.G., Prelock, P.A., & Messick, C.K. 1984. Symbolic play in normal and language-impaired children. *Journal of Speech and Hearing Research* 27:424–429.

Westby, C.E. 1980. Assessment of cognitive and language abilities through play. *Language, Speech, and Hearing Services in Schools* 11:154–168.

Intellectual Structure of Hearing-Impaired Children and Adolescents

Abraham Zwiebel

ognitive development in deaf individuals has been explained from numerous perspectives, two of which are Myklebust's (1964) organismic shift hypothesis and Furth's (1971) view that no difference exists between deaf and hearing subjects in conceptual performance, at least up to the level of concrete operative thinking. Myklebust hypothesized that deaf individuals are quantitatively equal to hearing individuals, but qualitatively inferior in that the deaf develop a more "concrete" and therefore less abstract intelligence. More recently, Moores (1982) concluded that deaf and hearing children are similar across a wide range of areas traditionally related to the study of cognitive and intellectual abilities.

The factor analytic approach has been one way to carry out research in the development of the cognitive structure of deaf individuals compared with that of hearing individuals.

Bolton (1978) compared the factor structures for deaf and hearing children, aged 3 to 10, based on the Hiskey-Nebraska Test of Learning Ability (H-NTLA). He concluded that the results of his work and other factor analytic studies generally agreed with Myklebust's organismic shift hypothesis and did not support Furth's position. Braden (1984) compared factors extracted from the normative samples of the Performance Scale of the Wechsler Intelligence Scale for Children (WISC-RPS) and the Hiskey-Nebraska Test of Learning Aptitude (HNTLA) with

This research has been supported by Israel Foundations trustees (a part of the Ford Foundation).

factors that emerged from normative samples of deaf individuals on these non-verbal intelligence tests. He reported that all sets of data supported arguments that deaf and hearing people do not exhibit major qualitative differences in nonverbal intellectual structure. More recently, Ljubesic (1986) investigated the factor structure in cognitive abilities of Yugoslav deaf children (ages 7.5 to 8.5 years) examined with the WISC and ITPA subtests adapted to Serbo-Croat. When factor analysis was performed on only nonverbal variables, the solution obtained was highly similar for both the deaf and hearing populations.

In a previous study conducted by the author (Zwiebel & Mertens 1985a), the Snijders-Oomen Nonverbal Intelligence Test (SON) was used as the measure of intelligence. This test has been adapted to Hebrew, and Israeli norms were created (Zwiebel & Rand 1978; Zwiebel & Mertens 1985b).

The SON is appropriate for assessing the intelligence of deaf children because

1. The ability of the experimenter to communicate the instructions does not affect the child's performance;
2. Heavily verbal tasks common to many intelligence tests are avoided; and
3. The test covers the entire intellectual span, including abstract thinking.

Table 1 summarizes the students' results on the SON.

The trend in the development of cognitive structure for deaf subjects has been found to be from a less organized to a more organized state of general intelligence and from a perceptual and visual orientation to a perceptual and abstract thinking orientation. As deaf children grow older, the perceptual component seems to merge into the general intelligence factor as the abstract thinking factor emerges. When coping with the abstract thinking problems of the nonverbal SON test,

TABLE 1   Factor Analytic Results on the Snijders-Oomen Nonverbal Intelligence Test for Deaf and Hearing Children by Age Level

Subscales	All Deaf Factor	Deaf (ages 6 – 9) Factor			Deaf (ages 10 – 12) Factor		Deaf (ages 13 – 15) Factor		Hearing (ages 10 – 12) Factor	
	1	1	2	3	1	2	1	2	1	2
Mosaic B	.56	.03	.90	.02	.04	.82	.65	.22	−.18	−.13
Block Design	.61	.56	.29	.05	.35	.40	.15	.66	.64	.40
Picture Memory	.57	.20	.06	.71	.61	.17	.39	.40	.69	−.09
Picture Series A	.58	.33	.38	.05	.57	.17	.57	.12	.04	.13
Picture Series B	.73	.95	.03	.06	.51	.32	.53	.56	.60	.27
Picture Analysis	.62	.33	.47	−.28	.56	.25	.67	.35	.00	.17
Figure Analysis	.44	.18	.08	−.21	.33	−.13	.25	.68	.37	.80

older deaf children seem to use abstract thinking skills rather than relying solely on perceptual skills. The most important difference between the deaf and hearing subjects of the same age was the weak presence of an abstract thinking component, accompanied by a strong perceptual factor in the deaf group. The deaf subjects appear to rely on visual-perceptual skills, while their hearing peers rely on abstract thinking skills. However, when hearing subjects are compared to a group of older deaf subjects, similar structures emerge on a general intelligence factor and on an abstract thinking factor.

One interpretation of the results is that the SON's visual stimuli may be processed more verbally by the hearing subjects and more visually by the deaf subjects. When coping with such visual stimuli, deaf individuals thus tend to use a more visual thinking technique (as is seen in the single factor in the deaf population as a whole). Overall, hearing subjects tend to use a verbal technique in coping with the same stimuli. The older deaf children, aged 13 to 15, appear to adopt a technique similar to that of the hearing.

The theoretical implications of these results suggest that neither Myklebust's nor Furth's positions accurately explain the intellectual development of deaf individuals. Since the previous study was conducted only with deaf children aged 6 to 15 and hearing children aged 10 to 11, our basis for comparison was limited. In order to explore alternative explanations more fully, the present study is expanded in the following ways:

1. By widening the age range in the deaf sample to ages 14–18;
2. By sampling of the same range (6–18) for the hearing children;
3. By using the same instrument (i.e., the SON).

By making these changes from the previous study, the entire course of development from elementary school to adulthood can be followed. Similarly, the addition of hearing children from the full age range allows a comparison with age-wise peers in the deaf population and an examination of the pattern of cognitive development as a function of response to nonverbal stimuli.

METHODOLOGY

The subjects consisted of 130 deaf children ages 14 to 18 with approximately equal numbers in each age group. The hearing sample consisted of 169 children (52% boys and 48% girls) ages 7, 9, 11, 13, 15, and 17 with approximately equal numbers in each age group. They were matched with the deaf population for socioeconomic background. The SON was administered individually to all subjects by trained psychologists who followed the test manual instructions. The administration was the same for both deaf and hearing subjects. Background information was collected from school files. Seven subtests of the SON were used in the study: MOSAIC B, Block design, Picture Memory, Picture Series A and B, Picture Analogy, and Figure Analogy.

RESULTS

A factor analysis with seven subtests of the SON was conducted on the data with VARIMAX as a rotated method on various sub-samples (i.e., separate age groups for hearing and deaf children). Table 2 reports the findings of a factor analysis on the data of hearing children ages 6 to 9 compared to those of hearing children from the previous study. The findings show a significant structural difference between the two populations. Hearing children already reveal a more organized structure at this age. Similarly, a "verbal" thinking factor that involves a memory component (Factor 1) was also found in this group. The second factor includes a more "visual" component. The LISREL VI program (Joreskog & Sorbom 1984), whose purpose is to test for goodness of fit, shows a significant difference between the data from the hearing group and the factorial model of the deaf group (X^2 = 58.23; df = 14; α = 0.000). Comparison of the findings of factor analyses of deaf children ages 13 to 15 with a group of hearing children of the same age shows a greater similarity within this age group than in younger children. Table 3 compares the findings of the deaf (n = 63) and hearing (n = 101) groups of high school age (14–18). A comparison of the two groups shows an almost perfect fit between them. The first factor includes an abstract thinking and mem-

TABLE 2   Factor Analytic Results of the SON for Deaf and Hearing Children Ages 6 – 9

Subscales	Hearing Factor		Deaf Factor		
	1	2	1	2	3
Mosaic B	.81	.05	.03	.90	.02
Block Design	.82	.28	.56	.29	.05
Picture Memory	.55	.29	.20	.06	.71
Picture Series A	.02	.91	.33	.38	.05
Picture Series B	.46	.70	.95	.03	.06
Picture Analogy	.32	.63	.33	.47	−.28
Figure Analogy	.78	.27	.18	.08	−.21

TABLE 3   Factor Analytic Results of the SON for Deaf and Hearing Children Ages 14 – 18

Subscales	Hearing Factor			Deaf Factor		
	1 (30.5%)	2 (16%)	3 (14%)	1 (36.4%)	2 (17.6%)	3 (14.8%)
Mosaic B	.08	.84	−.05	.24	.77	−.21
Block Design	.86	−.07	.23	.72	.05	.32
Picture Memory	.32	−.64	.00	.67	−.01	−.23
Picture Series A	.16	−.36	−.49	−.12	.82	.24
Picture Series B	.63	−.06	−.05	.80	.11	.05
Picture Analogy	.08	−.19	.85	.15	.02	.91
Figure Analogy	.80	−.11	−.19	.83	.01	.26

ory component; the second factor is perceptual; and the third is a more "visual" thinking component. The LISREL-VI method was also implemented. The findings indicate fit between the groups.

DISCUSSION

The general trend in the development of cognitive structure has been found to be identical in deaf and hearing children toward the end of the period of cognitive development. The formation of the structure of a general factor of intelligence that includes a "verbal" nucleus of formal thinking along with a perceptual factor appears gradually in the hearing group even at an early age. In the deaf group, in contrast, a structure like this begins to emerge only at ages 13 to 15. At ages 6 to 12 there is a slower formation of the structure. On the other hand, among the younger deaf children, there is evidence of a strong perceptual factor, along with a recognizable visual-perceptual orientation and cognitive mechanisms based more on this orientation.

The findings gain additional support through the use of the recently developed LISREL method. This technique permits scientific examination of goodness of fit for factorial structures. Comparing the relatively large groups of adolescents shows a significant fit between the structures.

The theoretical implications for the field of cognitive development of the deaf are even greater. As emphasized in the previous study, there is no confirmation either of Myklebust's theories nor of Furth's. Thus the internal structure of deaf and hearing individuals is identical at the end of the course of development, although the level of development across ages is different. These findings are identical to those of Braden (1984) even though he tested subjects on the performance section of the WISC, which does not include thinking tests. The findings of the present study are more extensive, however, since the SON includes a thinking component.

It is noteworthy that a comprehensive examination of a population of deaf children who use sign language and are educated through manual teaching methods could complement the picture and explain the reasons for the different rates of development of the two populations. Findings similar to the deaf groups in the present study will strengthen the generality of the theory with regard to the pattern of development of the cognitive structure of the deaf. In other words, lack of auditory language exposure and concentration on the visual channel could explain the slower process of formation of the verbal component, and deaf children depend on a strong perceptual component at an early age. Research results from signers who do not begin to form the "verbal" component until an older age level or who display a stable visual component during adolescence are likely to require a different and more far-reaching approach to explain the findings, one that is possibly closer to Myklebust's (Kelly et al. 1976; Tomlinson et al. 1978). This explanation argues for a special cognitive structure for the deaf, one that is visual and more natural and original. The cognitive structure with higher verbal loadings can be attributed to the influence of an oral environment or adaptation to the environment. A more venturesome interpretation, however, might claim that the deviation of the "natural" structure from its course eventually leads to lower performance scores in the deaf population in comparison to hearing peers, while deaf children exposed to a manual language at home (deaf children of deaf parents) and at school will perform at a level equal to hearing peers.

The overall significance of this research lies not only in its theoretical implications, but also in the better understanding of the techniques used by deaf children and adolescents, which will enable educators to raise deaf children's achievement levels in all areas.

REFERENCES

Bolton, B. 1978. Differential ability structure in deaf and hearing children. *Applied Psychological Measurement* 2(1):147–149.

Braden, J.P. 1984. The factorial similarity of the WISC-R performance scale in deaf and hearing samples. *Personality and Individual Differences* 5:403–409.

Furth, H.G. 1971. Linguistic deficiency and thinking: Research with deaf subjects, 1964–1969. *Psychological Bulletin* 76:58–72.

Joreskog, K.G., & Sorbom, D.S. 1984. *Analysis of linear relationships by the method of maximum likelihood.* Uppsala, Sweden: University of Uppsala.

Kelly, R.R., & Tomlinson-Keasey, C. 1976. Information processing of visually presented picture and word stimulation by young hearing-impaired and normal-hearing children. *Journal of Speech and Hearing Research* 19:628–638.

Ljubesic, M. 1986. A contribution to the study of the structure of cognitive abilities of the deaf. *International Journal of Rehabilitation Research* 9:290–294.

Moores, F.S. 1982. *Educating the deaf: Psychology, principles, and practices.* Boston: Houghton-Mifflin.

Myklebust, H. 1964. *The psychology of deafness.* New York: Grune & Stratton.

Tomlinson-Keasey, C., & Kelly, R.R. 1978. The deaf child's symbolic world. *American Annals of the Deaf* 123:452–458.

Zwiebel, A., & Mertens, D.M. 1985a. A comparison of intellectual structure in deaf and hearing children. *American Annals of the Deaf* 130:27–31.

———. 1985b. A factor analytic study of intellectual development in deaf and hearing children. In *Cognition, education, and deafness: Directions for research and instruction,* ed. D.S. Martin, 151–155. Washington, DC: Gallaudet University Press.

Zwiebel, A., & Rand, Y. 1978. *S.O.N. Test for Israeli deaf children: New norms and applications.* Bar-Ilan, Israel: Publications of Bar-Ilan University (Hebrew).

Symbolic Play Behaviors of Normally Developing Deaf Toddlers

Patricia E. Spencer
David Deyo
Natalie Grindstaff

C hildren's play has long been acknowledged to be a source of information about the content and sophistication of their thoughts. Symbolic play (sometimes called "pretend" or "pretense" play) is thought to be tied especially closely to the development of other representational or semiotic functions (Piaget 1962) and, as such, to provide an index of cognitive development or maturity (Bruner, Oliver & Greenfield 1966; Lowe 1975; McCune-Nicolich 1981; Nicolich 1977). Observations of play behaviors have been proposed to provide an alternative means of measuring the cognitive development of children with some form of language delay (Ungerer, Zelazo, Kearsley & Kurowski 1979). Thus, assessment of play behaviors could provide a helpful means of measuring the cognitive development of children with a significant hearing loss and concomitant delayed language acquisition. Use of such an assessment approach assumes, however, that neither language delay nor lack of auditory input during critical developmental periods negatively affects the level of play that a child demonstrates. Neither assumption has yet been shown to be valid.

Available studies of the play behaviors of deaf children raise doubts about the quality and quantity of their play compared to that of hearing children. Darbyshire (1977) reported that deaf children engaged in less pretend ("make-believe") play, produced fewer episodes of play in which one object is substituted for another, and generally exhibited less "mature" play than did hearing children. Other researchers have similarly reported that the symbolic play of deaf children was deficient or delayed for age (Gregory 1985; Higginbotham & Baker 1981; Singer & Lenahan 1976). In contrast, Mann (1985) found no qualitative differences in levels of play of deaf and hearing children when the language accompanying their play was excised from the analysis. She found a quantitative difference between the groups, however, with deaf children engaging in symbolic play less of the available time.

The source of differences between symbolic play of deaf children and hearing children has been suggested to be due to or associated with deaf children's language delay. Several authors (Casby & McCormack 1985; Pien 1985; Vygotsky 1978) have reported that deaf children with higher language skills show play behaviors beyond those of their peers with lower language skills. These findings suggest that, in the absence of any delay in language acquisition, deafness (i.e., the lack of auditory input) should have no negative effect on children's play behaviors.

Our study addressed this possibility by comparing symbolic play of hearing children with that of deaf children whose parents are deaf and use sign language fluently. Deaf children like those in our study have been found to develop language at normal rates in the visual-manual modality (Bellugi & Klima 1975). We predicted, therefore, that no differences would be found between the symbolic play of our deaf and hearing subjects. The lack of consistent auditory input throughout the sensorimotor period would therefore fail to have any negative effect on early symbolic abilities as shown in symbolic play.

METHODS AND PROCEDURES

Four deaf toddlers with deaf mothers and four hearing toddlers with hearing mothers participated. The children ranged from 24 to 28 months old. All mothers had graduated from college. Deaf children had congenital hearing losses in the severe/profound to profound range and were not using amplification. Their mothers used either ASL or a form of Sign English as their primary language. Hearing children were from English-speaking homes. All children were evaluated using either the Alpern-Boll Developmental Profile II or the Bayley Scales of Mental Development and were determined to be functioning developmentally within norms for age.

Twenty minutes of play between mother and child were videotaped in the family's home. Mother and child were provided with a box of toys containing most of those used by Nicolich (1977), and the mother was instructed to "play with [the child] just as you would when you have some free time during the day."

The coding system was based on that of McCune-Nicolich (1980, revised 1983) and included five levels of symbolic play (Figure 1). We modified the original system in order to allow differentiation between verbal and nonverbal preplanning of play activities and to elaborate somewhat the highest subcategory of play (5.3) so that it included both logical sequencing and preplanning of the first activity in the sequence. (See Spencer, Deyo & Grindstaff, 1990, for further description of the coding system.)

Before the tapes of the deaf dyads were coded, a deaf native signer prepared transcripts of the mother and child language. Inter-rater reliability, computed on three of the eight tapes, was 96.7 for assignment of play levels 2 and 3, and 77.8

LEVEL 1: PRE-SYMBOLIC
Child demonstrates correct function of object. No evidence of pretending.

LEVEL 2: AUTO-SYMBOLIC
Child pretends with an object. Play involves the child's own body and behaviors.

LEVEL 3: SINGLE SCHEME SYMBOLIC
Child extends play beyond self by (a) including other participants (mother, doll), or (b) pretending at activities normally performed by another person.

LEVEL 4: COMBINATIONS
Child combines several play behaviors which focus on an object of a theme.
    4.0   Single action repeated in different locations or on different objects.
    4.1   Single action repeated with different participants.
    4.2   More than one action is used with the same or related objects.
    4.3   More than one action is used with the same or related objects, and actions occur in a logical sequence.

LEVEL 5: PLANNED SYMBOLIC
Child shows evidence of preplanning play behaviors, or demonstrates object substitutions.[a]
    5.1   Preplanning or object substitution (nonverbal evidence).
    5.2   Preplanning or object substitution (verbal evidence).
    5.3   Preplanned 4.3 sequence.

---

[a] These categories were modified for the present study.

FIGURE 1   Levels of play behaviors. (Adapted from McCune-Nicolich 1980, Revised 1983)

for coding sequences of play behaviors at levels 4 and 5. Percent of agreement on the time of onset and termination of play behaviors (plus or minus one second) was 93%.

RESULTS

Group Differences

Table 1 displays individual data and group means for measures of symbolic play. Comparisons employing the Mann-Whitney U test showed no statistically significant group difference on any of the measures, including the percent of available time spent in symbolic play, the mean duration of a symbolic play episode, the highest productive level of play (highest level occurring at least twice in the session), percent of play episodes prompted by the mother, and the mean number of play themes engaged in each minute.

Because of the age of the participating children, patterns of occurrence of the higher levels of play (levels 4 and 5) were of the most interest to us. Table 2 shows that the groups also failed to differ on these categories, including the duration and frequency of related sequences of play behaviors (level 4) and the frequency of episodes for which preplanning was evident (level 5). There was a

TABLE 1   Characteristics of Symbolic Play Behaviors, Deaf and Hearing Subjects (Individual and Group Data)

	Deaf Subjects					Hearing Subjects				
	Lisa	Ann	Steve	Sally	X	Eva	Jen	Sue	Tony	X
I. Time in symbolic play (percentage of total time) % of SP	63	37	27	25	38.0	44	39	38	15	34.0
II. Mean duration of symbolic play episodes	55.1	20.0	21.9	33.2	32.6	37.9	46.2	62.1	12.9	39.78
III. Highest productive levels	5.3	5.3	5.1/2[1]	5.1/2	(NA)	5.1/2	5.1/2	5.1/2	4.2	(NA)
IV. Maternal prompts (percentage of total number of episodes)	16	11	23	30	20.0	12	14	34	35	23.8
V. Themes per minute of play	0.55	0.87	0.72	.80	0.74	0.90	0.90	0.24	2.25	1.07

[1] Levels 5.1 and 5.2 were not differentiated in the analysis because they differed only in mode of expression, not in symbolic level.

TABLE 2   Characteristics of Higher Levels of Symbolic Play, Deaf and Hearing Groups

	Deaf Subjects X (range)		Hearing Subjects X (range)	
I. Level 4 (combinations)				
1. Percentage of SP time	71.3	(59–78)	80.0	(53–90)
2. Number of level 4 episodes	7	(4–10)	6	(3–10)
3. Longest combination (number of behaviors)	9	(7–13)	8	(3–11)
4. Longest duration of combination (seconds)	188	(78–384)	204	(23–378)
II. Level 5 (preplanned)				
1. Percentage of SP time	37.5	(15–59)	24.8	(0–44)
2. Number of level 5 episodes	6	(2–10)	6	(0–9)
3. Percentage of level 5 episodes with verbal preplanning	59	(5–80)	89	(67–100)

nonsignificant tendency for the hearing children to provide more verbal evidence of preplanning than the deaf children. On that measure as on all others, however, there was considerable overlap between the two groups. In summary, the measures of the children's play behaviors seemed to represent that of *one* group rather than *two* different ones.

Individual Differences

Despite the lack of group differences, there was striking variation within each group of children on many of the measures. For example, some children in each group spent considerably more time playing symbolically than others within the same group. Regardless of hearing status, children who played more of the time also tended to have longer mean duration of play episodes ($r_s = .738$; $p <.05$) and spent a greater proportion of their play time engaged in level 4 play ($r_s = .643$; $p <.05$) and level 5 play ($r_s = .774$; $p <.05$). Both the proportion of play prompted by the mother and the number of play themes per minute were negatively, but nonsignificantly, related to the amount of time spent in symbolic play.

Informal review of the tapes suggested other variables that seemed to be related to a child's amount and level of symbolic play. In each group, the children who played most had mothers who tended to engage as active participants in the play themselves, going along with the pretend situation and playing assigned roles. These mothers tended to *follow* rather than to *direct* their children's attention focus and interest. Perhaps because of this feature, the interactive turn-taking between mother and child appeared to be smooth and nicely paced. In addition, these children produced more expressive language during the session than did their peers who engaged in less symbolic play.

The mothers of the children in each group who played the least amount of available time did not appear to value playing nor to enjoy it very much. This conclusion was suggested by their frequent interposition of more traditional "teaching" activities, even when the child was already engaged in a play episode. These dyads showed much less smooth turntaking and, in fact, mother and child were frequently engaged in separate activities with a separate attention focus. In general, the dyads did not seem to be "in synch"—the pace of their activity was not matched.

DISCUSSION

In contrast with earlier reports of diminished quality and quantity of symbolic play by deaf children, we found no differences between our groups of deaf and hearing toddlers. The deaf toddlers matched, indeed sometimes exceeded, the hearing toddlers in the amount of time spent in play as well as in the production of sequenced play and preplanned play.

Although our findings should be confirmed by studies employing larger groups of subjects, it does appear that deficiencies in play behaviors should not be considered a necessary or even an expected result of hearing loss. Deaf children who do show deficiencies in their symbolic play deserve to have further evaluation of organic and environmental factors that may be causing the deficiency.

Our findings may differ from other reports because of methodological differences between those earlier studies and our own. We analyzed naturally occurring play with a supportive adult rather than play with peers, who are less likely to be able to provide a supportive context. In addition, we used a free-play context rather than structured activities in which children would have had to comply with instructions from investigators. Our analysis was therefore based on behaviors produced in a more typical, naturally occurring context than was the case in most previous studies of deaf children's play.

An even more important source of the difference between our findings and earlier ones is that we studied a sample of deaf children with deaf parents. When a study purports to characterize effects of deafness, rather than of language deprivation, on development, we believe that the appropriate group to study is that of deaf children with deaf parents. These children's interactive and linguistic experiences with their parents are more similar to those of hearing children than are the experiences of deaf children with hearing parents (Meadow, Greenberg, Erting & Carmichael 1981; Spencer & Gutfreund, 1990).

Because of the importance for symbolic development of engaging in play activities, the sources of individual differences found within both groups of children in this study should be investigated in more detail. Variables of particular interest include the child's language level, the degree of contingency or reciprocity in mother-child interaction, and what we believe to be differences in the importance that various mothers accord the role of play in the child's development.

This and other available reports on the play behaviors of hearing and deaf toddlers indicate that symbolic play is the product of a complex interaction between cognitive, linguistic, and social factors. Because of this interaction, it does not appear that assessment of symbolic play can be assumed to provide an unbiased measure of a child's cognitive functioning, most especially if that measure is expected to predict future accomplishment. Assessment of play behaviors does, however, provide an important window through which we may observe the child's current functioning in a variety of domains that impact on development.

REFERENCES

Bellugi, U., & Klima, E. 1975. Aspects of sign language and its structure. In *The role of speech in language*, ed. J. Kavanagh & J. Cutting, 171–205. Cambridge, MA: MIT Press.

Bruner, J., Oliver, R., & Greenfield, P. 1966. *Studies in cognition*. Cambridge, MA:MIT Press.

Casby, M., & McCormack, S. 1985. Symbolic play and early communication development in hearing-impaired children. *Journal of Communication Disorders* 18:67–78.

Darbyshire, J. 1977. Play patterns in young children with hearing impairment. *Volta Review* 79:19–26.

Gregory, S. 1985. *The relationship between language development and symbolic play in deaf children*. Paper presented at IRSA conference, Brussels, Belgium.

Higginbotham, D., & Baker, B. 1981. Social participation and cognitive play differences in hearing-impaired and normally hearing preschoolers. *Volta Review* 83:135–149.

Lowe, M. 1975. Trends in the development of representational play in infants from one to three years—an observational study. *Journal of Child Psychology and Psychiatry* 16:33–47.

Mann, L. 1985. Play behaviors of deaf and hearing children. In *Cognition, education, and deafness: Directions in research and instruction*, ed. D. Martin, 27–29. Washington, DC: Gallaudet University Press.

McCune-Nicolich, L. 1980, rev. 1983. *A manual for analyzing free play*. Unpublished manuscript.

———. 1981. Toward symbolic functioning: Structure of early pretend games and potential parallels with language. *Child Development* 52:785–797.

Meadow, K., Greenberg, M., Erting, C., & Carmichael, H. 1981. Interactions of deaf mothers and deaf preschool children: Comparisons with three other groups of deaf and hearing dyads. *American Annals of the Deaf* 126: 454–468.

Nicolich, L. 1977. Beyond sensorimotor intelligence: Assessment of symbolic maturity through analysis of play. *Merrill-Palmer Quarterly* 23:89–101.

Piaget, J. 1962. *Play, dreams, and imitation*. New York: W.W. Norton & Co.

Pien, D. 1985. The development of communication functions in deaf infants and hearing parents. In *Cognition, education, and deafness: Directions in research and instruction*, ed. D. Martin, 30–33. Washington, DC: Gallaudet University Press.

Singer, D., & Lenahan, M. 1976. Imagination content in dreams of deaf children. *American Annals of the Deaf* 121:44–48.

Spencer, P., Deyo, D., & Grindstaff, N. 1990. Symbolic play behavior of deaf and hearing toddlers. In *Educational and developmental aspects of deafness*, ed. D. Moores & K. Meadow-Orlans, 390–406. Washington, DC: Gallaudet University Press.

Spencer, P., & Gutfreund, M. 1990. Directiveness in mother-infant interactions: Relationships with mother and infant hearing status. In *Educational and developmental aspects of deafness*, ed. D. Moores & K. Meadow-Orlans, 350–365. Washington, DC: Gallaudet University Press.

Ungerer, J., Zelazo, P., Kearsley, R., & Kurowski, K. 1979. *Play as a cognitive assessment tool*. Paper presented at Ninth Annual Interdisciplinary Conference on Piagetian Theory and its Implications for the Helping Professions. February, Los Angeles, CA.

Vygotsky, L. 1978. *Mind in society: The development of higher psychological processes*. Cambridge, MA: Harvard University Press.

Analysis

Kathryn P. Meadow-Orlans

A notable feature of the six papers in this section is the diversity of approach, methodology, and subject matter. A welcome review of Vygotsky's theory in relation to an understanding of deaf children's cognitive development contrasts with the other papers summarizing empirical data, where sample size ranges from the case study of a single pair of twins to the analysis of IQ scores of 120 deaf and 150 hearing Israeli adolescents. Methodologies include interviews with families, questionnaires administered to deaf students, and videotaped observations analyzed for behavioral and linguistic features. Altogether, the authors have contributed a rich and refreshing potpourri of viewpoints.

The Vygotsky paper by the Michigan State authors (Bonkowski, Akamatsu & Gavelek), provides a contrast to and continuity with the 1984 symposium. In 1984, a major paper by Irene Athey focused on Piaget, whose theories stress more formal structure in cognitive developmental processes, compared to Vygotsky's emphasis on process, interaction, and context. In fact, Moores' summary comments at the 1984 symposium called for researchers in the field of deafness to utilize Vygotsky's ideas when designing projects on cognitive development. As Bonkowski and her colleagues now agree, the translation of Vygotsky's ideas into research protocols is very difficult—a possible reason for his relative lack of influence. Indeed, attention to Vygotsky would lead to greater reliance on qualitative research methodology for the collection of either primary or secondary data and to the role of process in cognitive development. Additional emphasis might be placed on maternal behaviors that have a positive relationship with, for example, mastery motivation during infancy, or on teachers' classroom behaviors that have a positive relationship to academic performance of their deaf students.

223

Vygotsky's concept of the "zone of proximal development" refers to the cognitive tasks that may be learned most successfully. Bonkowski et al. make some interesting general suggestions about the implications of independent vs. assisted learning for deaf children. It would seem to be a logical and useful exercise for a researcher/educator team to build a proposed list of actual activities that would reflect the ZPD for deaf children. The plethora of generalizations and the paucity of concrete examples are characteristic of efforts to interpret Vygotsky's theory. As was suggested in the discussion of this paper at the symposium, Vygotsky has much in common with George Herbert Mead, whose seminal ideas are difficult to convert to a research mode. As a perspective, emphasizing the importance of interaction, context, social, and emotional components of cognitive development, these ideas have great significance for those interested in the development of deaf children. These authors have performed a service in summarizing the theory and suggesting some possible links to the study of deafness.

The Vygotsky paper also served as an interesting introduction to the one on family coping, contributed by the team from the University of Washington (Calderon, Greenberg & Kusché). This paper could well have been presented within a Vygotskian framework: Their data combined information obtained from mothers in a face-to-face interview setting with outcome measures reflecting deaf children's cognitive/academic performance. The effort to capture the effect of family attitudes and behaviors on deaf children's cognitive/academic performance is admirable. They measured a wide variety of parent, family, and child variables, illustrating the difficulty (and the high cost) of conducting research that examines context as well as performance in deaf children.

One important part of the "context" of deaf children's learning is the broader community or social system. In this study, that broader context is represented through an examination of the parents' social support network. Another aspect of the broader context for deaf children is the educational system that may (or may not) provide early intervention, including counseling for the parents and educational support for the child. These research findings show the importance of continuing to provide support for parents (after their children reach age five) as well as early intervention for the children. The positive relationship between mothers' beliefs in their ability to influence their child's development (internal locus of control) and the child's cognitive performance is an extremely important finding. The authors suggest that this result is positive from the point of view of educational intervention: mothers can be *taught* coping skills to enhance the child's educational experience, thereby increasing mothers' actual influence as well as their perceived influence.

"The understanding of time by deaf pupils" (by Irmina Kaiser-Grodecka from Jagiellonian University in Poland) evoked a great deal of interest among the symposium participants. It was clear that the participants who work with deaf children in educational or counseling settings agreed that the understanding and expression of time is a frequent problem for their students or clients. Michael Karchmer, Dean of Graduate Studies and Research at the Gallaudet Research Institute, reported that he has plans to replicate and expand the research reported by Kaiser-Grodecka. Questions to be explored include those related to the sign language skills of both questioners and student respondents. Kaiser-Grodecka explained that all instruction of deaf children in Polish schools is oral, and that few children are exposed to sign language. Her description of deaf education in Poland was reminiscent of the United States twenty years ago, before the acceptance of sign language as a medium of instruction and communication.

There are many other questions that might be profitably raised in this area: Would the deaf children of hearing vs. deaf parents respond differently to questions regarding concepts of time? Occasionally both deaf and hearing people will jokingly refer to the idea of "deaf time," suggesting a cultural difference in the way time is viewed. Clinical practitioners sometimes suggest that failure to keep appointments or to be "on time" is a way for clients or patients to control the therapist. For individuals who are often powerless to act independently, time may be both a psychological and a cognitive issue.

An interesting comment was made by a teacher of young deaf children after the symposium session. She recounted her daily routines with preschool students, specifically directed toward an understanding of past, present, and future actions and events. She uses several set phrases every day during show-and-tell sessions, such as "*After* that, we did such and such." It is rewarding for her when the young children begin using the phrases independently and appropriately to describe holiday outings with their families. This account of a teacher's classroom practice suggests the value of holding a symposium, or at least a series of sessions in future symposia, in which practitioners are given the opportunity to share innovative methods for promoting cognitive development in deaf students.

Schirmer's paper on the twin sisters specifically investigates the relationship between language and cognition. The author utilized techniques of linguistic analysis widely used with hearing children: Brown's stages of language acquisition as measured by mean length of utterance (MLU) and Halliday's categories of language function. Schirmer also analyzed the twins' imaginative play on a cognitive play scale. In every analysis performed, the deaf twin was functioning at a level below that of the hearing twin. A number of interesting questions and suggestions were made by members of the audience. For example, they were curious about the twins' interactions with the researcher, alone and together and with parents and teachers. In other words, what was the effect of *context* on the linguistic productions of the deaf and the hearing twin?

The difficulties of designing and conducting research with deaf children are illustrated again in this twin study. Because of the low incidence of deafness and the difficulties of determining a diagnosis early in life, subjects must be recruited over a long period of time or throughout a broad geographic area if significant numbers are to be located. These difficulties are multiplied when special characteristics (such as twin sets) are of interest. This point argues for wide collaboration among investigators in different institutions and perhaps an umbrella system of funding to permit large-scale research operations.

Spencer, Deyo, and Grindstaff examined play behaviors of another low incidence subset of deaf subjects: The deaf children of deaf parents. Although only four dyads are included in the reported study (matched with four mothers and children with normal hearing), they are continuing to recruit additional subjects in this ongoing project. Their research illustrates additional methodological difficulties of working with low-incidence groups. For example: this group is based at Gallaudet; while they have access to a large Deaf community from which to recruit subjects, those subjects may not be representative of the larger deaf population. The widespread use of American Sign Language by the mothers and children included in this research group makes the participation of deaf persons very important to the data analysis. Grindstaff, a native ASL user, described the research subjects and their language usage to symposium participants. This presentation, together with the ability of the audience to view one of the research videotapes, added background and meaning to the presentation of findings.

It is well known that fewer than 5% of deaf children have two deaf parents. How, then, can research with this population be expected to help in understanding the play behaviors and cognitive development of deaf children born to hearing parents? Day and her associates make a convincing case that it is important to try to separate the effects of access to *sound*, in the audiological sense, from the effects of access to *language*, as experienced by the four deaf children participating in their project.

The final paper in this group of six, Zwiebel's "Intellectual structure of hearing-impaired children and adolescents," illustrates the advantages of long-term commitment to this field of study. Zwiebel has been able to conduct a follow-up to research reported (with D. Mertens) at the 1984 symposium.

Factor analysis, the statistical technique Zwiebel had hoped to use, requires a large number of subjects. Although he recruited a substantial percentage of the deaf adolescents in Israel, his 120 subjects were not enough to conduct the definitive analysis he had hoped to achieve. One member of the symposium audience, Jeffery Braden, described the collaborative work he and Zwiebel are currently doing; they found that their similar studies had obtained *opposite* results. By comparing data sets and subdividing subjects by age, they expect to report additional analyses that should expand understanding of the cognitive development of deaf children.

As stated at the beginning of this analysis, these six papers address diverse topics and use many different research methods with a variety of approaches and conclusions. From the responses of symposium participants, and from the viewpoint of this commentator, "in diversity there is strength."

RESEARCH QUESTIONS

1. From infancy through adolescence, what specific cognitive tasks might be considered to delineate the "zone of proximal development" for deaf children? How might deafness render these tasks different at various stages of cognitive growth?
2. How do the timing, stress, and etiology of diagnosis of hearing loss affect the relationship of mothers' locus of control to deaf children's cognitive performance?
3. What is the relationship of deaf children's ability to express past and future time to their ability to sequence story pictures appropriately? What kinds of classroom interventions are most successful in helping deaf children understand time?
4. How is the temperament of both parents and children related to the linguistic performance of hearing and deaf twins?
5. How do deaf preschoolers with hearing parents, and hearing preschoolers with deaf parents, compare with the two groups reported by Spencer et al. regarding play behaviors and language production?
6. If age is an important determinant of performance on IQ tests, as Zwiebel and Braden suspect, are there additional differences in specific performance areas that are amenable to intervention? What kinds of classroom techniques are most effective in promoting particular skills reflected in the subtests used in Zwiebel's research? Does this area of research suggest a "critical period" for the acquisition of cognitive skills?

6

NEUROSCIENTIFIC ISSUES

Specialized Cognitive Function Among Deaf Individuals: Implications for Instruction

Helen B. Craig
Harold W. Gordon

This study analyzed the preliminary results of an ongoing three-year study of cognitive function and cognitive education among hearing-impaired persons and considers these results in the context of previous studies (Craig & Gordon 1988; McKee 1987). In the earlier studies, the cognitive profile of deaf individuals was found to differ significantly from that of normally hearing persons. Cognitive task performance was below average, as might be expected, for the verbal and sequential skills associated with the left hemisphere, but more importantly, performance was above average for the visual and spatial skills associated with the right hemisphere. In addition, reading and mathematics achievement directly correlated with this cognitive profile, especially with verbosequential performance. In potentially related investigations (Craig 1987; Martin & Jonas 1986), the systematic implementation of a thinking skills program, Feuerstein's Instrumental Enrichment (FIE), has been found significantly to improve reading and mathematics achievement among deaf students. FIE is a metacognitive program that includes a selective focus on several of the visuospatial and verbosequential features associated with specialized cognitive functions. Consideration of the FIE results and of their potential interaction with our findings on brain function formed the basis for the current investigation.

The purpose of this project was both theoretical and practical. The *theoretical*

This project is being supported by Grant #H133G80184 from the National Institute on Disability Rehabilitation Research (NIDRR), Office of Special Education and Rehabilitative Services, U.S. Department of Education.

231

goal was to determine whether the pattern of performance of specialized brain functions—the cognitive profile—differs in individuals who have normal vs. impaired hearing. The *practical* goal was to determine whether the cognitive profile of hearing-impaired students can help to predict which training materials and techniques will most facilitate their academic achievement. The objectives, then, are fourfold.

1. To explore further, in a cohort of congenitally profoundly deaf persons, the relative performance of cognitive functions associated with the left and right hemispheres;
2. To determine whether there exists a "critical period" for development of brain organization and/or a "critical degree of deficit" relating to differing ages of onset and differing degrees of hearing loss;
3. To explore the relationship between cognitive profile and academic achievement; and
4. To determine whether success in a training program in higher-order thinking (such as FIE) can be attributed to the nature of training material that favors specialized brain function—specifically, whether a match or a mismatch between materials and students' cognitive profiles will be most effective for improvement in academic achievement.

RATIONALE AND REVIEW OF PREVIOUS STUDIES

The main theoretical hypothesis underlying this series of studies was that congenital loss of auditory experience alters the cerebral development and the normal lateralization of specific cognitive tasks associated with brain function, particularly of neurosystems associated with the left cerebral hemisphere. It was further hypothesized that these developmental differences may well be a critical factor influencing the academic achievement of persons with profound and congenital hearing impairment; and, by extension, that intervention techniques that take into consideration the cognitive profile of each deaf student may improve academic achievement.

Underlying these hypotheses are two potentially interacting factors:

1. The identification of the left hemisphere as an analytic, serial, time-dependent processor, uniquely specialized for speech, writing, and other language skills (Bradshaw & Nettleton 1983); and
2. The observation that children whose hearing is significantly impaired, regardless of preferred communication mode, will miss out on a major portion of the highly sequential and temporal input that is conveyed auditorily. It is also reasonable to suppose that continued deprivation of serial stimuli may further reduce development of these processes in the left hemisphere, whereas increased reliance on visual sources, which are inherently less sequential than the auditory, may potentiate right hemisphere development.

METHOD

The current study involved two major components, cognitive evaluation and cognitive training, both conducted throughout the three-year period.

Evaluation Component

Approximately 200 deaf subjects were evaluated over the three years, divided evenly into 4 cells in a 2 x 2 matrix—age of onset (congenital or postlingual) by severity of hearing loss (profound or moderate-to-severe). The age range was 15 to 45 years, with Performance IQs above 80.

The major evaluation tool was the Cognitive Laterality Battery (CLB) (Gordon 1986). The CLB is specifically designed to measure the verbosequential and visuospatial functions attributed respectively to the left and right hemispheres and thereby to determine a subject's cognitive profile (i.e., the *relative* performance on tasks associated with the two hemispheres). The evaluation included the following items (the first two items are part of the CLB):

1. Four verbosequential tests, two measuring memory for sequencing (Serial Pictures and Serial Numbers), and two measuring word fluency (Word Production: Letters and Word Production: Categories);
2. Four visuospatial tests: Localization (of points in space), Orientation in Space, Form Completion (of incomplete silhouettes), and Touching Blocks.
3. Serial Squares, a nonverbal test of sequencing;
4. Sign Production: Hand Shapes, a non-English test of language fluency;
5. Tests of hand dominance and hand performance; and
6. Reading Comprehension and Mathematics Computation subtests of the Stanford Achievement Test (SAT) and the Vocabulary, Reading, Spelling, Language and Mathematics subtests of the California Achievement Test (CAT).

Training Component

Feuerstein's FIE program was selected as the experimental tool for the training component both because its thinking-skills emphasis is particularly pertinent to the goals of this study and because certain FIE instruments focus primarily on skills that may be considered either verbosequential or visuospatial. The FIE program provides a theoretically cohesive instructional plan and a comprehensive, targeted set of learning materials. Its fourteen cognitive instruments are a series of challenging problem-solving tasks in specific areas of cognitive development, such as spatial orientation; classification; and temporal, numerical, and transitive relations.

The instruments or activity groups used in this project were analyzed and operationally classified as either *visuospatial*—organization of dots, orientation in space, analytic perception, and representational stencil design; and *verbosequential*—instructions, temporal relations, numerical progressions, and transitive relations. The "comparisons" instrument, a composite of visuospatial/verbosequential skills, was included in equal portions for both training groups as a necessary step in the cognitive program from an instructional point of view.

Subjects for the training component were selected from a postsecondary transitional program for deaf students. These students, as part of their standard curriculum, received special training in thinking skills using FIE. All students in this study used each of the FIE instruments listed above, but in different proportions depending on the training group. Students were distributed into two training groups, one concentrating on FIE instruments that emphasized verbosequential skills and the other on those that emphasized the visuospatial. All students within the pool of potential subjects also were classified as primarily verbosequential or visuospatial, depending on their specialized cognitive performance on the CLB. Over three years, 48 subjects in all were selected, with 12 in each of the 4 cells of the 2 x 2 matrix—2 types of FIE training group (verbosequential or visuospatial) by 2 types of cognitive profile (again, verbosequential or visuospatial).

In the first year of this study, sixteen subjects were selected for training according to this experimental design—four in each of the four cells. Hearing loss, performance IQ, age, and sex distribution were comparable between the two training groups. All students in these groups received FIE training three days per week in one-hour sessions for 32 weeks. The same teacher, a certified teacher of the deaf who is fluent in Sign and fully trained in FIE, provided the instruction. Each group received the same number of pages overall, spent the same time on task for FIE, and followed the same sequence of training. Only the proportions of verbosequential and visuospatial material were varied.

RESULTS

First-year results from this ongoing project have been analyzed in relation to two major questions, the first from the evaluation and the second from the training component.

1. Can performance on tests of specialized cognitive function, as usually associated with the left or right hemispheres of the brain, predict achievement? and
2. Does improvement in achievement depend upon instructional type and/or cognitive profile?

Can cognitive function predict achievement? To date, analysis is complete on the evaluation of 35 deaf subjects, with the following results. On the Reading Comprehension subtest of the SAT, significant correlations were recorded with the verbosequential test of the CLB ($r = .462$, $p < .01$) and with the cognitive profile ($r = .398$, $p < .05$). In an analysis by CLB subtest, there were significant correlations between SAT reading and all but one of the verbosequential tasks. There was no correlation between reading and any of the visuospatial tasks. This finding is in agreement with previous results with deaf adolescents (Craig &

Gordon 1988) and with deaf college students (McKee 1987). In achievement test results on the CAT, the verbosequential tests of the CLB correlated significantly only with the Language Mechanics subtest ($r = .515$, $p < .05$). There were, however, significant correlations between many of the CAT subtests and the Fluency subtests of the CLB. The CAT total correlated with Word Production: Letters and Word Production: Categories, as did the CAT subtests of Vocabulary, Spelling, Language Mechanics, Language Expression, and Mathematics Computation. Again, there was no correlation between any of these tests and the visuospatial tasks of the CLB.

Results from the training component, at this point, are available on only a small portion of the 48 subjects projected for this project and are therefore offered here only as tentative directions for consideration. By July 1989, 14 subjects had completed both the FIE training program and the posttesting evaluation, 7 with a verbosequential focus and 7 with a visuospatial focus. Achievement results for both training groups showed significant growth in both reading and math from pre- to posttest time, a period of 6 months. Reading Comprehension Grade Equivalent (GE) on the SAT increased by .8 GE, from 5.1 to 5.9, and Mathematics Computation increased by 1.3 GE, from 9.0 to 10.3. By contrast, a similar but unmatched comparison group, in the same transitional program but not receiving FIE instruction, recorded no significant achievement gains.

Given the achievement gains noted above, a major question for this program remains: Does improvement in achievement depend on instruction type and/or cognitive profile? In other words, do students benefit more from instruction that matches their own cognitive profiles (e.g., visuospatial instruction for those with visuospatial profiles) or from mismatched instruction? Results on the Vocabulary subtest of the CAT did show significant three-way interaction ($p<.05$, $df = 1.9$) relating to this question. Subjects who had verbosequential profiles gained significantly from visuospatial (mismatched or contrasting) training, whereas those with visuospatial (matching) profiles did not. On the other hand, those with verbosequential profiles did not gain from the verbosequential (matching) training, whereas those with visuospatial (contrasting) profiles did.

IMPLICATIONS

The evaluation results from this project so far confirm earlier results. Performance on the verbosequential tasks associated with the left hemisphere predicts academic achievement, whereas visuospatial performance does not. It is still too early to draw definitive inferences from the instructional results. However, they do augment so far the evidence that Feuerstein's Instrumental Enrichment strengthens academic achievement for deaf students. Further, if the interaction results relating to training by profile hold up over the three years of this project, they would support training and early intervention that provide compensatory stimulation and practice for the less-developed hemisphere; that is, training methods that contrast with the cognitive profile.

REFERENCES

Bradshaw, J., & Nettleton, N.C. 1983. *Human cerebral asymmetry*. Englewood Cliffs, NJ: Prentice-Hall.

Craig, H.B. 1987. Instrumental enrichment: Process and results with deaf students. *Thinking Skills Newsletter*. Harrisburg: Pennsylvania Department of Education.

Craig, H.B., & Gordon, H.W. 1988. Specialized cognitive function and reading achievement in hearing-impaired adolescents. *Journal of Speech and Hearing Disorders* 53:30–41.

Feuerstein, R. 1980. *Instrumental enrichment: An intervention program for cognitive modifiability*. Baltimore: University Park Press.

Gordon, H.W. 1986. The Cognitive Laterality Battery: Tests of specialized cognitive function. *International Journal of Neuroscience* 29:223–244.

———. 1988. Specialized cognitive function and school achievement. *Development Neuropsychology* 4(3):239–257.

Martin, D.S., & Jonas, B. 1986. Cognitive modifiability in the deaf adolescent. (Available from ERIC Clearinghouse on Gifted and Handicapped Children, Document No. ED 276 159)

McKee, D.E. 1987. An analysis of specialized cognitive functions in deaf and hearing signers. Ph.D. diss., University of Pittsburgh.

Cortical Integration of Hemispherical Processes vs. Cognitive Processes in Deaf Children

Anna Knobloch-Gala

Neurophysiological and psychophysiological research and related psychological experiments have yielded a great deal of data concerning the functional differentiation of the cortical hemispheres. Nevertheless, fascination with the discovery of hemispheric asymmetry should not obscure an obvious phenomenon of interhemispherical communication through the corpus callosum. This tract, containing about two million nerve fibers, serves as an integrator of different functions of the hemispheres (Diamond 1980).

Integration is not a simple process of combining compound elements. Principles of integration in a hierarchical set derive from its structure and function. The author's model of cooperation between cortical hemispheres is based on J. Konorski's conception (Konorski 1969). Discussion of two independent systems of data interpretation should be treated as a specific intellectual experiment. In fact, division of the two aspects is not easy. Even persons who have undergone brain bisection preserve some forms of interhemispheric communication.

MODEL OF SIMULTANEOUS COGNITION

This method of data interpretation discerns mutual relations between all the events that happen to appear in the perceptual field at the same time. Even if the simultaneity is not full, the temporal elements are abandoned as insignificant. In this kind of cognition, the whole is primal and dominates the elements that create it. Concentration on details seems less important than comprehension of their

237

mutual relationships and application of definite synthesizing rules. Reality has a quantum and discrete character. "Here and now" is all that counts; the previous state and the results of the present state are neglected.

Simultaneous processes dominate visual perception. Apprehension of various mutual relationships and their simultaneous overlapping allows us to construct three-dimensional space.

MODEL OF SEQUENTIAL COGNITION

Sequential understanding of reality consists of recording temporal sequences of events or elements. In this case the duration of an event is significant together with the record of consecutive states or phases, and the order of appearing phenomena. Therefore, they are either transformations or trains of homo- or heterogeneous events.

The elements included in sequence are exactly defined, and analytical understanding of details is a natural approach to this interpretative procedure. Causal thinking is a final result of this activity. Sequential processes prevail in the processing of acoustic stimuli; hence the lack of aural experience may be an obstacle to conducting such operations. Sounds, however, are not the only elements having temporal/sequential characteristics. Organization of any kind of motoric activities is also strongly influenced by this component. This statement indicates an additional source of sequentiality experienced by the deaf.

SYNCHRONIZATION AND SEQUENTIALITY OF ACTIVITIES

Organization of activities may be related to mutual relationships on one hand and to sequence of events on the other. Synchronization requires special functional schemata in which we may abandon the duration of an activity, what should precede it, and what should follow it. We are concerned with what has to be performed simultaneously so that an appropriate effect of the activity is achieved.

It appears that the sequential aspect dominates an activity. The mutual system of single groups of muscles of both hands, legs, and the whole body (not to mention human activity in a larger context) is important, but it has a static character, while activity is connected with directed and ordered changes. Functional, sequential schemata define the order and duration of composed elements. A simple movement does not have to be the element; most frequently it is a synchronized structure composed of various components, which is feasible through integration taking place on various levels of cortical structure.

PHYSIOLOGICAL PREMISES OF CORTICAL PROCESSES INTEGRATION

In his work on integrational cerebral activity, Konorski (1969) presents fundamentals of perception and pays attention to the regularities occurring in the whole afferent system. He introduces the concept of the *gnostic unit*, a group of cells of various status in a cortical hierarchy, from receptor cells to the highest levels of cortical analyzer. A lower level communicates with a higher one according to the principles of convergence and divergence. In most cases, divergence prevails and results in the increase of units on a higher level.

Impulse integration, according to Konorski, does not take place on the same hierarchical level but in higher-order structures. Vertical communication clearly dominates the horizontal connections, and units of the same category are antagonistic to each other, thus favoring a precise and specific reception of information.

Worth mentioning are the investigations of brain structure and function carried out by means of deoxyglucose autoradiography (Kossut 1983) and their comparison with Konorski's theory. The investigations conducted in L. Sokoloff's laboratory in the USA (Sokoloff et al. 1979) indicate a column-like functioning of the cerebral cortex in mammals. Such a cortical structure confirms the existence of the vertical functioning systems assumed by Konorski.

While concentrating on the integrating cortical processes, Konorski pays particular attention to the creation of interanalyzer perceptual schemata; however, he does not take into account hemispherical differentiation. When he published his studies, the investigations of the split brain had just begun and were not yet well known. Now information about the split brain is available, but our knowledge concerning the physiology of interhemispheric communication is incomplete.

PRINCIPLES AND PATTERNS OF HEMISPHERICAL INTEGRATION

Our sense that the world is both spatial and continuous, fluently changing in time but also having a complex and multidimensional structure, seems to be obvious. However, this experience does not give us any indication of how the unification of the spatial and temporal aspects is achieved. Nevertheless, it indicates a certain neutrality and even points up the necessity of hemispherical integration.

The analysis of various activities may show which factors have sequential and which have simultaneous character. On this basis we may establish a hemispherical pattern indicating the participation of the left and right hemispheres in particular phases of their activity. Certain categorization and stricter assignment of patterns and types of activity should be expected. The next step should be a penetration of the psychological tests in this respect.

Domination and dichotomization are the main comprehensive categories in studies of interhemispherical interaction. However, we should remember that integration is reciprocal, including right hemisphere (RH) iconic structures into left hemisphere (LH) sequential procedures. The plasticity of the nervous system allows for the origination of a variety of different patterns that are more or less advantageous, appropriately fitting to reality and personal goals, and reasonable.

The nervous system offers limited structural possibilities. Most of the emerging systems are limited mainly by the capacity of short-term memory. Connection of structures in various states may enable one to overcome physiological barriers, though fixation of long sequences is not possible. If a certain number of elements are grasped simultaneously as a whole, later we may apply only the iconic representation of the group of elements. Such an icon is then treated as an element and may be used for the construction of next-generation structures.

Cognitive and operational schemata may consist of elements integrated within the same hemisphere (homogeneous) or may have data coming from both hemispheres (heterogeneous). The openness of the system and its liability of structures is an unquestionable opportunity for a multiple shaping of human experience, even under not-very-favorable conditions. Lack or deterioration of a certain modality of perception may be considered to be such an unfavorable situation. In the case of the deaf, it is a lack of aural experience. Many operational schemata in these conditions have to be shaped differently. This point refers particularly to activities requiring complex lateral integration, specifically speech.

CORTICAL INTEGRATION AND DEAFNESS

The influence of sensory defects on the shaping of cognitive processes was considered by Piaget (1927, 1956), Furth and Youniss (1966), and O'Connor and Hermelin (1978). These works suggest that spatial processes are disturbed in blind persons and temporal processes in deaf persons. Belmont, Karchmer, and Bourg (1983) wanted to see the differences in the scope of initial temporal/spatial orientation between deaf children and a control group of hearing children. Their experiment indicates that deaf children as a group are not homogeneous. Although the hearing children had initial sequential orientation, the deaf children differed among themselves. An attempt to change the orientation and present the material, disagreeing with the students' natural disposition, showed that deaf children, regardless of beginning results, always have difficulty in adapting to a situation of a different structure. These investigations undo existing stereotypes to some degree and give rise to new questions.

It is interesting to investigate what statements, experiences, or individual predispositions condition one and not another preorientation of the deaf, and also what makes free communication between the sequential/temporal and synchronic systems difficult.

Keeping in mind the problem of cortical integration, we should concentrate rather on the sequential and synchronic properties of a given modality. This point explains why comparison of operational schemata of hearing and deaf persons must omit this direct, perceptual aspect and instead go into operational status. Those activities that are equivocal are those whose auditive sequential elements are, for instance, exchanged for a sequence of gestures. When a sound sequence is exchanged for an iconic sign, we must acknowledge structural difference.

Accordingly, from the above statements we may formulate indices for educational application as follows:

1. If the lack of aural perception weakens the origin of sequential sche-

mata, a small child should be given an opportunity to acquire them in a different way.

2. Purposeful development of formal operation must include both temporal/sequential and spatial/simultaneous aspects of cognition.

3. Particularly important for deaf children is the shaping of experience that favors connection between formally and functionally different elements.

Structural Properties of Linguistic Systems Used by Deaf Persons

Interhemispheric exchange is particularly important for the organization of speech. It is commonly claimed that this activity is controlled by the dominant hemisphere (usually the left), but without cooperation from the other hemisphere the complex verbal net could probably never exist (Molfese 1983, and Dimond 1980).

The structure and psychophysiological features of each language have a unique system of sequential and simultaneous schemata. Any change of perception or control system implies significant differences in operational patterns, which should be taken into consideration in the analysis of language structure and acquisition in the deaf person. Natural sign language is a set of gestures symbolizing objects and imitating states and activities. These expressions have iconic character and are presented in an empirical order. The language is not phenomenologically transparent but has a very close approximation to the reality being represented. Such a language has been said by some not to allow abstract thinking. Before attempts at its inclusion in the European oral tradition, it had been excluded from the official educational systems.

Oral language has many advantages, and from the deaf person's point of view, one drawback—it is based on unheard sounds. In efforts to teach oral language, the fact that it enables communication with those who can hear is far more important than the cognitive argument. In practice, we notice that the deaf community not only protests against oral methods, but also questions other forms of communication. It is quite possible that the correct formal structure of oral language causes difficulties for deaf people because of the nature of its sequential and simultaneous heterogeneity, which goes beyond the average deaf person's receptive and expressive possibilities.

It is worth noting that in artificially created languages, frequently with one sign denoting a unitary object or state, one has to connect gesture icon with a sequence of fingerspelling. This process may be compared to writing with hieroglyphs and an ordinary alphabet at the same time. A meaning unit should never include sequential and simultaneous components at the same time. The basic sign should be homogeneous, the more so because empirical evidence shows that deaf persons have difficulties in performing interhemispherical operations. Higher-order expressions may have heterogenic form—a sentence may be a sequence of iconic signs while the general meaning of the sentence may refer to synchronic events. The optimal solution should be reached empirically, for only experience can provide the best solution to the problem.

SUMMARY

These considerations are the result of work on integration of specialized hemispherical systems. Although the problem of temporal and spatial organization of our experience is nothing new in psychological investigations, we must admit that only neuropsychological data showed how physiologically pertinent such differentiation is. For the sake of cognitive performance and efficient activity, the integration of the two systems is of great importance. Lack of aural experience puts a person in a slightly different situation in this respect. If the purpose of our theoretical or practical work is activation of deaf persons, we should also see this fundamental aspect connected with the organization of cortical processes.

REFERENCES

Belmont, J.M., Karchmer, M.A., & Bourg, J.W. 1983. Structural influence on deaf and hearing children's recall of temporal/spatial incongruent letter strings. *Educational Psychology* 3:3–4.

Dimond, S.J. 1980. *Neuropsychology: A textbook of systems and psychological functions of the human brain.* London: Butterwoods.

Furth, H.G., & Youniss, J. 1966. *Spatial and temporal factors in learning with deaf children: An experimental investigation of thinking.* Washington, DC: Catholic University of America.

Konorski, J. 1969. *Intergracyjna dzialalnosc mozgu* (Integrative activity of cortex). Warszawa: PWN.

Kossut, M. 1983. Radioaktywna dezoksyglukoza w badaniach aktywnosci mozgu. In *Nowe metody w badaniach mozgu.* Wroclaw: WPAN.

Molfese, D.L. 1983. Neural mechanisms underlying the processing of speech information in infants and adults. In *Neuropsychology of language, reading, and spelling,* ed. U. Kirk. New York: Academic Press.

O'Connor, N., & Hermelin, B. 1978. *Seeing, and hearing, and space, and time.* London: Academic Press.

Piaget, J. 1927. *The child's conception of time.* London: Routledge & Kegan Paul.

———. 1956. *The child's conception of space.* London: Routledge & Kegan Paul.

Sokoloff, I., Reivich, M., Kennedy, C., Des Rosiers, M., Patlak, C., Pettigrew, K.D., Sakurada, C., & Shinohara, M. 1979. The (14C) deoxyglucose method for the measurement of local cerebral utilization: Theory, procedure, and normal values in the conscious and anesthetized albino rat. *J. Neurochem* 32:15–22.

Cortical Organization and Information Processing in Deaf Children

Carol A. Kusché
Mark T. Greenberg

In order to develop a neurolinguistic model for cortical processing during reading, we collected data on 24 deaf children to support the following two hypotheses that several researchers, including ourselves, have proposed (Greenberg & Kusché 1989; Kusché 1985; Neville 1985).

1. Due to auditory deprivation, prelingual deafness may result in differences in the organization or reorganization of the brain as compared to that of individuals with normal hearing. These differences are believed to be reflected in aspects of functioning such as short-term memory and reading ability.
2. Differences in information-processing abilities among subgroups of deaf children may be related to differences between these groups in cortical organization and functioning.

A NEUROLINGUISTIC MODEL OF PROCESSING DURING READING

Our proposed neurolinguistic model of cortical processing during reading is based upon models proposed by Geschwind (1979) and Hynd (1986). We embellished upon these models, however, because they provided only partial descriptions and did not take into account certain processes that are necessary for reading. As noted by Kolb and Whishaw (1985), "A comprehensive model of language function must incorporate stimulation and lesion data and include subcortical struc-

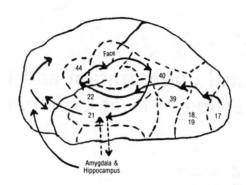

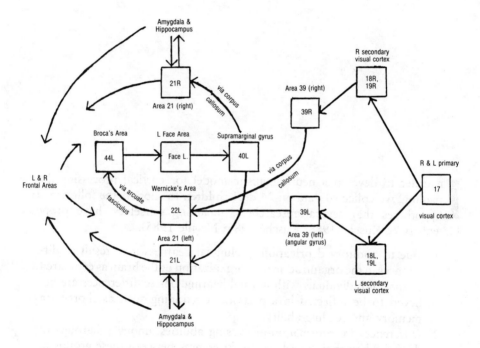

Area 17L & R → Areas 18, 19L & R → Area 39L & R → Area 22L → Area 44L → Face Area L → Area 40L → Areas 21L & R → amygdala, hippocampus, frontal lobes → feedback from frontal lobes

FIGURE 1   A proposed neurolinguistic model of cortical processing during normal reading.

tures as well as mechanisms of affective control. Such a model remains to be proposed" (p. 528).

Our model was developed first by reviewing the types of procedures that are utilized while reading. We then matched these processes to the corresponding areas of the brain (based on Brodmann's 1909 paradigm) that are believed to subserve these functions. (For a more comprehensive review, the reader is referred to Kolb and Whishaw 1985, and to the complete version of this paper). Finally, we drew a "map" to illustrate the sequential processing involved among these areas.

As can be seen in Figure 1, we proposed that information is relayed from the primary visual cortex (area 17) to the secondary visual cortex (areas 18/19) in both hemispheres, resulting in information from the retinal projections becoming interpreted as letters and perhaps words. From the secondary visual cortex, information proceeds to the angular gyrus (39) in both hemispheres, where visual short-term memory and spatial/location processing can be undertaken. Grapheme-to-phoneme translation and order-retention are then processed in Wernicke's Area (22) in the left hemisphere, and speech-motor programming and perhaps grammatical processing are undertaken in Broca's Area (44), again in the left hemisphere. From there the information is relayed to the left face area for subvocal phonetic processing, to the supramarginal gyrus (40) in the left hemisphere for phonetic short-term memory processing, and to area 21 in both hemispheres for long-term memory encoding, to the amygdala for affective associations, and to the frontal areas for associative processing. Information from the frontal lobes is then fed back to various regions of the brain.

Obviously, this process is very complex, involving numerous areas of the brain working in intricate coordination. To add to the complexity, it should be noted that although this model is presented as sequential, the brain is actually processing different units of information simultaneously and is continually integrating these units. We would also expect to find individual differences in reading processing within any large population, so that this model represents only an "average" reading model.

We believe that our reading model might prove useful in deafness research with regard to examining the cortical processing of subgroups of deaf subjects. For example, specific types of reading difficulties might be expected to be found with different types of processing. It might also be found that certain processing strengths are substituted for weaker areas (e.g., a visual-gestalt word-recognition function might be utilized in lieu of phonetic encoding, episodic memory might be used to compensate for poor verbal short-term memory, etc.). This model might be especially useful if used in conjunction with paradigms from neurological research (e.g., EEG studies) as well as from neuropsychological research. The model could have useful implications for educational interventions.

INFORMATION PROCESSING IN 24 DEAF CHILDREN

Subjects

The sample originally studied included approximately 50 children, but those under age 8 and those who had missing or unscorable data on any of the variables (with the exception of speech intelligibility) were excluded from these analyses. Future analyses are planned that will include a larger sample. The data were collected on 24 deaf elementary-school age children between 8 and 12 years of age (mean age = 9.5 years), 6 males and 18 females. Racial composition was 20

Caucasian, 2 Black, 1 Asian, and 1 other. All of these children received their education in self-contained Total Communication day classrooms for hearing-impaired children and were educated primarily in Manual English. Most of the children had early intervention preschool conducted in Total Communication, parent training, and hearing aids. None of the children were seriously multi-handicapped, all were diagnosed as deaf before the age of 3, and all had an unaided hearing loss equal to or greater than 70 dB in the better ear averaged across the speech range. The average unaided hearing loss was 95 dB, while the average aided loss was 56 dB. All of the children had hearing parents, and most of the parents knew some sign language.

Measures

Cognitive measures and rated characteristics were obtained for each child. All cognitive tasks were administered to the children in Total Communication by persons knowledgeable about deafness. These tasks included the following.

1. The Visual-Aural-Digit Span Test, adapted to a manual mode [VADS %Age] (Koppitz 1977). (The average score was found to be 23%)
2. The WISC-R Performance Scale [WISC-R Perf. IQ], deaf norms (Anderson & Sisco 1977; Wechsler 1974) (mean score = 111), which included the Block Design subtest ($X = 11$)
3. The Bender-Gestalt Test [Bender %Age] (Koppitz 1963, 1975) ($X = 34\%$)
4. The Stanford Achievement Test Reading Comprehension Subtest: Hearing-Impaired Version [Reading %Age] (Jensema, Schildroth & O'Rourke 1973; Madden, Gardner et al. 1972) (X score = 79%).

Teacher ratings (TR), based on a scale of 1 = very poor to 5 = excellent (compared to other deaf children of the same age), were obtained on each child's skills in the following areas: reading ($X = 3.3$), writing ($X = 3.2$), speech ($X = 2.7$), sign skill ($X = 3.5$), residual hearing ($X = 3.3$), and speechreading ($X = 3.6$). Speech intelligibility was also assessed by using a modified version of a simple sentence-reading test devised by Monsen (1978, 1981) (X = between poor and fair).

ANALYSES AND RESULTS

The first analysis was based on the assumption that the VADS Total Percentile Score represented a rough indication of functioning of the left temporal-parietal area, while the Block Design subscale score provided a rough estimate of functioning in the right temporal-parietal area. We hypothesized that significant correlations of these scores with other measures would suggest possible relationships of processing in these areas to other types of functioning. It should be emphasized, however, that these relationships would be associations only and could not be interpreted as being causally related.

The VADS Percentile Score and the Block Design Score were not significantly related to one another ($r = .12$), as would be predicted (see Table 1). These scores should therefore represent relatively independent contributions in their relationships to other variables. The Block Design Subtest was highly related to the WISC-R Performance IQ, while the VADS was not. This finding provides additional validation for a discriminative difference between the VADS and Block Design scores, but it should be noted that this finding is confounded by the fact that the score on the Block Design subtest is included in the total WISC-R Performance Score. The VADS and Block Design scores were roughly equally related to the Bender Percentile Score. This finding suggests that independent contributions from both the right and left hemispheres may be equally important with regard to performance on the Bender, even though this test is considered to be nonverbal. The VADS and the Block Design scores were also both significantly related to both reading measures (which again suggests the importance of both left and right processing), while only the VADS was significantly associated with writing skill (which suggests a somewhat greater reliance on left processing for writing). With regard to other rated characteristics, the VADS was related to speech intelligibility and residual hearing, while speechreading was equally related to both scores. Interestingly, teacher ratings of sign language skill were not significantly related to either measure.

A second set of analyses was based on grouping the 24 children according to whether they fell above or below the group mean for this sample on the VADS (23rd percentile) and the normative mean on the Block Design (scale score of 10) (see Table 2). Unfortunately, this grouping resulted in the inclusion of only one child in Group 4, so only three groups could be used in the analyses. (Scores for

TABLE 1   Correlations of VADS and Block Design Scores with Cognitive Measures and Rated Characteristics, and the Hypothesized Associations of Left and Right Temporal-Parietal Functioning (N = 24)

Measures and Characteristics	Left T-P (VADS)	Right T-P (Block Design)	Hypothesized Association to Left-Right T-P Areas
VADS Percentile Age	—	.12	
WISC-R Performance IQ	.18	.87***	
Bender Percentile Age	.51**	.50**	L & R
Reading Percentile Age	.47**	.40**	L & R
Reading (TR)	.48**	.35**	L & (R)
Writing (TR)	.51**	.25	L
Speech Intelligibility	.60**	.25	L
Speech (TR)	.33a	.06	(L)
Sign Skill (TR)	.05	.20	—
Residual Hearing (TR)	.37*	.11	(L)
Speechreading (TR)	.47**	.49**	L & R

$^a p = .06.$
$^* p \leq .05.$
$^{**} p \leq .01.$
$^{***} p \leq .001.$

TABLE 2   Comparisons of Three Subgroupings of Deaf Children on Selected Cognitive Measures and Rated Characteristics (N = 24)

Cognitive Measures	Group 1(N = 5)	Group 2(N = 11)	Group 3(N = 7)	Group 4(N = 1)[1]	Probability
VADS Percentile Age	10%	11%	48%	58%	.0001[b,c]
Block Design SS	8.0	11.8	12.7	7.0	.001[a,b]
WISC-R Performance IQ	97	115	117	95	.01[a,b]
Bender Percentile Age	13%	33%	51%	27%	.05[b]
Reading Percentile Age	43%	82%	96%	98%	.001[a,b]
Reading (TR)	2.0	3.2	4.0	5.0	.01[a,b]
Writing (TR)	2.0	3.1	4.0	5.0	.05[b]
Speech Intelligibility	25	30	44	—	.05[b,c]
Speech (TR)	2.2	2.6	3.0	4.0	NS
Sign Skill (TR)	2.8	3.7	3.3	5.0	NS
Residual Hearing (TR)	2.6	3.3	3.6	4.0	NS
Speechreading (TR)	2.8	3.5	4.3	4.0	.05[b]

Note. Group 1 = VADS Percentile Age < 23% and Block Design SS < 10.
  Group 2 = VADS Percentile Age < 23% and Block Design SS ≥ 10.
  Group 3 = VADS Percentile Age ≥ 23% and Block Design SS ≥ 10.
  Group 4 = VADS Percentile Age ≥ 23% and Block Design SS < 10.

[1] Because Group 4 contained only one case, it was not used in the statistical analyses. The scores for this case are included here only for purposes of illustration.
[a] Group 2 is significantly different from Group 1 at the .05 level.
[b] Group 3 is significantly different from Group 1 at the .05 level.
[c] Group 3 is significantly different from Group 2 at the .05 level.

the child in Group 4 are included in Table 2 for purposes of illustration only.) A series of one-way ANOVAS were conducted to examine differences between the three subgroups of deaf children. When ANOVAS were significant, Duncan's post hoc procedure (.05 level) was utilized to ascertain which groups were significantly different.

The group scores on the VADS, the Block Design, and the WISC-R Performance Scale were significantly different in the hypothesized directions, which merely provides a validity check for group organization. With regard to the Bender, Group 3 scored significantly better than Group 1 on both reading measures, while Group 3 scored higher than Group 1 on teacher ratings of writing ability. With regard to speech intelligibility, Group 3 scored significantly better than Groups 1 and 2. Finally, Group 3 scored higher than Group 1 on speechreading skill, while other teacher ratings showed no significant differences between groups.

DISCUSSION

Overall, we believe that our results support our hypotheses and contribute to similar findings that have been emerging recently in the literature. Further analyses utilizing a larger sample size are planned. One area that we did not address (but that we believe may be highly relevant with regard to subgroup differences) involves etiology; for example, children with congenital deafness may show or-

ganizational differences, while children with postcongenital/prelingual onset may show evidence of *reorganizational* phenomena that may be quite different.

REFERENCES

Anderson, R.J., & Sisco, F.H. 1977. *Standardization of the WISC-R Performance Scale for deaf children.* Office of Demographic Studies (Series T, No. 1). Washington, DC: Gallaudet College Press.

Brodmann, K. 1909. *Vergleichende Lokalisationlehre der Grosshirnrinde in ihren Prinzipien dargestellt auf Grund des Zellenbaues.* Leipzig: J.A. Barth. Cited by Kolb, B., & I.Q. Whishaw, 1985. In *Fundamentals of human neuropsychology.* 2d ed. New York: W. H. Freeman.

Geschwind, N. 1979. Specialization of the human brain. *Scientific American* 241:180–201.

Greenberg, M.T., & Kusché, C.A. 1989. Cognitive, personal, and social development in deaf children and adolescents. In *The handbook of special education: Research and practice*, 3 vols. ed. M.C. Wang, H.J. Walberg, & M.C. Reynolds, 95–129. Oxford, England: Pergamon Press.

Hynd, C.R. 1986. Educational intervention in children with developmental learning disorders. In *Child neuropsychology: Clinical practice* (vol.2), ed. J.E. Obrzut & G.W. Hynd, 265–297. San Diego: Academic Press.

Jensema, C.J., Schildroth, A.N., & O'Rourke, S.W. 1973. *Score conversion tables and age-based percentile norms for the Stanford Achievement Test, special edition for hearing-impaired students.* Washington, DC: Office of Demographic Studies, Gallaudet College.

Kolb, B., & Whishaw, I.Q. 1985. *Fundamentals of human neuropsychology.* 2nd ed. New York: W. H. Freeman.

Koopitz, E.M. 1963. *The Bender Gestalt Test for young children.* New York: Grune & Stratton.

———. 1973. *The Bender Gestalt Test for young children* (vol. 2). New York: Grune & Stratton.

———. 1977. *The Visual Aural Digit Span Test.* New York: Grune & Stratton.

Kusché, C.A. 1985. Information processing and reading achievement in the deaf population: Implications for learning and hemispheric lateralization. In *Cognition, education, and deafness: Directions for research and instruction*, ed. D.S. Martin, 115–120. Washington, DC: Gallaudet University Press.

Madden, R., Gardner, E.F., Rudman, H.C., Karlsen, B., & Merwin, J.C. 1972. *Stanford Achievement Test: Special Edition for Hearing Impaired Students.* New York: Harcourt Brace Jovanovich.

Monsen, R.B. 1978. Toward measuring how well hearing-impaired children speak. *Journal of Speech and Hearing Research* 21:197–219.

———. 1981. A usable test for the speech intelligibility of deaf talkers. *American Annals of the Deaf* 126:845–852.

Neville, H.J. 1985. Effects of early sensory and language experience on the development of the human brain. In *Neonate cognition: Beyond the blooming buzzing confusion*, ed. J. Mehler & R. Fox, 349–363. Hillsdale, NJ: Lawrence Erlbaum and Associates.

Wechsler, D. 1974. *Manual for the Wechsler Intelligence Scale for Children-Revised.* New York: The Psychological Corp.

Mastery Motivation in Deaf and Hearing Infants: A First Look

Robert H. MacTurk

T he idea that infants are motivated to engage their environment has only recently received empirical attention. Though White's (1959, 1963) influential papers provided the conceptual basis, it was not until the late 1970s that a concerted effort was made to operationalize the concept and develop a methodology appropriate for the study of the motivational characteristics of young infants (Jennings et al. 1979; Morgan et al. 1977).

The results of these early studies served to validate the methodology in terms of its relationships to standardize measures of competence (Yarrow, McQuiston et al. 1983; Messer et al. 1986), and parental influences on infants' motivation to master the environment (Jennings et al. 1979; McCarthy & McQuiston 1983; Yarrow, Morgan et al. 1982; Yarrow, MacTurk et al. 1984). These studies focused on infants' motivation to explore the inanimate environment, while more recent papers have addressed the social aspects of motivated behavior (MacTurk, Hunter et al. 1985; MacTurk, Vietze et al. 1985; Wachs 1987). These latter investigations established the importance of the social domain and provided a key to further understanding of the interface between cognition and personality.

Since the subjects of previous investigations of mastery motivation were all normally hearing infants, there are no data to indicate the possible influence of audition on this domain. Therefore, the purpose of this report is to examine the

The authors gratefully acknowledge the efforts of Ms. Victoria M. Trimm for her assistance in modifying the original coding system for this project and for the reliability coding.

motivational characteristics of a small group of deaf 12-month-old infants. Even though this report is exploratory in nature, we did have some expectations based both on anecdotal reports and on the results of an earlier pilot study of mother-infant interaction (Meadow-Orlans et al. 1987).

The deaf infants were expected to display an increased level of behaviors directed toward the experimenter or the mother. The prediction of a relative increase in social behaviors for the deaf infants in comparison with their hearing peers is associated with the prediction of a reduced level of motivated behavior attributed to a redistribution of object-directed and socially directed activities.

METHODS

Subjects

This report is based on 10 subjects: 7 deaf infants (4 girls and 3 boys) and 3 normally hearing infants (1 girl and 2 boys) who were seen when they were 12 months old. All the infants came from middle-income families with both parents present in the home. For the deaf infants, the mothers' mean age was 31.3 years and their education level was 15.3 years. The fathers' mean age was 33.7 years and their education level was 16.5 years. For the hearing infants, the mothers' mean age and education level were 34.5 and 18 years, respectively; the fathers' mean age and education level were 36 and 19 years. Two of the deaf infants have deaf parents, as does one of the hearing infants.

Procedures

Four mastery motivation tasks were presented in a fixed order for three minutes each. During the administration of the tasks, the infants sat on their mothers' laps at a feeding table, and the examiner sat across from the mother and the infant. In presenting the toy, the examiner demonstrated it to the infant, and if no interest was shown within the first minute it was demonstrated again. Afterwards, the examiner sat quietly while the child played with the toy, except to reposition the toy or to prevent it from being pulled off the table. Each mastery motivation assessment session was videotaped from behind a one-way mirror. These videotapes were coded using a system designed to capture the range of an infant's behavior in three categories: (1) behaviors directed toward the objects; (2) behaviors directed toward the mother or the experimenter; and (3) facial expressions of affect (crying/fussing, neutral, interest/excitement, and smiling/laughing). Each of the three categories of behavior were mutually exclusive and exhaustive within a category but not between categories.

The coding was performed at the individual behavior level and combined during the initial data-processing phase by adding the frequencies and durations to yield six primary measures of mastery motivation (Look, Explore, Persist, Social, Off-task, and Positive Affect).[1]

Measures of Mastery Motivation

Based on previous investigations of mastery motivation (Jennings et al. 1979; Yarrow, McQuiston et al. 1983), we chose to focus on nine measures—the six primary measures of mastery motivation and three latency measures that were derived from a separate series of analyses of the raw sequential data set.

1. Visual attention to the toys (Look)
2. Exploratory behavior (Explore)
3. Persistence on task-related activities (Persist)
4. Off-task behavior
5. Social behavior (Social)
6. Positive affect
7. Latency to task involvement
8. Latency to social behavior
9. Latency to positive affect

Reliability

Interrater reliability was assessed by having two trained observers independently code seven (out of a total of 40) toys. The percent of agreement for the object related behaviors was 86%, for Social, 92%, and for facial expressions, 78%.

RESULTS

Contrary to our expectations, no dramatic group differences were found for the measures of task engagement (Look, Explore, Persist, or Off-task) (Table 1). The deaf infants and the hearing infants displayed equal durations of persistent, task-related activities. Not only were the groups equally motivated to engage with the toys, but they also displayed a similar distribution of other toy-related behaviors.

TABLE 1   Means[1] and Standard Deviations for the Measures of Mastery Motivation for Deaf and Hearing Infants

Category	Deaf		Hearing	
	Means	SD	Means	SD
Look	31.5	14.5	27.0	17.0
Explore	62.4	23.9	62.3	25.0
Persist	57.9	23.6	68.8	37.3
Social	30.4	25.8	12.8	12.6
Off-task	6.4	10.6	10.1	11.7
Positive Affect	30.8	39.0	3.8	5.2
Latency to Task Engagement	8.5	15.8	3.5	4.7
Latency to Social	13.4	14.6	52.5	49.4
Latency to Positive Affect	96.1	61.3	151.5	44.6

[1] In seconds.

This finding suggests that hearing status is not important with regard to an infant's motivation to explore and learn about objects in the environment.

Given the absence of group differences for the measures of task-related activities, we were surprised to find that our initial prediction regarding social behavior was supported by the data. The major group differences appeared in the measures that tap the social/affective component of motivated behavior. The deaf infants spent close to 2.5 times longer engaged in socially-directed behaviors, that is, looking at the examiner and/or mother (both directly or in the mirror), than did their hearing peers. The deaf infants also spent 8 times longer laughing and smiling compared to the hearing infants. Not only did the deaf infants display longer durations in Social and Positive Affect, but they also did so with dramatically shorter latencies. The hearing infants spent 52 seconds engaged with the toy before attempting to involve the mother or examiner in their activities, compared to only 13 seconds for the deaf infants. A similar picture emerges for Latency to Positive Affect: The hearing infants spent approximately 2.5 minutes manipulating the object before smiling or laughing, while the deaf infants waited only 1.5 minutes. It appears that the deaf infants are more adept at integrating socially-oriented activities into their attempts to master the objects in their near environment. Even though they spent more time engaged in social behaviors and were quicker to do so, it was not at the expense of their task-directed activities.

The differences in the measures of social behaviors and positive affect prompted a series of additional analyses designed to examine the specific behaviors which preceded instances of Social/Positive Affect (e.g., lag sequential analysis).

For the Social category, we found that both Look and Persist had significant negative z-scores, suggesting an inhibitory effect on the infants' social behavior, regardless of their hearing status (Table 2). When the infants were engaged with the object, either visually or in active exploration, they were unlikely to proceed to a social behavior. This finding was not unexpected, since both Look and Persist typify a high degree of involvement with the toy.

This focused attention to objects has been shown to be a powerful marker of the infant's cognitive processes and has also been shown to represent a salient dimension of infants' interactions with objects during the last half of their first year of life (McCall et al. 1977; Lewis & Baldini 1979; Ruff 1984, 1986). A

TABLE 2 Conditional Probabilities and Z-scores for the Transitions from a Mastery Behavior to a Social Behavior for Deaf and Hearing Infants

Category	Deaf		Hearing	
	Probability	Z-score	Probability	Z-score
Look	13.9	−2.31[b]	4.5	−2.67[b]
Explore	22.9	1.98[a]	15.3	1.78
Persist	12.4	−6.36[c]	6.1	−4.28[c]
Off-task	30.2	3.08[b]	31.3	4.50[c]
Positive Affect	28.2	3.60[c]	0.0	0.0

[a] $z > 1.96, p < .05$.
[b] $z > 2.26, p < .01$.
[c] $z > 3.30, p < .001$.

similar pattern held for the transitions to Positive Affect, though the *z*-scores were attenuated, probably due to its comparatively low frequency.

Turning to the behaviors associated with an increased likelihood of Social, we found that Explore, Off-task, and Positive Affect tended to be a precursor to a socially-oriented behavior. This finding was particularly true for the deaf infants. For Off-task, both groups were about equally likely to follow with a Social, while the probability for the transition to Positive Affect was significant only for the deaf infants. The off-task behaviors imply boredom with the task at hand and the infants were, therefore, more likely to display an increased variability or openness to engage with the animate environment. The deaf infants were more likely to follow Positive Affect with a Social than were the hearing infants (in fact, that transition never occurred for the hearing infants). Although part of the reason may be the small number of infants in the hearing group, this finding remains unusual, primarily because one would expect socially oriented behaviors to be associated with laughing and/or smiling. This finding raises the possibility that the Positive Affect/Social axis may have a different psychological function for the deaf infants.

The Explore to Social transition was significant for the deaf infants and approached significance for the hearing group. This finding is particularly interesting both in terms of (1) when, in the course of object-related activities, social behaviors would be expected to appear, and (2) infants' management of their apparent need to maintain contact with the animate environment while simultaneously mastering inanimate objects.

DISCUSSION

These results support the following conclusions:

1. Deaf and hearing infants exhibit similar amounts of motivated behavior toward objects. Auditory contact with their surroundings is not a determining factor in attempts to master objects.
2. The deaf infants spent a longer period of time engaged in behaviors directed toward the experimenter and mother than did the hearing infants; they were able to do so without any apparent sacrifice to the deployment of their task- and goal-directed activities. This finding implies that the deaf infants were more skillful at integrating the competing demands of social- and object-oriented endeavors than were hearing peers.
3. The deaf infants engaged with the social environment and displayed a positive emotional response to the situation more quickly than the hearing infants. In addition, positive affect was more likely to be followed by a social behavior for the deaf infants. This finding indicates that the integration of social behaviors and object-oriented activities serves either a different function or a more potent function in the early development of deaf infants.

All the group differences were in the measures dealing with the infants' contact with the social environment. The deaf infants were more social, were faster to engage in a social behavior, and, when not actively engaged with the object, were more likely to move to a social behavior than their hearing peers. This conclusion suggests that as early as the first year of life, deaf infants have developed an important set of compensatory behaviors in an effort to obtain (presumably) the same amount of information from their environment through two sensory channels (visual and tactile) as the hearing infants obtain through three (auditory, visual, and tactile).

It is important to note that the integration of social behaviors into the stream of object-related activities is not solely a function of hearing status. Both groups of infants were almost equally likely to follow an Explore with a Social (Table 2). This finding suggests that at some level, all infants need to monitor their social environment. Furthermore, this monitoring (or social referencing [Feinman 1982; Feinman & Lewis 1983]) followed a predictable sequence of actions. Note that the transition associated with an increase in Social was from Explore—a set of behaviors considered in the current context to represent a more elementary level of mastery motivation. Clyman, Emde, Kempe, and Harmon (1986) typify this activity as "post-action referencing," which implies that the infants felt secure enough to explore the objects in the first place but still required some external affirmation with regard to their attempts to acquire more information concerning the properties of the toys (Feinman 1982; Klinnert, Campos, Sorce, Emde & Svejda 1983).

The existing literature has never addressed the possible effects of deafness as a means to investigate the influence of audition on the patterns of parent-infant interaction. Our data indicate that auditory contact with the environment is not a necessary condition for the infants' expressions of motivated behavior. There were no consistent differences either in the infants' persistence with objects or in the other measures of object interaction. The deaf infants may have developed a set of behaviors that offset the lack of auditory contact with the environment and that enable them to engage with and benefit from their interactions with their surroundings on an equal footing with their hearing peers.

In future studies we shall address the nature of the hypothesized compensatory mechanism and its developmental trajectory. It is obvious that its manifestations would not spring *de novo* at the onset of increased interest toward objects, but rather would have its precursors in the patterns of early parent-infant interaction. This data, which is currently being collected, offers the opportunity to understand the adaptations required of deaf infants to operate effectively in a world that presumes auditory contact.

NOTE

1. The coding scheme enabled us to assess individual behaviors (dropping, mouthing, looking at mother, etc.), which were determined, on an *a priori* basis, to constitute the subordinate categories of *look, explore, manipulate, task-directed, goal-directed, success, social,* and *off-task.* We formed the superordinate categories by summing *explore*

and *manipulate* into Explore and *task-directed* and *goal-directed* into Persist. The rationale for this pooling was based on the similarities between the behaviors in *explore*, *manipulate*, *task-directed*, and *goal-directed*. This pooling is analogous to the distinction that Weisler and McCall (1976) drew between motor-aided perceptual examinations and active physical interaction. *Explore* and *manipulate* were considered similar because of the general nature of the actions involved. Mouthing, touching, banging, and shaking were all behaviors that may be done with any toy and do not relate to particular toy properties. The *task-directed* and *goal-directed* categories, on the other hand, involved actions that were specific to an individual toy.

REFERENCES

Clyman, R.B., Emde, R.N., Kempe, J.E., & Harmon, R.J. 1986. Social referencing and social looking among twelve-month-old infants. In *Affective development in infancy*, ed. T.B. Brazelton & M.W. Yogman, 75–94. Norwood, NJ: Ablex Publishing Corp.

Feinman, S. 1982. Social referencing in infancy. *Merrill-Palmer Quarterly* 28:445–470.

Feinman, S., & Lewis, M. 1983. Social referencing at 10 months: A second order effect on infants' responses to strangers. *Child Development* 54:878–887.

Jennings, K.D., Harmon, R.J., Morgan, G.A., Gaiter, J.L., & Yarrow, L.J. 1979. Exploratory play as an index of mastery motivation: Relationships to persistence, cognitive functioning and environmental measures. *Developmental Psychology* 15:386–394.

Klinnert, M.D., Campos, J.J., Sorce, J.F., Emde, R.N., & Svejda, M. 1983. The development of social referencing in infancy. In *Emotion: Theory, research, and experience*, vol. 2, ed. R. Plutchik & H. Kellerman, 57–86. New York: Academic Press.

Lewis, M., & Baldini, N. 1979. Attentional processes as an individual difference. In *Attention and cognitive development*, ed. G.A. Hale & M. Lewis, 135–172. New York: Plenum Publishing Corp.

MacTurk, R.H., Hunter, F.T., McCarthy, M.E., Vietze, P.M., & McQuiston, S. 1985. Social mastery motivation in Down's syndrome and nondelayed infants. *Topics in Early Childhood Special Education* 4:93–109.

MacTurk, R.H., McCarthy, M.E., Vietze, P.M., & Yarrow, L.J. 1987. Sequential analysis of mastery behavior in 6- and 12-month-old infants. *Developmental Psychology* 23:199–203.

MacTurk, R.H., Vietze, P.M., McCarthy, M.E., McQuiston, S., & Yarrow, L.J. 1985. The organization of exploratory behavior in Down's syndrome and nondelayed infants. *Child Development* 56:573–581.

McCall, R.B., Eichorn, D.H., & Hogarty, P.S. 1977. Transitions in early mental development. *Monographs of the Society for Research in Child Development* 420 (3, Serial No. 171).

McCarthy, M.E., & McQuiston, S. 1983. *The relationship of contingent parental behaviors to infant motivation and competence.* Paper presented at the biennial meeting of the Society for Research in Child Development, April, Detroit, MI.

Meadow-Orlans, K.P., MacTurk, R.H., Prezioso, C.T., Erting, C.J., & Day, P.S. 1987. *Interactions of deaf and hearing mothers with three- and six-month-old infants.* Paper presented at the biennial meeting of the Society for Research in Child Development, April, Baltimore, MD.

Messer, D.J., McCarthy, M.E., Mcquiston, S., MacTurk, R.H., Yarrow, L.J., & Vietze, P.M. 1986. The relationship between mastery behavior in infancy and competence in early childhood. *Developmental Psychology* 22:366–372.

Morgan, G.A., Harmon, R.J., Gaiter, J.L., Jennings, K.D., Gist, N.F., & Yarrow, L.J. 1977. A method for assessing mastery motivation in one-year-old infants. *JSAS Catalog of Selected Documents in Psychology* 7:68. (No. 1517, 41 pp).

Ruff, H.A. 1984. Infants' manipulative exploration of objects: Effects of age and object characteristics. *Developmental Psychology* 20:9–20.

———. 1986. Components of attention during infants' manipulative exploration. *Child Development* 57:105–114.

Wachs, T.D. 1987. Specificity of environmental action as manifest in environmental correlates on infant's mastery motivation. *Developmental Psychology* 23:782–790.

White R.W. 1959. Motivation reconsidered: The concept of competence. *Psychological Review* 66:297–333.

———. 1963. Ego and reality in psychoanalytic theory. *Psychological Issues* 3:1–40.

Yarrow, L.J., Klein, R.P., Lomonaco, S., & Morgan, G.A. 1975. Cognitive and motivational development in early childhood. In *Exceptional infant 3: Assessment and intervention*, ed. B.Z. Friedlander, G.M. Sterritt, & G.E. Kirk. New York: Brunner/Mazel.

Yarrow, L.J., MacTurk, R.H., Vietze, P.M., McCarthy, M.E., Klein, R.P., & McQuiston, S. 1984. Developmental course of parental stimulation and its relationship to mastery motivation during infancy. *Developmental Psychology* 20:492–503.

Yarrow, L.J., McQuiston, S., MacTurk, R.H., McCarthy, M.E., Klein, R.P., & Vietze, P.M. 1983. Assessment of mastery motivation in the first year of life: Contemporaneous and cross-age relationships. *Developmental Psychology* 19:159–171.

Yarrow, L.J., Morgan, G.A., Jennings, K.D., Harmon, R.J., & Gaiter, J.L. 1982. Infants' persistence at tasks: Relationships to cognitive functioning and early experience. *Infant Behavior and Development* 5:131–142.

Yarrow, L.J., Rubenstein, J., & Pedersen, F.A. 1975. *Infant and environment: Early cognitive and motivational development*. Washington, DC: Halsted.

Analysis

Anthony B. Wolff

As cognitive science and neuroscience grow closer together, there has been a gradual increase in research on neurological and neuropsychological aspects of deafness. Such work is motivated by a number of questions, including

1. What is the effect of congenital deafness on brain development and/ or function?
2. Are particular educational strategies suggested by observed patterns of cerebral function or cognitive function in deaf students?
3. Are there general principles of cognitive or neurological development that can be learned from studying these phenomena in deaf subjects?

To a greater or lesser degree, each of the four papers in this chapter has addressed one or more of these issues.

It should be noted at the outset that none of the work reviewed here utilized physiological measurements. Two of these papers, those by Craig and Gordon and by Kusché and Greenberg, do report cognitive findings that provide at least a speculative functional view of some underlying neural mechanisms. The paper by Knobloch-Gala presents no data but instead discusses certain formal linguistic incongruities in some educational practices for deaf learners that may in turn conflict with the author's view of underlying neural organization. MacTurk and Trimm present interesting infant data that is not particularly germane to the understanding of neurological issues, but is quite relevant to questions of compensatory processes.

Craig and Gordon have now established a record of careful, systematic research that suggests the existence of some degree of cerebral reorganization, associated with specialized cognitive functioning, among their deaf subjects. Most notably, using Gordon's Cognitive Laterality Battery, they have demonstrated a superiority of deaf subjects over hearing subjects on certain purely visuospatial tasks. They also argue that the lower performance of deaf subjects on verbose-quential portions of their battery reflects a processing difficulty that is inherent in deafness. Taken at face value, this pattern of relative weakness for verbose-quential processes, and relative strength for visuospatial functioning, is suggestive of a pattern of atypical cerebral asymmetry that classically favors right hemispheric processes. Although one may question the validity of virtually any non-sign-based linguistic assessment procedure with deaf subjects (even when the instructions are signed, as they were in this case), the verbosequential tasks used here were quite free of syntactic demands, and only one involved a semantic process (categorical retrieval of lexical items). In any case, these possible objections do not negate the affirmative finding of enhanced spatial functioning among deaf subjects. These findings are also consistent with results reported by other laboratories, using both behavioral methods (Marcotte & LaBarba 1987) and electrophysiological methods (Wolff & Thatcher 1990), which have demonstrated cortical reorganization and enhanced right hemispheric functioning in deaf subjects.

In their paper, Kusché and Greenberg provide a restatement of the view that deafness may give rise to cerebral reorganization. They offer a theoretical model of the process of reading, which is not directly referenced in, and seems unrelated to, the later data-oriented portion of their article. However, a well-taken point in their speculative exposition is that the process of reading must involve numerous cortical areas. This view is not controversial and is consistent with the contemporary view of all complex human behaviors. It follows that cortical reorganization or functional alteration in any one or a combination of the relevant "modules" may give rise to modifications in the process of reading (or other complex behavior).

The animal sensory deprivation literature reveals that early deafferentation (removal or attenuation of sensory input), as well as environmental enrichment, can give rise to a host of modifications in cortical and subcortical cytoarchitectonics, neurochemistry, and behavior (e.g., Gyllensten, Malmfors & Norrlin 1966; LeVay, Wiesel & Hubel 1980; Rubel 1984; see also Renner & Rosenzweig 1987 for a general review of environmental effects on brain structure and function).

There is no logical reason to doubt that auditory deafferentation in the developing human should lead to similar developmental effects in the cerebral cortex. Further, given the multiplicity of neural connections to primary and secondary auditory cortex, there are numerous possible areas and modules that may be affected secondarily by the absence of auditory stimulation. This effect may result in altered functioning in virtually any cognitive domain, for example, memory, executive control, or sequencing.

The data offered by Kusché and Greenberg, although not clearly related to their speculative treatment of reading, do reflect the presence of some aspects of cognitive functioning that are not typical of hearing subjects. For example, despite above-average WISC-R Performance scores, one of their high-functioning groups attained below-average performance on the Bender-Gestalt test. The authors attribute that result to possible left-hemispheric aspects of this visually-based task. It is interesting that the same subgroup also performed poorly on a verbal memory task (the Visual-Aural-Digit Span Test), suggesting that other, nonvisual processes may contribute to performance on the presumably visual Bender. Whether the anatomic locus of this phenomenon is actually somewhere in the left temporal-parietal area, as the authors suggest, or elsewhere, remains to be seen. The present author and colleagues (Wolff, Kammerer, Gardner & Thatcher, in press) have found a similar pattern of sub-normative performance by intellectually above-average deaf subjects on the Developmental Test of Visual Motor Integration (Beery 1982)—a test similar to the Bender. These same subjects manifested numerous EEG differences from hearing subjects, spanning both left and right *intra*hemispheric occipito-parietal, fronto-temporal, and fronto-frontal regions, as well as *inter*hemispheric fronto-frontal and parieto-parietal pathways.

It would be pure speculation to attempt to relate which of these physiological observations may be "responsible" for any specific cognitive or behavioral finding. What does seem evident, as supported by various authors, including Kusché and Greenberg (as well as Craig and Gordon), is that certain tasks are performed differently by deaf than by hearing subjects, possibly reflecting systematic differences in cognitive style; moreover, there is mounting evidence that these differences may be related to a complex interaction of component neural processes that may be altered as a consequence of deafness.

Given that such differences exist, the question of their relevance still remains. The present results add to the accumulating data suggesting that a variety of cognitive tasks are performed differently, or that the distribution of skills is different among deaf persons than among hearing persons. For the educational or mental-health professional, greater diagnostic validity and precision should result from an increased understanding of "normal" functioning among deaf people. The use of such information as a baseline in the evaluation of a deaf individual is far more appropriate than the use of norms or baselines derived from experience with hearing subjects.

Alone among the present set of authors, Craig and Gordon have explored the implications of their work for intervention, in this case of an educational nature. Specifically, they utilized Feuerstein's Instrumental Enrichment in an effort to enhance academic functioning in their subjects. Preliminary analysis of their data reveals that the greatest functional improvement was obtained when subjects were given training in their weaker areas. That is, subjects stronger in visuospatial functioning improved academically when given training in verbosequential skills, and vice versa. However, training to the stronger area was not helpful, and even may have been detrimental. This finding suggests that Feuerstein's methods are of practical educational utility; furthermore, cerebral dominance measures may be useful in prescribing educational interventions for deaf students.

Knobloch-Gala's paper is also interesting in this connection. She raises the problem of deaf students being required to assimilate communications that blend more iconic elements with more symbolic elements. Further, she questions the appropriateness of such communication, on the grounds that it leads to dissonant demands for cerebral processing (e.g., left vs. right hemispheric processes). Although there is no convincing argument given to support a neurological objection to such educational and communicative practices, there is much sentiment in educational quarters to support this view. Perhaps empirical methods, such as those of Craig and Gordon and others, could be useful in suggesting which deaf individuals are most likely to benefit from a more simultaneous or visual style of presentation as opposed to a more sequential or oral one.

The presence of enhanced right-hemispheric function implies the existence of neural compensation in deaf subjects. The animal literature again provides some insight, as in demonstrating that postnatal sensory experience has a direct impact on the elaboration of brain circuits in the developing organism. Thus, the young deaf child may make greater use of visual and tactual input than the hearing child, resulting in compensatory cerebral adaptations. It is also reasonable to hypothesize that deaf children may alter their behavioral repertoires in such a way as to maximize the informational benefit of nonauditory sensory input.

The data presented by MacTurk and Trimm support this view. These authors observed normally developing twelve-month-old deaf infants interacting with several objects under carefully controlled conditions. The infants' activity was then coded for a number of categories, including exploratory behavior, persistence, positive affect, visual attention, and social behavior. Results suggested that in comparison to hearing infants, deaf subjects displayed more positive affect, slightly greater persistence, longer latency to engage in task, but shorter latency to engage in social interaction. Deaf subjects appeared more adept at integrating social/affective cues into the task environment.

It would seem improbable that these behavioral differences were due to neurological differences between deaf and hearing infants. It is more likely that the behavioral differences arise as a consequence of altered reward potency of various experiences for the deaf infant, as a consequence of lack of auditory stimulation and an attendant reliance on other modalities. To be consistent with the developmental literature, however, one would expect systematic differences in infant experience to give rise to altered cerebral circuitry and/or function. The work reported by MacTurk and Trimm, as well as other careful investigation of deaf infants, may thus provide a crucial link in our understanding of the ontogeny of cortical reorganization in deaf subjects.

Taken together, these papers contribute to the view that the experience of deafness results in a certain degree of neural, behavioral, and cognitive "reprogramming." However, nothing in this work, nor in that of other authors, provides a metric that could inform us as to the practical magnitude of these deaf/hearing differences. Clearly, a variety of factors contribute to cortical reorganization among deaf individuals. These factors include etiology, degree of hearing loss, age at onset, extent of early exposure to various communication systems, and deaf acculturation, among others. The influence of such variables on cerebral development and function needs to be made the subject of further inquiry.

More generally, current research is only beginning to point toward an understanding of the interactions among deafness, early experience, altered brain function, cognitive function, and behavioral adaptations. Further advances in physiological measurement techniques, as well as refinements in psychometrics, may eventually lead to increased knowledge of these interactions.

REFERENCES

Beery, K.E. 1982. *Revised administration, scoring, and teaching manual for the developmental test of visual-motor integration.* Cleveland: Modern Curriculum Press.

Gyllensten, L., Malmfors, T., & Norrlin, M.L. 1966. Growth alteration in the auditory cortex of visually deprived mice. *Journal of Comparative Neurology* 126:463–470.

LeVay, S., Wiesel, T.N., & Hubel, D.H. 1980. The development of ocular dominance columns in normal and visually deprived monkeys. *Journal of Comparative Neurology* 191:276–300.

Marcotte, A.C., & LaBarba, R.C. 1987. The effects of linguistic experience on cerebral lateralization for speech production in normal hearing and deaf adolescents. *Brain and Language* 31:276–300.

Rubel, E.W. 1984. Ontogeny of auditory system function. *Annual Review of Physiology* 46:213–229.

Wolff, A.B., Kammerer, B.L., Gardner, J.K., & Thatcher, R.W. 1989. The Gallaudet neurobehavioral project: Brain-behavior relationships in deaf children. *Journal of the American Deafness and Rehabilitation Association* 23:19–33.

Wolff, A.B., & Thatcher, R.W. 1990. Cortical reorganization in deaf children. *Journal of Clinical and Experimental Neuropsychology* 12:209–221.

7

COGNITIVE PROCESSES

Spontaneous Comparative Behavior and Categorization: The Links Between Mediated Interaction and Reading Comprehension

Janice Berchin

elping deaf persons to attain successful reading has always frustrated educators of the deaf. The discrepancy between reading achievement levels for hearing-impaired and hearing individuals is well documented in the literature (Furth 1966; Gentile & DiFrancesca 1969; Lane & Baker 1974). Studies documenting the achievement levels of hearing-impaired students over the last 10 years by the Gallaudet University Center for Assessment and Demographic Studies indicate that only 10% of the hearing-impaired children in the U.S. reach eighth grade reading level by age 14—the age at which the average hearing child achieves the same reading level (Trybus & Karchmer 1977; Allen 1986). The average reading level of deaf adults leaving school is approximately at the fourth grade. In addition, the population of congenitally deaf individuals tends to reach a plateau with regard to reading comprehension at age 13 or 14, with very little change through adulthood (DiFrancesca 1972).

READING COMPREHENSION

Most research has examined the linguistic abilities of deaf individuals in order to explain their difficulty in reading comprehension (Quigley et al. 1977; Hatcher & Robbins 1978). However, it is essential to examine the cognitive abilities necessary to develop the prerequisites for reading comprehension. Reading researchers have utilized schema theory (Rumelhart 1980) to help gain insight into how people read. This theory describes the formation of schemata (networks of concepts and their defining and associative links) and the use of schemata in terms of storing information in memory (semantic memory). The manifestation of schemata in printed text is the existence of cohesion between sentences (lexical cohesion) and larger units of text (main idea). Underlying the formation and use of schemata are the two cognitive functions of spontaneous comparison and the operation of categorization.

COGNITIVE PREREQUISITES FOR READING IN DEAF STUDENTS

To date there has been almost no research directly on schema development with deaf students. From studies by Gaines et al. (1981) and Kluwin et al. (1980), it can be concluded that deaf individuals do bring their world knowledge to bear on the reading task. However, a study by Strassman (1985) indicated that deaf subjects do not make use of their knowledge by spontaneously instantiating.

Although there have been a number of studies to investigate the association, sorting, and classification abilities of deaf individuals, the results have been inconsistent, depending on the variable being classified.

Ottem (1980) analyzed the cognitive studies and suggested a classification system of tasks and problems used in studies with deaf people. This classification demonstrated that the deaf and hearing perform equally well when required to show their understanding by referring to one of two minimum data. However, the deaf perform worse than their hearing peers when required to refer to both such data. This performance results in the cognitive deficiency mentioned by Feuerstein (1979) as an inability to hold two sources of information. This function is extremely important to keep intact since a successful reader needs to hold and integrate multiple pieces of information as he or she reads a text (activates and uses schemata) (Anderson 1981). This function is crucial for categorization, as well as for spontaneous comparative behavior (Feuerstein 1980).

MEDIATIONAL INTERVENTION

Feuerstein (1980) has developed a theoretical construct that explains the etiology of cognitive deficiencies among retarded performers. Feuerstein asserts that this construct, called mediated learning experience, is necessary for the development of organized, efficient cognitive structures. This "experience" involves the active interaction on the part of well-intentioned, caring adults who interpose themselves between the world of objects and events and the learner and, in so doing, "mediate" the stimuli so that each stimulus is changed as it reaches the organism. Research has shown the mediated experience to be highly applicable to the assessment of deaf individuals (Keane 1983; Keane & Kretschmer 1987; Katz 1984; Krapf 1985). In addition, Martin and Jonas (1986) found the Instrumental Enrichment curriculum, based on Feuerstein's theory, to be very effective for the deaf adolescent student in improving analysis of problem situations, finding sources of errors, completeness, organization, and planning in problem solving situations, reading comprehension, and abstract thinking. This construct however, had not been applied to specific academic content in the classroom.

Broadly, the purpose of the study was to investigate that particular application (i.e., the modifiability of a specific cognitive function and the transfer of the modified function to a specific academic content). More specifically, this study attempted to determine whether a chain of functional relationships exists between a particular method of interaction called mediated learning, a cognitive function called spontaneous comparative behavior, the operation of categorization, and the reading comprehension tasks of using lexical cohesion and finding the main idea (activation and use of schemata).

Effect and Transfer to Reading Comprehension

The overall research design for this study was a single-subject one, with multiple baselines across subjects. The Categorization Instrument from the Feuerstein Instrumental Enrichment Program (FIE) (Feuerstein 1980) mediational interaction treatment was applied in sequence across three profoundly deaf subjects. The probe battery consisted of five tests: A particular set of Spontaneous Comparison Cards, Categorization Cards, the Test of Verbal Abstraction, the Lexical Cohesion Test, and the Main Idea Test. Twelve sets of Spontaneous Comparison Cards were designed for use in each baseline/treatment session to obtain the data for the dependent variables.

Baseline instruction represented a direct-experience approach to testing categorization and used a Classification Workbook (Curriculum Associates Curricula 1981). Instruction continued until a stable baseline was established. The purpose of the probe battery was not only to examine the effect of a mediated learning experience on the acquisition of the ability to categorize and on the remediation of the cognitive function of spontaneous comparative behavior, but also to examine the transfer of that enhanced functioning to two reading tasks (lexical comprehension and main idea). The study investigated whether enhanced cognitive functioning would exhibit enhanced functioning in related reading tasks (lexical cohesion and main idea).

Three profoundly prelingually deaf youngsters between the ages of 11 and 13 served as subjects for this study. All subjects were enrolled in a school for the deaf and were reading between 2.0 and 2.5 grade level on standardized reading tests. In addition, the subjects were unable to compare spontaneously or to use the operation of categorization in screening testing.

The dependent variables, measured from the responses to the sets of Spontaneous Comparison Cards, were

1. The number of spontaneous comparative responses;
2. A score of spontaneous comparison involving the notion of connectivity;
3. The quality of the commonality and difference in the subjects' responses; and
4. The number of most salient verbs and class nouns that the subjects used.

Results indicated a positive treatment effect for all three subjects for all the dependent variables as well as for acquiring the operation of categorization. In addition, positive treatment effect was established for the near transfer of spontaneous comparison. However, a treatment effect was only evident for two subjects for one test of the near transfer of categorization and one subject for the other. The far-transfer results were inconsistent. Although there was an upward trend for all three subjects on the tests of lexical cohesion and main idea, a treatment effect was established for only one subject for one of the far-transfer tests.

CONCLUSION

The combined results of the dependent variables and the Spontaneous Comparison Cards from the Probe data support the contention that at least one cognitive function of deaf individuals can be significantly enhanced through a mediational approach to interaction. This finding is consistent with other research (Keane 1983; Krapf 1985; Martin & Jonas 1986), which suggests a wider applicability of this notion and the potential for long-term effects. In turn, these findings support the applicability of Feuerstein's (1979) theoretical construct of mediated learning in a hearing-impaired population.

A closer look at the transfer tasks provides more insight into the effect of mediation. A change in the directions for the transfer tests may have affected the results. The difference in directions represents a slight control of the input phase of the mental act. This finding may suggest that manipulation of the input can have a powerful effect on the output. This effect is consistent with the results of a study by Huberty and Koller (1984), which found that even minimum input control had a profound effect on the ability of hearing and deaf students to solve a cognitive task. The researchers concluded that "the deaf may have more difficulty with initial input of information than do hearing persons" (Huberty & Koller 1984) but that with minimal input control, significant increases in performance could be effected. In this view, then, input manipulation can be viewed as a form of mediation. Therefore, it can be concluded that all three subjects had a treatment effect for the transfer tasks. This conclusion also would be consistent with the findings of Strassman, Kretschmer, and Bilsky (1987), who found that in contrast to the hearing subjects, the deaf subjects in their study did not spontaneously instantiate in a reading task, but could when directed to do so (a manipulation of the input).

This study is offered as an initial investigation of the cognitive modifiability of a specific cognitive function and the transfer of that function to specific academic content. The results for this population indicate cognitive modifiability with the use of the mediated interaction for the cognitive function of spontaneous comparison. In the classroom, academic learning might be enhanced in the future by using this special interaction to remediate the cognitive deficiencies necessary for academic learning.

REFERENCES

Allen, T.E. 1986. Patterns of academic achievement among hearing impaired students: 1974 and 1983. In *Deaf children in America*, ed. A.N. Schildroth & M.A. Karchmer, 161–206. Boston: College-Hill Press.

Anderson, R. 1981. *A proposal to continue a center for the study of reading*. (Technical Proposal, 4 vols.). Urbana, IL: University of Illinois, Center for the Study of Reading.

DiFrancesca, S. 1972. Academic achievement test results of a national testing program for hearing impaired students, Spring 1971 (Series D, No. 9). Washington, DC: Gallaudet College, Office of Demographic Studies.

Feuerstein, R. 1979. *The dynamic assessment of retarded performers*. Washington, DC: Curriculum Development Associates.

———. 1980. *Instrumental enrichment: An intervention program for cognitive modifiability*. Washington, DC: Curriculum Development Associates.

Furth, H.G. 1966. *Thinking without language*. New York: Free Press.

Gaines, R., Mandler, J., & Bryant, P. 1981. Immediate and delayed story recall by hearing and deaf children. *Journal of Speech and Hearing Research* 24:463–469.

Gentile, A., & DiFrancesca, S. 1969. *Academic achievement test performance of hearing impaired students*. Washington, DC: Gallaudet College.

Hatcher, C., & Robbins, N. 1978. *The development of reading skills in deaf children*. Paper presented at the annual meeting of the National Reading Conference, November/December, St. Petersburg, FL.

Huberty, T., & Koller, J. 1984. A test of the learning potential hypothesis with hearing and deaf students. *Journal of Educational Research* 78:22–27.

Katz, N.M. 1984. Use of the learning potential assessment device for cognitive enrichment of a deaf child. *School Psychology Review* 13:99–106.

Keane, K. 1983. Application of mediated learning theory to a deaf population: A study in cognitive modifiability. Ph.D. diss. Teachers College, Columbia University.

Keane, K., & Kretschmer, R.E. 1987. Effect of mediated learning intervention on cognitive task performance with a deaf population. *Journal of Educational Psychology* 79(1):49–53.

Kluwin, T., Getson, D., & Kluwin, B. 1980. The effects of experience on the discourse comprehension of deaf and hearing adolescents. *Directions* 1(3):49.

Krapf, G. 1985. The effects of mediated intervention on advance figural analogic problem solving with deaf adolescents: Implications for dynamic assessment. Ph.D. diss. Temple University.

Lane, H.S., & Baker, D. 1974. Reading achievement of the deaf: Another look. *Volta Review* 76:489–499.

Martin, D., & Jonas, B. 1986. Cognitive modifiability in the deaf adolescent. Washington, DC: Gallaudet University. Typescript.

Ottem, E. 1980. An analysis of cognitive studies with deaf subjects. *American Annals of the Deaf* 125:564–575.

Quigley, S., Power, D., & Steinkamp, M. 1977. The language structure of deaf children. *Volta Review* 79:73–84.

Rumelhart, D.E. 1980. Schemata: The building blocks of cognition. In *Theoretical issues in reading comprehension perspectives from cognitive psychology, linguistics, artificial intelligence, and education*, ed. R.J. Spiro, B.C. Bruce, & W.F. Brewer, 33–58. Hillsdale, NJ: Lawrence Erlbaum Associates.

Strassman, B.K. 1985. Training an inferential and constructive reading process in deaf and hearing youngsters. Ph.D. diss. Teachers College, Columbia University.

Strassman, B.K., Kretschmer, R.D., & Bilsky, L.H. 1987. The instantiation of general terms by deaf adolescents/adults. *Journal of Communication Disorders* 20:1–13.

Trybus, R.J., & Karchmer, M.A. 1977. School achievement scores of hearing impaired children: National data on achievement status and growth patterns. *American Annals of the Deaf* 122:62–69.

Hearing-Impaired Students' Performance on the Piagetian Liquid Horizontality Test: An Analysis and Synthesis

Laurie Witters-Churchill
Lee A. Witters

Piaget and Inhelder (1956) examined from a developmental perspective whether or not children understood the concept of liquid horizontality—the principle that the surface of still water remains horizontal regardless of the tilt of the jar. They were concerned with children's ability to utilize external frames of reference for locating and comparing the positions and orientations of objects in space. They believed that this concept is an important milestone in a learner's cognitive development, since this skill is essential in the areas of science, mathematics, and geography (Copeland 1979).

Numerous studies have been conducted involving the principle of liquid horizontality. Developmentally, it has been demonstrated that children below the age of nine have considerable difficulty in perceiving and understanding this concept (Barna & O'Connel 1967; Beilin, Kagan, & Rabinowitz 1966; Ford 1970; Kelly & Witters 1981; Piaget & Inhelder 1956; Shantz & Smock 1966). A number of studies have reported that females appear to have considerably more problems than males in perceiving and understanding that liquid remains invariantly horizontal. Sex differences on this task have been documented with the adult population (Morris 1971; Rebelsky 1964; Willemsen & Reynolds 1973), college students (Kelly & Kelly 1977; Kelly & Kelly 1978b; Thomas & Jamison 1975; Thomas, Jamison, & Hummel 1973; Walker & Krasnoff 1978), and with elementary and junior high level children from both regular and gifted educational programs (Kelly & Kelly 1978a; Kelly & Witters 1981).

Few studies examining the principle of horizontality have been conducted with "exceptional" populations. In studies with hearing-impaired students by Witters-Churchill, Kelly, and Witters (1983) and Murphy-Berman, Witters, and

Harding (1985a, 1985b, 1986), the researchers reported that either no sex differences were found or that few differences across test items emerged. This result was true for both elementary and secondary hearing-impaired students and for children who were labeled as "gifted hearing-impaired." In addition, no sex differences were reported in a study with adolescents with severe social-emotional problems (Murphy-Berman & Witters 1987), nor with elementary and secondary learning-disabled students (Murphy-Berman, Witters & Schillerstrom 1988).

The present study analyzed and synthesized the current research that has been conducted in the area of hearing-impaired students' understanding of the liquid horizontality principle. Data were compared for normally hearing populations and other exceptional populations. A limited application of the meta-analysis procedure (Glass 1976) was used. This type of cognitive research is potentially interesting to educators, psychologists, and other professionals working with the hearing-impaired. First, it involves both visual-spatial and language concept tasks; Luria (1966, 1973) contended that the speech/language function regulates all the higher mental functions, including perception. Second, considerable developmental data are available for normally hearing subjects, giving a solid perspective on how people at different ages should perform these tasks. Finally, it can contribute to the knowledge base concerning the influence of a severe hearing loss on the cognitive processes. By using meta-analysis—a method for synthesizing empirical studies—the research questions that have been studied extensively may be clearly summarized.

METHODOLOGY

Analysis and synthesis focused on studies involving exceptional populations. An extensive literature search was conducted to identify studies appropriate for the present investigation. The primary data base for this search was the Educational Resources Information Center (ERIC); additionally, reference lists from relevant published articles were perused and the authors' personal files were searched. To be included, a study needed to meet these criteria: (1) subjects involved exceptional populations; (2) some form of liquid horizontality test was used; (3) quantitative data were provided; (4) data to calculate effect size and/or explained variance were included; and (5)information given was related to at least one of the major questions being considered.

After locating studies that met topical criteria, the investigators read for variables relating to the research questions. The following variables were noted: (1) developmental data; (2) training data; (3) gender data; and (4) test data. Each study was reviewed individually, and results were examined to ensure that separate samples were reported.

This search resulted in the discovery of only seven separate research studies that have investigated the liquid horizontality concept with exceptional populations. Of these, four studied hearing-impaired subjects (Murphy-Berman, Witters & Harding 1985a, 1985b, 1986; Robertson & Youniss 1969; Witters-Churchill, Kelly & Witters 1983), one studied gifted subjects (Kelly & Witters 1981), one studied adolescents with severe social-emotional problems (Murphy-Berman & Witters 1987), and one studied learning-disabled subjects (Murphy-Berman, Witters & Schillerstrom 1988). Unpublished studies were deliberately included in the synthesis in order to diminish the concern that available studies are biased toward significant effects while other studies remain in the file drawer (Rosenthal 1979). Twenty-three studies involving investigation of the liquid horizontality principle with hearing populations were reviewed for comparison purposes.

A major purpose of this study was to reanalyze the studies on cognitive gender differences with both "abnormal" and "exceptional" populations, and to report the magnitude of differences that exist between those "exceptional" males and females. Typically, the measure

$$d = \frac{M1 - M2}{SD},$$

where M1 and M2 are the same means of the two groups and SD is the average of the standard deviations of the two groups is used to report "effect size." For purposes of interpretation, Cohen (1977) considers a d of 0.20 to be small, a value of 0.50 to be medium, and a value of 0.80 to be large. An effect size of 0.50, for example, means that one group differed from the other by one-half a standard deviation.

Another measure of effect size that researchers frequently use to report magnitude is omega-squared (Ω^2). This measure was used to identify the proportion of the total variance in the population that was accounted for by gender differences. McNamara (1978) transformed the frequently used formula by Hays (1963) so that this measure may be calculated using statistics commonly reported in research journals (i.e., F, N, and n) and would not require a complete ANOVA table. From this calculation, the practical significance of the findings may be interpreted. Effect size d and omega-squared (Ω^2) were reported when sufficient information was provided.

RESULTS AND IMPLICATIONS

For hearing students, numerous studies suggested that children younger than nine have difficulty in perceiving and understanding that liquid remains invariantly horizontal. For those exceptional populations commonly labeled learning-disabled and those who are gifted, older (secondary) students did better than younger (elementary) students (Murphy-Berman, Witters & Schillerstrom 1988; Kelly & Witters 1981), thereby suggesting that these children are similar to normal children in development according to the Piaget stages. The study by Murphy-Berman and Witters (1987) with adolescents having social-emotional problems did not address the developmental variable. For the hearing-impaired population, Robertson and Youniss (1969) examined hearing-impaired and hearing children's abilities to perceive the horizontality of water level for two age groups, 8 to 9 years and 11 to 12 years. Their study showed similar patterns between the two groups. The younger, but not the older, hearing-impaired children performed significantly lower than the hearing subjects.

Furth (1973) argued that the results of the Robertson and Youniss study indicated only a slight retardation on the part of hearing-impaired children and concluded that a lack of linguistic experience has no substantial impact on a child's understanding of spatial transformation. The Murphy-Berman, Witters, and Harding study (1985b, 1986) argued that primary and intermediate-level deaf students may possess this type of spatial transformation in a manner quite similar to their older peers. If additional studies support this conclusion, a lack of linguistic experience would have little impact upon hearing-impaired elementary and secondary students' understanding of this cognitive concept.

An examination of selected studies revealed that the bottle shapes of the test instrument varied (i.e., rectangular jars, flasks, beakers, curved surfaces). Generally speaking, the shape of the bottle used in the test stimuli influenced performance. Some students did better with curved surfaces than with rectangular. In those studies using specific training activities with normal populations, student performance on the test improved.

As for exceptional populations, training improved performance for elementary and secondary gifted students (Kelly & Witters 1981), for adolescents with social-emotional problems (Murphy-Berman & Witters 1987), for elementary and secondary learning-disabled students (Murphy-Berman, Witters & Schillerstrom 1988), and for secondary hearing-impaired students (Witters 1980; Witters-Churchill, Kelly, & Witters 1983). These studies conducted with hearing-impaired students utilized a nonverbal training procedure in which the principle was demonstrated using visual aids.

Females from a variety of normal populations have been found to have more difficulty than males in perceiving and understanding the principle of liquid horizontality. A meta-analysis by Linn and Petersen (1985) revealed that males do perform better than females on several spatial perception tasks. Linn and Petersen noted, however, that the studies they reviewed reported that only about 5% of the variance in the water level task is attributable to sex. Researchers have speculated that cognitive sex differences observed in hearing populations on the horizontality task and on other tasks may be due to either biological or experiential factors. Among the biological hypotheses considered have been differences in genes (Bock & Kolakowski 1973; Thomas 1983; Vandenberg & Kuse 1979), hormones (Berenbaum & Resnick 1982; Petersen 1979), brain structure and function (McGlone 1980; Petersen 1982), and timing of puberty (Newcombe & Bandura 1983; Petersen 1983). Hypotheses concerning the effects of experiential factors and socialization processes on cognitive sex differences have included expectancies for success (Meehan & Overton 1986), parental expectations (Parsons, Adler, & Kaczala 1982), educational policies and practices (Fox, Tobin & Brody 1979), and academic experience (Kalichman 1987). Petersen (1982) cautions that while sex is a simple, easy-to-measure variable, it is clearly not merely genetic or even biological in nature, and recommends that investigations of sex-related differences not be limited to one subset of plausible explanations.

No sex differences were noted in studies with hearing-impaired and gifted hearing-impaired subjects (Murphy-Berman, Witters, & Harding 1985a 1985b, 1986; Witters 1980; Witters-Churchill, Kelly & Witters 1983). When similar studies were conducted with adolescents with social-emotional problems (Murphy-Berman & Witters 1987) and with elementary and secondary learning-disabled students (Murphy-Berman, Witters & Schillerstrom 1988), again, no sex differences were noted. Why sex differences would be found with "normal" but not with "exceptional" populations is open to speculation. It has been hypothesized by the authors in previous research (Murphy-Berman & Witters 1987; Murphy-Berman, Witters & Harding 1985) that socialization differences among these populations may contribute to some of the different patterns of findings obtained. Witters-Churchill, Kelly, and Witters (1983) speculated that perhaps hearing-impaired students' lack of linguistic sophistication shields them from some of the subtle gender biases present in the language, supporting the notion argued by Petersen (1982) and others that the gender-related differences reported in studies with "normal" populations may have more of an experiential basis than a biological one (Maccoby & Jacklin 1974).

Several important implications for both instruction and research are apparent from this study. First, it appears that training hearing-impaired and other exceptional children and youth in scientific reasoning with controlled hands-on experiments increases their understanding of the process of scientific investigations. Experimenting in the classroom is recommended to observe whether exceptional learners, including the hearing-impaired, accelerate or elaborate their learning on visual-spatial tasks to show their ability for learning required material and for generalizing to other situations with less effort than learning specific lower-order subject skills.

Second, providing multisensory approaches utilizing visual, auditory, and tactile stimulation with exceptional learners likely maximizes learning. The synthesized data suggest that hearing-impaired children can begin to represent spatial relationships appropriately at an early age, but they need practice in learning to disregard distracting spatial cues. Applying visual-spatial tasks to daily living situations strengthens exceptional learners' understanding of basic concepts in math, science, and geography. Provision of an environment in which learners can solve problems and regulate their own learning would appear to be desirable.

Third, working cooperatively with others on the visual-spatial tasks in the learning environment seems desirable for language development. It seems important to combine verbal ability with manipulation. Verbal ability is not always equal to functional ability. In the case of hearing-impaired learners, verbal ability (i.e., ability to state the rule of horizontality) was related to functional ability (i.e., ability to draw the horizontal water line), but was not always equal to it. Functional ability improved after nonverbal methods of training were provided.

Fourth, the pattern of results reported in this study suggests that hearing status, per se, may not be as influential a factor in affecting an individual's ability to make these specific types of spatial transformations as other cognitive and experiential factors that cut across hearing/deaf dimensions. Given the likelihood that socialization processes account for sex differences in performance on some tasks, recommendations to reduce this negative socialization are warranted.

The review of studies involving liquid horizontality research, including those with both hearing and hearing-impaired subjects, revealed the importance of reporting complete statistical data. Several studies had to be excluded from the synthesis because inadequate data were reported for calculating effect size and the explained variance. Providing sufficient information to allow replication would increase credibility for educational research and would facilitate meta-analysis and other empirical syntheses of existing knowledge. Specifically, studies should include

1. Sample size specification;
2. Problem statements and research hypotheses;
3. Exact probability values associated with the test of each statistical hypothesis;
4. Measurement concerns associated with reliability and validity; and
5. Complete data results that correspond to the conclusions entered in the published report.

Prejudice against the null hypothesis in published journals has been discussed and documented. It is recommended that research journals publish nonsignificant findings, and that all significant findings include measures of practical significance. It is recommended that a meta-analysis procedure be conducted with the 23 studies of hearing subjects identified in the present literature search, in order to determine the magnitude of the sex differences that have been reported. More studies with exceptional populations are needed to expand the existing data base and should also extend to other measures of cognition in order to support or refute the conclusions derived from the present synthesis.

REFERENCES

Barna, J., & O'Connel, D. 1967. Perception of horizontality as a function of age and stimulus setting. *Perceptual and Motor Skills* 25:70–72.

Beilin, H., Kagan, J., & Rabinowitz, R. 1966. Effects of verbal and perceptual training on water level representation. *Child Development* 37:317–329.

Berenbaum, S.A., & Resnick, S. 1982. Somatic androgyny and cognitive abilities. *Developmental Psychology* 18:418–423.

Bock, R.D., & Kolakowski, D. 1973. Further evidence of sex-linked major gene influence on human spatial visualizing ability. *American Journal of Human Genetics* 25:1–14.

Cohen, J. 1977. *Statistical power analysis for the behavioral sciences*. New York: Academic Press.

Copeland, R.W. 1979. *How children learn mathematics*. New York: Macmillan.

Ford, L. 1970. Predictive versus perceptual responses to Piaget's water line task and their relationship to distance conversation. *Child Development* 41:193–204.

Fox, L., Tobin, D., & Brody, L. 1979. Sex role socialization and achievement in mathematics. In *Sex related differences in cognitive functioning*, ed. M. Wittig & A. Petersen, 303–332. New York: Academic Press.

Furth, H.G. 1973. *Deafness and learning: A psychosocial approach*. Belmont, CA: Wadsworth Publishing Company.

Glass, G.V. 1976. Primary, secondary, and meta-analysis of research. *Educational Researcher* 5:3–8.

Hays, W. 1963. *Statistics for psychologists*. New York: Holt, Rinehart & Winston.

Kalichman, S.C. 1987. *Water running uphill: A closer look at sex differences in perceiving the invariant horizontality of liquids*. Paper presented at the annual meeting of the Southeastern Psychological Association, March, Atlanta, GA.

Kelly, J.T., & Kelly, G.N. 1977. Perception of horizontality by male and female college students. *Perceptual and Motor Skills* 44:724–726.

———. 1978a. Science activity centers: Basic concepts of the physical world. *Science and Children* 16(3):25–26.

———. 1978b. Some college students may have difficulty acquiring basic concepts necessary for understanding the physical world. *The Journal of College Science Teaching* 8:29–31.

Kelly, R., & Witters, L. 1981. Developmental and sex differences of gifted children's perception of liquid horizontality. *Journal for the Education of the Gifted* 4(2):85–96.

Linn, M.C., & Petersen, A.C. 1985. Emergence and characterization of sex differences in spatial ability: A meta-analysis. *Child Development* 56:1479–1498.

Luria, A.R. 1966. *Higher cortical functions in man*. New York: Basic Books.

———. 1973. *The working brain: An introduction to neuropsychology*. New York: Basic Books.

Maccoby, E., & Jacklin, C. 1974. *The psychology of sex differences*. Stanford, CA: Stanford University Press.

McGlone, J. 1980. Sex differences in human brain asymmetry: A critical survey. *The Behavioral and Brain Sciences* 3:215–227.

McNamara, J.F. 1978. Practical significance and statistical models. *Educational Administration Quarterly* 14:31–50.

Meehan, A.M., & Overton, W.F. 1986. Gender differences in expectancies for success and performance on Piagetian spatial tasks. *Merrill-Palmer Quarterly* 32(4):427–441.

Morris, B.B. 1971. Effects of angle, sex and cue on adults' perception of horizontal. *Perceptual and Motor Skills*, 827–830.

Murphy-Berman, V., & Witters, L. 1987. Performance of adolescents with social-emotional problems on the Piagetian water line task. Lincoln: University of Nebraska.

Murphy-Berman, V., Witters, L., & Harding, R. 1985a. The effect of giftedness, sex and bottle shape on hearing-impaired students' performance on the water line task. *Journal for the Education of the Gifted* 4:273–283.

———. 1985b. Hearing-impaired students' performance on the Piagetian liquid horizontality test. In *Cognition, education, and deafness: Directions for research and instruction*, ed. D.S. Martin, 47–49. Washington, DC: Gallaudet University Press.

———. 1986. The effect of bottle shape, bottle position and subject gender on intermediate-aged hearing-impaired students' performance on water line task. *Volta Review* 88:37–46.

Murphy-Berman, V., Witters, L., & Schillerstrom, C. 1988. Learning disabled students' perception of liquid horizontality: An examination of the effects of gender, development, and training. Unpublished manuscript.

Newcombe, N., & Bandura, N.M. 1983. Effect of age at puberty on spatial ability in girls: A question of mechanism. *Developmental Psychology* 19:215–224.

Parsons, J.E., Adler, T.F., & Kaczala, C.M. 1982. Socialization of achievement attitudes and beliefs: Parental influences. *Child Development* 53:310–321.

Petersen, A.C. 1979. Hormones and cognitive functioning in normal development. In *Sex-related differences in cognitive functioning: Developmental issues*, ed. M.A. Wittig & A.C. Petersen, 189–214. New York: Academic Press.

———. 1982. A biopsychosocial perspective on sex differences in the human brain. *The Behavioral and Brain Sciences* 5(2):312.

———. 1983. Pubertal change and cognition. In *Girls at puberty: Biological and psycho-*

social perspectives, ed. J. Brooks-Gunn & A.C. Petersen, 179–198. New York: Plenum Press.

Piaget, J., & Inhelder, B. 1956. *The child's conception of space.* London: Routledge and Kegan Paul.

Rebelsky, F. 1964. Adult perception of the horizontal. *Perceptual and Motor Skills* 19:371–374.

Robertson, A., & Youniss, J. 1969. Anticipatory visual imagery in deaf and hearing children. *Child Development* 40:123–135.

Rosenthal, R. 1979. The "file drawer problem" and tolerance for null results. *Psychological Bulletin* 86:638–641.

Shantz, C.M., & Smock, C.D. 1966. Development and distance conservation and the spatial coordinate system. *Child Development* 37:943–948.

Thomas, M. 1983. Familial correlational analyses, sex differences, and the linked gene hypothesis. *Psychological Bulletin* 93(3):427–440.

Thomas, H., & Jamison, W. 1975. On the acquisition of understanding still water is horizontal. *Merrill-Palmer Quarterly* 21:31–44.

Thomas, H., Jamison, W., & Hummel, D.D. 1973. Observation is insufficient for discovering that the surface of still water is invariantly horizontal. *Science* 181:173–174.

Vandenberg, S.G., & Kuse, A.R. 1979. Spatial ability: A critical review of the sex-linked major gene hypothesis. In *Sex-related differences in cognitive functioning: Developmental issues*, ed. M.A. Wittig & A.C. Petersen, 67–95. New York: Academic Press.

Walker, J.T., & Krasnoff, A.G. 1978. The horizontality principle in young men and women. *Perceptual and Motor Skills* 46:1055–1061.

Willemsen, E., & Reynolds, B. 1973. Sex differences in adults' judgment of the horizontal. *Developmental Psychology* 8:309.

Witters, L. 1980. Developmental and sex differences of secondary deaf students' perception of liquid horizontality. Master's thesis. University of Kansas Medical Center.

Witters-Churchill, L., Kelly, R., & Witters, L. 1983. Deaf students' perception of liquid horizontality: An examination of effects of gender, development and training. *Volta Review* 85:211–229.

Learning Disabilities and Deafness: Do Short-term Sequential Memory Deficits Provide the Key?

Bruce Marlowe

S ince the rubella epidemic in the mid-1960s, hearing-impaired children with additional handicaps have drawn increased attention from educators (Powers, Elliot & Funderburg 1987). As a result of the growing size of the hearing-impaired population with additional disabilities, assessment and intervention techniques have been designed to provide suitable services for this group, though almost exclusively for the most severely multihandicapped students (Funderburg 1982). Learning-disabled deaf students exhibit "less obvious additional handicapping conditions" (Funderburg 1982), yet they are the largest subgroup of multihandicapped hearing-impaired (MHHI) students receiving services in American schools (Craig & Craig 1985). However, many argue that they remain underserved because no agreed-upon method for identifying, assessing, or serving this population exists.

A basic deficiency in short-term sequential memory has been popularly hypothesized and well documented as a common trait of learning disabilities in the hearing population. Although researchers have explained various reasons for this consistent finding, there is little agreement about what features of sequential memory tasks are responsible for the poor performance of learning-disabled children.

Previous research has shown deficiencies in the short-term sequential memory ability of learning-disabled subjects (Lindgren & Richman 1984; Swanson 1977, 1982a; Torgesen 1986; Vellutino et al. 1973; Rudel & Denkla 1976). It is expected that the results of the study projected in this paper not only will be consistent with previous studies but also will go beyond it.

It is expected that the learning-disabled groups described below will perform less well than the two non-learning-disabled groups on a temporal-spatial matching task (Rudel & Denkla 1976) where memory for and integration of sequential information are required. Contradictory results have been found on "pure" sequential memory tasks. For example, some researchers have found that learning-disabled students perform as well as their nondisabled peers on the Knox Cube test and the Corsi Block test, neither of which has a linguistic or integration component (Guthrie & Goldberg 1972; Mann & Liberman 1984). Others have found no significant differences between learning-disabled students on sequential memory tasks where nonlinguistic items were used as stimulus items (McLeod & Greenough 1980; Vellutino 1977). Yet there is also a substantial body of research that has directly contradicted these findings. For example, many have provided evidence that even when linguistic and integration requirements are eliminated from the stimulus items or are statistically controlled, learning-disabled students consistently perform significantly poorer than do nondisabled students on tasks of short-term sequential memory (Swanson 1977, 1982b; Rudel & Denkla 1976).

A sequential memory task without an integration requirement (Rudel & Denkla 1974) will be described below. It is expected that this task will help to determine whether an underlying capacity deficit or a more general problem with integration of information is responsible for this difficulty that learning-disabled students experience on tasks of short-term sequential memory.

Initial research comparing the short-term memory abilities of hearing and deaf subjects provided evidence for significant differences between the two groups on successive processing tasks (Conrad 1965, 1970; Blair 1958). But, as more recent reviews make clear, the reported variability of sources does not reflect qualitative differences between the two groups in short-term sequential memory (Liben & Drury 1977; Anooshian 1979; McGurk & Saqi 1986). Rather, experimental differences are frequently a function of a variety of other factors, including the bias of the materials used, the linguistic content of the stimulus items, and the manner of presentation. When these factors are controlled, no differences appear between hearing and hearing-impaired subjects on tests of short-term sequential material. For example, the memorization and later retrieval of photographs of faces or nonsense shapes may require a nonverbal visual code for storage and later retrieval. Such nonacoustic stimulus items are recalled by hearing-impaired subjects with the same degree of success as by hearing subjects.

Short-term sequential memory deficits have been shown to effectively distinguish learning-disabled from non-learning-disabled individuals. When hearing and deaf subjects are compared on tasks of short-term sequential memory, the groups do not differ significantly. Because short-term sequential memory deficits are not normally part of the psychological profile of deaf learners, an examination of these processes provides a valuable point of departure for isolating learning disabilities in the deaf population.

BACKGROUND

Professionals working with hearing-impaired children have suspected since at least 1971 (Auxter 1971) that some students have learning disabilities in addition to their hearing impairment. Recently a survey form was sent to 105 administrators of programs for hearing-impaired students throughout the United States to determine the status of hearing-impaired students with additional learning disabilities (Powers, Elliot & Funderburg 1987). Data obtained from the survey indicate the existence of students who are "atypical in academic performance" compared to their same-age hearing-impaired peers. While the exact nature of these differences remains unclear, the authors of the survey report that 6.7% of the students served by the schools surveyed were identified as learning-disabled. Yet, less than 50% of the respondents provided specific criteria for the identification of learning disabilities within the hearing-impaired population, 19% did not respond to the item requesting criterial information, and nearly 33% of the respondents indicated that they had no criteria for the identification of such a group. In many ways this finding is not surprising.

Due to their hearing impairment, deaf children often have major language and communication difficulties that affect linguistic processing, academic achievement, and social-emotional development. Unfortunately, from a diagnostic perspective, these same general characteristics are observed in learning-disabled students among the hearing population. Thus, assessment of atypical academic performance among hearing-impaired students is a thorny problem, since typically they exhibit learning characteristics that appear similar to those of hearing students with learning disabilities. A major focus of this study is to examine what constitutes "atypical performance" among hearing-impaired students.

Because the hearing-impaired student population is so rife with potentially confounding variables that may affect their learning, it is extremely difficult to determine when deficiencies in academic achievement are the result of the hearing impairment and when they are caused by the presence of a learning disability. That is, questions in the assessment of hearing-impaired students with additional learning problems (that distinguish them from their hearing-impaired peers) must address issues such as degree of hearing loss, age of onset, etiology, past educational intervention, language experience, differences between deaf children of deaf parents and deaf children of hearing parents, and all the possible combinations of these factors. In effect, these various agents interact to create complex, confounding variables, making the accurate diagnosis of learning disabilities within the hearing-impaired population seemingly impossible.

Nevertheless, according to Powers, Elliot, and Funderburg (1987), and Craig and Craig (1985), a significant percentage of hearing-impaired students have been identified as learning-disabled nationwide. Because teaching strategies and classroom recommendations must differ for those hearing-impaired students suspected of having a learning disability, as they must for those learning-disabled students within the hearing population, it is necessary to establish formal rules of assessment for conducting differential diagnoses of learning-disabled hearing-impaired students.

Currently, three major obstacles block the path to consistent identification and assessment of those children who are learning-disabled and hearing-impaired.

1. The language of Public Law 94–142, which, while not necessarily excluding the possibility of identifying learning disabilities within the hearing-impaired population, makes identification extremely difficult;
2. The lack of any evidence, from experiments that use nondisabled hearing-impaired students as a control group, to substantiate the existence of a learning-disabled hearing-impaired population; and
3. The theoretical problem of definition and differentiation in the search for a more accurate classification schema for learning disabilities.

The most commonly accepted definition of "learning disabilities" is that endorsed by the federal government (Hallahan & Kaufman 1986; Faas 1983; and Lyon & Riscucci, in press) in 1977.

> "Specific learning disability" means a disorder in one or more of the basic psychological processes involved in understanding or using language, spoken or written, which may manifest itself in an imperfect ability to listen, think, speak, read, write, spell, or do mathematical calculations. The term includes such conditions as perceptual handicaps, brain injury, minimal brain dysfunction, dyslexia, and developmental aphasia. The term does not include children who have learning problems that are the result of visual, hearing, or motor handicaps, of mental retardation, of emotional disturbance, or of environmental, cultural, or economic disadvantage (*Federal Register*, December 29, 1977, p. 65083).

We note that the definition specifically "does not include children who have learning problems which are primarily the result of . . . hearing . . . handicaps. . . ." This exclusionary rule puts the burden of proof squarely on the shoulders of the diagnostician, who may be eager to label a hearing-impaired student as learning-disabled. In fact, no researcher has adequately identified a hearing-impaired student as learning-disabled by systematically distinguishing a set of atypical learning characteristics that could not be attributed to the student's hearing impairment.

Literature on learning disabilities within the hearing-impaired community is extremely scarce. It is dominated by teachers' rules of thumb for identification, remedial strategies, and suggestions for classroom observation and team evaluation. To date, there exists no experimental evidence documenting the existence of learning disabilities within the hearing-impaired population nor any generally accepted set of criteria for distinguishing such a group.

The tremendous variation within the hearing-impaired population contributes to this problem, and to a certain extent, so does the heterogeneity of students identified as learning-disabled within the hearing population. Further, the criteria for identifying learning disabilities within the hearing population vary from state to state, are not applied uniformly within states, and have come under considerable attack from a variety of researchers for being vague, imprecise, and inapplicable to many disability groups (Torgesen 1986; Adelman & Taylor 1986a, 1986b; Agozzine & Ysseldyke 1983; and Lyon & Riscucci, in press).

The literature on learning disabilities within the hearing-impaired population provides little guidance for educators of the deaf, and insufficient evidence of the occurrence of such a group for diagnosticians, school psychologists, researchers, and lawmakers. Currently, there exists no experimentally valid way to identify learning disabilities among students in the hearing-impaired population. Despite the tremendous variability of these students (including differences in the etiology of deafness, age of onset of deafness, primary means of communication, the degree of hearing loss, and all those additional factors that account for variability in the hearing population—IQ, educational experiences, etc.), it is presumed that learning disabilities do exist in the hearing-impaired population. In fact, such students are now being identified in record numbers.

However, because no experimental methods have been established to distinguish learning-disabled hearing-impaired students from their nondisabled peers, the existence of learning disabilities in the hearing-impaired population is neither clearly understood nor even recognized by many educators working with deaf students. As a result, students who are learning-disabled and hearing-impaired are not receiving those services and accommodations that the federal law guarantees to those students identified as learning-disabled in the hearing population.

PURPOSE OF THE STUDY

An experimental study was designed in order to

1. Determine whether a subset of hearing-impaired students with "atypical academic performance" yet equal intelligence can be distinguished from their same-age hearing-impaired peers using measures of short-term sequential memory; and
2. Validate a measure of short-term sequential memory as an accurate predictor for distinguishing learning-disabled from non-learning-disabled students in both the hearing and hearing-impaired populations.

METHODOLOGY

Subjects

A sample of 80 subjects from 15 to 19 years of age with normal (or higher) intelligence was selected for the study: 20 hearing, non-learning-disabled children (N) from one school in the Washington, DC, area; 20 hearing-impaired non-learning disabled children (HI) from the Model Secondary School at Gallaudet University; 20 hearing learning-disabled children (LD) from the Chelsea School in Silver Spring, Maryland; and 20 hearing-impaired children suspected of having learning disabilities (LDHI), also from the Model Secondary School at Gallaudet.

Procedure

Two "same-different" tasks were used. In the first task, temporal-spatial matching (TS), the subjects had to decide whether a linear pattern of dots presented on a computer screen was the same as a series of light flashes that they had just been shown. The second task, temporal-temporal matching (TT), required the subjects to respond to "same" or "different" for one pattern of light flashes followed by another. Subjects in each group made 40 comparisons; half the subjects in each group performed 22 TT tasks followed by 20 TS tasks, and half the subjects performed the tasks in the opposite order. Before each series, subjects received six practice matches in each task, with correction repeated four times or until all six practice items were correct.

Analysis

Error scores on the two tasks were subjected to a three-way analysis of variance with a repeated measure on the third factor. The three factors (Learning Status, Hearing Status, and Integration Component) each contained two levels. Mean error scores in all eight cells were compared. Both group and task differences were compared separately.

CONCLUSION

While the study was still in process at the time this volume went to press, the results are expected to have important implications for both researchers and practitioners in the field of special education. The reader who is interested in the full results of the study is invited to contact the author through the publishers for that information.

REFERENCES

Ackerman, P.T., & Dykman, R.A. 1982. Automatic and effortful information processing deficits in children with learning and attention disorders. *Topics in Learning and Learning Disabilities* 2:12–22.

Adelman, H.S., & Taylor, L. 1986a. The problem of definition and differentiation and the need for a classification schema. *Journal of Learning Disabilities* 19:515–520.

———. 1986b. Summary of the survey of fundamental concerns confronting the LD field. *Journal of Learning Disabilities* 19:390–393.

Algozzinem, B., & Ysseldyke, J.E. 1986. The future of the LD field: Screening and diagnosis. *Journal of Learning Disabilities* 19:394–398.

Amoriell, W.J. 1979. Reading achievement and the ability to manipulate visual and auditory stimuli. *Journal of Learning Disabilities* 12:562–564.

Anderson, J.R. 1983. *The architecture of cognition.* Cambridge, MA: Harvard University Press.

———. 1987. Skill acquisition: Compilation of weak-method problem solutions. *Psychological Review* 94:192–210.

Anooshian, L.J., & Bryan, J.M. 1979. The effects of early auditory deprivation on temporal perceptions: A comparison of hearing and hearing-impaired children on temporal pattern matching tasks. *Journal of Speech and Hearing Research* 22:731–746.

Auxter, D. 1971. Learning disabilities among the deaf population. *Exceptional Children* 4:573–577.

Bauer, R.H. 1977a. Memory processes in children with learning disabilities: Evidence for deficient rehearsal. *Journal of Experimental Child Psychology* 24:415–430.

———. 1977b. Short-term memory in learning disabled and nondisabled children. *Bulletin of the Psychonomic Society* 10:128–130.

———. 1982. Information processing as a way of understanding and diagnosing learning disabilities. *Topics in Learning and Learning Disabilities* 2:33–45.

Bayliss, J., & Livesey, P.J. 1986. Cognitive strategies of children with reading disability and normal readings in visual sequential memory. *Journal of Learning Disabilities* 18:326–332.

Blair, F.X. 1958. A study of the visual memory of deaf and hearing children. *American Annals of the Deaf* 102:254–263.

Blennerhassett, L. 1987. Experimental use of the WISC-R and WAIS-R verbal scales with hearing impaired adolescents. Paper presented at the National Association of School Psychologists, March, New Orleans, LA.

Butt, N. 1984. Memory training and reading. *Special Education: Forward Trends* 11:31–33.

Chi, M.T., & Gallagher, J.D. 1982. Speed of processing: A developmental source of limitation. *Topics in Learning and Learning Disabilities* 2:23–32.

Clarke, B.R., & Kendall, D.C. 1980. Learning disabled or hearing impaired? A folly of forced categories. *British Columbia Journal of Special Education* 4:13–27.

Cohen, R.L., Netley, C., & Clarke, M.A. 1984. On the generality of the short-term memory/reading ability relationship. *Journal of Learning Disabilities* 17:218–221.

Conrad, R., & Rush, M.L. 1965. On the nature of short-term memory encoding by the deaf. *Journal of Speech and Hearing Disorders* 30:336–343.

Conrad, R. 1970. Short-term memory processes in the deaf. *British Journal of Psychology* 61:179–195.

Cordoni, B.K., O'Donnell, J.P., Ramaniah, N.V., Kurtz, J., & Rosenshein, K. 1981. Wechsler adult intelligence score patterns for learning disabled young adults. *Journal of Learning Disabilities* 14:404–407.

Craig, W.N., & Craig, H.B., eds. 1985. Reference issue. *American Annals of the Deaf* 130:132–133.

Crowder, R.G. 1970. The role of one's own voice in immediate memory. *Cognitive Psychology* 5:365–373.

Cumming, C.E., & Rodda, M. 1985. The effects of auditory deprivation on successive processing. *Canadian Journal of Behavioral Sciences* 17:232–245.

Dodd, B., Hobson, P., Brasher, J., & Campbell, R. 1983. Deaf children's short-term memory for lip-read, graphic and signed stimuli. *British Journal of Developmental Psychology* 1:353–364.

Elbert, J.C. 1984. Short-term memory encoding and memory search in the word recognition of learning disabled children. *Journal of Learning Disabilities* 6:342–345.

Faas, L.A. 1983. *Learning disabilities: A competency based approach.* Boston: Houghton Mifflin Co.

Feagans, L., & Short, E.J. 1986. Referential communication and reading performance in learning disabled children over a three year period. *Developmental Psychology* 22:177–183.

Funderburg, R.S. 1982. The role of the classroom teacher in the assessment of the learning disabled hearing impaired child. In *The multihandicapped hearing-impaired: Identification and instruction*, ed. D. Tweedie & E. Shroyer, 61–74. Washington, DC: Gallaudet University Press.

Guthrie, J.T., & Goldberg, H.K. 1972. Visual sequential memory in reading disability. *Journal of Learning Disabilities* 5:45–50.

Hall, J.W., & Humphreys, M.S. 1982. Research on specific learning disabilities. *Topics in Learning and Learning Disabilities* 2:68–78.

Hallahan, D.P., & Kauffman, J.M. 1986. *Exceptional children: Introduction to special education*. Englewood Cliffs, NJ: Prentice-Hall.

Hammill, D.D., Leigh, J.E., McNutt, G., & Larsen, S.C. 1987. A new definition of learning disabilities. *Journal of Learning Disabilities* 20:109–113.

Hanson, V.L. 1982. Short-term recall by deaf signers of American Sign Language: Implications of encoding strategy for order recall. *Journal of Experimental Psychology: Learning, Memory and Cognition* 8:572–583.

Hatt, C.V., Obrzut, J.E., & Swanson, H.L. 1978. Simultaneous and successive syntheses: A factor analysis of speed of information processing. *Perceptual and Motor Skills* 46:1167–1172.

Kachman, B., & Rush, P. 1988. Learning disabilities in the deaf population: Evaluation, interpretation, and recommendations for practice. Paper presented at the National Association for School Psychologists, April, Chicago, IL.

Kass, C.E. 1982. Remedial strategies for age related characteristics of learning disability. In *The multihandicapped hearing-impaired: Identification and instruction*. ed. D. Tweedie & E. Shroyer, 85–94. Washington, DC: Gallaudet University Press.

Kelly, R.R., & Tomlinson-Keasey, C. 1976. Information processing of visually presented picture and word stimuli by young hearing-impaired and normal hearing children. *Journal of Speech and Hearing Research* 19:628–638.

Kirby, J.R., & Robinson, G.L. 1987. Simultaneous and successive processing in reading disabled children. *Journal of Learning Disabilities* 20:243–252.

Kolligan, J., & Sternberg, R.J. 1987. Intelligence, information processing and specific learning disabilities: A triarchic synthesis. *Journal of Learning Disabilities* 20:8–17.

Krakow, R.A., & Hanson, V.L. 1985. Deaf signers and serial recall in the visual modality: Memory for signs, fingerspelling, and print. *Memory and Cognition* 13:265–272.

Liben, L.S., & Drury, A.M. 1977. Short-term memory in deaf and hearing children in relation to stimulus characteristics. *Journal of Experimental Child Psychology* 24:60–73.

Lindgren, S.D., & Richman, L.C. 1984. Immediate memory functions of verbally deficient reading-disabled children. *Journal of Learning Disabilities* 17:222–225.

Lyon, G.R., & Riscucci, D. In press. Classification issues in learning disabilities. In *Learning disabilities: State of the art and practice*, ed. K. Kavale. San Diego, CA: College-Hill Press.

Mann, V.A., & Liberman, I.Y. 1984. Phonological awareness and verbal short-term memory. *Journal of Learning Disabilities* 17:593–599.

Martin, D.S., ed. 1985. *Cognition, education, and deafness: Directions for research and instruction*. Washington, DC: Gallaudet University Press.

McGurk, H., & Saqi, S. 1986. Serial recall of static and dynamic stimuli by deaf and hearing children. *British Journal of Developmental Psychology* 4:305–310.

McLeod, J., & Greenough, P. 1980. The importance of sequencing as an aspect of short-term memory in good and poor spellers. *Journal of Learning Disabilities* 13:29–33.

Mishra, S.P., Ferguson, B.A., & King, P.V. 1985. Research with the Wechsler digit span subtest: Implications for assessment. *School Psychology Review* 14:34–37.

National Joint Committee for Learning Disabilities. 1987. Learning disabilities: Issues on definition. *Journal of Learning Disabilities* 20:107–109.

Noelker, R.W., & Schumsky, D.A. 1973. Memory for the sequence form and position as related to the identification of reading retardates. *Journal of Educational Psychology* 64:22–25.

O'Connor, N., & Hermelin, B. 1973. Short-term memory for the order of pictures and syllables by deaf and hearing children. *Neuropsychologia* 11:437–442.

Olson, J.E., & Furth, H.G. 1965. Visual memory span in the deaf. *American Journal of Psychology* 79:480–484.

Powers, A., Elliot, R., & Funderburg, R. 1987. Learning disabled hearing-impaired students: Are they being identified? *Volta Review* 2:99–105.

Powers, A., & Harris, A.R. 1982. Strategies for teaching language and/or learning disabled hearing impaired children. In *The multihandicapped hearing impaired: Identification and instruction*, ed. D. Tweedie & E. Shroyer, 249–263. Washington, DC: Gallaudet University Press.

Pronovost, W., Bates, J., Clasby, E., Miller, N.E., Miller, N.J., & Thompson, R. 1976. Hearing impaired children with associated disabilities: A team evaluation. *Exceptional Children* 5:439–443.

Rosell, G.P. 1982. Learning disability assessment. In *The multihandicapped hearing impaired: Identification and instruction*, ed. D. Tweedie & E. Shroyer, 107–120. Washington, DC: Gallaudet University Press.

Rudel, R.G., & Denkla, M.B. 1976. Relationship of IQ and reading score to visual, spatial, and temporal matching tasks. *Journal of Learning Disabilities* 9:42–51.

Rugel, R.P. 1974. WISC subtest scores of disabled readers: A review with respect to Bannatyne's recategorization. *Journal of Learning Disabilities* 7:57–64.

Shroyer, C. 1982. Assessing and remedying perceptual problems in hearing impaired children. In *The multihandicapped hearing impaired: Identification and instruction*, ed. D. Tweedie & E. Shroyer, 135–147. Washington, DC: Gallaudet University Press.

Siegel, L.S., & Linder, B.A. 1984. Short-term memory processes in children with reading and arithmetic learning disabilities. *Developmental Psychology* 20:200–207.

Smith, R.W., Osborne, L.T., Crim, D., & Rhu, A.M. 1986. Labeling theory as applied to learning disabilities: Survey findings and policy suggestions. *Journal of Learning Disabilities* 19:195–202.

Swanson, H.L. 1977. Nonverbal visual short-term memory as a function of age and dimensionality in learning disabled children. *Child Development* 48:41–44.

Swanson, H.L. 1982a. Information processing theory and learning disabilities: A commentary and future perspective. *Journal of Learning Disabilities* 20:155–166.

———. 1982b. Information processing theory and learning disabilities: An overview. *Journal of Learning Disabilities* 20:3–7.

———. 1982c. Strategies and constraints. *Topics in Learning and Learning Disabilities* 2:79–81.

———. 1982d. Verbal short-term memory encoding of learners disabled, deaf and normal readers. *Learning Disability Quarterly* 5:21–28.

Swanson, H.L. 1983. A study of nonstrategic linguistic coding on visual recall of learning disabled readers. *Journal of Learning Disabilities* 4:209–216.

Swanson, H.L., & O'Connor, L. 1981. Short-term memory in deaf children in relation to verbal and dactylo-kinesthetic encoding. *The Journal of Psychology* 107:231–236.

Sternberg, R.J., & Wagner, R.K. 1982. Automization failure in learning disabilities. *Topics in Learning and Learning Disabilities* 2:1–11.

Torgeson, J.K. 1979. What shall we do with psychological processes? *Journal of Learning Disabilities* 12:16–23.

———. 1986. Learning disabilities theory: Its current state and future practice. *Journal of Learning Disabilities* 19:399–407.

Torgeson, J.K., & Dice, C. 1980. Characteristics of research on learning disabilities. *Journal of Learning Disabilities* 13:531–545.

Torgeson, J.K., & Goldman, T. 1977. Verbal rehearsal and short-term memory in reading disabled children. *Child Development* 48:56–60.

Torgeson, J.K., & Greenstein, J.J. 1982. Why do some learning disabled children have problems remembering? Does it make a difference? *Topics in Learning and Learning Disabilities* 2:54–61.

Torgeson, J.K., & Houck, D.G. 1980. Processing deficiencies of learning disabled children who perform poorly on the digit span. *Journal of Educational Psychology* 72:141–160.

Tweedie, D., & Shroyer, E.M., eds. 1982. *The multihandicapped hearing impaired: Identification and instruction.* Washington, DC: Gallaudet University Press.

Vellutino, F.R., Pruzek, R.M., Steger, J.A., & Meshoulam, U. 1973. Immediate visual recall in poor and normal readers as a function of orthographic linguistic familiarity. *Cortex* 9:368–384.

Vockell, E.L., Hirshoren, A., & Vockell, K. 1972. A critique of Auxter's "Learning disabilities among deaf populations." *Exceptional Children* 4:652–667.

Worden, P.E., Malmgren, I., & Galbourie, P. 1982. Memory for stories in learning disabled adults. *Journal of Learning Disabilities* 15:145–152.

The Influence of Information Structure and Processing Strategy on the Interpretation of Classroom Questions: A Microanalysis

Thomas N. Kluwin

Q uestioning is a ubiquitous educational strategy with its roots in antiquity; however, the use of question-asking as an educational strategy makes several strong assumptions about the capacities of the learner. It assumes that the question can be processed on the linguistic or grammatical level; it assumes that on a social and cultural level the role of the question will be perceived in the same way by all participants; but equally important, it assumes that the question will be interpreted on the cognitive level in the same fashion by both the question-asker and the respondent. In the context of processing information within the classroom, the question may not function as intended by tradition or the teacher.

A MODEL OF CLASSROOM INFORMATION PROCESSING

Four generalizations can be made about information processing in classrooms. First, the process of communication is a negotiated process in which both sides have options for controlling the flow of communication to achieve their particular goals. Second, in classroom communication, like any other type of communication, the underlying process is one of pattern matching, that is, incoming structures at different levels are compared with encoded or constructed structures. Third, what speeds the process of pattern matching is the use of various kinds of "expectation sets." Fourth, because communication in the classroom is transitory, the teacher uses stylized or conventionalized communication forms, such as patterns of asking questions, in order to convey his or her ideas.

Understanding resulting conversation is a mutually achieved result or, as Schegloff (1982) describes it, an interactional "achievement." It is an achievement because it is the result of a cooperative process between teacher and students in which both sides have roles and options that they can exercise (Winograd 1977). Extended talk is a mutually controlled incremental accomplishment over time, because all the text is not immediately available to the participants as it is in print, and the process is subject to the ill effects of extension through time. Meaning is not presented as on a billboard or a menu, but is produced through cooperation and redundancy.

Because classroom language cannot be read repeatedly as text can, and because structure is needed in processing, classroom language is characterized by certain kinds of verbal structures. Gall (1970) and others have pointed out that the questioning routine is a fairly universal form of behavior in classroom settings. Questions serve several functions in classrooms, including monitoring students' understanding, introducing new information, and modeling heuristics (Stevens, Collins & Goldin 1979; Collins 1977; Collins and Stevens 1981).

The second and third functions of classroom questions are more appropriate to our discussion. The question asking-answering routine is a device that teachers use to structure the verbal web of classroom discourse in order to aid students' processing of the content of the lesson; however, the success of this routine is based on the premise that the expectations of all the participants are being met.

DeBeaugrande (1980) provides us with fairly complete descriptions of expectation sets for classroom interaction, listing assumptions about shared world knowledge, shared rules of social behavior, conventional scripts, traits of the current situation, and episodic knowledge of shared experiences as instances of expectation sets. In this paper, we are using expectation sets to cover a wide range of processes from the construction of schema for integrating interpretations of sets of sentences to linguistically encoded social rules such as turn-taking or appropriate address forms.

Expectation sets can be used to match incoming information in at least two ways, by asking either "Are the sets similar?" or "Are the sets dissimilar?" (Thorndyke 1976). The second strategy is inherently more efficient, because the individual only has to find one mismatched element of a set in order to declare that the two sets are dissimilar. In order to establish similarity between two sets, *all* elements of the set must be identical. Further, by asking whether the sets are dissimilar, one only has to compare elements until a mismatch occurs instead of matching all elements. The basic operating principle is that the creation of expectation sets facilitates processing by reducing processing time. However, minimal monitoring of the appropriateness of the expectation set within a higher-order structure would lead to inappropriate subsequent processing.

To summarize, let us say that teachers use question-asking as a device to examine students' knowledge structure. Both teachers and students use expectation sets in order to facilitate the processing of classroom dialogue. The student's stored information is a kind of schema or macro-rule system for which we will appropriate Schank's (1982) theory of information processing. To make things even more complicated, the various subsystems have feedback loops that can alter processing values.

The question of how badly this system can go astray begs to be asked. In the following section, we will discuss the results of sincere and not-so-sincere attempts to exchange information when systems are out of synchronization, thus raising doubts about the utility of question-asking as an educational procedure.

This study examines how "experience" is differentially encoded by individuals in their cognitive systems and then brought forward to be used in the processing of new information, specifically classroom content. Using the general concept of "schema" or "scripts" as higher-level rules for organizing verbal behavior, this study examined the confusion that can result when different individuals pursuing different schema and using different verification rules attempt to exchange information about a verbal object—in this case, a paragraph of text.

DATA

The data for this analysis of classroom information processing consisted of five minutes of videotaped interaction between a deaf female teacher and eight deaf students in a secondary school English classroom at a residential school for the deaf (see Table 1). The particular segment that is analyzed was selected because the content was most amenable to an analysis of thought processes. This segment was specifically selected because it showed a clear instance of students working through a logical sequence.

To establish the context for this lesson, let us look at the text that the teacher and students were discussing. The text is reproduced below exactly as it appeared in the textbook.

The Scotts followed the rocky trail more than 2000 feet to the bottom of the canyon. All at once, Mr. Scott heard strange noises coming from the car's engine. He got out and found that the fan by the car's radiator had shaken loose. The blades of the fan had gashed the radiator in a dozen places. Water spurted from

TABLE 1   Student Subjects

Student	Age	Sex	Better Ear Average	Reading Level*
1	13	female	82dB	5.3
2	17	female	72dB	5.7
3	17	male	70dB	4.2
4	16	female	92dB	5.9
5	14	male	88dB	6.6
6	16	male	92dB	3.l3
7	17	male	68dB	5.8
8	17	male	90dB	4.2

* Stanford Achievement Test Hearing-Impaired Version (SATHI) Reading Comprehension Subtest Grade Equivalent Score.

the holes. Before Mr. Scott could pull off a hub cap to catch the water, it had disappeared in the hot sand.

The physical array of the material is important to understanding the confusion that will be described later in the students' processing of the teacher's questions.

There are three generalized memory-organizing packets (or MOPs) that might be applied to the general topic of "radiator failure" and a specific instantiation in this text which, while containing elements of all the generalized scenes, is quite different from any one of them. Table 2 presents three generalized MOPs—M-WINTER, M-SUMMER, M-DISASTER—and the specific MOP that can be inferred from the text itself.

As a negotiated process, understanding or misunderstanding in the classroom falls into two categories of sources of "errors." Within the category of student error, we can see dysfunction in three areas: Social rule failures, symbolic processing errors, and conceptual categorization errors. Within the category of teacher-processing errors, we see two general types of errors. First, there are simple physical limitations in the communication system, such as the case in which the teacher completely or partially misses a student utterance. Second, there are instances in which the teacher inappropriately categorizes the student's input, either because the student misrepresents his or her intent or because the teacher generates a question that is too vague for the immediate dialogue situation.

We saw no instances of social rule failures or symbolic processing failures by the teacher. This finding should not be assumed to be a universal case, since the particular teacher in this lesson was highly skilled at communicating in several modes and languages.

A fundamental confusion among the students in the processing of the text, and possibly the keystone for the entire progress of the interaction, may lie in the phrase "the fan by the car's radiator." The students either processed this input linearly, that is, they read to the end of the line and assumed that the line contained the entire meaningful unit, or they processed the complex passive expression and converted it to a simple active. Both hypotheses are plausible since young hearing-impaired readers have a tendency to respond to questions about text by using some kind of keyword or phrase-search heuristic that is print-oriented rather than meaning- or syntax-motivated.

In a considerable number of instances, according to our transcription, students did not conceptually categorize the question in an appropriate manner. These errors can be the result either of inappropriate categorization of the question or of inappropriate matching of an item with the questions because the student is using an inappropriate meta-MOP. In other words, there are cases of both the right information for the wrong question and the wrong information for the right question.

There were apparently two stages of processing during this lesson. The first was the accessing of a personal or idiosyncratic meta-MOP accompanied by accurate processing of the question; that is, the citation of the element from the meta-MOP would be correct if that meta-MOP had been under discussion. The next stage of the processing was a period during which the appropriate text-generated meta-MOP was used, but apparently it was used randomly. Either the

TABLE 2 Scene Structure for M-Radiator Failure

MOP	Preparatory	Enablement	Pre-condition	Side-condition	Action	Post-condition	Disengagement	Transitory
Winter	Previous water loss	Low water	Engine runs		Water boils out	Car stops	Raise hood	Locate water
Summer			High ambient temperature	Stuck in traffic	Water boils out	Car stops	Raise hood	Locate water
Disaster		Equipment damaged		High ambient temperature	Water loss	Car noise	Car stops	Locate damage
Text Specific	Fan loose	Fan cuts radiator	Wrong turn	Desert	Water loss	Car noise	Car stops	Drive on

text-generated meta-MOP had not yet been fully constructed and the students were trying to sort out the various elements of it, or the students had rapidly constructed an appropriate text-generated meta-MOP but were unsure of the intent of the teacher's questions. Both speculations are possible and may define different types of learners.

Considered in combination, we appear to have two types of meta-MOP generation—fast and slow or stable and unstable, and two types of intention resetting—stable and changing. Student #5 would be an example of fast meta-MOP generation and no intention resetting; he rapidly changed responses and had no trouble answering the teacher's questions. Student #4 would be an instance of a slow meta-MOP generator who was trying to reset the teacher's intention values at the end of the sequence. Except for student #1, the others would represent students operating under those two conditions (fast generation with intention resetting or slow generation without intention resetting) who produce similar kinds of behavior. The final stage is the process of developing the appropriate meta-MOP within a framework of recognizing the true intent of the teacher.

As has been said above, even when an individual possesses a relatively large amount of information about a topic, that person can inappropriately process new information through the assignment of the information to an inappropriate node, through an inappropriate association of the new verbal element within an appropriate superordinate node for the new information, or through the use of a completely inappropriate or inaccurate schema.

The continuous use of a buffer strategy would probably be extremely taxing for an individual, since such a strategy would require keeping everything in abeyance and would effectively stymie comprehension. An alternative would be to use a disconfirming strategy. The individual would activate the most appropriate available schema and then proceed to accept whatever matched the expectations generated by that schema and to ignore (rather than overtly reject or hold in abeyance) any disconfirming information. The basic strategy would be, "If it matches, attach it to a node. If no match occurs, ignore it." Based on this kind of strategy, one would expect to see internally consistent representation, but responses would be at odds with the structure of the speaker. This conclusion appears to fit the behavior of the students in this study.

REFERENCES

Collins, A. 1977. Processes in acquiring knowledge. In *Schooling and the acquisition of knowledge*, ed. R.C. Anderson, R.J. Spiro, & W.E. Montague, 330–357. Hillsdale, NJ: Lawrence Erlbaum Associates.

Collins, A., & Stevens, A.L. 1981. A cognitive theory of interactive teaching. In *Instructional design theories and models: An overview*, ed. C.M. Reigeluth, 187–203. New York: Academic Press.

deBeaugrande, R. 1980. *Text, discourse, and process.* Norwood, NJ: Ablex Publishing Corp.

Gall, M. 1970. The use of questions in teaching. *Review of Educational Psychology* 40:707–720.

Schank, R. 1982. *Dynamic memory*. New York: Cambridge University Press.

Schegloff, E.A. 1982. Discourse as an interactional achievement: Some uses of 'uh huh' and other things that come between sentences. In *Analyzing discourse: Text and talk*, ed. D. Tunnon, 71–94. Washington, DC: Georgetown University Press.

Stevens, A.L., Collins, A., & Goldin, S. 1979. Misconceptions in students' understanding. *International Journal of Man-Machine Studies* 11:145–156.

Thorndyke, P. 1976. The role of inferences in discourse comprehension. *Journal of Verbal Learning and Verbal Behavior* 15:437–446.

Winograd, T. 1977. A framework for understanding discourse. In *Cognitive processes in comprehension*, ed. M. Just & P. Carpenter, 63–88. Hillsdale, NJ: Lawrence Erlbaum Associates.

Constructive Processing in Skilled Deaf and Hearing Readers

Joan S. Pinhas

R ecent research has shown that inferential processing is an important cognitive skill in the acquisition of knowledge (Spiro 1980). The ability to draw inferences is crucial to recalling prose (Kintsch 1974; Paris & Carter 1973), adding structure to story meaning (Collins, Brown & Larkin 1980; Mandler & Johnson 1977), and understanding the reading comprehension skills of children (Kail et al. 1977; Wilson 1979; Wilcox & Tobin 1974; Gibson & Levin 1975). To date, little work has been carried out on deaf learners' inferential processing of written text, since inference, which requires abstract cognitive reasoning, had been considered too difficult for this population.

The tendency to ignore inference is surprising, since it is generally accepted that inference is critical for their successful reading comprehension. The available data from Davey, LaSasso and Macready (1983), and from Pinhas (1984) suggest that relatively unskilled deaf readers do have greater difficulty processing inferential information than their hearing counterparts. This study examined the inferential processing abilities of *skilled* deaf and hearing readers in order to de-

This work was supported in part by a grant from the SUNY Organized Research Initiatives Project and from the Nuala Drescher Affirmative Action Leave Program. I would like to thank the students at the National Technical Institute for the Deaf at Rochester Institute of Technology for their participation in the project and the faculty and staff in the Educational Research department for their assistance. Special thanks are extended to Keri McBride for subject recruitment and data collection. Thanks are also extended to David L. Olds for reviewing the manuscript.

termine what abilities they rely upon to process inferential information in written text.

HYPOTHESIS

According to constructive processing models of reading (Kintsch 1974), inferences are made while reading the text. We reasoned that skilled deaf readers, when presented with written text, may rely on alternative strategies, such as that identified by Wolk and Schildroth (1984), in which a question is matched in some way to information presented in the text. Such a strategy results in the inference being drawn at the time of questioning, rather than at the time of reading, as a constructive model of reading would predict. Thus, the deaf student reading written text was expected to process inferential information nonconstructively; the hearing reader was expected to process the same information constructively.

More specifically, we expected the deaf reader who is processing written text to show longer response times for inferential questions than for literal questions in both the immediate and delayed question conditions. Additionally, inferential questions should take longer to process in the delayed condition as opposed to the immediate condition. We expected the hearing reader to show shorter response times for literal questions than for inferential questions immediately after the material was presented, but to show equivalent response times for both types of questions after a delay in which the surface cues in working memory had faded. Furthermore, the hearing reader was also predicted to respond to the inferential questions with equal latencies in both the immediate and delayed conditions.

Response accuracy is not considered to be a sensitive measure of constructive processing. Previous research by Kintsch (1974) and Pinhas (1984) indicates that literal information is always retrieved more accurately than inferential information. Therefore, it was expected that for all subjects across both time intervals, literal questions would be responded to more accurately than inferential questions.

METHODS

Seventy-six deaf students who were reading at grade levels 9, 10, and 11, with a mean reading level of a 10.3 grade equivalent, were recruited from the National Technical Institute for the Deaf at the Rochester Institute of Technology. All students were identified as being prelingually deaf for unaided puretone averages of 500, 1000, and 2000 Hz, with a mean hearing loss of 94.48 decibels in the better ear. The mean age for the deaf subjects was 21.9 years.

Fifty-three hearing students, who were selected according to reading level, served as the comparison group. The mean reading level was 10.4 grade equivalent, with a mean age of 16.19 years.

The task consisted of reading four narrative stories and answering eight questions per story—four literal and four inferential questions. The questions were presented in two time intervals: 30 seconds and 20 minutes after story presentation, respectively, to allow for determination of when the inference was being formulated. All subjects participated in both intervals. The order of the intervals, question types, and truth value were counterbalanced.

The dependent measures were accuracy and response time (for correct responses only) to the two types of information. All data were analyzed by analysis of variance with repeated measures. The classification factors were hearing status (deaf, hearing), question type (literal, inferential), question interval (30 seconds, 20 minutes) and all interactions among these factors. Question type and question interval were within-subjects factors.

RESULTS

The test of the three-way interaction of hearing status x question type x question interval was non-significant. The hearing subjects performed as predicted in the 30-second interval, where the literal questions were responded to more quickly than the inferential questions ($p = .01$). However, rather than displaying the predicted equivalence in processing in the 20-minute interval, the hearing subjects continued to process literal questions more quickly than inferential questions in this time interval ($p = .02$). The hearing subjects did appear to be drawing the inference at the time of reading, however, because the time needed to process the inference was the same at both intervals. Thus, the hearing subjects performed as nonconstructive readers according to a strict interpretation of Kintsch's model.

Among the deaf subjects, the literal questions were responded to more quickly than the inferential questions in both the 30-second and 20-minute interval conditions. In addition, both literal and inferential questions had longer latencies in the 20-minute interval than the 30-second interval, as predicted.

Although the predicted three-way interaction was not significant, several significant main effects and two-way interactions elucidate our understanding of the data. The deaf subjects processed both literal and inferential questions more slowly than the hearing, across both time intervals ($p = .0000$).

Questions presented in the 30-second interval were responded to more quickly than questions in the 20-minute interval, regardless of hearing status and question type ($p = .007$). This main effect can be explained, however, by the hearing status x delay interval interaction ($p = .04$), where the longer latencies in the 20-minute condition were due almost exclusively to the deaf subjects.

Literal questions were responded to more quickly than inferential questions, regardless of hearing status and delay interval ($p = .0000$). Again, this main effect is accounted for by a hearing status x question type interaction, in which the effect of question type is concentrated among the deaf subjects ($p = .003$).

Analysis of the accuracy data revealed that literal questions were answered more correctly than inferential questions ($p = .0000$). Contrary to prediction, there were no differences between the deaf and hearing subjects in accuracy of response. Delay interval did not affect accuracy of responses, nor did it affect accuracy for either population.

DISCUSSION

As defined by Kintsch (1974), the hearing subjects in our study failed to read constructively. Specifically, the hearing subjects failed to show the accelerated literal response in the 30-second interval, presumably accounted for by working or auxiliary memory. This failure may be explained in part by developmental differences in subjects between the two investigations. Our subjects, who were high school students, were substantially younger than Kintsch's college-age subjects. The age difference may, in turn, be related to differences in subjects' reading abilities. The mean reading level of our hearing subjects was 10.4 grade equivalent. Kintsch's subjects were 40 college students recruited as part of an undergraduate course requirement with no available reading level information. It is likely that Kintsch's subjects were not only older but also more sophisticated readers who possessed a well-integrated set of reading skills that may result in more rapid literal processing abilities.

While the hearing subjects did not possess the accelerated literal responses necessary for constructive reading, they demonstrated equivalent latencies for inferential questions across both time intervals—an indicator that the inference was formulated during the reading process. This immediate formulation of the inference according to Kintsch is a critical component of the constructive process. Thus, the hearing subjects in our investigation demonstrated some of the skills critical to the constructive process while other skills remained absent. The meaning of the absence of rapid literal processing in reading requires further investigation. For example, does rapid literal processing allow the reader to spend more time searching for the deeper meaning of the text? If so, how rapid does the literal response have to be to allow deeper processing to occur?

Results for the deaf subjects are consistent with previous research, which shows that this population can, and indeed does, draw inferences in a written comprehensive task. The deaf students displayed a different response time pattern than did their hearing counterparts. First, the deaf students took longer than the hearing readers to answer both types of questions. One might argue that the longer latencies can be attributed to time needed for transcoding from written English to manual language, but this explanation is unlikely, since the time difference is approximately one second, insufficient for transcoding. The additional processing time may be an adaptive strategy in our sample, whose reading achievement is exceptional compared to most deaf students, as opposed to signaling a deficiency.

Second, the deaf students demonstrated longer latencies for inferential questions presented in the 20-minute interval compared to the 30-second interval, indicating that the inference was not formulated at the time of reading, but rather during questioning. This strongly suggests that these deaf students are processing inferences in a nonconstructive manner.

Recent work has shown that many skilled readers construct inferences at the time of questioning as opposed to doing so while reading (McKoon & Ratcliff 1986; Singer 1979). It is certainly feasible that some inferences are constructed automatically during reading, but it is difficult to determine which inferences are most likely to be made at the time of reading. This result is due to the vast number of possible inferences that can be drawn. Furthermore, some inferences are necessary if appropriate comprehension is to be obtained, while others are not as essential to text comprehension. In either case, the reader may choose to use a question as a cue to draw an inference as a means of efficiency, not because he or she is less skilled. The work of McKoon and Ratcliff (1986) suggests that inferences may be primed during the reading process but not actually formulated until specifically cued.

Thus, our results suggest that, although the deaf students did not exhibit the characteristics of the constructive reader, their pattern of processing may not be indicative of a deficiency in inferential processing. Considering that the deaf students were as accurate in their inferential responses as hearing students were, it may be that the processing difference exhibited by the deaf readers reflects an adaptive strategy.

Additional research is needed to validate the timing of inferential construction and the utility of such processing in overall text comprehension. Questions regarding how different types of inferences are processed, as well as the effect of retrieval conditions on such processing, need to be addressed for both hearing and deaf populations to explain more fully the nature of inferential processing and the role it plays in the reading process.

REFERENCES

Collins, A., Brown, J.S., & Larkin, K.M. 1980. Inference in text understanding. In *Theoretical issues in reading comprehension: Perspectives from cognitive psychology, linguistics, artificial intelligence and education*, ed. R.J. Spiro, B.C. Bruce, & W.F. Brewer, 385–407. Hillsdale, NJ: Lawrence Erlbaum Associates.

Davey, B., LaSasso, C., & Macready, G. 1983. Comparison of reading comprehension task performance for deaf and hearing readers. *Journal of Speech and Hearing Research* 26:622–628.

Gibson, E., & Levin, H. 1975. *The psychology of reading*. Cambridge, MA: MIT Press.

Kail, R., Chi, M., Ingram, A., & Danner, F. 1977. Constructive aspects of children's reading comprehension. *Child Development* 48:684–688.

Kintsch, W. 1974. The representation of meaning in memory. Hillsdale, NJ: Lawrence Erlbaum Associates.

Mandler, J., & Johnson, N. 1977. Remembrance of things passed: Story structure and recall. *Cognitive Psychology* 9:111–151.

McKoon, G., & Ratcliff, R. 1986. Inferences about predictable events. *Journal of Experimental Psychology: Learning, Memory and Cognition* 12:82–91.

Paris, S., & Carter, A. 1973. Semantic and constructive aspects of sentence memory in children. *Developmental Psychology* 9: 109–113.

Pinhas, J. 1984. Inferential processing in deaf and hearing readers. Paper presented to the American Speech-Language-Hearing Association, San Francisco.

Singer, M. 1979. Temporal locus of inference in the comprehension of brief passages: Recognizing and verifying implications about instruments. *Perceptual and Motor Skills* 49:539–550.

Spiro, R.J. 1980. Constructive processes in prose comprehension and recall. In *Theoretical issues in reading and comprehension: Perspectives from cognitive psychology, lin-*

guistics, artificial intelligence and education, ed. R.J. Spiro, B.C. Bruce, & W.F. Brewer. Hillsdale, NJ: Lawrence Erlbaum Associates.

Wilcox, J., & Tobin, H. 1974. Linguistic performance of hard of hearing and normal hearing children. *Journal of Speech and Hearing Research* 17(2): 286–293.

Wilson, K. 1979. Inference and language processing in hearing and deaf children. Ph.D. diss., Boston University.

Wolk, S., & Schildroth, A. 1984. Consistency of an associational strategy used on reading comprehension tests by hearing-impaired students. *Journal of Research in Reading* 7:135–142.

Interactions Between Language and Mathematics with Deaf Students: Defining the "Language–Mathematics" Equation

Eleanor Hillegeist
Kenneth Epstein

The Gallaudet University School of Preparatory Studies serves students who do not have the mathematical and English language skills necessary to begin the university's undergraduate liberal arts program. Many preparatory students exhibit an inadequate level of skill development and a poor understanding of mathematical concepts in algebra and geometry. More than half the students fail the university's waiver test in Algebra I, and more than 90% fail the geometry waiver test. Most students in the Algebra I classes do very well, while students enrolled in Algebra II and Geometry do not. Reasons for the relative lack of success of the more advanced students are not well understood. We believe that one explanation involves a combination of the increasing abstractness and complexity of the mathematical concepts and the difficulty of finding an effective language in which to teach and learn those concepts.

The languages to be considered are the language of mathematics and the language of learning and instruction. The language of mathematics is a precise, symbolic notation system. The language of instruction is the language used in textbooks and by instructors who use some combination of English and American Sign Language (ASL). The language of learning for our students may be ASL, English, a foreign language, a combination of ASL and English, or some nonsystematic variety of English. As mathematical concepts and procedures become increasingly abstract and complex, students' success in learning mathematics depends on how successful they are in integrating these three languages. As the mathematics becomes more difficult, mismatches among these three languages will tend to interfere with learning and may be an important part of the reason that college-age deaf students are less successful in the more advanced mathematics courses.

In this paper we consider the literature on learning mathematics and the interactions between language and the development of mathematical concepts and skills. Following the literature review are the results of a pilot study designed to explore the effect of the levels of complexity and abstraction in English and in the language of mathematics on student performance. The final section of this paper discusses what the literature and results of the pilot study suggest about the teaching-learning process in algebra with college-age deaf students.

REVIEW OF LITERATURE

Resnick, Cauzinille-Marmeche, and Mathieu (1987) provide a cognitive approach to understanding how students learn algebra. They remind us that "number is a strictly cognitive identity . . . people must reason about objects that exist only as mental abstractions" (p. 170). Algebraic symbols and rules provide a formal representation system for communicating mathematical ideas and procedures. Bell, quoted in Moses (1984), says that the generality of mathematics and its freedom from specific content are accomplishments of abstraction and logical reasoning.

Several investigators have attempted to delineate cognitive and linguistic factors related to mathematics performance. Cohen (1971) identified four cognitive factors: language, memory, logical reasoning, and visual-spatial abilities. Earp and Tanner (1980) reported that a student's success in mathematics is inextricably interwoven with the student's level of language sophistication. Aiken (1972) claimed that success in mathematics depends upon understanding of mathematical vocabulary, syntax, semantics, and function. Some research on spoken language has assumed that students who have production problems may have difficulty with one or more aspects of mathematics. Hall and Tomblin (1978) found that language-impaired subjects scored significantly lower than those with production deficits. The authors suspected that the language of instruction may have accounted for some of the problem but that general problems of symbolic representation, including nonlinguistic symbols, should be investigated.

Studies of language minority students have shown that the mathematical achievement differences between the language-minority and language-majority students in the United States are pronounced (Cocking & Chipman 1987). Stone (1988) reported that experience and observation at the National Technical Institute for the Deaf clearly demonstrate that deaf students have difficulties understanding the language of mathematics. She believes that the mismatch between the everyday language of the students and the language of instruction accentuates the problem for hearing-impaired students. Stone suggests that greater exposure to the language of the classroom and to the language of mathematics is necessary to enhance student performance in mathematics. Research with hearing-impaired individuals suggests that apparent cognitive-processing problems may be linguistic-conceptual differences rather than an inherent inability to think abstractly (Levine 1976; Martin 1985; Wolff 1985).

The literature suggests that relatively good language skills are necessary to learn mathematics successfully. Differences in the language of instruction and the language of learning can interfere with the teaching-learning process. Also, the evidence clearly shows that deaf college students should be able to learn more abstract algebra and more advanced mathematics. To improve instructional strategies in mathematics, a better understanding of the role of complexity and abstraction in language and mathematics is needed.

SUMMARY OF PILOT STUDY RESULTS

For the purposes of this investigation, mathematical expressions containing variable terms and coefficients were defined to be more abstract than those composed of numeric terms or coefficients. Mathematical complexity increased as the number of operations required to solve the problem increased. Language abstraction and complexity increased as the directions increased from three-word statements to conditional sentences to conditional sentences containing a clause. We hypothesized that problems embedded in conditional sentence constructions would be more difficult than similar problems given with simple three-word directions. The first pilot study was conducted with students enrolled in both Algebra I and Algebra II, who were given a linear-equations test and a quadratic-equations test, both including 25 questions grouped to vary the level of language and mathematical abstraction. Mathematical complexity was investigated only in the quadratic test, since the problems in the linear-equations test required one operation to solve the equation.

We considered results in three ways. First, we sought trends based on the difficulty of the items considered as a single group. Second, we compared difficulties of different item types within each group as defined by the level of language and mathematical abstraction. Third, we considered item difficulties of similar item types across abstraction groups.

On the linear-equations test, trends are clear. Division and multiplication problems were more difficult than addition and subtraction problems. Mathematically more abstract items, such as $X - T = C$, were more difficult than the more concrete items, such as $X + 3 = 7$. These results were true regardless of the level of language abstraction. From student performance on the linear-equations test, we conclude that *mathematical abstraction is a more potent source of item difficulty than language abstraction.* If there had been a systematic language effect, we would have expected problems embedded in conditional sentences to be more difficult than the mathematically equivalent problems grouped with simple sentence directions. The data did not show these differences.

The same basic combinations of language and mathematics abstraction were used to analyze the quadratic-equations test. In addition, one grouping of items embeds the problems in a complex conditional sentence, increasing the level of language complexity, and there are differences in mathematical complexity as well as in abstraction within each group. The most difficult items on the quadratic-equations test were those embedded in the complex/abstract language group.

Among the other test items, the more mathematically complex and abstract items were more difficult than those that were less so, even though the easier items were embedded in more abstract language. These data suggest that the conditional language construction can be ignored, or that it is relatively easy when compared with the effect of replacing numbers with variables in these types of problems.

As a follow-up to the first study, the quadratic test was given to Algebra II students only. Selected data from the second sample were combined with data from the first study to yield a combined sample of 66 students. The combined scores represent students who were sufficiently confident of their abilities to attempt to solve at least one problem in the most demanding group. The overall mean score of (10.2 of 25) clearly shows that the quadratic test was very hard for the students. An analysis of right/wrong scoring for the sixty-six students supports the findings of the first study. Abstract, complex mathematics is more likely to make a problem difficult than the abstraction or complexity of the language in which the problem is embedded. As in the first study, abstract, complex mathematical problems embedded in complex language structure were difficult for all the students. These results suggest that there are independent thresholds of language and mathematical complexity and abstractness that interfere with students' abilities to solve problems.

DISCUSSION

The test data demonstrate in a structured and controlled manner that students have problems dealing with the rule-governed, symbolic language of mathematics. The most difficult test items were those that were more representative of formal mathematics language. What are some of the implications of this study for further research?

Clearly we need to be more precise in describing deaf students' mathematical behavior. We need more structured research to identify specific conceptual problems common to many students. We must clarify the interaction of spoken, written, and sign language in communicating mathematics to deaf students. More research is needed to explain the cognitive processing that underlies our students' mathematical behavior.

How do we apply concepts of general cognitive psychology to understand how deaf students process sequential and spatial materials to access the concepts of higher mathematics? We need to develop cooperative relationships between mathematics educators and researchers in communication, cognitive science, linguistics, and mathematics in order to understand the cognitive components of the interaction among the several language systems involved in the teaching and learning process. The gap between classroom applications and research is too large. Together, instructors and researchers can develop teaching strategies that reflect understanding of the integral relationships among the context of mathematics, and the cognitive factors in communication that are required to meet the needs of hearing-impaired students.

REFERENCES

Aiken, L., Jr. 1972. Language factors in learning mathematics. *Review of Educational Research* 42:359–385.

Bloomquist, C.A., & Allen, T.E. 1988. Comparison of mathematics test item performance by hearing and hearing-impaired students. Paper presented at the annual convention of the American Educational Research Association, New Orleans, LA.

Brown, J.S., & Burton, R.E. 1978. Diagnostic models for procedural bugs in basic mathematical skills. *Cognitive Science* 2:155–192.

Cawley, J.F. 1985. *Cognitive strategies and mathematics for the learning disabled.* Rockville, MD: Aspen Systems Corporation.

Cocking, R.R., & Chipman, S.F. 1987. Conceptual issues related to mathematical achievement of language minority children. In *Linguistic and cultural influences on learning mathematics,* ed. R.R. Cocking & J.R. Mester, 17–46. Hillsdale, NJ: Lawrence Erlbaum Associates.

Cohen, R. 1971. Arithmetic and learning disabilities. In *Progress in learning disabilities.* Vol. 2, ed. H.R. Myklebust. New York: Grune & Stratton.

Cossio, M. 1977. The effects of language on mathematics placement scores in metropolitan colleges. *Dissertation Abstracts International* 38(7):4002A.

Dawe, K. 1984. A theoretical framework for the study of the effects of bilingualism on mathematics teaching and learning. Paper presented at the Fifth International Congress on Mathematical Education, Adelaide, Australia.

DeAvila, E.A. 1988. Bilingualism, cognitive function, and language minority group membership. In *Linguistic and cultural influences on learning mathematics,* ed. R.R. Cocking & J.R. Mester, 101–121. Hillsdale, NJ: Lawrence Erlbaum Associates.

Earp, N., & Tanner, F. 1980. Mathematics and language. *Arithmetic Teacher* 28:32–34.

Goldberg, E., & Costa, L.D. 1981. Hemisphere differences in acquisition and use of descriptive systems. *Brain and Language* 14:144–173.

Grove, C., & Rodda, M. 1984. Receptive communication skills of hearing impaired students: A comparison of four methods of communication. *American Annals of the Deaf* 129:378–385.

Hall, P., & Tomblin, J. 1978. A follow-up study of children with articulation and language disorders. *Journal of Speech and Hearing Disorders* 43:227–241.

Janvier, C. 1987. Problems of representation in the teaching and learning of mathematics. *Topics in Learning and Learning Disabilities* 1:19–30.

Levine, E.S. 1976. Psychological contributions. In *A bicentennial monograph on hearing impairment: Trends in the U.S.A.,* ed. R. Frisina, 23–33. Washington, DC: A.G. Bell Association.

———. 1988. Psychological contributions. In *A bicentennial monograph on hearing impairment: Trends in the USA,* ed. R. Frisina, 23–33. Washington, DC: A.G. Bell Association.

Lochhead, J., & Mestre, J. 1988. The ideas of algebra, K-12. In *1988 Yearbook of the National Council of Teachers of Mathematics,* 127–135. Reston, VA: National Council of Teachers of Mathematics.

MacNamara, J. 1966. *Bilingualism in primary education.* Edinburgh, Scotland: Edinburgh University Press.

———. 1967. The effects of instruction in a weaker language. *Journal of Social Issues* 23:121–135.

Martin, D.S. 1985. Enhancing cognitive performance in the hearing-impaired college student: A pilot study. In *Cognition, education and deafness: Directions for research and instruction*, ed. D. S. Martin, 176–179. Washington, DC: Gallaudet University Press.

Matz, M. 1982. Toward a process model for high school algebra errors. In *Intelligent tutoring systems*, ed. D. Sleeman & J.S. Brown, 25–50. London: Academic Press.

Mauer, S.B. 1987. New knowledge about errors and new views about learners: What they mean to educators and more educators would like to know. In *Cognitive science and mathematics education*, ed. A.H. Schoenfeld, 165–187. Hillsdale, NJ: Lawrence Erlbaum Associates.

Moses, J. 1984. Neurological analysis of calculation deficits. *Focus on Learning Problems in Mathematics* 6:1–12.

Pea, R.D. 1987. Cognitive technologies for mathematics education. In *Cognitive science and mathematics education*, ed. A.H. Schoenfeld, 89–122. Hillsdale, NJ: Lawrence Erlbaum Associates.

Poizner, H., Klima, E.S., & Bellugi, U. 1987. *What the hands tell us about the brain.* Cambridge, MA: Bradford Books/MIT Press.

Resnick, L.B., Cauzinille-Marmeche, E., & Mathieu, J. 1987. Understanding algebra. In *Cognition processes in mathematics*, ed. J.A. Sloboda & D.Rogers, 169–203. Oxford, England: Clarendon Press.

Rodda, M., & Grove, C. 1987. *Language, cognition and deafness.* Hillsdale, NJ: Lawrence Erlbaum Associates.

Schoenfeld, A.H., ed. 1987. *Cognitive science and mathematics education.* Hillsdale, NJ: Lawrence Erlbaum Associates.

Silver, E.A. 1987. Foundations of cognitive theory and research for mathematics problem-solving instruction. In *Cognitive science and mathematics education*, ed. A.H. Schoenfeld, 221–240. Hillsdale, NJ: Lawrence Erlbaum Associates.

Spanos, G., Rhodes, N.C., Corasaniti, D., & Crandall, J. 1988. Linguistic features of mathematical problem solving: Insights and applications. In *Linguistic and cultural influences on learning mathematics*, ed. R.R. Cocking & J.P. Mester, 221–240. Hillsdale, NJ: Lawrence Erlbaum Associates.

Stone, J.B. 1988. Intention and convention in mathematics instruction: Reflections on the learning of deaf students. In *Linguistic and cultural influences on learning mathematics*, ed. R.R. Cocking & J.P. Mester, 63–71. Hillsdale, NJ: Lawrence Erlbaum Associates.

Wolff, A. 1985. Analysis. In *Cognition, education, and deafness: Directions for research and instruction*, ed. D.S. Martin, 79–81. Washington, DC: Gallaudet University Press.

The van Hiele Levels of Geometric Thought Among Deaf Undergraduate Students

Vicki Kemp

E uclidean geometry plays a special part in the mathematics curriculum. In this course, the student is learning more than just isolated geometric facts. The student is being introduced to a mathematical system in which geometric facts are joined in a logical and coherent way. For many educators, the goal of teaching Euclidean geometry is to expose students to the deductive nature of reasoning—the framework that ties one fact to another.

Geometry is viewed by many students, deaf and hearing alike, as a difficult course, largely because of proof writing. These students say they "get by" by memorizing certain logical arguments or the entire proof of a theorem. Geometry teachers see their students failing to learn. Shaughnessy and Burger (1985) confess that "despite our best efforts to teach them, even the most capable algebra students may struggle and get through geometry by sheer will power and memorization" (p. 149).

According to the results of the Gallaudet University Mathematics Waiver Test, administered during the 1988 orientation week to all newly enrolled undergraduates, at least 95% of these students failed the geometry section. Hence, the students were required to take a remedial course in Euclidean geometry (MAT 039) at Gallaudet. This course is traditionally structured around deductive logic with an emphasis on proof writing, typical of a formal geometry course in sec-

---

This paper was a part of the author's dissertation for George Mason University. Partial support for this study was provided from Gallaudet University's Small Grant Fund, Office of Graduate Studies and Research.

ondary school. Student performance in this course has not been encouraging. During five semesters (Fall 1986 to Fall 1988), between 51% and 67% of the deaf students enrolled in MAT 039 received a final course grade of WD, D+, D, or F. Before this study, no research on reasons for or ways to reduce these failure rates has existed.

A review of data and research relating to deaf students reveals very little empirical research dealing with deaf students in geometry. However, there is clearly a serious educational problem in the geometry course. This study attempts to bridge that gap.

THEORETICAL FRAMEWORK

In the late 1950s, Pierre van Hiele and the late Dina van Hiele-Geldof evolved a structure for and experiment with thought levels in order to help students develop insight into geometry. They asserted that there are five consecutive levels of thought in the development of geometric understanding. A student's thinking moves sequentially from the basic level (visualization), where geometric figures are simply observed in their totality, to the next level (analysis) where the parts or components of the figure are perceived; the third level (informal deduction), a student establishes the interrelationships of properties both within figures and among figures; the fourth level (formal deduction), a student understands the logical structure of a proof; at the highest level (rigor), the student works in a variety of axiomatic systems.

Besides describing student levels of cognition in geometry, the van Hiele theory also implies how effective instruction could be organized in order for students to overcome cognitive difficulties in learning geometry. For this reason, this study attempted to provide a baseline discussion of the deaf students' difficulties with the geometry course in terms of the van Hiele levels before and after such a course, and to answer three research questions:

1. In what way are deaf undergraduate students distributed with respect to the van Hiele levels prior to a course in Euclidean geometry?
2. To what extent are deaf undergraduate students distributed with respect to the levels after completing a course in Euclidean geometry?
3. Is there a significant difference in deaf students' subsequent levels between those in classes receiving maximum emphasis on proof writing vs. those students in classes experiencing a minimum?

METHOD

The setting for this study was Gallaudet University in Washington, D.C. One hundred seventy-five deaf undergraduate students were the subjects. The research was conducted during a one-semester (fifteen week) course of MAT 039 (Euclidean geometry) that met for three hours per week. The learners were those deaf students who failed the university's diagnostic geometry test and were enrolled in one of the twelve sections of MAT 039. Hence these students were required to take MAT 039.

All ten geometry instructors used the same textbook. The instructors also met to coordinate the course materials that they would cover during the semester. The instructional process was characteristic of the lecture type that is common in university classrooms. Lessons were primarily expository in format, and assignments were from the textbook. All the instructors were fluent in sign language and had at least three years of experience in teaching geometry to the deaf.

A quasi-experimental pretest-posttest design was used for this study. The van Hiele geometry test, designed by the Cognitive Development and Achievement in Secondary School Geometry Project (CDASSG), was used to determine the deaf students' van Hiele levels. Due to the questionable nature of van Hiele level 5: Rigor, only the first 20 test items (Level 1 through level 4) of this test were used in this study. The reliability and validity of this test are detailed in the author's dissertation (Kemp, 1990).

All participating sections of geometry course MAT 039 took the van Hiele geometry test during the first week of the fall 1988 academic semester and again during the final exam week of that semester. The van Hiele test was designed to determine the van Hiele level of each student.

CLASSIFICATION OF DEAF STUDENTS INTO van HIELE LEVELS

A student was identified to be at van Hiele level n (any of the four levels) if the student correctly answered at least four out of five test items at level n and at all lower levels. Otherwise, a pseudolevel n was assigned to a student who correctly answered at least four out of five at level n, but not at all lower levels. A level 0 was assigned to a student who did not reach the criterion on van Hiele level 1, the first level. A student classified at pseudolevel 2 was considered to be one who had attained level 2, but had not mastered level 1.

Of the 156 subjects who took the pretest, 96% were assigned a van Hiele level. Of the 133 subjects who took the posttest, 90% were assigned a van Hiele level.

SUMMARY OF RESULTS

At the beginning of the geometry course, a large majority of the deaf students were assigned levels 0 and 1. Between 45% and 51% of the subjects were assigned level 0; in comparison, between 39% and 44% of the subjects were assigned level 1 (Table 1). Only one student was classified as level 3 and no one achieved level 4 at the beginning of the geometry course. Thus, if the geometry course demanded level 4 thinking, a large majority of these deaf students were *entering* the course three or four levels below the requirement.

TABLE 1   Distribution of Students on the van Hiele Geometry Test Based on Pretest Scores

Level	All Subjects (N = 156)	Subjects Who Took the Pre- and Posttests (N = 114)
Level 0	79 (51%)	51 (45%)
van Hiele Level 1	61 (39%)	50 (40%)
Pseudolevel 2	4 (3%)	4 (3%)
van Hiele Level 2	8 (5%)	6 (5%)
Pseudolevel 3	1 (.5%)	1 (1%)
van Hiele Level 3	1 (.5%)	1 (1%)
Pseudolevel 4	2 (1%)	1 (1%)
van Hiele Level 4	0	0

After the students completed the geometry course, the number at level 0 and level 1 decreased compared to the pretest (Table 2). However, a large majority of deaf students continued to be assigned level 0 or level 1 after completing the course.

After the posttest, approximately 15% of the deaf students were assigned van Hiele level 2, 5% were assigned pseudolevel 3, and 2% were assigned pseudolevel 4. No deaf students were found to be at van Hiele levels 3 or 4.

It appears that a plurality of deaf students are at level 0 or level 1, both at the outset of the course and at the end of it, with very little variation with respect to changes in the van Hiele levels. About 13% decreased their levels, about 60% remained at the same levels, and 27% increased their levels. Although the geometry course required van Hiele level 4 thinking in order to understand proofs, no deaf students, according to the van Hiele geometry test, were found to be functioning at such a level.

Although all the subjects in the study were being instructed in geometry, the amount of time devoted to proof-writing varied greatly among the ten instructors in Euclidean geometry, according to information obtained during interviews at the end of the course. An attempt was made to determine the role that proof-

TABLE 2   Distribution of Students on the van Hiele Geometry Test Based on Posttest Scores

Level	All Subjects (N = 133)	Subjects Who Took the Pre- and Posttests (N = 114)
Level 0	45 (34%)	40 (35%)
van Hiele Level 1	53 (40%)	42 (37%)
Pseudolevel 2	7 (5%)	7 (6%)
van Hiele Level 2	19 (14%)	17 (15%)
Pseudolevel 3	7 (5%)	6 (5%)
van Hiele Level 3	0	0
Pseudolevel 4	2 (2%)	2 (2%)
van Hiele Level 4	0	0

writing played in the students' changes in van Hiele levels. Three groups of students devoting different amounts of time to proof-writing were selected, based on the instructors' responses during interviews. The three groups were determined by averaging the percentages of time devoted to proof-writing (1) in the classroom, (2) on homework assignments, (3) on quizzes, tests, or graded papers.

At the outset of the course, deaf students who devoted the maximum amount of time to proof-writing primarily were classified as level 0. In contrast, the group of students who devoted the minimum amount or the average amount of time to proof-writing were primarily classified as level 1. At the end of the course, at least one-fourth of all students, regardless of the amount of time devoted to proofs, improved by one or two levels, and at least 58% of the students remained at the same level (Table 3).

The deaf students who spent the minimum amount of time doing proof-writing in their geometry courses proved to be the most improved group in terms of changes in van Hiele levels at pre- and posttest. This group was followed closely by the group of students who spent the maximum amount of time in proof-writing. However, no statistically significant differences were found among the three groups with respect to changes in the van Hiele levels and amount of time devoted to proof-writing in the course.

Conclusions regarding the emphasis on proof-writing in the classroom cannot be accurately made, due to independent factors that may have affected the results. The group who received the minimal amount of emphasis on proof-writing had taken geometry previously, had prior proof experience before taking the geometry course at Gallaudet, scored a higher score on the university's diagnostic test, and scored at higher levels on the SAT-HI Reading and SAT-HI Mathematical Applications, than did the groups doing an average or maximum amount of proof-writing in the classroom.

DISCUSSION

It became clear from the results of this study that deaf undergraduate students were entering the geometry course at Gallaudet University at lower van Hiele

TABLE 3 Distribution of Students' van Hiele Levels and Pseudolevels by Grouping According to Amount of Time Devoted to Proof-writing in the Geometry Course

| Level | at most 20% | | 30% to 35% | | at least 45% | |
| | Pretest | Posttest | Pretest | Posttest | Pretest | Posttest |
	(n = 22)		(n = 64		(n = 28)	
Level 0	7(32%)	5(23%)	27(42%)	23(36%)	17(61%)	12(43%)
van Hiele Level 1	11(50%)	9(41%)	30(47%)	23(36%)	9(32%)	10(36%)
Pseudolevel 2	1(4%)	0	3(5%)	4(6%)	0	3(11%)
van Hiele Level 2	3(14%)	5(23%)	2(3%)	10(16%)	1(3.5%)	2(7%)
Pseudolevel 3	0	2(9%)	1(1.5%)	3(5%)	0	1(3%)
van Hiele Level 3	0	0	1(1.5%)	0	0	0
Pseudolevel 4	0	1(4%)	0	1(1.5%)	1(3.5%)	0

levels than was expected. At least 45% of these students were not able to recognize or name figures by their global appearance. In addition, another 45% of these students recognized or named figures, but could not explicitly identify properties of these figures, such as "a rhombus has four equal sides," or "a square has four right angles and equal sides." Hence, a large majority of these deaf students were not prepared to think at the level required in the traditional geometry course in which proof-writing was expected to be learned.

After one semester of geometry instruction, at least 60% of the deaf undergraduate students remained at the same van Hiele level at which they entered the course. The course demands van Hiele level 4 thinking, but no student entered at this level. Thus, the students were not able to make progress. This finding may explain the obstacles to the students and to the teachers in geometry classrooms. While students are thinking at lower levels, their teachers are confronting them with problems that require vocabulary, concepts, and thinking at higher levels. Hence, there is a teaching/learning gap between the teacher and the student. As a result, the student may only memorize the theorems, proofs, and geometric concepts in order to "get by" in the geometry course.

The conventional approach in teaching Euclidean geometry to deaf undergraduate students does not bring these students to van Hiele level 4 at the end of the course. In fact, no deaf students in this study were assigned van Hiele levels 3 or 4 at the end of the geometry course. In addition, the amount of time that instructors devoted to proof-writing in class, out of class, and on their student's evaluations, indicated no significant differences in van Hiele level attainment among the three groups of students. Regardless of the instructor's emphasis on proof-writing, the deaf student tended to remain at the same van Hiele level throughout the course.

REFERENCES

Burger, W.F., & Shaughnessy, J. M. 1986. Characterizing the van Hiele levels of development in geometry. *Journal for Research in Mathematics Education* 17(1):31–48.

Fuys, D., Geddes, D., and Tischler, R. 1985. *An investigation of the van Hiele model of thinking in geometry among adolescents.* Final report of the NSF-RISE van Hiele Project at Brooklyn College. Research in Science Education (RISE) Program of the National Science Foundation, Grant No. SED 7920640. Washington, DC: National Science Foundation.

Han, T.S. 1986. The effects of achievement and attitude of a standard geometry textbook and a textbook consistent with the van Hiele theory. Ph.D. diss., University of Iowa, 1986. *Dissertation Abstracts International* 47:3690A. University Microfilms No. 86–28106.

Hoffer, A. 1979. *Geometry: A model of the universe.* Menlo Park, CA: Addison-Wesley Publishing Co.

———. 1983. Van Hiele-based research. In *Acquisition of mathematical concepts and processes,* ed. R. Lesh & M. Landau, 205–227. New York: Academic Press.

Kemp, V. 1990. The van Hiele levels of geometric thought and achievement in Euclidean geometry among deaf undergraduate students. Ph.D. diss., George Mason University, Fairfax, Virginia.

Mayberry, J.W. 1981. An investigation in the Van Hiele levels of geometric thought in undergraduate preservice teachers. Ph.D. diss., University of Georgia, 1979. *Dissertation Abstracts International* 42:2008A. University Microfilms No. 80–23078.

Senk, S.L. 1983. Proof-writing achievement and van Hiele levels among high school geometry students. Ph.D. diss., University of Chicago, 1983. *Dissertation Abstracts International* 44:417A. University Microfilms No.T28618.

———. 1985. How well do students write geometry proofs? *Mathematics Teacher* 78(6):448–456.

Shaughnessy, J. M., & Burger, W.F. 1985. Spadework prior to deduction in geometry. *Mathematics Teacher* 78(6):419–428.

Usiskin, Z. 1982. *Van Hiele levels and achievement in secondary school geometry*. Final Report of the Cognitive Development and Achievement in Secondary School Geometry Project (CDASSG). Chicago: University of Chicago. ERIC Document Reproduction Service No. ED 220–288.

van Hiele-Geldof, D. 1984a. The didactics of geometry in the lowest class of the secondary school. Ph.D. diss., In *English translation of selected writings of Dina van Hiele-Geldof and Pierre M. van Hiele*, ed. D. Geddes, D. Fuys, & R. Tischler. Washington, DC: National Science Foundation (Grant No. SED 7920640). (Original work published in 1957.)

———. 1984b. Didactics of geometry as learning process for adults. In *English translation of selected writings of Dina van Hiele-Geldof and Pierre M. van Hiele*, ed. D. Geddes, D. Fuys, & R. Tischler. Washington, DC: National Science Foundation (Grant No. SED 7920640). (Original work published in 1958).

van Hiele, P.M. 1958–59. La signification des niveaux de pensee dans l'enseignement par la methode deductive (The significance of level of thought in teaching by the deductive method), trans. A. van Twembeke. *Mathematica & Pedagogia* 16.

———. 1959. *Development and learning process: A study of some aspects of Piaget's psychology in relation with the didactics of mathematics*. Institute of Education, University of Utrecht, No. XVII. Groningen, Holland: J.B. Wolters.

———. 1984a. A child's thought and geometry. In *English translation of selected writings of Dina van Hiele-Geldof and Pierre M. van Hiele*. ed. D. Geddes, D. Fuys, & R. Tischler. Washington, DC: National Science Foundation (Grant No. SED 7920640). (Original work published in 1959).

———. 1984b. The problem of insight in connection with school children's insight into the subject matter of geometry. In *English translation of selected writings of Dina van Hiele-Geldof and Pierre M. van Hiele*, ed. D. Geddes, D. Fuys, & R. Tischler. Washington, DC: National Science Foundation (Grant No. SED 7920640). (Original work published in 1957).

———. 1986. *Structure and insight: A theory of mathematics education*. Orlando, FL: Academic Press.

van Hiele, P.M., & van Hiele-Geldof, D.A. 1958. A method of initiation into geometry at secondary schools. In *Report on methods of initiation into geometry*, ed. H. Freudenthal, 67–80. Subcommittee of the International Commission on Mathematical Instruction for the Netherlands, Report No. III. Groningen, Holland: J.B. Wolters.

Williams, E. 1980. An investigation of senior high school students' understanding of the nature of mathematical proof. *Journal for Research in Mathematics Education* 11:165–166.

Wirszup, I. 1976. Breakthroughs in the psychology of learning and teaching geometry. In *Space and geometry: Papers from a research workshop*, ed. J.L. Martin & D.A. Bradbard, 75–97. Columbus, OH: ERIC/SMEAC.

Memory and Metamemory in Deaf Students

Hing Fung Tsui
Michael Rodda
Carl Grove

T he memory capabilities of deaf students have been studied extensively; however, no comprehensive picture has emerged because of several problems. It is difficult to define memory, for it is not a unitary concept, but instead involves a variety of theoretical models. The research questions asked at the outset of most of the studies seem to have adopted the assumptions of the structural and process models. Yet the target of investigation has frequently been the problem of representation or encoding, since audition is assumed to be related to sequential processing and hearing loss to spatial processing (e.g., O'Connor & Hermelin 1972, 1973; Hermelin & O'Connor 1973; Beck, Beck & Gironella 1977; Lake 1981; Das 1983). The search for differences between the deaf and the hearing has predominated, and little information is available on the underlying mechanism for the often-reported inferior performance of the deaf. The studies that explored sign-informational and syntactic effects on memory (e.g., Liben, Newell & Posnansky 1978; Tweney & Heiman 1977; Tweney, Heiman & Hoeman 1978) are in fact reactions to a deep-rooted controversy regarding the linguistic status of sign language. Beneath the controversy is another more basic theoretical argument about the relationship between language and cognition.

Inevitably, the formulation of research questions is constrained by the adopted theoretical model; therefore it is important to have frameworks that address

This paper was based on the doctoral dissertation of H. F. Tsui. The participation of the students of the Alberta School for the Deaf and R.J.D. Williams Provincial School for the Deaf of Saskatchewan are thankfully acknowledged.

pertinent aspects comprehensively. What we term as memory may include various phenomena and processes, as the recent metacognitive models of Flavell (Flavell & Wellman 1977) and Brown (1975, 1978) have suggested. The metacognitive models have provided invaluable conceptual refinements for researchers. If one's focus is on development, then efforts should not be wasted on the basic processes, such as memory span. If one is intent on an inclusive view, then general cognitive schema, voluntary strategies, and metamemory (knowledge of memory and executive strategies) all would be taken into consideration. The newly emergent knowledge structure argument of Chi (Chi & Reese 1983; Chi & Ceci 1987) and the Vygotskyan notion of internalization (Vygotsky 1978) are also complementary to the general metacognitive paradigm.

Based on these metacognitive and cognitive theories, the purpose of the present research was to obtain a holistic descriptive profile of the interaction among the different variables, i.e., retrieval, encoding, strategy, declarative metamemory, task conditions, knowledge, and age.

THE RESEARCH STUDY

The subjects were 24 severely to profoundly deaf students, between the ages of 9 and 20, with bilateral sensorineural loss.

Declarative metamemory was investigated with four slightly modified subtests from Kreutzer, Leonard, and Flavell's (1975) interview—story list, study plan, retrieval event, and opposites-arbitrary. A systematic scoring scheme was also developed for the subtests. The responses were rated by three independent raters.

Encoding was tested with a spatial position vs. temporal position task. Three cards with either three digits or three letters were placed face down in a row. Each card was exposed for one second and put back in the original position. The temporal order of exposure did not occur from left to right or right to left in all trials, and the second one never corresponded to the spatial middle position. Detailed instruction and practice were given. After each presentation, the subject was asked either a "spatial middle" question or a "temporal middle" question. Overall performance and confusion error pattern were analyzed.

Semantic knowledge was assessed in the pretest word review. The words used had high imagery value derived from a pilot study. Also, the words were within a designated word-frequency range, each having six or seven letters.

Retrieval was investigated with free recall of a clusterable word list and paired-associate recall of prototypically associated items and non-prototypically associated items. The words used in these two tasks were the same ones as in the word review.

The use of clustering strategy and serial strategy was analyzed from the free-recall protocols using two statistical procedures. To obtain an index of the working memory capacity, the digit span forward test was taken from WISC-R (Wechsler 1974) with some procedural modification. A color sequence matching task was used as an interpolated task between tests as well as an informal context for behavioral observation. The testing was conducted by the first author and interpreted by a sign language interpreter for each individual subject.

SUMMARY OF RESULTS

The results indicated that the working-memory capacity of the deaf subjects was depressed. However, this finding, which has often been reported, should not mislead one to think that the "memory" of the deaf is totally deficient. The encoding and retrieval processes were interpreted in terms of the concepts of Flavell and Wellman (1977) (i.e., production deficiency, production efficiency, and mediation deficiency).

Inefficiency in encoding was reflected in the results. However, overall, the results did not suggest a spatial bias, that is, a mediation deficiency of temporal processing was not evident. When the sample was broken down into three age groups for contingency analysis, different patterns were discerned. In terms of mediation, some of the oldest subjects manifested a temporal processing deficiency; in contrast, the youngest subjects showed some spatial processing deficiency. In terms of production, the middle group seemed to be characterized by production deficiency. Also, an interesting finding was the significant negative correlation between spatial position encoding and retrieval event, which suggested that reflective thinking is essential for the inhibition of spatial preference.

Appropriate strategy use was shown to be critical for free-recall. High performance on free-recall correlated positively with clustering strategy, and clustering was influenced more by knowledge than by declarative metamemory. In the contingency analysis, both the oldest and the youngest subjects were found to be less proficient in clustering, which could be explained in terms of production deficiency or production inefficiency.

The effect of task difference was shown in the paired-associate test. Ceiling performance was observed on the prototypic items, indicating a highly automatic process. Performance on the non-prototypic items probably was associated with rehearsal, as shown in the positive and significant correlation with digit span, which was in turn correlated positively and significantly with temporal position recall.

Metamemory-memory relationship was found in free recall among the word-related memory tests. It was interpreted that memory tasks that did not invoke strategy use would not show correlation with metamemory. The high correlation between declarative metamemory and word review suggested that metamemory as measured in the present research shared common roots in long-term semantic memory. Age trend was observed on metamemory in general, with different patterns on the various subtests. The less optimal performance of some oldest subjects on three subtests might suggest some developmental lag in light of expected performance.

In general, the issue of knowledge structure development seemed to be pertinent to the memory development of the deaf students, which strongly agreed with the theory of Chi and her colleagues (e.g., Chi & Reese 1983) that memory development is in fact knowledge development.

One aspect that was not investigated in the present research was another component of metamemory (i.e., the executive strategies such as monitoring and planning for future retrieval). In the informal observation, the subjects displayed different studying styles and use of time; all these factors might reflect the underlying executive strategies that merit further exploration.

DISCUSSION

The present research suffered from many limitations, such as sample size, length of tests, and test-retest reliability. However, more adequate paradigms were utilized which at least pointed to the right questions to be asked. It appeared that the perennial question of spatial vs. temporal processing could not be answered if viewed as a perceptual problem. The present research exposed the possibility that this problem is in fact a conceptual or metacognitive issue.

The memory performance of deaf individuals often has been shown to be inferior to that of the hearing, yet what is "good" memory? The interpretive focal points provided by Flavell—mediation/production deficiency or production inefficiency of strategies—serve very well in answering that question (Flavell & Wellman 1977). This model of Flavell suggested that one should look into the mechanisms but not at the surface performance. A comprehensive investigation would require attention to all possible variables and their complex interaction; this kind of approach is especially necessary in dealing with disabled individuals, since the salience of the disability may occlude the researcher's targets. A more unfortunate consequence would be the stereotyping of the disabled person's cognitive ability. From the present study, it was shown that some tasks were more age-dependent, while others were knowledge-dependent or strategy-mediated. Instead of finding differences between the hearing and the deaf, more efforts must be directed toward finding the mechanisms beneath both efficient and inefficient performance of a particular kind of task.

The fact that knowledge was found to be critical is very encouraging to educators of the deaf, because knowledge is transmissible and transmutable. Granted that most of our deaf students are experientially deprived, perhaps we are left with the responsibility of finding better means of transmitting knowledge and enabling students to assimilate knowledge metacognitively.

REFERENCES

Beck, K., Beck, C., & Gironella, O. 1977. Rehearsal and recall strategies of deaf and hearing individuals. *American Annals of the Deaf* 122:544–552.

Brown, A.L. 1975. The development of memory: Knowing, knowing about knowing, and knowing how to know. In *Advances in child development and behavior*, ed. H.W. Reese, vol. 10, 103–152. New York: Academic Press.

———. 1978. Knowing when, where, and how to remember: A problem of metacognition. In *Advances in instructional psychology*, ed. R. Glaser vol. 1, 77–165. Hillsdale, NJ: Lawrence Erlbaum Associates.

Chi, M.T.H., & Ceci, S.J. 1987. Content knowledge: Its role, representation, and restructuring in memory development. In *Advances in child development and behavior*, ed. H.W. Reese, vol. 20, 91–142. New York: Academic Press.

Chi, M.T.H., & Reese, E. 1983. A learning framework for development. In *Contributions to human development: Vol. 9. Trends in memory development research*, ed. M.T.H. Chi, 71–107. Basel: Karger.

Das, J.P. 1983. Memory for spatial and temporal order in deaf children. *American Annals of the Deaf* 128:894–899.

Flavell, J.H., & Wellman, H.M. 1977. Metamemory. In *Perspectives on the development of memory and cognition*, ed. R.V. Kail & J.W. Hagen, 3–34. Hillsdale, NJ: Lawrence Erlbaum Associates.

Hermelin, B., & O'Connor, N. 1973. Ordering in recognition memory after ambiguous initial or recognition displays. *Journal of Psychology* 27:191–199.

Kreutzer, M.A., Leonard, C., & Flavell, J.H. 1975. An interview study of children's knowledge about memory. *Monographs of the Society for Research in Child Development* 40(1). Serial No. 159.

Lake, D. 1981. *Syntax and sequential memory in deaf children*. Ph.D. diss., University of Waterloo, Ontario, Canada.

Liben, L.S., Newell, R.C., & Posnansky, C.J. 1978. Semantic and formational clustering in deaf and hearing subjects' free recall of signs. *Memory and Cognition* 6:599–606.

O'Connor, N., & Hermelin, B. 1972. Seeing and hearing in space and time. *Perception and Psychophysics* 11(1A):46–48.

———. 1973. The spatial or temporal organization of short-term memory. *Quarterly Journal of Experimental Psychology* 25:323–343.

Tweney, R.D., & Heiman, G.W. 1977. The effect of sign language grammatical structure on recall. *Bulletin of the Psychonomic Society* 10:331–334.

Tweney, R.D., Heiman, G.W., & Hoeman, H.W. 1978. Psychological processing of sign language: The effects of visual disruption on sign intelligibility. *Journal of Experimental Psychology: General* 106(3):255–268.

Vygotsky, L.S. 1978. Mastery of memory thinking. In *Mind in society*, ed. M. Cole, V. John-Steiner, S. Scribner, & E. Souberman, 38–51. Cambridge, MA: Harvard University Press.

Wechsler, D. 1974. *Manual for the Wechsler Intelligence Scale for Children-Revised*. New York: Psychological Corporation.

Analysis

Robert Lee Williams

I n their paper for this volume, Hillegeist and Epstein state that "apparent cognitive-processing problems may be linguistic-conceptual differences rather than an inherent inability to think abstractly." It is a measure of how far we have come since the first Symposium on Cognition, Education and Deafness (1984) that such caveats are now scarcely necessary. According to Tsui, Rodda, and Grove in their description of the view of Soviet psychologists, "Rather than from a deficiency perspective, the research perspective is [now] more akin to that of cross-cultural variation." The papers in this chapter are both descriptive and prescriptive. Explanations for the disparity in performance between deaf and hearing students are explored, and possible remedies are offered. The topics in this chapter flow easily from mathematics to cognition to reading and to the complex interplay among them.

Those who are unfamiliar with deaf persons and deafness often assume that deaf persons will excel in the area of mathematics in the same way that foreign students often do in American universities. The common misconception is that mathematics is "language-free" or at least "language-fair." Unfortunately, this notion is not the case.

The papers in this chapter by Kemp and by Hillegeist and Epstein address the difficult topic of mathematical reasoning in deaf students. Both point out the difficulty that deaf students have with geometry. Kemp focuses her attentions specifically on the development of geometric thought in deaf undergraduate students. She indicates that van Hiele describes five levels through which one must progress towards full understanding of geometry: visualization, analysis, informal deduction, formal deduction, and rigor. It would appear that van Hiele's system follows the necessary protocol to be called a true stage theory. Stage theories must show an invariant sequence that is more than just an innate unfolding, an underlying structure that accounts for a variety of behaviors at a specific stage (no matter how varied they may be), and a clearly presented description of how each stage prepares the way for succeeding stages. As Kemp says, "the structure of a certain level is constructed from and incorporates the prior levels. . . ."

Clearly, van Hiele's stages go hand-in-hand with Piaget's stages, and the role of formal operations is critical. However, neither van Hiele nor Piaget clearly explained the role of formal instruction. Piaget believed that children move through the stages in a process of active discovery, but at the same time formal operations seem to be more common in students who have had formal training in, for example, the sciences. Even with formal training it appears that students who are at the first or second van Hiele level are doomed to fail when they take geometry. Is this result due to the courses being taught at the third or fourth level and the gap being too great for the students to close? If these reasons apply, then one would expect a tremendous difference in an Individualized Education Plan (IEP) in which a teacher could locate a student's level of reasoning and then adapt the course, as opposed to a lecture format in which the teacher presents the information at a fixed and predetermined level.

Hillegeist and Epstein point out that three languages are involved in learning mathematics, "the language of mathematics, the language of instruction, and the language of learning . . . success in learning mathematics depends on how successful each student is in integrating [these languages]." A number of research possibilities are raised in this paper. Clearly, an interesting idea would be to compare classes in which both teacher and student are communicating in American Sign Language with those classes in which both are using spoken English as well as with those classes in which there is a mismatch. This process would allow us to ferret out the validity of the later statement: "Relatively good language skills appear to be necessary to successfully learn mathematics . . ." as opposed to the problems of "limited life experiences upon which to draw to derive meaning from new concepts or to fully understand example problems." Additionally, one would wonder what proportion of the problems that deaf university students encounter with mathematics (see article by Kemp) could be attributed to a long-term problem with mathematics at the arithmetic level (a difficulty that will be difficult to solve at the university level). Hillegeist and Epstein further suggest that ". . . errors . . . appear to indicate that the student focused on the surface structure of a mathematical statement rather than on its meaning."

One of the positive aspects of bringing together professionals from different areas of research is finding common threads linking different fields. In the paper by Pinhas, deaf and hearing readers are compared on the basis of their abilities to process inferential information in written texts. The key here is less the difference between hearing and deaf readers and more the difference between skilled and unskilled readers. A skilled constructive reader "draws inferences while reading the text [while] a nonconstructive reader is assumed to draw the inference at the time of questioning or not at all." To see if this hypothesis could account for some of the difficulty that deaf students have in reading, research participants in this study were examined in a variety of tasks involving variable intervals between reading and questioning. Pinhas indicates that previous research suggests that deaf students have more difficulty in processing inferences than do hearing students, but as yet the causes are unclear. Pinhas's present study finds that while the deaf students seem to have the same level of accuracy in processing inferential information, they take longer to do so. As Pinhas states, this finding could "reflect an adaptive strategy." Deaf students who have had lifelong problems with reading may have had lifelong instructions to "take your time" and "it's better to be slow and careful than fast and careless." These caveats, applied at different times to different situations, make it difficult to draw meaningful conclusions from such data.

The notion of adaptive strategies would be a good introductory description of the paper by Kluwin. Students tend to arrive in the classroom using different methods and/or different schemas when dealing with questions from the teacher. Looking at a variety of script theory, Kluwin finds that a difference between a teacher's meta-MOP (memory organizing packet) and a student's meta-MOP can result in the teacher asking a sensible question, and the student giving a sensible answer that does not coincide with the teacher's question because he or she is following a different script. A typical classroom scenario: "The confusion of the student is apparent in the instability of his responses. When the appropriate meta-MOP was brought into play, it was not appropriate to the requirements of the question, thus producing a series of unique utterances until the student eventually lapsed into silence." Thus goes another day in the classroom.

Imagine this scenario on a global level, and we may have a clue to the difficulties plaguing students in Kemp's geometry classes. It is likely that the different meta-MOPs used by student and teacher arise from a tangle involving both different levels and different varieties of life experiences as well as simple linguistic miscommunication. Again, this finding could be examined by looking at a variety of combinations in the classroom and especially by comparing classrooms where this happens frequently vs. infrequently. As Kluwin points out, "for some students, the traditional Socratic dialogue may be an inappropriate instructional device." However, all teachers have had the occasional student who uses the Socratic method on the teacher, carefully, in a manner reminiscent of the television game show "Jeopardy," giving answers and soliciting questions.

Another aspect of reading is discussed by Tsui, Rodda, and Grove. In their conclusion they point out research suggesting that "the poor reading performance of the deaf [student] may reflect the failure of the educational system to teach the meaning of reading." This stern indictment is an easy one to make. If the students cannot read and the responsibility of the educational system is to teach them to read, then it is clear where the blame lies (assuming we do not want to blame the victim). It is far more difficult to suggest a means by which the problem can be alleviated. Tsui, Rodda, and Grove draw upon works by Vygotsky and Erickson in suggesting a number of approaches and strategies that must be explored, including work on "prerequisite knowledge-schemata building, a bimodal (sign and oral languages) interlingual format of instruction, and turn-taking metacognitive monitoring." While some of these notions (e.g., a bimodal [sign and oral languages] interlingual format of instruction) may be controversial and even contraindicated by earlier papers in this volume, they most certainly point the way for future research.

Berchin examines another micro-aspect of reading, specifically categorization and its modifiability via mediated learning experience (MLE). In her research, MLE was shown to enhance students' categorization performances. If one takes as a given that categorization is an important aspect of reading, then the potential for improvement is clear. This paper and others seem to hold out the promise of real classroom programs to improve reading skills in deaf students. The question open for further research then becomes whether all the effort involved in effecting these small gains will amount to a major elevation in reading scores—whether the game will be worth the candle. Optimistically, it may be that the gestalt will come together and the gain will be significant.

Volumes of research and lore discuss gender differences in verbal and mathematical skills. The article by Witters-Churchill and Witters seems to follow a growing trend toward finding fewer or smaller gender differences among special populations. In this case the task was a Piagetian liquid horizontality test. Males typically do better on this test than females, although the size of the difference is a matter of dispute. The authors believe that "the visual-spatial task of drawing a water line correctly for various bottle rotations also involves considerable language mediation." This kind of research ties in with the earlier papers in this chapter that relate language proficiency to mathematical skill. The relationship, if it exists, is incredibly complex and certainly under some dispute. The notion that gender differences noted in the "normal" vs. "special" populations may be a result of social learning only in the normal population also has been suggested. One might imagine that "special" populations would be less sensitive to the prejudices of modern society. On the other hand, there seems to be no evidence that this reduced sensitivity is the case. Further, there is no reason to believe (1) that there is less sexism in schools for the deaf than public schools, or (2) that deaf students are any less sensitive to its effects.

Witters-Churchill and Witters also examine the effects of training—a topic that Kemp also examines. While Kemp pointed out the difficulties involved in moving low van Hiele-stage students to higher stages of geometric thought, these authors suggest that improvement in performance on Piagetian tasks with special populations has been noted. This finding may suggest a qualitative difference between the skills required in the two tasks.

Marlowe's paper addresses the problem of diagnosing learning disabilities in hearing-impaired individuals. One index of a learning disability is a deficiency in short-term sequential memory. If differences on this task can reliably separate learning-disabled hearing-impaired individuals from their non-learning disabled counterparts, it could provide diagnosticians with an invaluable tool. This possibility is especially important because PL94−142 makes it clear that any designated learning disability not be the "result of visual, hearing, or motor handicaps . . . or cultural or economic disadvantage." The performance deficit among hearing-impaired individuals relative to hearing individuals is now thought to be due to "bias of the materials used, the linguistic content of the stimulus items, and the manner of presentation." A properly cleaned-up short-term sequential memory task would allow diagnosticians to separate the effects of a deaf person's language and culture on the task from the effects of a possible learning disability.

In the past, psychologists have been criticized for examining human behavior through a microscope and thereby missing the big picture. In this area of research, at this time, it would seem that this approach is appropriate. All the research in this chapter points toward the need to unravel the complex weave of language, culture, cognition, gender, and deafness. This unraveling may have to be done thread by thread.

RESEARCH QUESTIONS

1. How important is congruity between the communication mode of the teacher and that of the student in acquiring mathematical concepts?
2. Would it be possible to develop a type of "language-free" mathematical instruction that would put deaf students on an equal footing with hearing students?
3. What role can computer-assisted individualized instruction play in the development of mathematical reasoning?
4. To what extent are van Hiele's stages an "unfolding" as opposed to the result of formal instruction?
5. How would one go about adapting geometry proofs to fit ASL? Is there a "Whorfian" problem here?
6. How much of deaf students' difficulties with university mathematics is caused by weak "mathematical infrastructure," i.e., weak arithmetic skills?
7. What are the important differences in deaf students' learning a language where words are initially sounded out, as opposed to an Asian language in which learning the characters is more dependent upon memory?
8. If there is a general short-term memory deficit that accounts for a number of academic difficulties in many deaf students, is there a general, underlying, and basic ability that could be enhanced in deaf students that would improve both their reading and their mathematical abilities?
9. What factors contribute to a lack of gender differences in special populations?
10. Given the myriad factors that make up the complex task of reading, which are amenable to training, which are truly significant in their contributions, and which are global in that they affect a variety of cognitive tasks?

8

COGNITIVE INTERVENTION PROGRAMS

A Program to Enhance the Social Cognition of Deaf Adolescents

Mimi WheiPing Lou
Elizabeth S. Charlson

A high proportion of deaf individuals have been reported to experience difficulties in social functioning. Through group testing and case studies of deaf persons, researchers have correlated deafness with a host of maladaptive personality characteristics, including impulsive behavior, egocentrism, lack of empathy, overt aggression, lack of self-esteem and conduct and adjustment disorders (Bachara et al. 1980; Craig 1965; Eabon 1984; Evans 1987; Gibson 1984; Harris 1978; Hirshoren & Schnittjer 1978; Levine 1981; Meadow 1984; Sarlin & Altshuler 1977). In addition, research indicates that deaf individuals may have great difficulty in understanding the perspective of other people (Kusché & Greenberg 1983; Lou 1987) and understanding social rules and morals (Nass 1964; DeCaro & Emerton 1978). One explanation that has been offered for these socio-emotional problems is experiential deprivation. Losses and gaps in social experience are pervasive for deaf individuals because of significant limitations in their ability to communicate with others, especially in the family and at school. In the model of Feuerstein (1980) we might suggest that the best way to compensate for these kinds of experiential lacunae would be with "mediated intervention."

This paper describes a social-cognitive program that provides and structures opportunities to think about people and about psychological and social issues in a guided way. We have described the program as a social-cognitive one because our aim has been to provide opportunities for mediated learning in the social domain. By social cognition we mean not only social knowledge and problem-solving ability, but more broadly and fundamentally, understanding and reasoning about people, relationships, and social events. We hypothesized that if a program of mediated intervention can raise levels of social cognition, then improved social and social-emotional functioning will follow. The program we have been developing focuses on two particular aspects of social cognition: role- or perspective-taking and person perception or conceptualization. Perspective-taking refers to the ability to take and simultaneously coordinate a variety of perspectives on a particular situation. Person conceptualization has to do with the degree of sophistication (depth and complexity) of a person's understanding of self and others. We believe these two dimensions to be central to independent reasoning in the social domain. A third focus for the program was communication, by which we mean the ability to share meaning with another, not language per se.

METHODS

Pilot Programs

Initial versions of this program have been piloted with three groups. The first program was piloted with a small group of deaf adults receiving vocational-rehabilitation services, and more recently, with classes of hearing impaired students at two different high schools. The adult group (Group I) included four deaf V-R (vocational rehabilitation) clients (2 men, 2 women), with two hearing group leaders/guides. This program ran for seven weeks, meeting twice a week in sessions lasting an hour and a half. In order to ensure that the group members would faithfully attend sessions, and because the program was highly experimental and still under active development, each member was given $10 at the end of each session as reimbursement for travel costs and as some compensation for their time. All sessions, with the exception of a picnic, were held at the Center on Deafness in San Francisco. These sessions were videotaped for purposes of program development, review, and revision. Each session began with a fifteen-minute period for informal socializing over coffee and refreshments. The food and drinks were then removed for the program activities. Usually two different types of activities occurred during each session, while each activity itself or versions of it continued across several sessions. Before the program began and again after it ended, each member was interviewed to assess two aspects of their level of social cognition: role- or perspective-taking and person conceptualization. The interview and analysis is described below under *Procedures*.

A second and third version of the program were piloted with hearing-impaired high school students. The second program (Group II) included four boys and five girls, but one of the girls attended school for only three of the days when the program took place. For most of the program the boys and girls met consecutively in separate groups. Their schedules had been arranged by student request to permit sex-specific classes because sex education was planned for three days of the week that the social cognition program did not take over. Three additional sessions of boys and girls were also held so as to permit joint, full-class discussion of one particular program activity. The program was offered to each group twice a week for a class period (45 minutes) for twelve weeks. All sessions took place in the resource classroom and were videotaped. The deaf education teacher (a hearing fluent signer) led Group B (the boys' group) while co-leading Group A (the girls' group) with a counselor (a hearing Licensed Clinical Social Worker who was also a fluent signer) from the University of California Center on Deafness. In addition, the teacher's aide (a deaf woman) often participated in the boys' group, while a student teacher (a hearing woman, fluent signer) replaced the regular teacher for several of the last group sessions. As with the adult group, each student was interviewed before and after the program using the social cognitive protocol.

The third program (Group III) was held in another high school classroom. This group met twice weekly with boys and girls together, but some students were only able to attend the group once a week. A social worker led the group with very little involvement from the classroom teacher who chose to participate in only a few activities. These students met over a 7-month period. Students were interviewed before and after the program as well.

PROCEDURES

The Social-Cognitive Interview

This interview was designed to assess three specific aspects of social cognition: perspective-taking ability, social-causal reasoning, and personal conceptualization. In order to elicit levels of perspective-taking, interviewees were told three different stories involving a number of protagonists and were then questioned about the feelings and thoughts of each protagonist. Their answers for each story were then scored separately for one of the following levels of perspective-taking, based on the work of Robert Selman (1971; Selman & Byrne 1974) and of Marvin Feffer (1959; Feffer & Gourevitch 1960).

1. *Level 0. Egocentric.* Psychological perspectives undifferentiated. No distinction between personal interpretation and "correct" perspective.
2. *Level 1. Subjective.* Psychological perspective of Subject and Others separated and recognized as potentially different, but readable by situation. Cannot coordinate perspectives.
3. *Level 2. Self-reflective. Reciprocal.* Can reflect on Subject's behavior and motivation from Other's perspective. Individual roletaking. Sequential roletaking.
4. *Level 3. Mutual. 3rd Person:* Can abstractly step outside interaction and simultaneously and mutually coordinate perspectives of Subject and Other(s). Generalized other perspective.

Person conceptualization was assessed in the second part of the interview when individuals were asked to describe separately three different people: someone they liked very much (e.g., a best friend), someone they disliked, and themselves. Analysis of levels of person conceptualization was based on the descriptive work of Peevers and Secord (1973) and Livesley and Bromley (1973). Sophistication and depth of person conceptualization were scored for one of the following five levels:

> *Level 1.* Objective information: geographic, appearance, heal family, friends, occupation, behavior, incident, routine. Egocentric: behavior focused on subject. Global judgment.

> *Level 2.* Evaluative of any of the above. More personally informative but not descriptive of personality: roles, activities, interests, preferences. Feelings and reactions (transient).

> *Level 3.* Personality traits, implied dispositions. Abilities, skills, achievements. Beliefs and values.

> *Level 4.* Traits or dispositions that are modified, qualified, specified, or elaborated.

> *Level 5.* Traits or dispositions that are explained psychologically.

The interviews were scored by the second author. The first author independently scored 20% of the interviews. Interrater reliability was >.80 within one-half point on role-taking scores and >.80 on person conceptualization.

The Social-Cognitive Program

The program differed from other educational curricula in that the intent was not to instruct, but rather to make salient considerations for ways of thinking (i.e., to mediate learning about social events and people). Thus, a number of principles guided the development and selection of program activities. These included the importance of activities that were natural, having meaningful real-life consequences. This feature also meant that rewards were intrinsic to the social actions taken by an individual rather than arbitrarily tied to behavior by an external authority. Another guiding principle was that authority-subordinate distinctions within the group would be minimized. Thus, the program leaders functioned more as "guides" or "mediators" who participated in the various program activities equally with the other members of the group, rather than as teachers or outside authorities. Correspondingly, the group members were viewed as active, responsible participants, not as mere passive followers.

The major principle guiding the program was that learning could occur without explicit teaching. Thus, activities were structured to elicit thinking about others without necessarily providing ultimate and correct solutions. Most of the program activities were games rather than lessons with didactic instruction. In addition, wherever possible, interactions within the group were used for discussion and learning. While we had a purpose for each of these activities, this purpose was usually not made explicit to the group members, i.e., the "point" or lesson of each activity was not told to the group.

There were three major types of activities: (1) those focused on improving communication; (2) those focused on raising levels of person conceptualization; and (3) those focused on increasing perspective-taking. Some activities addressed more than one aspect of social cognition at a time. In addition, there were some activities that included a focus in social problem-solving.

RESULTS

Overall, all participants improved significantly in role-taking ability from pretest to posttest ($p < .01$), while person conceptualization scores remained relatively constant. By intervention group, the high school students in Group II made the greatest improvement in role-taking scores ($p < .01$). Group I participants also improved from pretest to posttest in role-taking although the improvement was not quite statistically significant ($p < .06$). Although Group III had the greatest number of group meetings, their role-taking scores did not significantly improve. Person conceptualization scores did not improve.

DISCUSSION

It appears that the kind of "mediated social experience" approach described here is promising, but we are well aware that much needs to be done before such a social-cognitive program can be rigorously evaluated. First, we believe that the program itself can be much improved, and that the activities and the group processing of the activities are still in the early stages of development. Our expectation is that as the program continues to be experimental, the group guides will constantly rework it. Moreover, we expect that the program will benefit from the diverse training and experience of the leaders, and thus we are intentionally having different types of professionals (including counselors, teachers, clinical social workers, and professionals) lead different groups. We believe that the involvement of teachers in the high school program is critical. Although Group III had the longest duration of intervention, the teacher did not actively support the program, and the students in this classroom were not guided to generalize their experiences in the group to activities throughout the school day. We believe that this lack of support limited the effect of the group experience to a minor change in role-taking.

The accurate assessment of social cognition and social functioning also must be improved. Our social-cognitive interview does not capture all the types of changes that guides and teachers noted in group members. In addition to continuing to develop the program itself, we are also developing a behavior-ranking instrument to assess change in social interactions and understanding.

REFERENCES

Bachara, G., Raphael, J., & Phelan, W. 1980. Empathy development in deaf pre-adolescents. *American Annals of the Deaf* 125:38–41.

Craig, H. 1965. A sociometric investigation of the self-concepts of the deaf child. *American Annals of the Deaf* 110:456–467.

DeCaro, P., & Emerton, R. 1978. *A cognitive-developmental investigation of moral reasoning in a deaf population.* Paper presented at the American Educational Research Association, Toronto, Ontario, Canada.

Eabon, M. 1984. *On the relationship between impulsivity and field-dependence in hearing-impaired children.* Paper presented at the Annual Meeting of the Midwestern Psychological Association, Chicago.

Evans, J.W. 1987. The treatment of emotional problems associated with hearing impairment in childhood and adolescence. In *Expanding horizons: Psychosocial interventions with sensorially-disabled persons.* ed. B. Heller, L. Flohr, & L. Zegans. New York: Grune & Stratton.

Feffer, M.H. 1959. The cognitive implications of role-taking behavior. *Journal of Personality* 27:152–168.

Feffer, M.H., & Gourevitch, V. 1960. Cognitive aspects of role-taking in children. *Journal of Personality* 28:383–396.

Feuerstein, R. 1980. *Instructional enrichment: An intervention program for cognitive modifiability.* Baltimore, MD: University Park Press.

Gibson, J. 1985. Field dependence of deaf students: Implications for education. *Cognition, education, and deafness: Directions for research and instruction,* ed. D. Martin. Washington, DC: Gallaudet College Press.

Harris, R. 1978. The relationship of impulse control to parent hearing status, manual communication, and academic achievement in deaf children. *American Annals of the Deaf* 123:62–67.

Hirshoren, A., & Schnittjer, C. 1979. Dimensions of problem behavior in deaf children. *Journal of Abnormal Child Psychology* 7:221–228.

Kusché, C., & Greenberg, M. 1983. The development of evaluative understanding and role-taking in deaf and hearing children. *Child Development* 54:151–157.

Levine, E. 1981. *The ecology of early deafness.* New York: Columbia University Press.

Livesley, W.J., & Bromley, D.B. 1973. *Person perception in childhood and adolescence.* London: John Wiley & Sons.

Lou, M. 1987. *Social cognitive functioning in deaf adolescents and young adults.* Paper presented at the Society for Research in Child Development, Baltimore, MD.

Meadow, K. 1984. Social adjustment of preschool children: Deaf and hearing, with or without other handicaps. *Topics in Early Childhood Special Education* 3:27–40.

Nass, M. 1964. Development of conscience: A comparison of the moral judgments of deaf and hearing children. *Child Development* 35:1073–1080.

Peevers, B.H., & Secord, P.F. 1973. Developmental changes in attribution of descriptive concepts of person. *Journal of Personality and Social Psychology* 27:120–128.

Sarlin, M., & Altshuler, K. 1977. On the interrelationship of cognition and affect: Fantasies of deaf children. *Child Psychiatry and Human Development,* 95–103.

Selman, R.L. 1971. Taking another's perspective: Role-taking development in early childhood. *Child Development* 42:1721–1734.

Selman, R.L., & Byrne, D.F. 1974. A structural-developmental analysis of role-taking in middle childhood. *Child Development* 45:803–806.

Cognitive Enhancement of Hearing-Impaired Postsecondary Students

David S. Martin
Bruce S. Jonas

R esearch with hearing-impaired persons has documented that there are no basic differences between their range of cognitive abilities and that of the general population, and that any inferiority in cognitive performance may be accounted for by experiential and linguistic deficits as well as by communication handicaps (Levine 1976).

During recent years, a specially developed program entitled Instrumental Enrichment (IE) (Feuerstein 1980) has become available in the United States, developed by the Israeli Piagetian scholar Reuven Feuerstein. This classroom intervention program for adolescents and adults uses content-free paper-and-pencil exercises to correct deficient cognitive functions and to provide the prerequisites for learning and problem-solving, such as analytic perception, projection of virtual relationships, orientation in space, comparison, temporary relation-ships, hierarchical relationships, syllogistic thinking, categorization, synthesis, and sequential progression.

HYPOTHESES

The following hypotheses were advanced as potential outcomes of using the Instrumental Enrichment Program with the experimental sample of hearing-impaired college students.

Hearing-impaired college students working on a regular and systematic basis with the exercises in the Instrumental Enrichment Program for two years will:

1. Demonstrate significantly higher logical reasoning in comparison with a control group, as measured by results on the Raven's Standard Progressive Matrices (Raven 1960) at the end of the research period.
2. Demonstrate significantly better achievement in reading comprehension in comparison with a control group, as measured on the Stanford Achievement Test, Hearing-Impaired (SAT-HI) (Madden 1972).
3. Demonstrate significantly better achievement in mathematics concepts in comparison with a control group, as measured by the SAT-HI.
4. Demonstrate significantly better achievement in mathematical computation in comparison with a control group, as measured on the SAT-HI.
5. Demonstrate improved organization in their production of a written essay as judged by a team of trained independent judges.
6. Within the experimental group, students whose hearing loss dates from age 2 or before will show significantly greater improvement in scores in logical reasoning as measured by the Raven's Matrices, when compared with students whose hearing loss dates after age 2.

GROUPS

In the Fall of 1985 (year one), 91 experimental subjects were identified in the classes of the seven experimental instructors who made a commitment to training in the methods of Instrumental Enrichment—the experimental treatment. Ninety-one control subjects were also identified, matched on age of onset of hearing loss, degree of hearing loss, and gender. As a result of naturally expected student attrition at the college level, four different lengths of experimental intervention exposure occurred—a four-semester experimental group, a three-semester experimental group, and two two-semester groups (1985–86 and 1986–87).

In the fall of 1986 (year two), those individuals in the original control group who had not returned to college were identified; a great many control subjects did not return for their second year (the group was reduced from 91 to 55). The same assessment was made of the experimental subjects from the first year, and again, considerable attrition occurred (from 91 to 75). The control group, of course, consisted of individuals who, throughout the two-year period, had no exposure to the experimental treatment.

RESULTS

The results show that for the first comparison, IE students significantly gained more than control students, averaging 1.9 points to the control group's 0.7 points, after controlling for the effects of the pretest. A second comparison revealed no trend between two and four semesters of IE groups. Hence, Hypothesis 1 was supported: Gains for the IE students were significantly greater than those for the controls in logical reasoning.

On the SAT-HI Reading Comprehension results for the posttest administration, insufficient pretest information was available for experimental subjects. Based on our previous research, we assumed that matched samples among hearing-impaired students are comparable among such standardized tests (Martin & Jonas 1986). The results indicated significantly higher scores for the IE group (634.99) vs. the control group (621.4). The two- to four-semester comparison of IE exposure showed no significant pattern within the experimental subgroups. Hypothesis 2 was therefore supported in that the IE group did significantly better in reading comprehension than the control group. Scaled, rather than grade-equivalent, scores are reported because they are invariant across different levels.

On the SAT-HI Math Concepts posttest means, results showed that (1) IE students scored significantly higher than control students (698.9 vs. 678.1) and (2) that four-semester IE students score significantly higher than two-semester students (720.1 vs. 690.5).

This result was expected, since the content of the Math Concepts test requires the students to use principles of logic and analogic activities that occur repeatedly throughout IE instruction and more frequently as IE instruction moves into the second year. Hence, Hypothesis 3 was strongly supported in that both the presence and the duration of IE instruction had a significant impact on performance in Math Concepts.

On the SAT-HI Math Computation, the results show significantly higher scores for the IE group (711.7) compared to the control group (689.0). The two-to-four semester comparison shows a greater gain for the four-semester group (726.5), vs. the two-semester group (707.5), but this comparison did not reach statistical significance, perhaps due to the low sample sizes compared (11 four-semester students vs. 26 two-semester students). Hence, Hypothesis 4 was supported in that the IE group as a whole demonstrated significantly better performance in math computation in comparison with controls.

On the Gallaudet University Writing Placement test, a test of grammatical usage, word choice, and organization, the data do not show any significant differences between the IE and control groups. The comparison between two- and four-semester IE groups (3.7 vs. 8.6) does approach statistical significance ($p = .0891$). Hence, Hypothesis 5 was somewhat ambiguously supported; we cannot support an overall effect of the IE training, but within the IE group, additional exposure did increase gain scores in writing.

Hypothesis 6, that there will be a greater improvement in logical reasoning by prelingually deaf experimental students compared with postlingually deaf experimental students, was not supported.

INTERVIEW DATA

The investigators interviewed randomly selected experimental subjects as well as the instructors in the experimental group. These data were used to assist in the interpretation of the statistical findings and to broaden the base of information on the results of the experiment beyond paper-and-pencil instruments.

Students

Students were asked to respond to the question "In what ways have you changed your thinking since you started to use Instrumental Enrichment?" Five of the twenty randomly selected experimental subjects responded that they were not aware of any change; an additional two students said only that they were concerned about the amount of time that Instrumental Enrichment seemed to "take away" from learning English. The remaining thirteen students all replied in some form that they believed that their thinking patterns had become more careful or systematic or less impulsive.

Experimental Instructors

During the interviews with the experimental instructors, the key question was "What types of responses to the program did you see happening in your students in the experimental group?" Instructor responses to this question helped to elaborate further on the above student responses. Instructors' observations revealed that, by March 1987, experimental students began to demand that their instructors give them verbal elaboration on any response, thus reflecting the same elaborative style the instructor had been trying to model for them. Instructors reported that no such demands were made by experimental students during the first semester of the experiment. Instructors also reported that students argued with one another during class, whereas previously they had merely accepted what the instructor said or what other students said without question.

It is clear from these reports that the program enhances verbal elaboration behaviors; experimental group instructors reported no such responses from students in non-Instrumental Enrichment classes.

The second key question in the interviews with IE faculty was "What overall changes do you see as a result of the experiment?" The following points were made by faculty interviewees:

1. Students in the experimental group began to feel the "strength" of their reasoning powers.
2. The students in the experimental group moved further ahead into higher level English and math than had been the case in previous years with similar groups that did not have Instrumental Enrichment.
3. Students demonstrated more confidence in themselves during examinations.
4. Students began to be able to use more than one piece of information at a time in activities requiring that behavior.
5. Test scores on teacher-made tests demonstrated that students had begun to "reason better."
6. Students stopped giving up on difficult academic problems or being depressed about their difficulty.
7. Students became better notetakers; they began to ask the instructor to stop and let them take notes instead of the instructor having to stop and remind them to do so (this is an important issue in teaching

deaf students, who are normally unable to take notes during a lecture because of the need to pay attention visually).

8. Students at first resented the nonverbal materials in the program, feeling that the materials were for younger students; but by the end of the third semester, students said they saw the value of nonverbal materials and began to ask for more practice in the nonverbal instruments as well as in the verbal ones.

9. Instructors said that they believed their own style of teaching had changed permanently as a result of the training, in the direction of allowing more "wait-time" for student responses in discussions, using more cognitive terms in their teaching, and demanding higher-level responses from their students during discussions.

Thus, these data also demonstrate that important changes were taking place beyond what was noted in the test scores reported earlier:

1. For the younger adult learner in the collegiate environment, a systematic cognitive skills program places students in situations where they can begin to believe that they can think, which is an important factor in their self-confidence as learners. This conclusion is especially critical to the deaf college student, who frequently has a problem with self-confidence in comparing himself or herself with hearing students.

2. No significant alterations of sequence in cognitive skills instruction were needed for adapting cognitive-skill programs for hearing-impaired, as compared with hearing, college students.

3. This program of systematic cognitive instruction leads students to mediate for each other, to the point where this peer mediation gradually becomes a supplement to the mediation carried out by the instructor.

4. Instrumental Enrichment as an intervention may assist in making some of the linkages between the visual and the verbal code systems for the hearing-impaired learner; this conclusion was based on the observed easy interaction back and forth between those two modalities on the instruments as noted by experimental group instructors, by comparison with their observations of the same students at the beginning of the experiment. Once again, this conclusion is fundamentally important in regard to the hearing-impaired college student who must make transitions on a regular basis between those two modes if he or she is to be successful in the collegiate learning environment and in the world beyond college.

5. The implementation of a cognitive skills instruction program at the college level is made administratively difficult by the flexible scheduling and optional course election that is permitted in the collegiate environment; systematic ensured instruction in cognitive skills is far more difficult in that environment than in the secondary school. Cognitive skills instruction should therefore be made a regular part of at least one course in any hearing-impaired college student's program so that all students have this systematic experience.

6. All, not some, hearing-impaired college students can benefit from cognitive skills instruction; the positive changes noted in experimental subjects were general and not limited to those whose pretest scores or individual characteristics fell into any low, medium, or high range.

7. Trained IE instructors tend to persist in their interest in implementing the teaching of thinking skills.

8. While it is administratively efficient for cognitive skills instruction to be the responsibility of one single academic department in which students must take courses (e.g., English), it is far better to have cognitive skills instruction embedded across all subjects and across several departments to which students will be exposed. If departments work together to take responsibility for cognitive skills instruction, the burden is spread and the student benefits by seeing the connection between generic cognitive skills and a variety of subject areas.

For many years, educators of the deaf have been concerned with raising the cognitive performance of their students. Systematic implementation of a specially-developed cognitive education program with in-depth faculty development appears to be an appropriate approach to this problem. It is essential that educators of hearing-impaired students at all levels, but especially at the college level, now take note that the cognitive potential of such students can indeed be raised. This conclusion is most essential and hopeful for the future of the hearing-impaired learner.

REFERENCES

Brown, W. F. 1964. *Effective Study Test*. San Marcos, TX: Effective Study Materials.

———. 1983. *Study Skills Survey*. San Marcos, TX: Effective Study Materials.

Dansereau, D.F., et al. June 1975. Effective learning strategy program: Development and assessment. Final Report. *Resources in Education*. ERIC Document No. ED 111 740.

Drever, J., & Collins, M. 1928. *Performance tests of intelligence*. Edinburgh: Oliver & Boyd.

Feuerstein, R. 1980. *Instrumental enrichment: An intervention program for cognitive modifiability*. Baltimore: University Park Press.

Feuerstein, R. 1984. *Instrumental enrichment*. Baltimore: University Park Press. A thinking skills curriculum disseminated through Curriculum Development Associates, Washington, DC.

Levine, E.S. 1976. Psychological contributions. In *A bicentennial monograph on hearing impairment: Trends in the U.S.A.*, ed. R. Frisina, 23–33. Washington, DC: A. G. Bell Association.

Madden, R., et al. 1972. *Stanford Achievement Test for Hearing-Impaired Students*. New York: Harcourt Brace Jovanovich.

Martin, D.S. 1981. "Thinking Skills Survey." Unpublished manuscript. Washington, DC: Gallaudet University.

———. November 1984. Infusing cognitive strategies into teacher preparation programs. *Educational Leadership* 42(3):68–72.

Martin D.S., & Jonas, B. December 1986. Cognitive modifiability in the deaf adolescent. *Resources in Education*. ERIC Document No. ED 276 159.

Raven, J.C. 1960. *Standard progressive matrices*. New York: The Psychological Corporation.

Vernon, M. 1968. Five years of research on the intelligence of deaf and hard-of-hearing children: A review of literature and discussion of implications. *Journal of Research on Deafness* 1(4):1–12.

Weinstein, C.E. April 1977. Cognitive elaboration learning strategies. *Resources in Education*. ERIC Document No. ED 144 953.

Weinstein, C.E., et al. August 1980. Training versus instruction in the acquisition of cognitive learning strategies. *Resources in Education*. ERIC Document No. ED 208 018.

Weinstein, C.E., et al. 1981. Training versus instruction in the acquisition of cognitive learning strategies. *Contemporary Educational Psychology* 6(2):159–166.

Implications from the Cognitive Paradigm for Teacher Effectiveness Research in Deaf Education

Donna M. Mertens

L eaders in teacher education have recognized a shift in the image of the teacher to that of "thoughtful professional" or "reflective thinker" (Carnegie Commission Task Force 1986; Holmes Group 1986). Along with this shift in the teacher's image has come a shift in the research paradigm used to investigate teacher effectiveness (Peterson 1988; Shavelson 1988). For the past decade, the most vigorous program of research on teaching has been the process-product model of research (Shulman 1986). However, the emerging image of the teacher as a thoughtful professional suggests a need for researchers to use one of the emerging approaches to research, such as the cognitive paradigm (Peterson 1988).

The purpose of the present paper is to examine the implications of the cognitive paradigm for research in teacher effectiveness in deaf education. First, a historical perspective of the paradigm shift from the process-product model to the cognitive model is presented. Second, a conceptual framework for the cognitive model is used to examine researchable topics and appropriate methodologies. Third, variables that are unique to deaf education are discussed, and suggestions are made for future research.

HISTORICAL OVERVIEW OF PARADIGM SHIFT

In the process-product research model, investigators used an atheoretical approach to correlate teacher behaviors with student outcomes (Shulman 1986).

Thus, effective teaching was defined as a composite of variables that correlated highly with student achievement. However, there was little evidence that any one teacher had ever carried out the behaviors in that composite collective pattern. Also, experimental studies that trained teachers in the desired behaviors did not always indicate that they used those behaviors or that the behaviors were consistently related to achievement. Because of the atheoretical nature of the approach, researchers were unable to explain why particular combinations of behavior led to gains and others did not. For this reason, the process-product model is "losing intellectual vigor within the research community" (Shulman 1986), and researchers have shifted to the cognitive model in order to examine the mediators of learning between teacher behavior and student performance.

CONCEPTUAL FRAMEWORK FOR THE COGNITIVE MODEL

Weinstein and Mayer (1986) developed a framework for describing the teaching-learning process from the cognitive perspective. This framework included teacher characteristics (what the teacher knows), learner characteristics (what the learner knows), teaching strategy, learning strategy, encoding process (how the information is processed), learning outcomes, and performance (how learning is evaluated). Peterson (1988) recommended adding general and content-specific categories of cognitional and meta-cognitional knowledge to the model. In other words, to learn effectively in a classroom, students need to have both general knowledge strategies for learning and acquiring information during classroom instruction and content-specific knowledge of strategies that enable them to learn the specific subject matter. At the meta-cognitive level, learners must have a self-awareness that includes both general and content-specific cognitive processes and strategies.

Definition of Researchable Topics

Teachers' and students' thinking are important objects of study within the cognitive model (Peterson 1988). Wittrock (1986) identified six topics that relate to student mediation of classroom events: perceptions and expectations, attention, learning and memory, comprehension and learning strategies, and meta-cognitive strategies. An example related to teacher expectations can illustrate the difference between the process-product approach and the cognitive model of research.

Researchers using the process-product approach have reported inconsistent findings concerning the effect of high expectations on student achievement (Wittrock 1986). Cognitive researchers would ask such questions as: Did the teachers convey their expectations to the students? Did the students perceive the teachers' expectations? Did the students try to change their behavior? If these conditions exist, then the self-fulfilling prophecy will be observed. This point implies that some students will manifest this effect and others will not.

Clark and Peterson (1986) frame the cognitive researcher's question as: Do teachers who are effective in producing positive gains in student achievement differ in their patterns of interactive decision-making from teachers who are less effective in promoting student achievement? This definition of a researchable topic is very different from asking whether the number of times a teacher performs a specific behavior (e.g., uses positive reinforcement) will affect achievement.

Methodological Implications

Use of the cognitive paradigm has implications for the importance of the subject matter being taught, the level and type of teachers' and students' knowledge, the design of the study, the dependent variable, and the data collection method. Because both general and content-specific cognitive and meta-cognitive strategies are used in the teaching-learning process, cognitive researchers have expressed a need for more consideration of the subject matter being taught (Clark & Peterson 1986; Peterson 1988; Shulman 1986). Cognitive researchers view standardized tests as inappropriate dependent measures because they lack sensitivity to the actual teaching-learning unit under study. Shavelson et al. (1986) recommend looking at within-group variation, studying subgroups, and examining the response patterns and strategies that students use to approach the test.

Cognitive and meta-cognitive knowledge can be obtained through interviews that provide insight into self-awareness of mental processes used in the classroom (Peterson 1988). Clark and Peterson (1986) describe the method of "stimulated recall," which consists of replaying a videotape or audiotape of a teaching episode to enable the viewer to recollect and report on his or her thoughts and decisions during that episode. Peterson and her colleagues (Peterson & Swing 1982; Peterson, Swing, Braverman & Buss 1982) used the stimulated recall method with fifth- and sixth-graders. They found that student reports of understanding (i.e., an ability to make a judgment about their understanding) were positively related to the number of seatwork problems they got correct. Peterson and her colleagues (Peterson, Swing, & Stoiber 1986; Swing, Stoiber & Peterson 1988) tested the hypothesis that process variables related to understanding were amenable to manipulation. Math teachers were taught techniques for the thinking skills of defining, describing, comparing, thinking of reasons, and summarizing. They found that "lower ability" children in the experimental classes improved more in their math skills than did "high ability" children. The low ability children in the control group showed little strategic thinking; they could not explain how they got their answers, and the answers they did get were wrong.

Martin and Jonas (1986) studied the effects of teaching cognitive skills from the Instrumental Enrichment Program (Feuerstein 1980) to deaf adolescents and reported significant improvement on such standardized tests as the Raven's Progressive Matrices Test and the Stanford Achievement Test.

IMPLICATIONS FOR DEAF EDUCATION RESEARCH

Thus, although researchers in deaf education study cognitive topics (*cf.* Martin 1985, 1989), they have yet to apply the cognitive paradigm fully to the design of their research on teacher effectiveness. No matter what paradigm is used to guide research in deaf education, several variables uniquely associated with hearing-impaired subjects must be considered (Mertens 1990).

1. Family background characteristics (e.g., hearing status of parents; communication mode used in the home);
2. Subject background characteristics (e.g., age of loss, cause of loss, degree of loss, additional handicaps, communication skills);
3. School or school district conditions (e.g., size of hearing-impaired student enrollment, support services, expenditures);
4. Within-school conditions (hearing-impaired student-teacher ratio);
5. Instructional personnel characteristics (e.g., signing ability, training, and experience working with deaf students);
6. Student attitudes (e.g., impulsivity, internal/external control);
7. Student placement (e.g., residential, mainstreamed, self-contained); and
8. Instructional personnel, including teachers and interpreters (e.g., communication mode used).

Thus, the researcher must realize the heterogeneity of the deaf population, and therefore all reports of cognitive research must make clear exactly what the characteristics of the subjects and the context are. To address the problem of generalizability in such contexts, Lincoln and Guba (1985) recommend that researchers provide "thick description," i.e., a narrative developed about the context in such detail that judgments about the degree of fit or similarity may be made by others who may want to apply all or part of the findings elsewhere.

A second issue in applying the cognitive paradigm in deaf education arises from the unique communication system used, particularly in mainstreamed classrooms. Data collection becomes more complicated because of the communication triad, i.e., teacher-interpreter-student. If the stimulated recall method is used, the researcher would need to videotape the teacher, the interpreter, and the student. This procedure might be done by having one camera on the teacher and another on the interpreter-student dyad. However, the impact of such an arrangement on the people involved is a sensitive issue.

Another challenge that the researcher faces is coding the data. Klima and Bellugi (1979) developed a transcription system that was modified by Erting (1982) to code signed videotapes—a very labor-intensive and time-consuming process. Thus the questions of sample size, comparison groups, and number of observations conflict with the traditional experimental model of research. Obtaining funds to support such research is difficult because both the Office for Educational Research and Improvement (Kilgore 1986) and the National Science Foundation (Tressel 1987) continue to include the criteria of generalizability and comparison groups as bases for awarding funds.

IMPLICATIONS FOR FUTURE RESEARCH

Researchers in deafness and cognition will need to formulate questions regarding what the teacher knows, what the student knows, how the student mediates the information received from the teacher, and what impact these factors have on performance (Weinstein & Mayer 1986). Increased attention also will need to be given to the subject matter being studied (Shulman 1986; Peterson 1988).

Leaders in cognitive research have warned against the use of standardized tests as dependent measures (Shavelson, Webb & Burstein 1986; Shavelson 1988). Instead researchers should look at student response patterns and strategies used to approach problem-solving. This need presents a logistical problem in applying this concept to deafness research in that frequently the number of deaf students in a class is very small. If data are collected from several classrooms, the teacher-made tests of performance may not be appropriate across classrooms.

Interviews are used frequently in cognitive research to access the mental processes of students and teachers (Clark & Peterson 1986; Peterson 1988). The stimulated recall method has been shown to be a very effective method of obtaining information about thought processes. However, this method presents logistical problems in deafness research because two cameras would be required to record the activities of the teacher, student, and interpreter. Coding, analysis, and interpretation of the information would require excellent understanding of sign language and would be very time-consuming. This need has implications for sample size, resources required, and number of observations that are feasible.

Analysis by subgroups is recommended in cognitive research (Shulman 1986). In deafness research, the multiplicity of variables that must be considered adds to the complexity of this task (Mertens 1990). Lincoln and Guba's (1985) advice concerning "thick description" would be well heeded by researchers in deafness to make clear exactly the type of subjects who are in the study and, thus, aid in the transferability of results.

Moving from the traditional experimental research model to the cognitive approach to research will require researchers in deafness to adapt more than just their research methods; this shift has political and economic implications as well. As long as funding agencies continue to insist on generalizability, large samples, and comparison groups, it will be difficult to obtain support for research based on the cognitive paradigm. However, as Shulman (1986) pointed out, providing feedback to teachers about their pupils' thinking may be the most useful way to produce positive changes in teachers and student learning. This question is empirical, and the work of the leaders in the educational research field suggests that this method will be useful in bringing about the changes in educational practice and outcomes we seek in the education of deaf learners.

REFERENCES

Carnegie Commission Task Force 1986. *A nation prepared: Teachers for the 21st century.* The report of the Task Force on Teaching as a Profession. New York: Carnegie Corporation.

Clark, C.M., & Peterson, P.L. 1986. Teachers' thought processes. In *Handbook of research on teaching*, ed. M.C. Wittrock. New York: Macmillan Publishing Co.

Erting, C. 1982. *Deafness, communication, and social identity: An anthropological analysis of interaction among parents, teachers and deaf children in a preschool.* Ph.D. diss. Washington, DC: American University.

Feuerstein, R. 1980. *Instrumental enrichment: An intervention program for cognitive modifiability.* Baltimore, MD: University Park Press.

Holmes Group, Inc. 1986. *Tomorrow's teachers: A report of the Holmes Group.* East Lansing, MI: Author.

Kilgore, S.B. 1986. Personal communication from the Director, Office for Educational Research and Improvement, U.S. Department of Education.

Klima, E., & Bellugi, U. 1979. *The signs of language.* Cambridge: Harvard University Press.

Lincoln, Y.S., & Guba, E.G. 1985. *Naturalistic inquiry.* Beverly Hills, CA: Sage Publications Inc.

Martin, D.S., ed. 1985. *Cognition, education and deafness: Directions for research and instruction.* Washington, DC: Gallaudet University Press.

————. 1989. *The second international symposium on cognition, education, and deafness: Working papers.* Washington, DC: Gallaudet University.

Martin, D.S., & Jonas, B. 1986. Cognitive modifiability in the deaf adolescent. *Resources in Education.* ERIC Document No. ED 276 159.

Mertens, D.M. 1990. A conceptual model for academic achievement: Deaf student outcomes. In *Educational and developmental aspects of deafness,* ed. D. Moores & K. Meadow-Orlans, 25–72. Washington DC: Gallaudet University Press.

Peterson, P.L. 1988. Teachers' and students cognitional knowledge for classroom teaching and learning. *Educational Researcher* 17(5):5–14.

Peterson, P.L., & Swing, S.R. 1982. Beyond time on task: Students' reports of their thought processes during classroom instruction. *Elementary School Journal* 82(5):481–491.

Peterson, P.L., Swing, S.R., Braverman, M.T., & Buss, R. 1982. Students' aptitudes and their reports of cognitive processes during direct instruction. *Journal of Educational Psychology* 74(4):535–547.

Peterson, P.L., Swing, S.R., & Stoiber, K.C. 1986. Learning time vs. thinking skills: Alternative perspectives on the effects of two instructional interventions. Program Report 86–6. Madison: Wisconsin Center for Education Research.

Shavelson, R.J., Webb, N.M., & Burstein, L. 1986. Measurement of teaching. In *Handbook of research on teaching,* ed. M. C. Wittrock. New York: Macmillan Publishing Co.

Shavelson, R.J. 1988. Contributions of educational research to policy and practice: Constructing, challenging, and changing cognition. Presidential address at the annual meeting of the American Educational Research Association, New Orleans, LA.

Shulman, L.S. 1986. Paradigms and research programs in the study of teaching: A contemporary perspective. In *Handbook of research on teaching,* ed. M. C. Wittrock. New York: Macmillan Publishing Co.

Swing, S.R., Stoiber, K.C., & Peterson, P.L. 1988. Thinking skills vs. learning time: Effects of alternative classroom-based interventions on students' mathematics problem solving. *Cognition and Instruction* 5(2).

Tressel, G.W. 1987. Personal communication from the Director of the Division of Materials Development, Research, and Informal Science Education, National Science Foundation.

Weinstein, C.F., & Mayer, R.F. 1986. The teaching of learning strategies. In *Handbook of research on teaching.* ed. M.C. Wittrock. New York: Macmillan Publishing Co.

Wittrock, M.C. 1986. Students' thought processes. In *Handbook of research on teaching,* ed. M. C. Wittrock. New York: Macmillan Publishing Co.

Using Cooperative Learning and Concept Maps with Deaf College Students

Angela O'Donnell
Dinaz Adenwalla

T his chapter reports on a preliminary investigation of the potential of two information processing tools (*scripted cooperative learning* and *concept maps*) to address the need to develop methodologies in curricular areas outside the traditional areas of investigation and the need for instruction in cognitive strategies.

Research on the education of the deaf has been oriented largely toward "issues" and has focused on developing curricula. Teaching methodologies have largely focused on teaching reading, language, and speech (Moores 1982). Traditional subject matter areas (e.g., science) have received little attention. Also, there has been relatively little research on the teaching of cognitive skills to the hearing-impaired (Martin 1985). It is being recognized that there is a need to study strategy training for college students in general (McKeachie 1988). The need for such training for hearing-impaired students may be even more critical (Martin 1985).

SCRIPTED COOPERATIVE LEARNING

Scripted cooperative learning is a method of structuring the cooperative learning activities of pairs of students. The word *script* is used as if it were a theater script, specifying the roles of the participants and the activities in which they engage. Scripted cooperation can be used with a variety of tasks, such as writing, reading, and working in a science laboratory. In this investigation, scripted cooperation was used as a strategy for reviewing material presented in a biology laboratory class. After the instructor presented information, students were assigned to work in pairs. One partner then recalled the first half of the material the teacher had presented, and the other partner tried to provide feedback on errors. Partners then changed roles for the second half of the material.

While cooperative learning of some kind has been used in almost every classroom, the critical part of scripted cooperation is the script that regulates the activities of the participants. The sequence of activities results in the controlled activation of specified cognitive processes (see Dansereau 1988 for details of this approach). Students who have studied using scripted cooperative learning have consistently outperformed students who work alone (O'Donnell et al. 1985, 1986; Hall et al. 1988). They have expressed more positive attitudes toward learning than individualistic learners (O'Donnell et al. 1987), and they have acquired skills that resulted in improved performance on a transfer task (McDonald et al. 1985).

POTENTIAL OF SCRIPTED COOPERATION FOR DEAF STUDENTS

The use of scripted cooperation by deaf students has enormous potential. First, its use as part of classroom instruction relieves the teacher of some of the responsibility for transmitting information, freeing up time to monitor students and provide special help to those who need it. Another important benefit is the potential of scripted cooperation to promote positive affect towards the instructional context. Too often the early experiences of deaf children in school are dominated by failure. Continued failure has been shown to be associated with increased absenteeism and dropout rates among hearing students (Moos & Moos 1978). The use of cooperative learning can certainly improve the chances of success for deaf students.

CONCEPT MAPS

Concept maps (also known as knowledge maps) are two-dimensional representations that can be used to improve the presentation of information. Idea units are contained in nodes and connect to other ideas (Figure 1). The use of concept maps in presenting information to deaf students may help to bypass some of the difficulties that many of them commonly experience in processing text. Moores (1982) noted that deaf students have difficulty with subject matter that relies on knowledge of English. He further noted that in curricular areas involving traditional academic subjects (e.g., history) the tendency has been for teachers to rely on texts and other materials designed for students with normal hearing, potentially exacerbating deaf students' difficulties in these subject areas.

Concept map presentations can reduce the syntactic complexity of information as compared to text presentations of the same information. In addition, the use of concept maps makes the structure of the information apparent, signaling

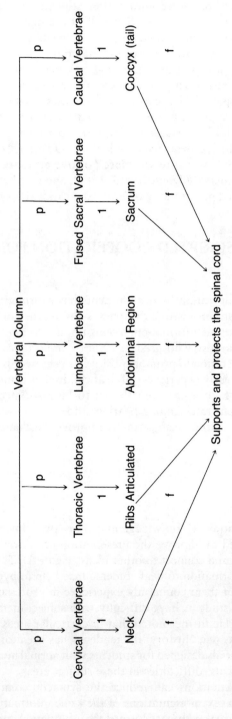

Key to Links: p = part; 1 = leads to; f = function.

FIGURE 1   Example of a concept map.

the main ideas and informing students about the interrelationships of ideas and the logical connections between higher-order and lower-order concepts (Armbruster & Anderson 1984; Alverman 1986; Darch, Carnine, & Kameenui 1986). A further potential advantage of using knowledge maps is that they allow the learner to use both spatial and verbal cues in the acquisition and retrieval of information. Research with hearing college students indicate that the use of concept maps in the presentation of information enhances learning (O'Donnell, et al. 1988; Rewey 1988). The use of "mapping" as a learning strategy has also been shown to be successful with hearing-impaired students (Long & Aldersley 1984).

The use of concept maps may reduce the syntactic complexity of the material, improve the organization of the information, highlight the main ideas and how they connect to lower-order ideas, and make easily apparent the ordering of events.

EXPERIMENT 1

The participants were 43 undergraduate students at Gallaudet University who were enrolled in three laboratory sections of an introductory biology course. Two of the three sections were assigned to the cooperative condition; students in the third section worked individually. In all classes, the instructor presented material on the structure and function of cells in animals and plants. Students were then assigned randomly to cooperative dyads and were presented with instructions on how to cooperate (if in cooperative groups) or how to review independently (if in the individual group). In each cooperative dyad, partner A reviewed the material about the plant cell, and partner B was responsible for the material about the animal cell. All students completed an in-class exercise. The instructor then presented information about the mitosis of plant and animal cells. Students again reviewed the material either cooperatively or individually and completed an in-class exercise. One week later, students took a test on the material covered.

RESULTS AND DISCUSSION

Achievement on the in-class exercises and on the delayed test were used as dependent measures in subsequent analyses. In addition, performance on questions related to the structure and function of cells (to which the students had been exposed previously) and performance on those questions related to mitosis (to which the students had not been exposed previously) were analyzed separately. Using the dependent measures listed above, a series of planned comparisons was conducted. Comparisons were made between individuals and dyads and between the two groups of dyads.

The difference in achievement between individuals and dyads on the in-class activities approached statistical significance $t(40) = 1.8$, $p = .07$ (see Table 1 for means and standard deviations). Despite the additional information-pro-

TABLE 1   Experiment 1: Means and Standard Deviations[a] on
Classwork, Total Score and Subcomponents of Posttest

Group	n	Classwork	Posttest		
			Total Score	Structure/ Function	Mitosis
Individuals	14	31.3(16.3)	21.2(4.0)	7.5(0.52)	6.0(2.8)
Cooperative Dyads I	13	39.4(16.5)	21.7(4.3)	7.0(1.70)	8.5(3.2)
Cooperative Dyads II	16	42.3(15.0)	26.1(4.5)	7.4(1.60)	9.6(2.3)

[a] Standard deviations are in parentheses.

cessing demands involved in using a new method of learning (cooperative learning), students working in cooperative dyads completed the in-class exercises better than individual students. The contrast between the two cooperative groups did not approach significance.

On the total score from the delayed test, the difference between dyads and individuals approached significance, $t(33) = 1.8$, $p = .078$. A significant difference was found between the two dyad groups, $t(33) = 2.69$, $p = .01$. Although cooperative learning appeared to be beneficial overall, the difference between the two dyadic groups indicated that positive effects associated with the technique are not placebo effects and that cooperative learning may not work for everyone.

No significant differences were found in the material related to the structure and function of the cell, the material to which the students had been exposed previously. Significant differences were found, however, for the analysis of the questions related to mitosis (i.e., the new material presented in the laboratory class). Dyads significantly outperformed individuals, $t(33) = 3.02$, $p < .01$. The performance of the two groups of dyads did not differ significantly from each other. These results indicated that cooperative learning is effective as a means of acquiring new information.

As the experiment described above was preliminary in nature, we did not collect any data with respect to students' attitudes toward the use of cooperative learning. A second experiment was conducted to provide information about student attitudes and to examine the effects of presenting lecture information in the form of concept maps.

EXPERIMENT 2

A total of 34 participants enrolled in 3 sections of an introductory biology laboratory course served as the participants for the second experiment. Two of the class sections were assigned to cooperative conditions, and students in the third section were assigned to work individually.

The instructor presented a concept map showing information about the human skeleton. Students then cooperatively or individually reviewed the material presented. At the end of the class, students completed a practice test on the material and responded to a questionnaire that assessed their reactions to the cooperative or individual review and their attitudes toward the concept map. Students took a test on the material during a subsequent class period.

RESULTS AND DISCUSSION

The dependent measures used were achievement on the in-class exercise, performance on the practice test, and performance on the delayed test. Data were analyzed using planned comparisons. Relevant contrasts were those between the cooperative and individual groups and between the two groups of cooperative dyads. Individuals significantly outperformed the dyads on the completion of the in-class exercise, $t(31) = 3.4$, $p < .01$. Significant differences were also found between the two groups of dyads, $t(31) = 3.04$, $p < .05$. The dyads in the 8 a.m. section of the biology laboratory performed significantly worse than the other group of dyads.

No significant differences were found on the practice test, although one of the cooperative groups achieved the highest mean performance. Although students in this group (see Table 2 for means and standard deviations) did not complete the in-class exercises as well as the individuals, they did perform better on the practice test, indicating that learning did occur.

Finally, significant differences were found between the two dyadic groups on the delayed test on the material presented in the class. Again, dyads who took the early morning section performed significantly worse than the other group of dyads, $t(31) = -2.25$, $p < .05$. No difference was found for the comparison of individuals and dyads. All the students responded favorably to the use of concept maps as a method of presenting information, and those who engaged in cooperative learning expressed positive attitudes toward the experience and a desire to have continued experience with the technique. In this second experiment, we did not find a particularly positive effect for cooperative learning over individual learning. However, it may be that dyads in this particular experiment were cognitively overloaded by having to learn how to learn cooperatively and how to learn from a new presentation format.

TABLE 2   Experiment 2: Means and Standard Deviations[a] of Classwork, Practice Test, and Posttest

Group	n	Classwork	Practice Test	Posttest
Individuals	14	28.78(11.5)	15.57(5.5)	27.85(6.17)
Cooperative Dyads I	12	19.33(3.36)	17.42(2.9)	28.17(5.06)
Cooperative Dyads II	8	19.25(3.19)	13.63(4.9)	20.38(8.86)

[a] Standard deviations are in parentheses.

DISCUSSION

The research reported here demonstrated that scripted cooperative learning and the use of concept maps in the presentation of information have potential to improve the learning of deaf students in a college biology laboratory class. Cooperative learning did not work for all students. One group of students who were assigned to a cooperative review condition performed poorly. This performance may have been due to the time the class was scheduled (8 a.m.). It is possible that this particular group of students simply was not motivated. The performance of this group on all class tests was worse than the comparison groups in the experiment.

Informal observations of cooperating students indicated that many students felt uncomfortable with the cooperative task. Students in the second experiment who worked cooperatively expressed higher levels of anxiety related to the learning task than those who worked alone. Despite these feelings, students believed that cooperative learning was a good learning strategy. Many of the students who participated in this experiment came from mainstreamed high-school programs and reported that this activity was their first experience in working with other students on an academic task. More training in how to use the cooperative strategy is necessary, especially when a new method of presenting information is also involved.

Students responded very favorably to the use of concept maps as a method for presentation of information. The effects of cooperative learning and the use of concept maps were somewhat confounded in the research reported here. Further research is necessary to evaluate each of these techniques more thoroughly.

REFERENCES

Alverman, D.E. 1986. Graphic organizers: Cuing devices for comprehending and remembering main ideas. In *Teaching main idea comprehension*, ed. J.F. Baumann, 210–226. Newark, DE: International Reading Association.

Armbruster, B.B. & Anderson, T.H. 1984. Mapping: Representing informative text diagrammatically. In *Spatial learning strategies: Techniques, applications, and related issues*, ed. C.D. Holley & D.F. Dansereau, 189–212. Orlando, FL: Academic Press.

Dansereau, D.F. 1988. Cooperative learning strategies. In *Learning and study strategies: Issues in assessment, instruction, and evaluation*, ed. C.E. Weinstein, E.T. Goetz, & P.A. Alexander, 3–10. San Diego, CA: Academic Press.

Darch, C.B., Carnine, D.W., & Kameenui, E.J. 1986. The role of graphic organizers and social structure in content area instruction. *Journal of Reading Behavior* 18:275–295.

Hall, R.H., Rocklin, T.R., Dansereau, D.F., Skaggs, L.P., O'Donnell, A.M., Lambiotte, J.G., & Young, M.D. 1988. The role of individual differences in the cooperative learning of technical material. *Journal of Educational Psychology* 80:172–178.

Long, G. & Aldersley, S. 1984. Networking: Application with hearing-impaired students. In *Spatial learning strategies: Techniques, applications, and related issues*, ed. C.D. Holley & D.F. Dansereau, 109–126. Orlando, FL: Academic Press.

Martin, D.S 1985. Enhancing cognitive performance in the hearing-impaired college student: A pilot study. In *Cognition, education, and deafness: Directions for research and instruction,* ed. D.S. Martin, 176–179. Washington, DC: Gallaudet College Press.

McDonald, B., Larson, C.O., Dansereau, D.F., & Spurlin, J.E. 1985. Cooperative dyads: Impact on text learning and transfer. *Contemporary Educational Psychology* 10:369–377.

McKeachie, W. 1988. The need for study strategy training. In *Learning and study strategies: Issues in assessment, instruction, and evaluation,* ed. C.E. Weinstein, E.T. Goet, & P.A. Alexander, 3–10. San Diego, CA: Academic Press.

Moores, D.F. 1982. *Educating the deaf: Psychology, practices, and principles.* 2nd. ed. Boston: Houghton Mifflin.

Moos, R.H., & Moos, B.S. 1978. Classroom climate and student absences and grades. *Journal of Educational Psychology* 70:263–269.

O'Donnell, A.M., Dansereau, D.F., Hythecker, V.I., Larson, C.O., Rocklin, T.R., Lambiotte, J.G., & Young, M.D. 1986. Effects of monitoring on cooperative learning. *Journal of Experimental Education* 54:169–173.

O'Donnell, A.M., Dansereau, D.F., Lambiotte, J.G., Hall, R.H., Skaggs, L.P., Rewey, K.L., & Peel, J.L. August 1988. *Concept mapping: Impact on text recall and performance.* Paper presented at the Annual Meeting of the American Psychological Association, Atlanta, GA.

O'Donnell, A.M., Dansereau, D.F., Rocklin, T.R., Lambiotte, J.G., Hythecker, V.I., & Larson, C.O. 1985. Cooperative writing: Direct effects and transfer. *Written Communication* 2:307–315.

O'Donnell, A.M., Dansereau, D.F., Hall, R.H., & Rocklin, T.R. 1987. Cognitive, social/affective, and metacognitive outcomes from scripted cooperative learning. *Journal of Educational Psychology* 79:431–437.

Rewey, K.L. 1988. *The effects of scripted cooperation and knowledge maps on the processing of technical information.* Master's thesis, Texas Christian University, Fort Worth, TX.

ASL Intervention Strategies for Teachers

David A. Stewart

The value of using ASL to enhance classroom instruction has probably always been recognized by some teachers in the field. This point is especially true of deaf teachers, many of whom teach at the secondary level. But for other teachers the prospect of using ASL raises the very real concern not only of learning it but also of how to use it effectively in their classrooms. To assist teachers in their use of ASL in the classroom, a four-year demonstration Total Communication Project was established at three hearing-impaired programs at the elementary, middle, and high school levels in a midwest school district. The goal of the project is to prepare teachers to be consistent in their use of English and American Sign Language. In accordance with the school district's language policy, English is used as the primary language of the classroom, with a modified form of Signed English used to provide a visual representation of grammatically correct English; and ASL is used as a means of assisting and intervening in communication processes (Stewart 1988). At all times the project emphasizes the need to maintain an environment in which students are exposed to consistent linguistic input.

There has been little investigation of the instructional effectiveness of ASL or of the logistics of an English/ASL bilingual approach. However, research with hearing individuals reveals that bilinguals have greater comprehension of stories presented in their stronger language and that decoding efficiency is slower in the

This paper was made possible through Research Implementation Grant No. G008730145 from the United States Department of Education, Office of Special Education Programs.

nondominant language (Dornic 1979, 1980; Mcnamara & Kushnir 1971); students who learn concepts in two languages become more flexible and better able to handle these concepts, and students who understand instructional materials are more likely to succeed in school (Engle 1975; Ramos, Aquilar & Sibayan 1967). Hence, language context may facilitate deaf individuals' access to meaning (Morariu & Bruning 1985). Martin (1985) suggested that

> cognitive intervention programs for hearing-impaired children should recognize and use language in a systematic manner since linguistic deficits of hearing-impaired are considered to be partly responsible for some of their difficulties in cognition (p. 8).

Thus, one option for ASL intervention is that it be a constructive means of increasing deaf students' comprehension of instructional information.

Two further considerations in deriving an acceptable definition for ASL intervention were 1) how specific or broad the definition should be, and 2) whether the intervention would focus on a student's comprehension or on production abilities. The first of these considerations was answered by deriving a framework for ASL intervention from the field of language intervention. For example, Fey (1986) stated that language intervention occurs when

> some intervention agent (clinician, teacher, parent, sibling, etc.) stimulates or responds to a child in a manner that is consciously designed to facilitate development in areas of communication ability that are viewed as being at risk for impairment (p. 49).

Because of the variety of ways in which ASL can be used in the classroom and the lack of longitudinal research to substantiate the claims of any one method, a broad definition for ASL intervention along the lines of Fey is most appropriate.

The question of whether a student's comprehension or production abilities would be the focus of the intervention was answered by a policy decision by the school district. Its major educational goal is to promote the development of English language skills and academic achievement, which focused the instructional use of ASL on facilitating comprehension of the materials being presented. Thus ASL intervention, as defined for this project, refers to the *processes by which an intervention agent (e.g., teacher, language specialist) uses ASL in interactions with deaf students after determining that ASL is necessary to facilitate comprehension in a particular discourse situation.*

To accomplish this outcome, the intervention agent must first analyze a discourse situation to determine the need to use ASL. If ASL is necessary, the agent then uses ASL for a length of time dictated by the initial discourse factors that suggested its use. After this intervention period, the agent then switches back to using an English-based sign code. Hence, the nature of a discourse situation reveals the potential contribution of ASL to enhancing comprehension in agent-student interactions.

It should be obvious that almost all classroom situations can be conducive to the use of ASL intervention strategies. Thus, teachers must be prepared to analyze a diverse range of both instructional and noninstructional circumstances that would include teacher-initiated discourse (e.g., introduction of a lesson, explanation of instructions), student-initiated discourse (e.g., spontaneous remarks, questions), and discourse stemming from an outside agent (e.g., the public address system, a visitor). Also included would be situations resulting from students' interactions with printed materials. A teacher, while examining written responses to a story that a student had read, might notice a pattern of misinterpretation of the story. The teacher might then decide that translating the story into ASL would increase the student's comprehension.

ASL INTERVENTION PROGRAM

The ASL intervention program is still in its developmental stage, a process that may take as long as five years or more to complete. The value of describing it at this time is that it illustrates a way to help teachers incorporate ASL skills into their instructional repertoire. Hence, the four ASL intervention strategies described below are components of an initial attempt to use ASL as an intervention tool.

Use ASL Intervention when Certain Discourse Situations Arise

Support for this principle was drawn from research on the effects of context on teachers' communication behavior (Stewart, Akamatsu & Bonkowski 1988). In their exploratory study, Stewart et al. revealed that teachers' communication behaviors appeared to be influenced consistently by the nature of a discourse situation. Specifically, they found that teachers were more likely to incorporate ASL characteristics into their signing behavior when the situations involved conducting class business; sense of humor; introduction to a topic; repeating an explanation; and miscellaneous comments not related to the lesson or to class business. Thus, teachers were instructed to consider using ASL during such situations.

Use ASL Intervention to Facilitate Comprehension of Instructions

Although broadly defined, this strategy is not to be used indiscriminately whenever a student indicates a lack of understanding of instructions printed in English. Nonetheless, teachers must take measures to insure that their students do understand the objectives of the task at hand and then determine whether maintenance of an English-based instruction posssibly at the expense of comprehension is warranted.

Use ASL Intervention to Enhance the Meaning of English Phrases

The school district uses a modified form of Signed English that includes several ASL characteristics, such as verb directionality (e.g., I-MET-HIM), inflection of signs to distinguish between noun and verb pairs (e.g., CHAIR/SIT), incorporation of numbers in pronouns (e.g., TWO-OF-US), incorporation of numbers in time (e.g., TWO-WEEKS-FROM-NOW), and negative incorporation (e.g., DON'T-WANT) (Stewart 1988). A key component of this process is that teachers give explicit instructions to their students on the relationship of a manual sign (e.g., YOU-TWO) to its printed equivalent (e.g., *two of you = you two*). This strategic use of explicit instructions has been shown to facilitate the growth of print knowledge (Andrews & Mason 1986).

In addition to using these ASL characteristics, teachers are encouraged to use ASL phrases to clarify or emphasize the meaning of English phrases. For example, after signing in English *The street was packed with people*, the teacher has the option of following with the ASL translation in which the classifier for many people and the appropriate facial expression for many are used.

It is neither necessary nor practical for teachers always to translate English phrases simply for the sake of emphasizing a point. Analogous to this strategy are situations in which individuals will rephrase spoken utterances when they feel that a listener did not fully understand what they have said. Thus, to enhance comprehension, teachers retain the option of rephrasing utterances in English.

ASL Intervention Should Be Used Experimentally in Situations Determined by the Teacher

Teachers need to learn for themselves when and how ASL best increases instructional effectiveness. It is not proposed here that teachers should be restricted by a set of specified situations for using ASL. There is much to be learned about the pedagogical application of ASL, and teachers are in an ideal position to experiment in this area. Some possibilities for experimentation are dual presentation of stories in English and ASL in subject areas where a premium is placed on comprehension of concepts (e.g., science, social studies), and discussions of deaf culture and deaf heritage issues. Teachers' experiments with ASL intervention will be carefully observed to determine both the advantages and disadvantages of the particular strategies they employ.

Time evaluation of teachers' use of ASL intervention strategies has not yet been completed. Each teacher kept a record of the application of ASL intervention strategies. Information was compiled through checklists on frequency and type of ASL intervention, observations from researchers who team taught with the teachers, teacher interviews and written reports, weekly discussions with all teachers, transcriptions of videotapes, and interviews with students. These records provide a basis for refining certain strategies, creating new ones, and evaluating advantages and disadvantages of this English/ASL bilingual education strategy.

CONCLUSION

It is recognized that a lack of research on the instructional use of ASL means that time will be needed to resolve logistics and issues involved in ASL intervention. In addition, practitioners in the field generally do not, as yet, fully understand the ramifications of using ASL on a full-time basis in the classroom. Thus, by using ASL as a means of intervening in and assisting classroom communication processes, a situation is created through which the use of ASL will be guided in part by what past research on ASL has shown, and at the same time teachers will have the freedom to explore the use of ASL in enhancing their own instructional effectiveness.

Thus far, teachers and administrators have appreciated the effort that the research community has made to connect research with practice. The consensus is that training in communication skills will be a critical determinant of effective teaching. Once we have determined the ability of teachers to implement various communication strategies in the classroom and once the attendant effects on students' academic and language performance have occurred, we will be in a better position to understand the relationship between communication and learning processes.

Also, in view of the difficulty that many hearing individuals have encountered in learning ASL, it might not be feasible for all teachers in our project to become fluent in ASL. This concern, along with many others, will be evaluated at the end of the project.

This project attempts to investigate the pedagogical effect of using a sign code (manually coded English) and a sign language (ASL) in the classroom. This investigation should reveal insights into many other related issues, such as the ability of teachers to learn ASL and to code English in signs, the effects of using two different languages in the classroom, attitudes toward ASL intervention, the complex nature of visually represented English in signs, the conceptual function of signs, the appropriate age for introducing ASL intervention, and the role of fingerspelling as an instructional tool. Ultimately, it is expected that empirical evidence will begin to replace unsubstantiated rhetoric as a guideline for how language and communication systems can best be used in Total Communication classrooms.

REFERENCES

Andrews, J., & Mason, J. 1986. Childhood deafness and the acquisition of print concepts. In *Metalinguistic awareness and beginning literacy*, ed. D. Yaden & S. Templeton, 277–290. Portsmouth, NH: Heinemann.

Dornic, S. 1979. Information processing in bilinguals and some selected issues. *Psychological Research* 40:329–348.

———. 1980. Information processing and language dominance. *International Review of Applied Psychology* 29:119–140.

Engle, P.L. 1975. The use of vernacular languages in education: Language medium in early school years for minority language groups. *Papers in Applied Linguistics: Bilingual Education Series*. Arlington, VA: Center for Applied Linguistics.

Fey, M. 1986. *Language intervention with young children*. San Diego, CA: College-Hill Press.

Mcnamara, J., & Kushnir, S. 1971. Linguistic independence of bilinguals: The input switch. *Journal of Verbal Learning and Verbal Behavior* 10:480–487.

Martin, D. 1985. Enhancing cognitive performance in the hearing-impaired college student: A pilot study. In *Cognition, education, and deafness: Directions for research and instruction*, ed. D. Martin, 176–179. Washington, DC: Gallaudet University Press.

Morariu, J., & Bruning, R. 1985. A contextualist perspective of language processing by prelingually deaf students. In *Cognition, education, and deafness: Directions for research and instruction*, ed. D. Martin, 88–90. Washington, DC: Gallaudet University Press.

Ramos, M., Aquilar, J., & Sibayan, B. 1967. *The determination and implementation of language policy*. Philippine Center for Language Study Monograph Series: 2. Quezon, Philippines: Alemar/Phoenix.

Stewart, D. 1988. *A model communication and language policy for total communication programs for the hearing-impaired*. Occasional Paper No. 125. East Lansing: Michigan State University, Institute for Research in Teaching.

Stewart, D., Akamatsu, C.T., & Bonkowski, N. 1988. Factors influencing simultaneous communication behaviors in teachers. *ACEHI Journal/LeRevue ACEDA* 14:43–58.

Application of Technology to Cognitive Development

Louise Wilson

Verbal reasoning is necessary for a person to be able to process and utilize information and, in today's world, information utilization is becoming an increasingly important skill. Due to the exponentially expanding knowledge base, the ability to recall is no longer as important as the ability to access and use knowledge efficiently. For the child whose language development is impaired by hearing loss, the task is significantly more challenging, yet equally important.

Recent work in cognition, particularly information-processing theory, has been important in explicating the mental processes used in storing and accessing knowledge. Information-processing theorists view the mind as a central processor. Content or declarative knowledge, and skills or procedural knowledge, are stored in the brain in organized networks of related information and connected to one another at common points (Gagne 1985). Unfortunately, the ability to organize knowledge in this way is seldom taught, and the learner who does not develop good processing strategies naturally is left to reason much less effectively.

EFFECTIVE INSTRUCTION

Recent attempts to teach cognitive strategies to children have met with some success (Palincsar & Brown 1987). For example, work in learning theory has demonstrated the value of metacognitive awareness during learning. Metacognition is the process of knowing how to know—of understanding the thought processes that go into how one reasons in a particular type of situation.

362

Work with children, with and without learning difficulties, has demonstrated that heightened metacognitive awareness positively contributes to learning (Palincsar & Brown 1987). Think-aloud protocols, increased learner awareness of task demands, and training in the appropriate application of cognitive strategies have resulted in significant gains, particularly in students with learning problems (DeBernard & Ferber 1986; Papert 1980; Martin 1984).

Direct Instruction (DI), another approach with demonstrated positive outcomes, involves instructional strategies designed to promote active student participation in the learning process by means of frequent questioning, consistent feedback, extensive practice, and built-in high levels of success (Gersten et al. 1987). Theoretically, active participation in learning creates and reinforces pathways in memory, which facilitates recall.

High levels of interaction in a typical classroom group setting are often impractical to achieve, however. It is generally not possible for more than one or two students to be actively engaged in discussion, questioning, or feedback at any one time. Yet, where effective instructional strategies have been intentionally incorporated into daily practice, student success has followed (Wang 1987).

It is important, therefore, to look for tools that will enable teachers to incorporate and build upon known effective strategies. Though the invasion of computers into education over the past two decades has been significant in its intensity and promise, expectations about the value of this technology for learning have not been fully realized. The application of computer technology to the classroom has focused more on redoing what teachers already do well and not enough on what the technology can do uniquely.

It is becoming apparent that new applications of technology are needed, especially in areas such as cognitive development, where it has been difficult to develop skills by means of traditional approaches. There is also a need for computer-aided learning to be developed for group instruction. Two applications addressing these areas will be described in the next sections. The first, application of group-based technology to instruction, is already being researched. The second is a theoretical model and involves instruction of students in the development of a knowledge base for an expert system.

GROUP-BASED COMPUTER-ASSISTED INSTRUCTION

The first application is in a study utilizing direct instruction strategies and a group-based interactive technology system called Discourse. Discourse is a group-based classroom system involving a single IBM computer and a classroom set of individual student keyboards with digital readout screens, called "Study Coms." The teacher operates the computer, using it to program answers, display questions on a large public display screen, and run audio-visual equipment. Students respond to questions by typing answers into their Study Coms and receive feedback in the form of a flashing light and/or beep. All student responses are displayed on the teacher's monitor, and one or more can be displayed publicly on the public display screen. Group and individual responses and scores can also be printed out at the conclusion of the lesson. Discourse allows all students to respond to all questions asked of the class during group instruction or on independent seat-work activities.

In the fall of 1988, a research study was conducted in a public school in St. Paul, Minnesota using the Discourse Group Instructional System to instruct a group of hearing-impaired students in mathematical estimation and rounding strategies. The purpose of this study was to demonstrate the value of a group-based computer system to the application of direct-instruction principles.

Daily instruction involved presentation of a series of practice items, visually displayed either on the public display screen or by overhead transparency. Students entered responses into individual Study Coms, receiving feedback if responses were correct or changing responses that were incorrect. Following group instruction, additional problems were worked individually from a worksheet, again with responses entered into Study Coms.

Techniques of direct instruction were employed as part of every lesson. Intensive questioning, participatory learning, immediate feedback, and extensive rehearsal were primary pieces of the instructional design. The significance of the application of DI techniques in this study was the apparent extent to which they could be readily applied to a large group using a group-based, interactive system. The Discourse System made possible the effective implementation of question-answer, corrective feedback, and active learning strategies to a group of fifteen hearing-impaired students, all interacting at once—a situation not possible either in a traditional classroom setting or with typical one-on-one computer-assisted instruction software.

Group data collected during the instructional sessions revealed a high percentage of responses to the teacher's questions. An average of 32.4 questions were asked in each 50-minute instructional session. An average of 97% of the students responded to each question, and 94.4% of the responses were correct. This level of correct response is attributable partly to the structured nature of the questions and partly to the children's motivation to respond correctly. Each student knew it was possible to respond to every question and that a correct response would result in reinforcement, creating a strong incentive to answer correctly.

Pre- and posttest data demonstrated significant growth in learning the material on estimation and rounding. Mean results of 39% correct on the pretest grew to 83% on the posttest and 86% on a six-week retention test.

The potential impact of a system like Discourse for enhancing group instruction is one example of how instructional technology can contribute to education. The opportunity to implement elements of direct instruction in a precise way within group settings is a powerful advantage and one that needs broader implementation and further study.

EXPERT SYSTEM KNOWLEDGE BASES

A second application of technology to cognitive development involves teaching students to create simple knowledge bases for an expert system. This approach is still a theoretical concept, at least as it relates to the hearing-impaired, and does not involve the study of hardware or software specifically as much as it applies theories of system development to the development of higher-order reasoning in students.

Hearing-impaired students need the structure and reinforcement of direct instruction-type strategies, but they also need opportunity to develop and utilize higher-order thinking skills. Metacognitive awareness of higher cognitive skills and strategies for applying them to problem-solving may need to be taught using direct methods of instruction, but students then need to apply the learned strategies independently. The development of an expert system knowledge base is an intriguing vehicle for both developing and applying higher-order cognitive skills.

One of the more exciting and prolific fields of computer application today is artificial intelligence (AI), which on a broad scale is an attempt to create computer programs that are programmed to mimic the reasoning capabilities of humans. Intelligent systems do not operate the same way as the tightly programmed systems typical of educational software. Instead they are supplied with knowledge bases that are fluid and able to manipulate knowledge in a variety of ways depending on the user's needs and the input provided.

Expert systems, a subset of Artificial Intelligence, are designed to incorporate expert knowledge in a given domain and to interact with users who need to tap into that knowledge to solve a problem. An expert system is composed of stored knowledge (the knowledge base) and the mechanism for manipulating that knowledge to solve problems (the inference engine). The inference engine component can be purchased as a shell, or authoring system, eliminating the need for programming. The student organizes the knowledge base and enters it into the shell in three segments:

1. a set of possible decisions;
2. a set of questions to be asked of the user in order to make a decision; and
3. a set of rules that tie the answers to the decisions.

A few researchers are beginning to look at the value of student-created knowledge bases as a tool for learning (Trollip & Lippert 1987; Starfield et al. 1983; Bigum 1985), though most studies to date have focused on college-age or adult subjects. There is speculation, however, that this technique is also appropriate for children. The translation of a simple body of knowledge into the questions, rules, and decisions needed to solve problems with that knowledge establishes the necessary connections in memory between declarative and procedural aspects of the subject matter. This process also makes explicit the causal and inferential reasoning necessary to apply the knowledge to problem solving (Bigum 1985).

Once the decisions, questions, and rules are written, they are entered into the expert system shell, after which the expert system can be run. The computer will display the questions, allow the user to enter answers, parse the answers into the established rules and, when sufficient information has been received, produce a decision. The shell will also find errors in logic in the rules that have been entered and tell the programmer (or student) to correct them. The proof of the correctness is in the running of the program. The knowledge set must be well organized, and the cause-effect relationships and logic patterns must be clearly established or the expert system will not run.

In relation to the education of deaf children, the potential of this concept seems to hold real promise. It combines the opportunity to develop higher-order causal and logical thinking with a very structured approach. The process can be a step-by-step guided one through which the "expert" teacher guides the group, or it can be a cooperative project in which student groups work independently. The use of logic trees or flow charts can provide a visual, structured representation of the logic and make writing the rules a very concrete task. The pleasure of organizing a body of knowledge into a logical set and then seeing it operate as part of a computer program is highly motivating. Additionally, the exposure to this important technological tool is a step toward more sophisticated technological awareness.

CONCLUSION

Knowing how we know is as important as knowing. In these days of information explosion, it may be *more* important than knowing. People today have to understand how to access information, organize it, and put it together to solve problems. Educators must dedicate themselves to giving children a sound base of knowledge and the ability to access that knowledge in order to make intelligent decisions. This point is especially important when working with those for whom the natural processes of input so necessary for language and cognitive development are impaired.

The technology available today offers creative, far-reaching opportunities for accomplishing our task. The field of computer technology is expanding quickly beyond the early applications, and we have an opportunity in our field to apply innovative new approaches to enhance the strategies we already know to be effective. Applying what we do best to the best of technology opens vast fields of opportunity.

REFERENCES

Bigum, C. 1985. *Expert systems in educational research*. Unpublished manuscript. Deakin University, School of Education. Victoria, British Columbia.

DeBarnard, A.E. & Ferber, G.P. April 1986. *The teaching/learning process of handicapped children in the microcomputer environment*. Paper presented at the Annual Convention of the Council for Exceptional Children, New Orleans, LA.

Gagne, E.D. 1985. *The cognitive psychology of school learning*. Boston: Little, Brown & Company.

Gersten, R., Carnine, D., and Woodward, J. 1987. Direct instruction research: The third decade. *Remedial and Special Education* 8(6):48–56.

Martin, D. S. 1984. Enhancing cognitive performance in the hearing-impaired college student: A pilot study. In *International symposium on cognition, education, and deafness: Working papers*, ed. D.S. Martin. Washington, DC: Gallaudet University.

Palincsar, A.S., & Brown, A. 1987. Advances in improving cognitive performance of handicapped students. In *Handbook of special education: Research and practice, Vol. 1.* ed. M.C. Wang, 93–112. New York: Pergamon Press.

Papert, S. 1980. *Mindstorms.* New York: Basic Books.

Starfield, A.M., Butala, K.L., England, M.M., & Smith, K.A. 1983. Mastering engineering concepts by building an expert system. *Engineering Education*, November, 104–107.

Trollip, S.R., & Lippert, R.C. 1987. Constructing knowledge bases: A promising instructional tool. *Journal of Computer-Based Instruction* 14(2):44–48.

Wang, M.C. 1987. Toward achieving educational excellence for all students: Program design and student outcomes. *Remedial and Special Education* 8 (3):25–34.

Analysis

Kenneth Epstein

Cognitive intervention programs represent the ever-present problem in education of putting theory into practice. We all know that ideas that succeed beautifully in a well-controlled laboratory environment often fail when applied in normal classrooms. Yet, despite the difficulties and disappointments, it is critically important that application projects continue and that their results be completely and carefully reported. Practitioners need to know which techniques show the most promise, and they need to learn about errors to avoid. Researchers need to know how their theories hold up outside the laboratory so that theoretical work can grow and be enriched by applied results. The programs described in this chapter provide a rich source of information and deserve our careful consideration.

It is useful to consider the broad framework of cognitive science and its impact on education before attempting to address cognitive intervention programs and deafness. One may rely heavily on recent review articles by Nickerson (1988) and Shuell (1986) to help summarize the rapidly expanding literature. The work by Donna Mertens (1989) also provides an excellent overview of the impact of the cognitive point of view with respect to how we look at teachers and the teaching-learning process.

Learning, from a cognitive point of view, involves changes in knowledge. Contrast this point of view with the behavioristic view that defines learning as a change in observable behavior. The cognitive view interprets behavioral change as a result of a change in knowledge.

The cognitive focus on knowledge also focuses attention on the individual. One is less concerned with changing the environment in the hope of providing an appropriate reinforcement for desired behavior; rather, one asks how to change the learner so that he or she will demonstrate the desired behavior.

Learners are active participants in the learning process. We tend to organize information in ways that are meaningful to us as learners, often in ways that are surprising to our teachers. Learning is a constructive process, building on existing knowledge. We depend on our prior knowledge to help us learn new knowledge. We think about what we are doing as we learn. We continually employ meta-cognitive processes such as planning, setting goals and subgoals, actively selecting the stimuli on which to focus our attention, and choosing strategies to help us learn and remember.

In considering the teaching-learning process, the cognitive point of view changes the focus from what the teacher and students do to what they know and how they act based on their knowledge. Teachers are active, thinking participants along with their students. In addition to traditional observations of student behavior and student achievement, the cognitive point of view demands that one study what the teacher and student know, how they communicate their understandings and misunderstandings to each other, and how teachers change their instructional strategies to meet the changing conditions in the classroom. To learn effectively, learners must have general knowledge and learning strategies as well as content-specific knowledge and learning strategies. Learners must employ general metacognitive strategies to guide their learning, but they must also apply metacognitive strategies that are specific to the content under study. The more effective teachers are those who are aware of the active, information-processing nature of the learning process—they are alert and constantly adjusting to their students.

What does this cognitive view of learning and of the active learner suggest for instruction? What are the instructionally relevant areas that we should be investigating? Nickerson (1988) identified seven topics that require attention as we consider thinking and instruction:

1. Basic processes (classification, generalization, seriation, deduction, etc.);
2. Domain-specific knowledge (what we already know about a domain and how that influences subsequent learning);
3. Knowledge of domain-independent normative principles of reasoning (general principles learned from the study of subjects such as logic, geometry, grammar, and classical languages);
4. Knowledge of domain-independent informal principles and rules of thought (heuristics, general problem-solving strategies, etc.);
5. Metacognitive knowledge (knowledge about human cognition, knowledge of one's own cognitive strengths, weaknesses, and monitoring and control processes);
6. Values, attitudes, dispositions, styles (one's tendency to be reflective, open-minded, and objective); and
7. Beliefs (beliefs about one's own capabilities and the value of improving one's thinking).

Building on Mertens' (1989) analysis, several additional topics emerge that are particularly relevant to an interest in teaching:

1. Teacher planning, decision-making, theories, and beliefs;
2. Domain-independent and domain-specific knowledge and metacognitive strategies for both teachers and learners; and
3. Methodology for assessing teaching effectiveness and for identifying the characteristics of effective learning environments.

Mertens (1989) also provides a breakdown of some of the most important variables specific to development of cognitive intervention programs for deaf learners:

1. Family background characteristics (e.g., hearing status of parents; communication mode used in the home);
2. Subject background characteristics (e.g., age of hearing loss, cause of loss, communication skills, degree of loss, presence of additional handicaps);
3. School or school district conditions (e.g., size of hearing-impaired student enrollment, expenditures for hearing-impaired programs, support services provided);
4. Within-school conditions (e.g., hearing-impaired student-teacher ratio, process of making student placement decisions);
5. Instructional personnel characteristics (e.g., signing ability, training, and experience in working with deaf students);
6. Student attitudes (e.g., impulsivity, attitude toward communication, internal/external control);
7. Student placement (e.g., residential school, day school with self-contained classes, mainstreamed classes);
8. Instructional personnel performance by both teachers and interpreters (e.g., sign mode used); and
9. Family support variables (e.g., adaptation to deafness, family involvement/interaction, expectations) (p. 827).

Mertens' concerns about language are explicitly addressed in David Stewart's (1989) work. The program he describes uses American Sign Language (ASL) intervention as part of a bilingual total communication program:

> ASL intervention refers to the processes by which an intervention agent (e.g., teacher, language specialist) uses ASL in interaction with deaf students after determining that ASL is necessary to facilitate comprehension in a particular discourse situation (p. 864).

The goal is not to teach ASL *as a language*. The major language goal is to *promote English language skills*. However, ASL is recognized as the language understood by many students. Hence, it can be used to help with understanding in the classroom.

Stewart presents evidence and makes a convincing argument for instruction in the students' first language, and the program he describes has the potential to become a model for bilingual ASL/English instruction. However, the most important part of his paper lies in the questions he raises about the cognitive implications of ASL interventions. At the most basic level, he points out that we really do not understand how signed languages are processed and whether the information processing is basically the same or very different from that of spoken language. Further, we don't know the effects on comprehension of switching communication modes and languages and of routinely using two kinds of languages—a signed representation of spoken English and ASL—in the classroom.

Stewart recognizes that evaluation of the program he describes is very difficult because of the multitude of factors that could affect outcomes. For example, suppose comprehension improves because students understand ASL explanations better than explanations presented in English. Will better retention follow? How will the language change be demonstrated in students' understanding, classroom behavior, and academic performance? How can one design evaluation studies to investigate the many confounding factors that will be part of an instructional system incorporating ASL?

The programs described by Martin and Jonas (1989) and O'Donnell and Adenwalla (1989) are both examples of explicitly applying theory to practical intervention programs. The Martin and Jonas study of the Instrumental Enrichment program describes it as a "classroom intervention program for adolescents and adults [that] uses content-free paper-and-pencil exercises to correct deficient cognitive functions and provide the prerequisites for learning and problem-solving. . . ." O'Donnell and Adenwalla describe knowledge mapping and scripted cooperation—intervention programs that apply theories of memory and metacognition to instruction. Both programs reported student benefits, but both also reported practical problems.

In considering the results of these projects, and any projects designed to demonstrate effectiveness in an operational setting, one cannot ignore the practical problems over which the researcher has little or no control. Implementing programs such as these is extremely difficult. They require dedicated faculty who are willing to volunteer their time for training and willing to do much special preparation. They also require a cooperative and supportive administration, willing to give faculty the flexibility to participate and, in the case of Instrumental Enrichment, able to afford the cost of program materials. Ideally, instruction in *all* courses should reinforce skills such as those learned from Instrumental Enrichment activities, employ knowledge-mapping techniques to organize and present information, and encourage scripted cooperation to help students process new information more effectively. In reality, most students have one or two experimental classes using these kinds of interventions. Their other classes are unlikely to help them see how to use their newly developing skills in other content areas. Perhaps most important of all, these programs require that instructors and students *believe* that they are worthwhile. Instrumental Enrichment activities use class time that instructors and students may feel is better spent on completing course requirements. Scripted cooperation requires students to assume new active roles in the learning process. Students may not believe it is worth their time to learn to think. Thinking is hard work, and it is not immediately obvious how it relates to achieving a high grade-point average.

These two projects are illustrative of Sternberg's (1986) warnings about expecting too much from cognitive intervention programs. He lists several areas that could endanger attempts to apply cognitive theory to instruction. If the cognitive theory is not comprehensive, valid, or relevant to the instructional needs, it will not be useful. "Perhaps the single greatest source of disappointment in the application of cognitive principles to educational practice is the absence of an instructional theory to mediate the link between cognitive theory, on the one hand, and educational practice, on the other (p. 378)." Instructional theories must be improved and modified to fit the cognitive point of view. There must be a match between theory, student and teacher abilities, and motivation. Theories often assume that students and teachers will be highly motivated and that they will have a certain amount of competence in the field to be taught. Often these assumptions are subtle and implicit. If the students and teachers do not meet the expectations of the theory, applied projects may fail.

Lou and Charlson's (1989) social cognition program incorporates active learners, domain-independent skills applied to domain-specific problems, and group activities that emphasize metacognitive skill development. The program is particularly important because it explicitly addresses values and beliefs. Nickerson criticizes the "teaching thinking" field for the lack of programs dealing with values and beliefs. Too often, he points out, individuals choose not to use their problem-solving skills or think carefully because it would require considering another's point of view or because it might challenge one's own beliefs. The social cognition program is to be commended for addressing values, beliefs, attitudes and perceptions directly. Person conceptualization activities helped students understand themselves and others better. Perspective-taking activities focused on the ability to coordinate a variety of perspectives simultaneously.

It appears as though this latter project is also working. However, many of the project goals involve subtle changes in behavior, especially outside the classroom. These kinds of goals are difficult to measure. Assessment techniques, especially those that address one's perceptions of others, require continued refinement and may be confounded by differences in the English and ASL ways of expressing descriptions of others. It is also clear that a considerable amount of time is necessary to meet the project goals adequately. Pressley, Schneider, and Borkowski (1989) point out that it is impossible to produce good information processors with short-term interventions; years of appropriate instruction are necessary. Similarly, programs designed to improve social cognition must anticipate the need for considerable instructional time in order to achieve noticeable results.

Wilson (1989) describes how technology can dramatically change learning environments. The Discourse System permits much higher levels of interaction and feedback than are possible in classrooms without this kind of technological support. Her proposal that students build expert systems takes advantage of technology to encourage students to make explicit their understanding of a content area. Both programs use computers and computer software as tools to incorporate into instruction ideas from research in cognition.

Wilson's examples hint at the potential of technology. Batson's (1988) work with the Electronic Networks for Instruction (ENFI) Project is another good example. Technology may help break down language and communication barriers, it may make it possible to enrich the variety of modes in which instruction is presented, and it may make it possible for learners to be more actively involved in their learning. Pea (1987) provides a valuable framework for thinking about the role of technology in helping students learn to think mathematically. His ideas can be generalized to other content areas as well.

Nickerson (1988) begins his article by asking whether our efforts to apply the results of cognitive science research to teaching are worthwhile:

> The question that arises, in light of history, is whether there are reasons to believe that the current efforts to give the teaching of thinking top priority on the education agenda have any better chances of success than did those of the past. My answer to this question is a cautious yes, for three reasons: (1) the need to succeed is more urgent today than it was in the past, (2) research in cognition and learning is yielding useful results, and (3) technology has the potential to mitigate some of the logistic and practical constraints that have determined many of the characteristics of past and present educational practice (pp. 6–7).

This author shares Nickerson's optimism and believes his reasons for optimism are especially relevant to education of the deaf. Deaf people must be empowered to reach their full potential if they are to succeed in the present and future technological world. Political and social pressures and the growing expectations within the deaf community require a vigorous response from the educational community. Education for the deaf simply must improve.

Fortunately, the quality and quantity of research related to education and deafness are increasing. Researchers and practitioners are also slowly including others who have not traditionally been associated with deafness. Such contact and collaboration are necessary for research in deafness and deaf education to mature.

In sum, the papers in this chapter demonstrate that instructional practice can be informed by the results of research related to cognition. These successes, combined with the more mature and diverse research base, the promise of technology, and the need for improved education for deaf individuals, all provide a strong basis for optimism.

REFERENCES

Batson, T. 1988. *An imaginative use of computer networks to improve learning on campus: The five-university ENFI consortium.* Paper presented at EDUCOM 88.

Nickerson, R.S. 1988. On improving thinking through instruction. In *Review of research in education: 15.*, ed. E.Z. Rothkopf. Washington, DC: American Educational Research Association.

Pea, R. D. 1987. Cognitive technologies for mathematics education. In *Cognitive science and mathematics education*, ed. A. Schoenfeld. Hillsdale, NJ: Lawrence Erlbaum Associates.

Pressley, M., Schneider, W. & Borkowski, J.G. 1989. *Good information processing: What it is and how education can promote it.* Paper presented at the annual convention of the American Educational Research Association.

Shuell, T. 1986. Cognitive conceptions of learning. *Review of Educational Research*, 56(4):411–436.

Sternberg, R.J. 1986. Cognition and instruction: Why the marriage sometimes ends in divorce. In *Cognition and instruction*, ed. R.J. Dillon & R.J. Sternberg. Orlando, FL: Academic Press.

RESEARCH QUESTIONS

Topics for research appear implicitly throughout this analysis. Choosing those topics that are most important is an impossible task, since there is so much to do. However, some high-priority topics for research related to cognitive intervention programs in the immediate future would be

1. Language: We must know more about the role of language in instruction for deaf students. Obviously, ASL and its appropriate role in the classroom need to be studied. Also there are more fundamental questions related to the language base that students bring with them to instruction; for example, "How do students who did not hear or see language until they were 2, 3, or older process information?"
2. Knowledge: How does a student's pre-instruction knowledge about a subject relate to his or her ability to learn new knowledge? How can we identify and work with student misconceptions? What are the relationships between domain-independent and domain-specific skills and knowledge?
3. Technology: What is the role of technology in future instruction in the teaching of thinking to deaf students?
4. Assessment and Evaluation: What new assessment and evaluation tools do we need in order to understand the effectiveness of cognitive intervention programs?

9

PROGRAMS FOR APPLIED RESEARCH

The eight papers in this special section on Implementation represent a variety of experientially based activities within educational institutions that are working actively to improve the cognitive functioning of deaf learners at one or more age levels. Each paper describes a particular approach or intervention, and each in its own way is based on defensible cognitive theory. In addition, some of these presentations have grown out of research experiments and are now applying their results in an instructional environment; others are pilot programs of strong promise that could and should lead to broad-based data collection to systematically analyze their true effects. All reflect the encouraging spirit of interest among educational practitioners in developing explicit and planned means by which the cognitive capacity of the deaf learner can be enhanced.

Because each of these papers represents an independent effort at implementation, and because they cut across all the themes in the prior sections of this volume, they are not given the unifying analysis that accompanies the other groups of papers in this volume. The reader is encouraged to contact these authors for further details about implementation and documentation. It is hoped that the circle of practitioners working with such programs can widen in the years ahead.

David S. Martin, Editor

A Piagetian Model for Observation of Verbal, Nonvocal, and Nonverbal Cognitive Behavior in Hearing-Impaired Infants and Young Children

Kathee M. Christensen

It is difficult to assess the cognitive strengths and communicative potential of profoundly, congenitally deaf infants and toddlers. Typical preschool tests and scales focus on a limited set of developmental steps that are easily discerned in young children who have normal hearing. No empirical evidence supports the notion that these developmental milestones are equivalent for children with severe to profound hearing losses. In fact, several studies point out the danger in using tests designed for hearing children to predict or measure functional levels of deaf children (Martin 1985). A child who seeks to understand his or her world primarily through the sense of sight, without full benefit of natural auditory stimuli, may manifest cognitive and communicative strengths in ways that differ from children with normal hearing. Teachers and clinicians who can observe and understand the qualitative communicative variances of deaf infants and toddlers will have valuable information regarding the strategies these children employ to learn and to attempt communication. A format for the observation and analysis of nonverbal, nonvocal, and verbal cognitive behavior of deaf children is an important tool for those individuals responsible for the assessment and education of young, deaf children.

A PIAGETIAN MODEL

Piaget (1959) has taught us that children must construct their own knowledge and assimilate new experiences in ways that make sense to them. This activity occurs despite the fact that an experience may make sense to the adult mind in a way that differs dramatically from its interpretation by the child. An example is the little boy who, when observing the fluffy white clouds at the end of a rainstorm, thought of his bathtub sponge and said, "Look, Mommy, the clouds are all squeezed dry!" This analogy was logical for the two-year-old and a humorous anecdote for his mother. The wise adult probably will not launch into a lecture about the scientific fundamentals that cause changes in weather, but will instead note the young child's creativity and appreciate his attempt at figuring out a complicated phenomenon. A teacher who understands the developmental stages of Piagetian theory will view the incident as an example of Stage II behavior and add that bit of information to her overall view of the child. We know that simply telling a child a fact will not ensure the understanding or retention of that fact, nor will presenting a child with a dictionary ensure the child's acquisition of language. How children develop cognitively and communicatively is a fascinating subject that only recently has received substantial attention in educational research.

The ways in which thoughts can be communicated are many and varied. Children communicate through body movement, posture, gesture, facial expression, eye contact, and physical appearance. In turn, adults communicate to them in the same ways. Often what we say to a child is less important to that child than the way we say it. Nonverbal communication in the classroom is vital to the overall understanding of communication and cognitive potential. A Piagetian approach to assessment of communication and cognitive development allows the observer to record and evaluate both nonverbal and verbal behavior within the parameters of the four-stage epigenetic model that Piaget described.

Stage I is called the sensorimotor stage and is divided into six substages. Although early in his career Piaget assigned age approximations to his model, current theory disregards any attempt to attach specific age equivalents to the stages or substages. Some children may develop earlier than others; however, the important point is that development occurs and proceeds in a logical, orderly, but somewhat flexible manner. Stage I development is highlighted by the demonstration of object permanence and causality, among other examples of cognitive behavior. It is critical for teachers of deaf and deaf-blind children to be able to observe such behaviors as they occur spontaneously with or without the support of language. A deaf infant or toddler may prefer to display intentional behavior and symbolic play through nonverbal rather than verbal or vocal instruments. Deaf-blind infants may need extended, guided practice with tactile exploration before naturally exhibiting object permanence.

Gestures used for communication can be observed in both deaf and hearing children who have developed to substage 6 of the sensorimotor stage. These communicative gestures indicate that the child has advanced in the understanding of symbolic meaning to the extent that preoperational cognitive behavior is emerging. In fact, some research has suggested that sequencing abilities are first manifested in gesture (Thal & Bates 1988). Children who have meaningful linguistic input at this stage can be expected to use words for self-expression and as tools to gain a desired end. Children without comprehensible linguistic input will explore ways to understand and make themselves understood nonverbally. Creative use of nonverbal instruments such as gesture, gaze, vocalization, body position, and facial expression become apparent to a sensitive observer. It is at this point that a prelinguistic child may be penalized on formal cognitive assessments that expect verbal responses as the only correct responses. Even so-called nonverbal measures may, in fact, be influenced by the test taker's lack of verbal sophistication. It is important to stress that sign language and fingerspelling are verbal modes, and children who have learned these communicative options should be able to perform successfully on verbal measures that are presented by competent users of manual communication. Children who have learned neither sign language nor a form of majority language communication are at risk for cognitive misdiagnosis as early as Stage I, substage 5 and thereafter.

Prelingually deaf children have been observed to exhibit Stage III nonverbal cognitive behavior. An example is nine-year-old Jorge from Mexico, who came to a clinic with his mother for assessment and possible placement in a communication therapy program. The university where the clinic is located has been compared to a maze. This young man and his mother parked in the parking structure and proceeded to follow the maze, across the overpass, up the steps, right for one block, across the street, left for one block, down the steps, into the clinic, and down two halls to the writer's office (a complicated track for most visitors). After the initial assessment, the mother and the writer turned to one of the forms that the mother needed to complete. Since she spoke very little English, we were both absorbed in the task of communication. When we looked up a few minutes later, Jorge had disappeared. A search of the clinic ensued, with all hands called out to search for Jorge. Eventually, a graduate student came to our door and said, "There's a little boy in the parking lot and I think he's deaf. He's wearing hearing aids." Further conversation verified that Jorge, obviously ready to go home, had made the journey through the maze and back to his mother's car entirely on his own.

This action was a clear example of reversibility, although not a word was spoken. It is possible to observe concrete operations such as reversibility, classification, seriation, and conservation in a prelingually deaf child, but only if the teacher or clinician is 1) thoroughly comfortable with the Piagetian model and how it is interpreted, and 2) the child is given opportunities to demonstrate cognitive behavior in a variety of settings over time. Obviously, more systematic investigation into such cognitive functions in the deaf learner is now essential.

CONCLUSION

In the Piagetian model, all learning comes about as a direct result of active participation by the learner in the learning situation. Current research in language and cognition has suggested the existence of local homologies that function in early cognitive development. These modules cut across language and other aspects of cognitive functioning (Thal & Bates 1988). The theory of multiple intelligences (Gardner 1983) has provided another interesting model that can be applied to early identification of cognitive strength through other-than-verbal means.

All education is based on experience, but not all experiences are equally educational. Teachers must consider the quality of a planned educational experience and the potential outcome for the student. Each new experience will be perceived in relation to the child's cognitive level and experiential background. An effective teacher can determine the child's functional cognitive level and present new challenges within an overall model of cognitive development, providing motivation at an appropriate level of disequilibrium for the individual learner. The child will be encouraged to make personal discoveries and understand that these discoveries may or may not match exactly with the discoveries of peers in the classroom. There are many ways to solve problems. Nonverbal means may be as successful as verbal strategies if they are recognized and respected.

John Dewey once said that "to discover what is really simple and to act upon the discovery in an exceedingly difficult task." Teachers can accept the challenge of seeking the simple acts that children use naturally to communicate and to demonstrate thoughts, opinions, and creative problem-solving strategies. If teachers can learn to observe nonverbal cognitive behavior and use that information in planning appropriate classroom activities, the task of facilitating language acquisition will be more successful for all concerned.

REFERENCES

Gardner, H. 1983. *Frames of mind: The theory of multiple intelligences.* New York: Basic Books.

Martin, D.S., ed. 1985. *Cognition, education and deafness: Directions for research and instruction.* Washington, DC: Gallaudet University Press.

Piaget, J. 1959. *The language and thought of the child.* 3rd ed. London: Routledge & Kegan Paul.

Thal, D. & Bates, E. 1988. Language and gesture in late talkers. *Journal of Speech and Hearing Research* 31:115–123.

Improving Cognitive Performance Through Mathematics Instruction

Charles H. Dietz

M any programs designed to improve the cognitive performance of students require a substantial commitment of class time. This requirement especially applies to Feuerstein's Instrumental Enrichment Program (FIE) (Feuerstein 1980). While indications are that FIE is somewhat effective with deaf students (Martin 1984), the time, money, staff commitment, and training required to make the program accessible to most students in a school program is often considerable. For this reason, such programs are begun in schools, but their continued and extended use is often in question.

In mathematics, many deaf students tend to be procedural and rigid in their thinking. This kind of thinking has been encouraged, if not caused, by a traditional mathematics curriculum organized around skills and focused on outcomes. Mathematics programs in the United States generally have been questioned as to their effectiveness in providing students with the necessary thinking skills to solve problems (see McKnight et al. 1987; Dossey et al. 1988). A limited mediated experience-base, along with a procedurally oriented mathematics program, has resulted in especially poor problem-solving performance and restricted thinking behaviors for many deaf students. Cognitive training and better mathematics instruction could help to alleviate these difficulties.

Methods of providing a cognitively oriented mathematics program are being explored with students in the Postsecondary Enrichment Program (PEP) at the Model Secondary School for the Deaf at Gallaudet University. Designing lessons and classroom experiences around a taxonomy of cognitive behaviors, Feuerstein's concepts of a mediated learning experience, with bridging and major mathematical relationships, might make it possible to strengthen both cognitive and mathematical education for the students. The goal of this program is to provide instruction in cognitive modification, similar to FIE, along with and embedded in meaningful mathematics instruction.

COGNITION AND MATHEMATICS

Typical mathematics instruction is teacher-focused, answer-oriented, and often unrelated to student experience. Class organization frequently consists of a review of homework, introduction to a new method or idea with numerous examples, followed by a new assignment, some of which is done as individual work during the class time. The emphasis is on carrying out computations and single-step word problems. Very little opportunity is given to the student to use higher-order cognitive skills or to investigate mathematical relationships.

A cognitively oriented mathematics program provides these opportunities. Cognitively oriented mathematics instruction, as envisioned in PEP, focuses on discussion and use of cognitive functions as defined by Feuerstein (Feuerstein 1980) and on major mathematical concepts and relationships (Table 1). The clear, precise communication of these concepts and relationships in discussion and writing is emphasized. Frequently, classroom activity centers on collaborative learning experiences and investigations. Each problem or activity may involve several days to a week. As opportunities arise, applications of the cognitive functions and the mathematical relationships to other curricular areas and students' own experiences are shared.

As one type of activity consistent with such cognitively oriented mathematics instruction, a series of pilot instruments has been designed and used with PEP students. Each activity has a major mathematics concept and one or more cognitive function as its basis. Students work in groups and with the teacher. The experiences are used as a center of discussion around which to tie together mathematics and the cognitive functions involved. "Bridging" (i.e., relating the mathematics concepts and the cognitive functions to life situations to which they apply) is always a major component of the discussion. These activities are being developed to illustrate one way in which cognitively oriented mathematics instruction can take place.

Table 2 shows *Pentominos*, the first in a chain of instruments that are centered on the idea of pentominos (Picciotto 1984). This instrument begins with a challenge problem that is often vague, broad, and somewhat beyond the students' abilities to solve directly. The purpose of the problem is not only to challenge students, but also to establish the value and need for the concepts and cognitive functions involved. Through discussion in groups and as a class, students are encouraged to identify sources of difficulty in solving the challenge problem. There might be words they need to have defined; perhaps the nature of the solution is not clear; they might not be familiar with the relationships involved. By examining the remaining portion of the page, students are encouraged to infer the meaning of the unfamiliar words from context, the nature of the solution, and possible strategies for developing a solution.

TABLE 1   Instrumental Enrichment Cognitive Functions

I. Gathering all the information we need (Input)
   1. Using our senses (listening, seeing, smelling, tasting, touching, feeling) to gather clear and complete information (clear perception).
   2. Using a system or plan so that we do not skip or miss something important or repeat ourselves (systematic exploration).
   3. Giving the thing we gather through our senses and our experience a name so that we can remember it more clearly and talk about it (labeling).
   4. Describing things and events in terms of where and when they occur (temporal and spatial referent).
   5. Deciding on the characteristics of a thing or event that always stays the same, even when changes take place (conservation, constancy, and object permanence).
   6. Organizing the information we gather by considering more than one thing at a time (using two sources of information).
   7. Being precise and accurate when it matters (need for precision).
II. Using the information we have gathered (Elaboration)
   1. Defining what the problem is, what we are being asked to do, and what we must figure out (analyzing disequilibrium).
   2. Using only the part of the information we have gathered that applies to the problem and ignoring the rest (relevance).
   3. Having a good picture in our mind of what we are looking for or what we must do (interiorization).
   4. Making a plan that will include the steps we need to take to reach our goal (planning behavior).
   5. Remembering and keeping in mind the various pieces of information we need (broadening our mental field).
   6. Looking for the relationship by which separate objects, events, and experiences can be tied together (projecting relationships).
   7. Comparing objects and experiences to others to see what is similar and what is different (comparative behavior).
   8. Finding the class or set to which the new object or experience belongs (categorization).
   9. Thinking about different possibilities and figuring out what would happen if you were to choose one or another (hypothetical thinking).
   10. Using logic to prove things and to defend your opinion (logical evidence).
III. Expressing the solution to a problem (Output)
   1. Being clear and precise in your language to be sure that there is no question as to what your answer is. Put yourself into the shoes of the listener to be sure that your answer will be understood (overcoming egocentric communication).
   2. Thinking things through before you answer instead of immediately trying to answer, making a mistake, and then trying again (overcoming trial and error).
   3. Counting to ten (at least) so that you don't say or do something you will be sorry for later (restraining impulsive behavior).
   4. Making sure that, if you can't answer a question for some reason even though you know the answer, you don't fret or panic. Leave the question for a little while and then, when you return to it, use a strategy to help you find the answer (overcoming blocking). (Feuerstein 1980)

During the initial discussion on the *Pentominos* page, students can be guided to the idea that pentominos have something to do with shapes made using five squares. By making cardboard squares available, the teacher suggests that it might be an effective strategy to experiment with various shapes using these squares. Finally, the major questions suggest a plan of action for simplifying the original problem by reducing the number of squares involved and searching for relationships that could be useful in responding to the challenge problem.

TABLE 2   PENTOMINOS

Challenge Problem
    Find and draw all possible pentominos.
Goal
    To find all possible shapes that can be made by a group of squares.
Material
    A set of cardboard squares
Major Questions
    How many possible shapes can be made using only three squares?
    How many possible shapes can be made using only four squares?
    Students are encouraged to write down a plan that they believe would respond completely to this problem.
Plan Your Strategy

In early instruments, students develop this plan with the teacher. After some experience, students are asked to write their own plans through discussion in their groups. The formal plan is always developed before work begins on solving the problems.

In all discussions, the teacher uses appropriate and specific vocabulary related to the mathematical concepts and the cognitive functions. Correct and clear vocabulary reinforces the need for appropriate labels as an aid to clear thinking and provides students with the tools for precise communication about their ideas and their thinking.

After class discussion and planning, students attempt to solve the problem in their groups by applying the strategies discussed, if possible, and revising the plan if necessary. While the groups are working, the teacher will observe and mediate where necessary. Mediation is that process in which the teacher asks probing questions and makes suggestions that may assist a group toward a solution without explicitly leading the group to a specific solution. The group's working time may vary from half an hour to several days, depending on the task involved.

When groups have completed their work and written their report, the class again meets together to discuss the problem and the results obtained, to discuss the cognitive functions used in the investigation, and to bridge to other areas of the students' experience in school and in other aspects of their lives. This concluding discussion, which also could span several days, is the heart of the activity. Through the mediated discussion, the students are led to see the mathematical relationships and the applications of the cognitive functions involved.

During the Pentominos activity, there will certainly be opportunities to discuss explicitly the cognitive processes of clear perception, systematic exploration, labeling, analyzing disequilibrium, planning behavior, projecting relationships, overcoming egocentric communication, and overcoming trial and error (Table 1). While not all of these functions are introduced and discussed in detail in any one activity, the teacher selects those considered appropriate for that class.

This activity is followed by two others dealing with area and perimeter concepts and volume. Each of the two activities to follow provides the students opportunities both to extend the strategies to slightly new situations and to apply them to cognitive functions discussed in the first activity.

While the amount of time taken up with instruction using these instruments is considerably more than is typically used to teach the mathematical concepts involved, the nature of the activities allows instruction in the recognition and use of the cognitive functions involved—a process that is difficult to do in traditional mathematics instruction.

Student reactions to these instruments have been mixed. The activity is quite different from the mathematics instruction they have experienced before. They initially experience frustration in confronting challenging problems. On the other hand, most students do learn to enjoy the challenge when they realize that finding a unique, single answer to a problem is not always required and is not the point of the activity. Most students, finding that in groups they can solve difficult problems they could not solve individually, become excited about confronting more problems.

The discussions associated with the activities have provided the teacher with a way to help students become aware of various cognitive functions. There are not yet enough activities available to constitute a complete program in the cognitive functions. In fact, it is questionable whether one would want to develop an entire mathematics program around such instruments. However, this type of instrument, along with increased classroom emphasis on good problem-solving and instruction focusing on understanding mathematical relationships, might be an effective component of an overall school program that emphasizes cognitive functioning.

REFERENCES

Dossey, J.A., Mullis, I.V.S., Lindquist, M.M., & Chambers, D.L. 1988. *The mathematics report card - are we measuring up? Trends and achievement based on the 1986 National Assessment* (Report No. 17–M-01). Princeton, NJ: Educational Testing Service.

Feuerstein, R. 1980. *Instrumental enrichment: An intervention program for cognitive modifiability.* Baltimore, MD: University Park Press.

McKnight, C.C., Crosswhite, F.F., Dossey, J.A., Kifer, E., Swafford, J.O., Travers, K.J., & Cooney, T.J. 1987. *The underachieving curriculum: Assessing U.S. school mathematics from an international perspective.* Champaign, IL: Stipes Publishing Company.

Martin, D.S. 1984. Cognitive modification for the hearing impaired adolescent: The promise. *Exceptional Children* 51(3):235–242.

Picciotto, H. 1984. *Pentomino activities.* Palo Alto, CA: Creative Publications.

Philosophy: The Fiber of Deaf Education

Maura J. Geisser

The Philosophy for Children program was created by Matthew Lipman of the Institute for the Advancement of Philosophy for Children (IAPC) at Monclair State College in New Jersey (Lipman et al. 1980). The program was developed to enhance the thinking skills of hearing children in grades 3 through 10. In this program, teachers engage students in philosophical discussions of novels in which the characters discover the power of logic and the benefits of thinking analytically (Rembert 1985).

Implementation of this program at the Rhode Island School for the Deaf began as an attempt to bridge the gap observed between the verbal and written work of deaf students, to enable them to think more reflectively and more critically. We began using the program with high school seniors. The rigid thought processes and opinions of the seniors caused us to present the program earlier in our high school curriculum to juniors and sophomores in the hope of increasing the students' flexibility in dealing with ambiguity and in question formation. We found that the younger the children were, the more open to alternative possibilities and the more tolerant they were of other's beliefs, and eventually we used the program with nine-year-old deaf students.

When students are presented with information, they may not necessarily comprehend it and make it part of their repertoire. Facts that are largely unrelated seem meaningless to the student and to "real life." So one must look at the concepts and their underlying causes and reasons.

One day, a group of students came into a philosophy class from social studies, where they had been learning facts about cotton in the South and the effects it had on pre-Civil War America. None of the students had ever seen a cotton plant.

We went outside on that cold fall day, searching for cotton fibers; we found seeds, berries, dead plants, and milkweed pods, but no cotton. After examining the milkweed pods in answer to the question "What for?" (the ASL equivalent of "What is this for?") the students said the milkweed was like cotton and that it had seeds and fibers inside a pod that popped open in the heat. Analysis of the information and concrete samples from the "field trip" yielded a discussion on the differences and similarities between the milkweed fiber found in the yard and the cotton fiber studied in the social studies class. The class tried to discover why cotton could not grow in Rhode Island. Back in the classroom some students said it was too cold to grow cotton, but some still insisted that cotton could grow in Rhode Island. We then added up all the warm days when one could plant in June, July, August, September, and October and found approximately 122 days, much less than the 200 warm days required to grow cotton—a fact learned in social studies. They discovered the reasons to be climate and time for maturation; therefore, cotton cannot grow in Rhode Island. But it was not until they actually *saw* a cotton plant and cotton seeds that they truly understood the comparisons. In some ways the two plants were the same but in other ways very different.

The success of using the Philosophy for Children program was seen in the hearing-impaired children's ability to think critically, but the problem of helping them think and reason logically is very difficult, since it ties the linguistic system to the thought processes. The students used the novel *Harry Stottlemeier's Discovery* from the program for one year; the following year the same students took *Harry* again, this time from the point of view of inquiry, emphasizing logical reasoning. The students needed to be able to understand and categorize all the sentence structures and what NPs (subjects and objects) and VPs (predicates) were before they could deal with quantifiers (*each, generally, all but one, almost never,* etc.) and certainly before they could deal with syllogistic, logical, and hypothetical statements. Lipman stated that "infants begin to explore, deliberate, infer, and inquire well before the acquisition of language. As verbal behavior emerges, it is both grammatical and logical: children acquire the 'rules' of logic and grammar along with words and their meanings" (Lipman et al. 1980).

THE RELATIONSHIP OF PHILOSOPHY AND LOGIC TO LANGUAGE STRUCTURE

How does one go about teaching logic to hearing-impaired children? It would seem a fairly easy task to teach categorizations of statements beginning with *all, no,* and the in-between area of *some.* It would also seem that all one would have to do is present sentences with those quantifiers to children, and they would easily begin the task of formal operations, since we would be dealing with very simple English sentences. For example, one student, Kelly, said: "Fruits are not things. All things are not things. All things are things, but some are not things." This statement is a contradiction. The point is that the student should be competent in saying or writing language with good structures and have an understanding of the varying semantic functioning and phrasing of words within a sentence. In order to comprehend, analyze, and use syllogisms, one must first clearly understand the basics of standardization in order to see that some conclusions could be false, contradictory, or invalid. All this understanding is necessary for students to make clear decisions and value judgments. "Having knowledge of a given discipline is not the same as knowing how to think critically" (Hayward 1987, pp. 367–368).

Although the same students' abilities to inquire, discuss, agree or disagree, give reasons, think reflectively, and make inferences from information were increasing and developing in a critical and creative way, still they seemed to be failing to comprehend the logical process of standardization. One line of investigation was to look at the linguistics or grammar of the sentences as well as at the semantics or conceptual relationships of the English language. Grammar in this sense means a set of rules that will generate all expressions allowable in the language.

Before the students could deal with quantifiers, they had to be able to categorize the different kinds of sentences and the structures that make up the sentences. This categorization and organization of things into related groups must be represented clearly and consistently. Bruner explained that there are

> ... three universal properties of base-structure grammar, properties as characteristic of the child's grammar as of the adult's subject-predicate relations, verb-object relations, and modification. Each of these presupposes an underlying logical form that can be simply stated. (Bruner et al. 1966, pp. 42–43)

In logical terms, then, the subject is a function of the predicate. Logical standardization is based on the form *quantifier, noun phrase (NP), verb (V)* or *linking verb (LV)*, and *noun phrase*. This sequence in our curriculum was called Pattern 4.

We used five basic linguistic patterns for structuring simple sentences:

Pattern #1: NP + V (adverb)
Pattern #2: NP + V + NP
Pattern #3: NP + LV + Adj.
Pattern #4: NP + LV + NP
Pattern #5: NP + LV + Adv. (Blackwell et al. 1978, pp. 69–73)

> Thus, language provides the building blocks that make arguments possible, and this demands some comments on those aspects of language that are crucial to the construction and evaluation of ordinary arguments. Here clarity, precision, the rejection or misleading euphemisms and the unambiguous use of language are prerequisites for good argument, and they require the elimination of questionable classifications, vagueness and equivocation. (Groahke & Tindal 1986, pp. 303–304)

If students could categorize different sentences according to their grammatical structure in linguistic terms, then they could deal with the ambiguity and variety of the vocabulary that makes up the different elements of the sentence, whose functions change because of the semantic content. Language usage presupposes that there are specific cognitive processes that are necessary for its use. To be competent in language usage, the individual must both use analysis in determining how a word or phrase functions and be able to understand the meaning of the sentence by a synthesis of all its parts.

The students read and signed simultaneously *Harry* and *The Blind Men and the Elephant* (Lipman 1982) and were asked to give their ideas, which were then written on the overhead projector or chalkboard and discussed. The students said that there was a problem in the story, using as examples the sentences *The trunk was not a snake, The ear was not a fan,* and *The tail was not a rope.* These sentences identified problems in sequence, in logic, and in semantics. The students were asked to look carefully and see if there were any similarities in these sentences. When they agreed there were, the sentences were written on a chart and hung on the wall. Then, the students were asked to put the sentence in the form noun phrase (NP) + linking verb (LV) + noun phrase (NP). If a child is supposed to be able to standardize sentences in the form NP + LV + NP, and if the word after the noun is not a noun but rather an adjective or adverb, then the student must realize this fact and put the adjective or adverb into a relative clause with a noun. Bruner stated that "the conventional superordinate category emerges governed by logical rules of inclusion, exclusion, and overlap" (Bruner et al. 1966). Oleron showed that, for the deaf, this "idea of common class is hardly ever expressed in abstract form" (1972).

Once the students were comfortable with this process of syntactic analysis and putting words in the NP + LV + NP sequence, then they could look at a sentence and try to categorize it by quantifier and then standardize it and state what it meant. The quantifiers *all* and *some* were easier. The quantifiers *no* or *some, are not,* and *only* were extremely difficult for the hearing-impaired students. (The part/whole concepts involved in using *all, some,* and *no* are closely related to those involved in using fractions.) The student must clearly understand that if there is one example (no matter how small or unimportant) that is different or one exception to the statement, the speaker or writer cannot say *all,* but must instead say *some.* Only then will the reader or hearer know that the statement does not represent "all." Concrete experiences represented as Venn diagrams were helpful in representing these sentences.

LOGICAL RELATIONSHIPS AND VENN DIAGRAMS

Venn diagrams were found to be enormously helpful in dealing with relationships. The students could represent iconically what had first been worked out concretely. Then students could discuss part/whole or overlapping relationships and attempt to write sentences to represent the diagrams. Since there are three kinds of "turn about" relationships dealing with differences of kind and degree in chapter 7 of *Harry,* as well as "carry over" relationships when two sentences are combined, then some combinations containing a relationship are true, some are false, and others are indeterminate. The concept of stated relationships posed a difficulty for these students.

Summer is warmer than spring.
Spring is warmer than winter.
Therefore, *Summer is warmer than winter.* (Lipman 1984).

The students observed that certain words were the same in all three sentences. It was easy to eliminate the middle term, but then the students had absolutely no idea of the relationships involved or how to draw a conclusion. Iconically we represented it as:

NP	LV	relationship	NP	LV	relationship	NP
Summer	is	*warmer than*	Spring	is	*warmer than*	Winter

Students were asked to analyze the parts of the sentences and then to label the NP, the LV, and the relationship. Next they were asked if the relationship (big, small, warm, cold) was the same, since it might not be. One of the pairs of sentences might use the relationship "big," and the other "small," which would necessitate rewriting the sentence until the relationship was the same.

NP	LV		NP	LV		NP
Summer	is	*warmer than*	Spring	is	*warmer than*	Winter

_____ 1 _____/ _____ 2 _____/

These are the two given relationships, and now they needed to find a third relationship, a new sentence using the same relationship.

NP	LV		NP	LV		NP
Summer	is	*warmer than*	Spring	is	*warmer than*	Winter

_____ 1 _____/ _____ 2 _____/
_____ 3 _____/

Thus the third sentence (or conclusion) would be *Summer is warmer than winter*. Then the students could decide if the conclusion was true or false.

If there are two relationships and the relationships are different, one cannot draw a conclusion using the above method. Thus
The USA is larger than Mexico.

The USA is smaller than the USSR.

The students observed that the relationships were different in the two sentences and that three countries were involved. The students set up these sentences, analyzed and labeled them, and changed the second relationship. Changing the relationship involved using Venn diagrams.

NP	LV	relationship	NP
The USA	is	larger than	Mexico

NP	LV	relationship	NP
The USSR	is	larger than	U.S.A.

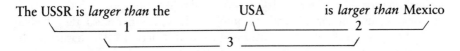

The USSR is *larger than* the USA is *larger than* Mexico

Thus, the conclusion would be *The USSR is larger than Mexico*, and it could be represented as

It was and is necessary for the students to observe the whole picture, a piece within another larger piece of the whole.

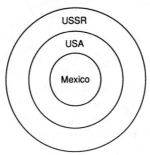

Then the students wrote out the sentences, this time using the other relationship, and figured out the conclusion.

1. *Mexico is smaller than the USA.*
2. *The USA is smaller than the USSR.*

Again they set up their relationships.

NP	LV	relationship	NP	LV	relationship	NP
Mexico	is	*smaller than*	USA	is	*smaller than*	USSR

The conclusion was that Mexico is smaller than the USSR. The children needed to see that both expressions, *Mexico is smaller than the USSR* and *The USSR is larger than Mexico*, mean the same thing. Here the problem of semantics arose again. The deaf students will say that these are two different sentences and cannot mean the same thing, regardless of proof by concrete experiences and Venn diagrams. Factual information, measurements of size and distance, and statistics were all used as verification for students who still did not understand or did not believe it was possible.

It is our basic supposition that this philosophical skill of inquiry must necessarily include the linguistic skills of sentence structure, reversals, and syllogistic sentences as well as the semantics of language as prerequisite for philosophical dialectical relationships. Oleron (1972) indicated that "concepts are basic to such mental operations as judgment and reasoning; and on the other hand, they depend for their information on other operations such as abstraction." The nature of the concept of noun phrases is bound up in the definition and function of the determiner and the quantifier. This point is extremely crucial.

Blackwell (1988) said "the NP is critical in philosophical issues as clear philosophical reasoning is essentially a matter of semantic consistency. In Syllogisms the critical factor is the quantifier in the NP." Thus, there must be the cognitive act plus the language system. Oleron observed that "progress in the use of language and of abstract terms should contribute to the development of conceptual thinking" (1972). If the language base is inadequate or deficient, as in the approximate two-year language delay of the deaf, then these children cannot handle, comprehend, nor accommodate the totally abstract. These abstract concepts depend on print for their explanation. Thus, the deaf child who cannot use print easily cannot deal with these formal abstract concepts without prior language work.

CONCLUSION

We found that by stressing the basic linguistic structure grammatically, deaf students could categorize sentences through similarities. Through analysis the students learned to determine how words are phrased, how they function, and what some of the semantic relationships entail. The students then made great progress in creating reversals and standardizing sentences. Because they could determine which words were nouns or quantifiers, the students could build paradigms of vocabulary for each category. The use of Venn diagrams helped the students clarify relationships and represent them in an understandable and enjoyable way.

Progress was slower in drawing conclusions from information taken from stories. If the information was organized and structured for the students and the inferences made, then they could go through the process of drawing conclusions more easily. It was extremely difficult for them to draw inferences and conclusions if no structure was presented. The students had gone through the process of exposure and were beginning to achieve the level of recognition that necessarily comes before representation.

The students' ability to look at information and concepts from different perspectives increased. The need had arisen for them to use the skills they had learned and to apply them to their daily interactions.

We firmly believe that all subjects can and should be taught reflectively and philosophically, through a Socratic approach. The search and discovery of meaning in a simple fiber like cotton can begin a cognitive revolution, and we can see that philosophical concepts hold together the fabric of curricula.

REFERENCES

Blackwell, P., Engen, E., Fischgrund, J., & Zarcodoolas, C. 1978. *Sentences and other systems: A language curriculum for hearing-impaired.* Washington, DC: Alexander Graham Bell Association.

Blackwell, P. 1988. *Rhode Island School for the Deaf Language Goals.* Providence: Rhode Island School for the Deaf.

Bruner, J. 1977. *The process of education.* Cambridge: Harvard University Press.

Bruner, J., et al. 1966. *Studies in cognitive growth.* New York: John Wiley & Sons.

Cowley, J. 1983. *The red rose.* New Zealand: Shortland Publications.

Dewey, J. 1916. Experience and thinking. In *Democracy and education.* New York: Macmillan Publishing Co.

Geiger, G.R. 1958. *John Dewey in perspective.* New York: Oxford University Press.

Geisser, M.J. 1985. Philosophy: A key to the deaf mind. *Thinking, The Journal of Philosophy for Children* 6(2):36.

Groahke, L., & Tindal, C. 1986. Critical thinking: How to teach good reasoning. *Teaching Philosophy* 10(4):301–318.

Hayward, A. 1987. Review of "Teaching students to think critically: A guide for faculty in all disciplines." *Teaching Philosophy* 10(4):367–368.

Holmes, E.F. 1977. *Amy's goose.* New York: Harper & Row.

Jackendoff, R. 1986. *Semantics and cognition.* Cambridge: MIT Press.

Lipman, M. 1982. *Harry Stottlemeier's discovery.* Montclair, NJ: First Mountain Foundation.

———. 1984. *Philosophical inquiry.* 2d ed. (Manual for *Harry*) Montclair, NJ: First Mountain Foundation & University Press of America.

Lipman, M., Sharp, A.M., & Oscanyan, F. 1980. *Philosophy in the classroom.* 2d ed. Philadelphia, PA: Temple University Press.

Mayer, M. 1968. *If I had.* New York: Dial Press.

McDermott, G. 1975. *The stone cutter.* New York: Viking Press.

McKee, D. 1986. *The hill and the rock.* New York: Puffin Books.

Oleron, P. 1972. Conceptual thinking of the deaf. In *Language in thinking*, ed. P. Adams, 43–49. New York: Penguin USA.

Quigley, L. 1981. *The blind men and the elephant.* New York: Charles Scribner's Sons.

Rembert, R. 1985. Philosophical inquiry among hearing-impaired students. In *Cognition, education, and deafness: Directions for research and instruction.* ed. D. S. Martin, 185–187. Washington, DC: Gallaudet University Press.

St. Exupery, A. 1982. *The little prince*, trans. K. Woods. New York: Harcourt Brace Jovanovich.

Scheffler, I. 1973. *Reason and teaching.* London: Routledge & Kegan Paul.

Silverstein, S. 1964. *The giving tree.* New York: Harper & Row.

Sizer, T.R. 1985. *Horace's compromise: The dilemma of the American high school.* Boston: Houghton Mifflin Co.

Tanz, C. 1978. *An egg is to sit on.* New York: Lothrop, Lee & Shepard Books.

Williams, M. 1983. *The velveteen rabbit.* New York: Holt, Rinehart & Winston.

Cued Speech and Language Acquisition: The Case of Grammatical Gender Morpho-Phonology

Catherine Hage
Jesus Alegria
Olivier Perier

S peechreading is a difficult task for deaf people, and it is all the more so for the young deaf child who has to acquire language from his hearing parents' model, which is basically provided through the lips. Words with identical or similar lip images, the so-called "invisible" phonemes, and the distortions induced by co-articulation are the main factors that make speechreading on its own unreliable, unfit to allow clear perception of spoken language and consequently a poor support for language acquisition.

Cued Speech (CS), designed by Cornett in 1967 and adapted to French under the name of Langage Parle Complete (LPC), is a set of systematic manual gestures made near the mouth while speaking, aimed at eliminating these drawbacks of speechreading. The combination of these gestures or cues with the normally available speechreading information is supposed to produce clear and precise visualization of spoken language.

Currently available data show that school children familiar with CS can use it efficiently to understand spoken language, since sentences presented with CS are better understood than similar sentences presented without cues. This has been shown for English Cued Speech by Nicholls and Ling (1982) and for its French version by Perier, Charlier, Hage, and Alegria in 1984. These results demonstrate that CS is indeed efficient in reducing the ambiguities inherent in speechreading.

At present there are little systematic data concerning the possibility of developing an ordinary language competence using CS as a source. Current observations of several profoundly deaf children with whom CS has been used consistently from the very beginning suggest that it develops that competence. Their spoken language understanding reaches levels closely approximating those of normally hearing children of the same age. However, no systematic analyses of their linguistic abilities are available to date, nor is it yet clear what cognitive mechanisms are involved in the processing of CS information.

A series of experiments probing the cognitive question has been carried out, utilizing the priming paradigm in a lexical decision task on written material (see Alegria, Lechat & Leybaert 1988 for a preliminary report). The underlying hypothesis was that CS could contribute to the establishment of visual representations, giving access to the corresponding words, equivalent to the phonological ones built up through audition in hearing children. Until now these experiments have not yielded clear-cut results. This situation might be due to the fact that too few children with whom CS was utilized from infancy were available for those studies. It is intended to resume and expand investigations along this line now that more and more CS-raised children are reaching reading competency.

Another current line of study in this laboratory is the collection of data concerning features of the language acquisition process. We plan to study a series of problems selected because they are recognized as especially difficult for deaf children educated by traditional aural-oral methods or by Total Communication. Some aspects of the linguistic competence precociously acquired by the normally hearing child are absent in the deaf, perhaps because of the opacity of speech-reading signals. Typical French language morphology is usually expressed by affixes that are difficult to perceive in speechreading. Moreover, function words such as articles, prepositions, logical connectors, etc. which serve syntactic purposes, are often unstressed monosyllabic words. It is well established that deaf children have greater difficulties with these than with the so-called "open class" items like nouns, adjectives, verb radicals, etc. The general hypothesis underlying the present research is that CS, inasmuch as it reveals the entire oral message, should have specific effects upon morpho-syntactic development.

Most of the available literature on the mastery of morpho-syntax has been done in English and, not surprisingly, relate to problems encountered in the endings *-ing, -ed, -s, -er, -est,* for example. Studies bearing on knowledge of morphology in orally educated deaf students conclude that 19-year-old deaf subjects fail to reach the level of 9-year-old hearing controls (Cooper 1967). More recently a study dealing with some fine aspects of Italian morpho-syntax shows a delayed development in tasks involving clitic pronouns and a qualitatively different pattern of results in the use of articles, but a normal development in pluralization (Taeschner, Devescovi & Volterra 1988).

Grammatical gender in French is a good example of morpho-syntactic information that is partially carried by word endings. Several studies have demonstrated that word endings do intervene in deciding whether a French word is masculine or feminine (Seguin 1969; Tucker, Lambert & Rigault 1977; Desrochers, Paivio & Desrochers 1989). Studies on the acquisition of grammatical gender by normally hearing children have shown that by the age of three they exploit the difference between typically feminine word endings such as *-ine, -aille,* and *-ette,* and masculine ones such as *-oir, -eau,* and *-on,* to determine the grammatical gender of words (Karmiloff-Smith 1979).

Models of grammatical gender development assume that children progressively associate word endings with other syntactic markers, such as articles that precede nouns in French. Grammatical gender mastery is a typical example of morpho-syntactic rules that hearing children acquire effortlessly through simple immersion from infancy in their mother language. Mastery of gender has not been studied with deaf children. It is generally taken for granted that this is an ability to which deaf children have a limited access.

This experiment dealt with the ability of profoundly deaf children who have had intensive CS practice to determine grammatical gender by using the morpho-phonological cues present on word endings. The hypothesis is that CS, because of its capacity to reveal critical information, could play a specific role in the acquisition of this ability.

The experimenter presented the subject with series of pictures representing words while naming them in CS. The child had to repeat the word, adding the corresponding masculine or feminine article. The items were 60 nouns, half of them selected from the children's current vocabulary and the other half made up of infrequently-used words not in the children's lexicon. Ten words in each category had typical feminine endings, ten others had masculine ones, and the last ten were unmarked (i.e., their endings were neither typically feminine nor typically masculine). Half of the unmarked words were masculine and the other half feminine.

Nine subjects participated in the experiment. They were all prelingually profoundly deaf (more than 90 dB mean loss). They have had intensive CS practice. Six of them have had CS at home before the age of two. The other three have had CS only at school, but for at least eight years.

The mean percentage of correct responses for familiar words reached 97%, 89%, and 89% in the masculine, feminine, and unmarked conditions respectively, indicating that the subjects do master grammatical gender and that they correctly utilize the corresponding article. These results alone do not allow us to know whether the child determines the grammatical gender of the words using phonological cues or whether they are known by heart. To establish the exact origin of these correct responses, the results concerning unfamiliar items must be considered. The corresponding scores in this case reached 73%, 78%, and 50% correct. These results show that the subjects are totally unable to determine the gender of the unmarked items. Indeed, correct responses for 50% of the unmarked words correspond exactly to the chance level. The performance, however, increases in a substantial and significant manner from unmarked to marked items (Wilcoxon, $p <.025$; unilateral). This result demonstrates that without phonological gender cues, the child cannot decide whether a noun is feminine or masculine, except for the familiar words. If such cues are introduced, as in the unfamiliar but marked items, the child can then give a correct answer.

In conclusion, subjects know the grammatical gender of words from two different sources, one lexical and rote-based, and the other productive, through a rule-based process. Let us briefly comment on each and speculate on their possible origins.

The difference in performance between familiar and unfamiliar unmarked words compels us to introduce the notion of a lexical source of knowledge about grammatical gender. With the unfamiliar unmarked words, the child cannot base a response on morpho-phonological cues, because they do not exist. In this case, the children were totally unable to determine the gender of the items. Therefore, that ability with familiar words indicates that children have stored them in association with a label concerning their gender.

Because lexical knowledge about gender is absent in unfamiliar items, the performance obtained with marked unfamiliar words implies an authentic generative competence exclusively based on morpho-phonological cues. The results on those items were not perfect, indicating that the association between word endings and grammatical gender is only partially established and/or partially productive. More work is necessary to explore this alternative.

The acquisition of gender probably follows a sequence in which the child first memorizes a series of forms from his parents' speech and progressively invents rules that generate these forms productively. Connectionists' accounts of language development have recently tried to eliminate this distinction between rote and rule-based sources of performance (see Rumelhart & McClelland's [1986] well-known work on the acquisition of the English past tense). Pinker and Price (in press) have pointed out a number of problems with this unified account and have argued that distinct mechanisms are necessary. Whatever the issue of this debate, the important point concerning the role of CS in morpho-syntactic development is that in any case the system needs a set of noun words with a complete phonological representation of each, and an independent way to classify them into gender categories. This second function could be carried out by associating with each noun the accompanying masculine or feminine article (and the other determiners, which are also marked for gender). For both the article and the phonological mark carried by the noun itself, CS is particularly efficient. The present data, though preliminary, suggest that the above mechanism is at work. It is necessary to compare these results with those of adequate control subjects who have not been exposed to CS. However, given the usual low levels of achievement of deaf children in this domain, it is not unreasonable to suppose that CS has played an important part in allowing the subjects to achieve grammatical gender mastery through a cognitive process similar to the one used by normally hearing children.

REFERENCES

Alegria, J., Lechat, J., & Leybaert, J. 1988. Role du LPC dans l'identification des mots chez l'enfant sourd: Theorie et donnees preliminaires. *Glossa*, 9:36–44.

Cooper, R.L. 1967. The ability of deaf and hearing children to apply morphological rules. *Journal of Speech and Hearing Research* 10:77–86.

Cornett, R.O. 1967. Cued speech. *American Annals of the Deaf* 112:3–13.

Desrochers, A., Paivio, A., & Desrochers, S. 1989. L'effet de la frequence d'usage des noms inanimes et de la valeur predictive de leur terminaison sur l'identification du genre grammatical. *Revue Canadienne de Psychologie* 43(1):62–73.

Hage, C., & Alegria, J. L'acquisition du genre grammatical chez l'enfant expose au LPC: Resultats preliminaires. Communication presentee au Premier Congres International du LPC, Bruxelles, 26–27 Novembre 1988.

Karmiloff-Smith, A. 1979. A functional approach to child language. Cambridge, England: Cambridge University Press.

Nicholls, G.H., & Ling, D. 1982. Cued Speech and the reception of spoken language. *Journal of Speech and Hearing Research* 25:262–269.

Perier, O., Charlier, B., Hage, C., & Alegria, J. 1988. Evaluation of the effects of prolonged Cued Speech practice upon the reception of spoken language. In *The education of the deaf: Current perspectives*, ed. I.G. Taylor, 616–628. Kent, England: Croom Helm Publishing.

Pinker, S., & Price, A. In press. Rules and connections in human language. In *Parallel distributed processing: Implications for psychology and neurosciences*, ed. R.G. Morris. Oxford: Oxford University Press.

Rumelhart, D.E., & McClelland, J.L. 1985. On learning the past tenses of verbs. In *Parallel distributed processing: Exploration in the microstructure of cognition, Volume 2: Psychological and biological models*, ed. J.L. McClelland, D.E. Rumelhart & The PDP Research Group. Cambridge: Bradford Books/MIT Press.

Taeschner, T., Devescovi, A., & Volterra, V. 1988. Affixes and function words in written language of deaf children. *Applied Psycholinguistics* 9:385–401.

Teaching Metacognitive Reading Comprehension Techniques to Gallaudet University Freshmen

Robert E. McDonald

The reading difficulty of college textbooks is a challenge faced by all college students. However, in facing this challenge, many deaf college students lack the comprehension strategies they need to make textbook study profitable and efficient. A recently developed reading-comprehension course for Gallaudet University freshmen gives them practice in using a set of comprehension techniques that they may immediately apply to their textbook study in other courses.

The reading comprehension of students entering Gallaudet's English program is tested using the Degrees of Reading Power Test (DRP). Mean Instructional-Level scores for that group have recently ranged between 62 and 64. The reading difficulty of textbooks is about 70 DRP units, a level at which many Gallaudet freshmen experience frustration. Although students take the DRP test again at the end of the new course, it is not specifically aimed at improving performance on this test. At present, scores on the DRP have no bearing on course grades.

Instead, the new course is seen as a cornerstone for future programs promoting improved reading comprehension and learning throughout undergraduate studies. Planning is already under way to train tutors to help students apply this course's reading-comprehension techniques to studies across the disciplines. Plans are also being made to help instructors across the disciplines to exploit metacognitive-comprehension techniques in the work required in their courses. In other words, developers of the course believe that wide application of these techniques should be valued over short-term improvement in test performance.

Description of the Course

The course is designed around the assumption that reading is not so much a process of decoding text as it is a process of *constructing meaning*—by drawing together the reader's relevant prior knowledge, the cues of the text, and its context. To promote active construction of meaning, students are given frequent opportunities to predict meanings, to ask teacher-like questions, to summarize, and to explain relationships between ideas. These four essential devices of comprehension derive from the work of Palincsar and Brown, and were selected for this course because the four processes entail most of the major skills of comprehension. To these the designers of the course have added vocabulary management techniques.

Predicting, questioning, summarizing, and explaining are practiced within the context of two overarching class activities: the Multiple Reading Strategy and conceptual mapping or graphing, usually instructor-led activities.

The Multiple Reading Strategy

The Multiple Reading Strategy (MRS) is essentially a way of getting students to read a text several times, each time with a different purpose. It leads the students through several processes: predicting the contents of the text; a timed reading to discover the main idea and perhaps the main supporting points; an untimed reading for fuller comprehension, and validation of the predictions.

Prediction of the contents of the text is intended to activate students' schemata and prepare them to read actively. The object of the timed reading for main and supporting ideas is a mental or graphic outline of the text (some instructors may use the activity as the basis for a conceptual web that can later be elaborated by students). Following the untimed reading, the class returns to the predictions to see which were accurate, and here it is intended that students recognize that they were able to make valid predictions, that predictions improve engagement with the subject and therefore promote better comprehension, and that even irrelevant predictions help one attend to new information.

Conceptual Graphing

Conceptual graphing or "mapping" is an opportunity for students to create a new schema for the information of the reading material. To the linear dimension of outlines and summaries, graphing adds a spatial dimension that is thought to involve deeper mental processing of the information. The practice has obvious links with the architectural metaphors used by ancient orators in the process of *memoria*, the memorizing of the arguments of a speech, and it has long been used as a recall technique by test-takers and writers. But the full importance of ideas and their relationships has yet to be fully understood.

Students who are new to this activity or who have done conceptual mapping in lower grades tend to begin with simple web or wheel graphs, arranging supporting ideas around a central subject or main idea. However, faced with complex text structures and the models of the instructor, they soon recognize these early attempts as little more valuable than an exploded list. Subsequent elaborations begin to reflect not only connections between ideas, but also larger organizing principles such as cause-effect or problem-solution.

Depending on the place in the course and the difficulty of the reading material, conceptual graphs may be completed by the class, started by the class and finished by groups, pairs, or individuals, or done entirely by individuals. Often graphs are started in class, finished for homework, and shared in the following class.

Comprehension Monitoring

Comprehension monitoring is usually managed by students working in pairs. It draws heavily on the work of Palincsar and Brown, but one difference from Reciprocal Teaching is that the instructor in this course is usually not a member of the pair. Class size and the pace and intensity of college-level work would prevent instructors from monitoring the comprehension of individual students more than a few times during the course. However, the students in this course are adults and can be trained to monitor comprehension in a very short time. Even before they develop much expertise at it, it seems a worthwhile activity. They are active, they accept responsibility for their own learning, and they take pleasure in assisting each other's learning.

Students alternate in the roles of comprehension monitor and responder. During this activity, the monitor may refer to the text and the conceptual graph. The responder tries to answer the monitor's questions from memory, but they may both consult the text to resolve disagreements. Monitors are trained to ask questions about the central idea and supporting points (summarizing), about relationship between ideas or especially difficult points (explaining), and they may finally ask responders to predict outcomes of situations discussed in the readings or to relate ideas of the reading to their personal lives or previous knowledge.

One may ask what sense it makes, after all the work of MSR and conceptual graphing, to begin comprehension monitoring. Does this activity not go back over the same territory? For the responder it partly does, but this time the responder is working from memory of the material and the graph. As one instructor has expressed it, making the graph creates schema; monitoring requires the new schema to be used. Moreover, the monitor puts pressure on the responder's understanding that usually leads to elaboration of schemata and may also lead to revisions of the conceptual graph.

If the primary activity of the responder in this paired work is cognition (the process of constructing meaning), then the primary activity of the monitor is metacognition (assessing the process, recognizing breakdowns in comprehension, and knowing enough about the reading process to choose alternate techniques when comprehension fails). The intention of repeated practice is that students will internalize the activity and be able to apply it to their own reading both in and outside this course.

Initial reactions to the new course from both students and instructors are positive, although some instructors are frustrated by the feeling that gains shown by students in class are not strongly enough reflected in gains on the DRP test.

Gains during early offerings of the course have ranged between 3.7 and 4.8 DRP units.

Teaching this course has involved learning a new set of teaching behaviors, and to support each other in this process, instructors meet for at least an hour a week to discuss methodology, practice the techniques offered to students, share materials, and develop tests. After the first semester instructors decided to put together an instructors' workshop for the beginning of the following semester with the purpose of introducing new instructors to the course and sharpening the skills of veterans. That workshop was attended by thirteen instructors in the Fall 1989 semester (all of those scheduled to teach the course), and it has grown to three full days of activity.

Instructors find this a stimulating course to teach. They see students taking a much more active role in learning than in courses where cooperation is not encouraged. They also feel that the dialogue and collaboration with other instructors is enriching and sustaining. As more and more instructors have the opportunity to practice metacognitive comprehension techniques, it seems appropriate for the techniques to be tapped in other studies across the disciplines. Such continuity would give students a greater sense of the fundamental coherence of studies in different disciplines and would offer opportunities for faculty members to strengthen links of collegiality.

REFERENCES

August, D. L., Flavell, J.H., & Clift, R. 1984 Comparison of monitoring of skilled and less skilled readers. *Reading Research Quarterly* 20:39–53.

Heimlich, J.E., & Pittelman, S.D. 1986. *Semantic mapping: Classroom applications.* Newark, Delaware: International Reading Association.

Hoffman, J.V., & Rutherford, W.L. 1984. Effective reading programs: A critical review of outlier studies. *Reading Research Quarterly* 20:79–92.

Palincsar, A.S., & Brown, A.L. 1984. Reciprocal teaching of comprehension-fostering and comprehension-monitoring activities. *Cognition and Instruction* 2:117–175.

Patching, W. et al. 1983. Direct instruction in critical reading skills. *Reading Research Quarterly* 18:406–418.

Pearson, P. D., & Gallagher, M.C. The instruction of reading comprehension, *Contemporary Educational Psychology* 8:317–342.

Pearson, P. D., & Johnson, D.D. 1972. *Teaching reading comprehension.* New York: Holt, Rinehart & Winston.

Pearson, P. D., & Spiro, R. 1982. Toward a theory of reading comprehension instruction. *Trends in research in teaching.* New Brunswick, NJ: Rutgers University Press.

Stewart, O., & Tei, E. 1983. Some implications of metacognition for reading instruction. *Journal of Reading* October, 36–43.

Weinstein, C.E., & Rogers, B.T. 1986. Comprehension monitoring: The neglected learning strategy. *Journal of Developmental Education* 9(1):6–29.

Whimbey, A., & Lockhead, J. 1982. *Problem solving and comprehension.* 3rd ed. Philadelphia: Franklin Institute Press.

Early Intervention and Cognitive Development in Deaf Individuals

Richard C. Nowell

For some years there have been various programs available to provide early intervention for deaf children, especially in the form of parent training. These programs in general have focused on attacking the primary and most obvious influence of deafness—delayed and inadequate language development in oral and written English. The widely accepted view of Piaget (1966) that sensorimotor learning is the basis for later cognitive and language learning and that learning requires active participation by the learner seems to contradict an emphasis in early intervention with deaf children on the reception and expression of speech and the general development of "language skill."

Based upon Piagetian theory, we may conclude that the deaf child's early cognitive growth, like that of the hearing child, is based largely upon nonverbal experiences, even though an effective verbal communication system will contribute greatly to making learning processes more effective and more efficient. Most current early education approaches, however, are largely designed to optimize the potential of verbal development (usually translated as English development and often as oral English).

The tasks facing educators of deaf children are

1. to develop an educational framework that provides the appropriate goals for early intervention activities;
2. to identify the most critical components of early intervention on which to focus limited resources in the educational system; and
3. to develop specific strategies that will optimize the effectiveness of early intervention.

Obviously these tasks are extensive and beyond the constraints of this text. However, let us address them briefly by discussing some aspects of developing a framework for such a program and presenting specific strategies for direct intervention and service delivery concerns. Our primary goal is to suggest sensible strategies for optimizing outcomes for deaf people in terms of accepted theoretical constructs and practicality in providing specific services.

In determining desired goals for a cognitively oriented early intervention program, research does not clearly define for us the relationships of specific cognitive differences between deaf and hearing children (see, for example, Liben 1978) to educational and daily life-skill functioning (Wolk 1985). However, there is a general consensus that our educational system is not succeeding in producing deaf graduates who are functioning as close to their potential as is needed to succeed as well as hearing people in postsecondary education or on the job. There also seems to be a consensus that the "system" is to blame more than the actual hearing disability. Therefore we must seek to enrich the cognitive program for the deaf child. The suggestion here is that we must start with early intervention programs, given the likelihood of continued influence on later programming.

Although there are obviously important concerns regarding influences of early intervention on socioemotional and language development, the effects of methods of intervention on cognition are also critical. If cognitive development is seen as a natural result of intervention affecting language development and parent support, the benefits for cognition will not be optimal. If intervention strategies are basically oriented around the development of communication and language, cognitive development may suffer.[1]

A general intervention model based on the previously stated theory would be one couched in a Piagetian developmental framework, stressing the sequential development of skills and the child's active, self-directed participation, even though within the developmental framework, behavioral techniques may be used to facilitate the learning of individual tasks. In general, a program must encourage disequilibrium to promote cognitive development (Athey 1985)—a situation directly opposed to the typical controlled teaching used by many parents of deaf children.

Strategies

Most cognitive programming seems to be focused on the secondary and postsecondary deaf student. Although cognitive programming has limited application in early intervention programs, we do know from research in this area that such programming can be successful.

---

[1] The focus of this paper is on cognition. A strong argument may be made that the most important aspect of any intervention is its effect on the affective development of the individual and the family. We personally believe in a program that seeks to meet the psychological needs of the deaf child's parents and to help that child to grow up well-adjusted and happy. There is no reason why both cognitive and affective needs cannot be met in the same program, although we have not addressed the affective realm here.

Specific techniques for stimulating cognitive abilities in deaf infants and toddlers need to be developed, applied, and studied. The following are only a few suggestions to initiate this effort. They are not meant to exclude other approaches because there is no evidence that they cannot be applied in the context of current approaches, and, indeed, many programs already use some related techniques.

Provide an Enriching Environment

For the deaf infant or toddler, the environment should be as stimulating as possible. Tendencies on the part of parents to be more protective of deaf children, reservations by parents about taking the child outdoors because of embarrassment, other adjustment problems related to the child's deafness, and any other situations that restrict the child's exposure to the world must be overcome. Obviously one implication is that parent counseling may be crucial to the cognitive development of the child as well as to the mental health of the parents. Parents should be encouraged to provide all types of experiences for the deaf child despite their reservations as to whether the deaf child receives as much benefit as the child who can hear.

Foster Communication[2]

To encourage deaf children to communicate, some type of response should be required from them in situations where parents often provide for children's needs without any request made by the child. During general communication, parents should use a systematic delay approach to give children an opportunity to respond and to help them learn that communicative actions are important and expected (Downing & Siegel-Causey 1988). Parents and other family members must not only initiate communication directly to the child, but also in turn must give the child their undivided attention, making it evident that some type of response is expected. By recognizing the child's gesture, actions, facial expression, and body posture, by interpreting these expressions, and by responding to the child's intended message in some way, parents are reinforcing behaviors that will be a basis for later language learning. Professional training of parents may be necessary to establish this process.

Structure Play

Play is the real business of young children, aiding in physical and social development. It is also a source of stimulation for early cognitive development. Visiting the home and training parents to be more attentive to the elements involved in

---

[2] Portions of this section are taken from a grant application to the U.S. Office of Special Education, entitled "Demonstration Project for Early Intervention with Hearing-impaired Infants and Toddlers and their Families in a Rural Environment." Much of the communication technique was developed by Dr. Muriel Munro.

play situations will help them to make play a better learning experience for the deaf child.

Develop Representational Thought and Distancing

Perhaps the most important aspect of cognitive intervention in the early years is the use of techniques that help the child deal with objects, actions, or events in a time-space context that is different from the present. Copple, Sigel, and Saunders (1979) call situations or actions that require this cognitive action by the child *distancing*. Although discussions of the application of distancing seem to assume that the child can use verbal labels, there may be ways to accomplish the intent of the method without using spoken words or signs. For example, actual photographs or other pictorial representations could be used with deaf infants and toddlers in the same way they are used with some multihandicapped deaf children (Murdza & Nowell 1980). In general, the principles used in the application of communication boards with other populations may be helpful in developing communication and thinking skills in young deaf children.

Use an Effective Communication System

Quigley and Kretschmer (1982) state that one of the primary concerns in facilitating successful education of deaf children is an early effective communication system. This statement seems to be supported within the theoretical and applied context discussed here. That is, how is a deaf child to receive the important information required to develop cognitive functions without effective communication patterns? Given the general advantages of a sign system (Greenburg 1978) and evidence that early oral intervention may be ineffective (Goppold 1988), logic seems to call for the early use of sign language with deaf infants and toddlers. Grant (1987) suggests that it is the content and function of language that is most important in the early years of the deaf child's life, not the form. The importance of form comes later. No one in the field denies that it is desirable for deaf children to develop oral communication. Oral language skills, however, must not be developed at the expense of early cognitive development. Effective communication, as early as possible, is crucial.

Many children who in the past would not have been able to use their hearing effectively can do so now because of better amplification and auditory training techniques. For those children who cannot use their hearing as at least a strong supportive system, the need for sign language in early years seems obvious. There will always be some children who do not clearly fall into one of these two groups, and there will be children whose parents will insist that oralism be used exclusively, despite a poor prognosis for effective communication in the early years. For these children, using representative materials similar to the communication boards used by other disabled children may provide the communication necessary for early cognitive stimulation. This technique may in fact be useful as well for signing and successful oral deaf children.

Be Aware of Socioemotional Concerns

As we continue to see increases in early intervention and specialists continue to train parents to work with their deaf children, we must be aware of the danger of substituting teaching for the parents' other roles. As parents ask us what is most important for them to do now that they know their child is deaf, the appropriate response is "to be a good parent—to provide a loving, caring environment in which the child can grow up." Early cognitive development is important and the parents' roles are crucial, but they must not become teachers first and parents second, or the effects on the deaf child may not be positive.

These suggestions, then, constitute a system for promoting planned cognitive growth in the young deaf child. Readers are urged to experiment with this list and amplify it in their efforts to maximize that cognitive development.

REFERENCES

Athey, I. 1985. Theories and models of human development: Their implications for the education of deaf adolescents. In *Cognition, education, and deafness: Directions for research and instruction*, ed. D.S. Martin, 22–26. Washington, DC: Gallaudet University Press.

Copple, C., Sigel, I.E., & Saunders, R. 1979. *Educating the young thinker: Classroom strategies for cognitive growth*. New York: Van Nostrand.

Downing, J.E., & Siegel-Causey, E. 1988. Enhancing the non-symbolic communicative behavior of children with multiple impairments. *Language, Speech, and Hearing in Schools* 19:338–348.

Goppold, L. 1988. Early intervention for preschool deaf children: The longitudinal academic effects relative to program methodology. *American Annals of the Deaf* 133:285–288.

Grant, J. 1987. *The hearing impaired: Birth to six*. Boston: College-Hill Press.

Greenburg, M.T. 1978. Attachment, behavior, communicative competence, and parental attitudes in preschool deaf children. Ph.D. diss., University of Virginia.

Liben, L.S. 1978. Developmental perspectives on the experiential deficiencies of deaf children. In *Deaf children: Developmental perspectives*, ed. L.S. Liben, 195–215. New York: Academic Press.

Murdza, S., & Nowell, R.C. 1980. The use of language boards with multiply handicapped, hearing impaired children. In *A handbook on the education of multiply handicapped, hearing impaired children*, ed. R.C. Nowell, 57–63. University Park, PA: Pennsylvania State University. ERIC Document No. ED193 834.

Piaget, J. 1986. *The psychology of intelligence*. Totowa, NJ: Littlefield, Adams & Co.

Quigley, S.P., & Kretschmer, R.E. 1982. *The education of deaf children: Issues, theory, and practice*. Baltimore, MD: University Park Press.

Wolk, S. 1985. A macroanalysis of the research on deafness and cognition. In *Cognition, education and deafness: Directions for research and instruction*, ed. D.S. Martin, 202–208. Washington, DC: Gallaudet University Press.

The Interaction of Mental Imagery and Cognitive Styles in the Retention of Prose Among Deaf College Students

Fatemeh Olia

T he question of how learners could benefit most from their classroom experiences remains an exciting area of investigation and a particular challenge when the educational needs of special learners are addressed. Among many variables existing in the instructional setting, learners' field dependent/independent cognitive styles—especially their ability to construct mental imagery—have been interesting topics for research in recent years. These two variables in terms of retention of verbal information are suggested to be interactive and predictive of individuals' learning outcome among hearing individuals (Walker, O'Leary & Chaney 1979; Carrier, Joseph, Krey & LaCroix 1983). This study examined the role of field dependent/independent cognitive style and induced mental imagery as a learning strategy in retention of prose among deaf learners. The ability of deaf learners to construct mental images was hypothesized to vary according to the learners' field dependent/independent cognitive styles. Further, it was hypothesized that those deaf learners who can actively form clear and relevant mental images can retain verbal information more successfully.

The first variable—mental imagery—refers to the images that exist in visual, auditory, or even kinesthetic form in one's mind. The use of mental images, produced voluntarily or as a result of direct instruction, can be considered a mental skill when an individual tries to receive, retain, or recall information, or to solve problems. To illustrate, the reader should try to remember the sensation of the early morning spring breeze, mentally locate the state of Rhode Island, or compare an orange with a lemon in color, weight, and texture. The conclusion from these exercises is that much of our thinking happens in the form of mental pictures with or without our conscious effort. Aristotle said, "The soul never thinks without a mental picture."

Some people are more skillful than others in using imagery intentionally in their mental activities, and as a result they are more successful in recalling and retaining information. Most important, they are also more successful in solving problems. The ability to create mental images is part of one's cognitive development, similar to the development of language and motor behavior. Piaget (1952) explained that imaginal abilities develop as a result of neurological differentiation during the pre-operational stage of a child's cognitive growth. He asserted that a certain degree of neurological maturation is necessary before thinking can also be represented in the form of images. Gradually, as the brain develops, the left and right hemispheres become clearly lateralized and specialized in certain functions: The left hemisphere processes verbal and sequential information, and the right processes imaginal-patterns. The revival of interest in research on mental imagery after 50 years of neglect was primarily stimulated by the extensive work of Paivio (1972). Recently, mental imagery instruction and training to facilitate learning and retention has gained special attention (Kosslyn 1975; Paivio & Foth 1970; Paivio, Yuille & Smythe 1966; Simon 1972; Sternberg & Weil 1980; Thorndyke & Stasz 1980). Most often the training involves specific programs to improve the vividness of voluntarily produced images (Richardson 1983), similar to training for drawing lessons. Research involving deaf learners also demonstrates the facilitative potential of mental imagery in learning under different conditions (Heinen & Stock 1974; Kelly 1976; Parasnis 1980; Reese & Parkington 1973).

The second variable examined in this research was the role of field dependent/independent cognitive styles in the individual's learning of verbal information. Cognitive styles are the "characteristic, self-consistent modes of functioning that individuals show in their perceptual and intellectual activities" (Witkin et al. 1971). Field dependence/independence refers to one's ability to disembed organized perceptual and intellectual tasks. A field dependent (FD) individual perceives parts of an organized task to be fused with the overall whole, while a field independent (FI) individual analyzes a task and can disembed the parts as discrete from the organized ground.

One of the oldest known visual games, Tangram, can be used to demonstrate (Read 1965). Tangram is an ancient Chinese puzzle consisting of seven simple pieces in geometrical shapes that can be put together in an extraordinary variety of ways. As one tries to solve a Tangram puzzle, one should observe the mental technique used. Is perception so dominated by the overall structure of the puzzle that it deters the learner from finding the location of each piece in the whole organization of the form? Or in the mind's eye, can the learner position, lift, move, and locate the place of each piece in the *background* of the complete design? Those who fall in the first category could be assumed to be FD or global thinkers; those in the latter would be FI or analytical thinkers.

Most often the test for field dependent/independent cognitive styles is the Embedded Figures Test (Witkin et al. 1971). The test consists of 18 complex figures and several simple forms. The participant is to find the previously seen designated simple form within a complex design. The scores range from 0–18, lowest to highest, respectively; however, the median varies from one group to another. To be FD or FI is not to occupy a distinct location on the continuum of 0–18, but instead to be somewhere about the two poles within several points below or above the median. In general, research has indicated that we all become more field independent as we go through the educational system that teaches us to make outlines, to design projects step by step, and to think analytically. Witkin et al. (1971) conclude that dependent/independent cognitive styles are not IQ-related, although they are influenced by the individual's sex, age, and social-cultural background. Furthermore, field dependent/independent cognitive styles exist in persons who are born handicapped in one or both sense modalities (Fiebert 1967; Witkin et al. 1968).

In this research project, three major questions were examined.

1. Does induced mental imagery enhance retention of verbal information significantly when given through signed English?
2. Learners with which cognitive style, field dependent or field independent, are significantly better in retention of information when presented in signed English and lecture form?
3. Is there an interaction effect between induced mental imagery and field dependent/independent cognitive styles?

The participants were 72 undergraduate deaf students between the ages of 18 and 25. They were divided into two groups—one receiving mental imagery instruction and the other no mental imagery instruction. At the beginning of each session the subjects in the experimental group received a brief training program in effectively forming mental images when presented with verbal information, while the control group was given training in relaxation techniques. Following the training program both groups watched three videotaped short stories, each with five paragraphs in signed English. There was a 15-second pause after each paragraph during which the experimental group was instructed to form mental pictures, while the control group relaxed. A multiple-choice test on the three stories and the Embedded Figures Test were given to students at the end of the session.

The subject's scores on the EFT ranged from 0–18, with a median of 9. To establish two distinct groups of FD and FI, those scoring 9 were excluded from the sample. Statistical analysis of the data indicated that forming mental images, regardless of the individual's cognitive style, enhances retention of verbal information significantly at the .034 level of confidence. A significant variable in retention of verbal information was cognitive style. The difference between the FD mean scores of 11.26 and 13.15 for FI was significant at almost the .01 level. The analysis of data also showed an interaction between the variables of cognitive styles and mental imagery. Both FD and FI participants benefited from imagery instruction; however, the field-independent group scored significantly higher than the field-dependent group.

The purpose of the study was to test the role of mental imagery in the retention of verbal information among deaf learners in a classroom setting. The overall conclusion from the study was that the production of self-generated mental images facilitates mental skill in retention of verbal information. Two specific inferences could also be made: The conventional lecture method seems more appropriate for FI learners than for FD learners, and FI learners can benefit significantly more from mental imagery instruction than can FD learners.

Another implication from this study would be the need to introduce instructional materials and strategies in more than one format to satisfy the learning needs of both FD and FI learners. Moreover, learners should be encouraged to form mental pictures while attending lectures, considering that this technique is easy and quick to teach.

REFERENCES

Carrier, C., Joseph, M.R., Krey, C.L., & LaCroix, P. 1983. Supplied visuals and imagery instructions in field independent and field dependent children's recall. *Educational Communication and Teaching Journal* 31(3):153–160.

Fiebert, M. 1967. Cognitive styles in the deaf. *Perceptual and Motor Skills* 24:319–329.

Heinen, J.R., & Stock, W.A. 1974. Modality-specific imagery and associative learning in the deaf and hearing. *Bulletin of the Psychonomic Society* 4(5a):462–464.

Kelly, R. 1976. Deaf children's hemispheric processing of words and pictures visually presented to the hemifields. *Dissertation Abstracts International* 37(7b):3664.

Kosslyn, S.M. 1975. Information representation in visual images. *Cognitive Psychology* 7:341–370.

Paivio, A. 1972. A theoretical analysis of the role of imagery in learning and memory. In *The function and nature of imagery*, ed. P.W. Sheehan. New York: Academic Press.

Paivio, A., & Foth, D. 1970. Imaginal and verbal mediators and noun concreteness in paired associate learning: The elusive interaction. *Journal of Verbal Learning and Verbal Behavior* 9:384–390.

Paivio, A., Yuille, C., & Smythe, P.C. 1966. Stimulus and response abstractness, imagery and meaningfulness, and reported mediators in paired-associate learning. *Canadian Journal of Psychology* 20:362–377.

Parasnis, I. 1980. The effect of imagery on memory for signs and words. *Dissertation Abstracts International* 41(6b):2367.

Piaget, J. 1969. *The origin of intelligence in children*. New York: Basic Books.

Read, R.C. 1965. *Tangrams 330 Puzzles*. New York: Dover Publications, Inc.

Reese, H.W., & Parkington, J.J. 1973. Intralist interference and imagery in deaf and hearing children. *Journal of Experimental Child Psychology* 26:165–183.

Richardson, A. 1980. Imagery: Definition and types. In *Imagery: Current theory and human memory*, ed. A.A. Sheikh. New York: St. Martin's Press.

Simon, H.A. 1972. What is visual imagery? An information processing interpretation. In *Cognition in learning and memory*, ed. L.W. Gregg. New York: John Wiley & Sons.

Sternberg, R.J., & Weil, E.M. 1980. An aptitude X strategy interaction in linear syllogistic reasoning. *Journal of Educational Psychology* 72:226–239.

Thorndyke, P.W., & Stasz, C. 1980. Individual differences in procedures for knowledge acquisition from maps. *Cognitive Psychology* 12:127–175.

Walker, M.R., O'Leary, M.R., & Chaney, T.M. 1979. Influence of cognitive style on an incidental memory task. *Perceptual and Motor Skills* 48:195–198.

Witkin, H.A. 1950. Individual differences in ease of perception of embedded figures. *Journal of Personality* 19:1–15.

Witkin, H.A., & Oltman, P.K. 1968. Cognitive style: International journal patterning in congenitally totally blind children. *Child Development* 39:768–786.

Witkin, H.A., Oltman, P.K, Raskin, E., & Karp, S. 1971. *Embedded Figures Test manual.* Palo Alto, CA: Consulting Psychologists Press.

Problem-Solving: A Vehicle for Developing Metacognition in Hearing-Impaired Students

Glenda J. Senior

Metacognition refers to the "deliberate conscious control of one's own cognitive actions" (Brown 1980, p. 453), which implies an active control over knowledge that has been acquired almost subconsciously. Many hearing-impaired students, like their hearing peers, have been exposed to schooling that places an emphasis on the answer rather than on the process by which an answer is reached. Thus, these students have had limited experience in analyzing their cognitive actions in order to develop a conscious awareness of and control over them. This paper proposes problem-solving as a suitable vehicle for identifying and developing metacognitive skills in low achieving hearing-impaired college students.

Problem-Solving and Academic Performance

Although Bloom and Broder (1950) recognized that several factors may account for academic achievement differences between "high" and "low aptitude" college students, a preliminary study of the problem-solving processes of such students led these authors to conclude: "It was our judgment that the differences in their success in problem-solving were as marked as the differences in their academic achievement . . . [and] some of the differences in achievement could be accounted for by differences in methods of attacking problems" (p. 25).

Investigation into covert thinking processes cannot be accomplished unless the subject makes his or her thought processes overt. In order to determine relationships between the products and the processes of thought, Bloom and Broder (1950) trained their subjects in the method of "thinking aloud." Using their results, they were able to categorize the characteristics of "good" and "poor" problem-solvers based on students' understanding of the problem presented, ability to use relevant knowledge, and approaches and attitudes toward the solution.

Whimbey (1975) is similarly interested in the processes of thinking, especially those involved in problem-solving and reading comprehension. A proponent of cognitive therapy, Whimbey maintains that poor problem-solving behavior can be identified and improved with practice. Because mental activities are carried out covertly, cognitive therapy requires that the students "externalize the thinking activities of problem-solving so that they can be demonstrated and practiced in full view." (Whimbey 1975, p. 116)

Feuerstein (1980) is also interested in how a child learns and solves problems (the process) rather than in what is learned (the product). Working with late adolescents and young adults, Feuerstein uses the term "retarded performer" to describe the individual whose cognitive behavior results in a poor intellectual performance. That is, according to Feuerstein it is the *performance* and not the *capacity* of the individual that is retarded. He considers intelligence as a "dynamic self-regulatory process that is responsive to external environmental intervention" (p. 2) and advocates that "except in the most severe instances of genetic and organic impairment, the human organism is open to modifiability at all ages and stages of development" (p. viii).

Feuerstein has developed a cognitive intervention program called Instrumental Enrichment (IE) consisting of a series of paper-and-pencil instruments, each of which focuses on a specific cognitive deficiency and is designed to change the cognitive structures of retarded performers and improve the active participation of these individuals in the learning process.

Problem-solving occurs in all phases of daily activities and is increasingly necessary in the work place. Because many of the strategies and cognitive processes used during problem-solving have a direct impact on learning, test-taking, and assignments, the author became involved in the development and teaching of a Thinking Skills course that addresses student weaknesses in these areas. The course "Reading and Thinking in Science and Technology," developed for deaf students, is offered at the Rochester Institute of Technology. The course has three components (lecture, Instrumental Enrichment, and problem-solving); this discussion focuses exclusively on the problem-solving component.

The purpose of the required individual problem-solving component is twofold: To provide students with problem-solving experiences in a non-threatening environment and to assist students in the analysis of their cognitive actions and problem-solving behavior so that they may capitalize on their strengths and improve their weaknesses by developing a conscious *control* over their actions. In these sessions, the student is the problem-solver and the instructor acts as an observer and a facilitator. The student reads and thinks aloud during the working of a problem while the instructor monitors and mediates the student's processing and assists with the identification of behaviors and strategies used.

Observation of Problem-Solving

Three word problems taken from the Whimbey and Lochhead card sets (1986) will be used to illustrate difficulties encountered in the problem-solving situation that manifest themselves in other areas of academic endeavor (Figure 1).

Problem 5   Dracula hates daylight more than Wolfman unless Frankenstein hates daylight more than Dracula. In that case Wolfman hates daylight more than Dracula but less than Mummy. Mummy hates daylight more than Dracula but less than Frankenstein. Show a diagram of the monsters ordered according to their hatred of daylight.

Problem 6   The Great Lakes differ in both their areas (measured in square miles) and their depths. However these two dimensions do not keep step perfectly. For example, Lake Michigan is exceeded in depth only by Lake Superior, but is exceeded in area by both Lake Superior and Huron. Lake Superior is by far the largest and deepest of the Great Lakes, but Lake Ontario, which is the smallest in area, is deeper than both Lakes Huron and Erie. Lake Erie is larger than Lake Ontario but it is not only shallower than Huron it is also shallower than Ontario. Show the order of the Great Lakes according to depth.

Problem 13   Boris, Irwin and Steven are engaged in the occupations of librarian, teacher, and electrician, although not necessarily in that order. The librarian is Steven's cousin, Irwin lives next door to the electrician. Boris, who knows more facts than the teacher, must drive 45 minutes to visit Irwin's house. What is each man's occupation?

FIGURE 1   Problems from the Whimbey and Lochhead card sets.

Problem 6, about the area and depth of the Great Lakes, may reveal not only a number of vocabulary difficulties but also the ability or inability of a student to focus on relevant data. Many students fail to recognize that two parameters, depth and area, are given; or they experience difficulty in separating the data into categories. Part of the difficulty lies in inattention to the question being asked, along with impulsivity in attacking the problem. Students often make the assumption that all data need to be used.

In the individual problem-solving sessions, the instructor's role is to act as the student's monitor, questioning in order to identify exactly what the question asks and how that question relates to the data given. The problem-solver should then try to name the two categories (parameters) of information given and suggest how to bring the relevant data to the fore. Students use different strategies to do this. Some cross out the irrelevant information; others underline the relevant information. Whatever strategy is used, the end result is the focusing of attention on only the data needed to solve the problem.

At this juncture, sentence structure, phrases, and vocabulary items become an obstacle for many low-aptitude students. For example, *is exceeded in depth only by* and *is not only shallower than* are phrases that cause deaf students a great deal of confusion, while *dimensions, shallower, exceeded* and *according* may be unknown words. After working with the instructor to clarify these areas of concern, the student then turns to paper and pencil to arrive at an answer. The most usual approach is to set up a continuum with the extremes of depth marking the ends. Even at this point, some students have difficulty identifying the parameter involved and naming the extremes. For example, a student may label one end of the continuum *depth* and the other *not deep* instead of identifying depth as the parameter and shallow vs. deep as the extremes.

Bridging these concepts to an example within a student's academic major, e.g., the range of temperature over which a biological reaction can occur, helps to anchor the concept more firmly and provide an application of the knowledge. In summary, this problem helps the student understand and identify the categories "depth" and "area," the parts of the data that are relevant to the question, and a suitable strategy for working the problem.

Problem 5 illustrates another problem that uses a continuum and requires identification of a parameter for its solution. Students have difficulty with this problem for a number of reasons, commonly the identification of the parameter under examination as hatred of daylight. The extremes may be named *hates daylight more* vs. *loves daylight more, daylight* vs. *nightlight, dark* vs. *bright* or *most* vs. *more*. Although this misidentification of the extremes may appear to be a trivial point, students who cannot name the extremes in a problem such as this one tend to be vague and imprecise in other areas of their work. To complicate this problem further, the terms *unless* and *in that case* may present a source of difficulty for students who often do not recognize them as "if . . . then" conditional propositions. By helping the student to identify and to separate the two alternatives, the instructor facilitates the student's analysis of the problem. A third source of difficulty lies in the structure of the second sentence. Students are sometimes unsure whether Mummy hates daylight more than Dracula or more than Wolfman.

A number of student difficulties are revealed by a study of problem 13. A few students initially use an order-of-mention strategy, concluding that Boris is the librarian because he is mentioned first. Some students make assumptions about the relationship between Boris and Irwin, saying that they must be cousins because they visit each other, while other students are convinced that cousins would live next door to each other. Some students insist that Steven is the librarian and must therefore know more facts than the teacher. These assumptions indicate that students do not easily recognize the boundaries of a problem, with the result that they become locked into one way of looking at the data given. Although the assumption that Boris is the librarian because a librarian would know more facts than a teacher does not prevent them from solving this particular problem, students need to be aware that this inference is based on their opinion and is not a fact stated in the problem.

Implications

The characteristics of good and poor problem-solvers were elicited and compared in the Bloom and Broder studies (Bloom & Broder 1950). Whimbey (1975) noted a similar correlation between the problem-solving characteristics of poor problem-solvers and low IQ. Inactivity, inability to draw upon prior knowledge, jumping to conclusions, lack of perseverance, inaccuracy in reading, poor attention to detail, vague understanding of the problem, and lack of checking behavior are among the types of error noted in the problem-solving situation (Whimbey & Lochhead 1986). Reber and Senior (1985) found marked similarities between low-achieving deaf students and the characteristics of poor problem-solvers identified by these authors.

The cognitive difficulties identified are not confined to the problem-solving situation but manifest themselves in other areas of academic work such as the ability to separate fact from opinion, find the main idea, and make logical statements using the information at hand. To cite a specific example, when asked to list the advantages of nuclear power based on text they had read about it, several students listed only the disadvantages because they were personally opposed to nuclear power. This type of behavior reflects an inability to focus on the question, to recognize the limits of the assignment that implies a separation of fact and opinion, and to focus on the relevant data contained in the text.

Developing Metacognitive Skills

"Self-monitoring for accuracy has a special significance for intelligence because of the relatively long sequence of covert activities involved in reasoning and comprehension" (Whimbey 1975, p. 137). Thus, during problem-solving sessions, the instructor initially acts as the student's self-monitor to make the student aware of the cognitive skills being used and to help the student recognize and value these skills. Over time, the student gains experience and confidence and begins to take on self-monitoring.

Students receive several benefits when they recognize and develop cognitive skills. First, the student becomes more actively involved in learning and becomes a manipulator and organizer of information. The problems in identifying the parameters under consideration are forerunners to developing the skills of generalization and comparison. Second, checking behavior tends to improve as students reread, check what is given, check and clarify the question, and consider the reasonableness of the answer. Third, students begin to identify relevant and irrelevant data and discriminate between them, and then they develop strategies for bringing relevant data to the forefront.

The author proposes that formal training for deaf college students in metacognition via problem-solving offers a mechanism by which these students can become more actively involved in monitoring their own learning behavior. By transferring particular skills acquired during problem-solving to the general learning process, deaf students should be able to improve their academic performance.

REFERENCES

Bloom, B.S., & Broder, L.J. 1950. Problem-solving processes of college students. *Supplementary educational monographs*. Chicago: University of Chicago Press.

Brown, A. 1980. Metacognitive development and reading. In *Theoretical issues in reading comprehension*, ed. R. Spiro, B. Bruce, & W. Brewer, 453–481. Hillsdale, NJ: Lawrence Erlbaum Associates.

Feuerstein, R. 1980. *Instrumental enrichment: An intervention program for cognitive modifiability*. Baltimore, MD: University Park Press.

Reber, D., & Senior, G. 1985. Steppingstones to thinking: A pilot project. *Teaching English to deaf and second-language students* 3(3):5–11.

Whimbey, A., & Lochhead, J. 1986. *Problem solving and comprehension.* Hillsdale, NJ: Lawrence Erlbaum Associates.

Whimbey, A., & Whimbey, L.S. 1975. *Intelligence can be taught.* New York: E.P. Dutton & Co.

10

METHODOLOGICAL ISSUES IN
DEAFNESS RESEARCH

Methodological Issues in Deafness Research

M. Diane Clark
Harry W. Hoemann

Researchers in deafness have many concerns in common. To address them, a special discussion session, with about forty participants, took place during the Second International Symposium on Cognition, Education, and Deafness. The major topics the group addressed were

1. the need for a clearer description of what researchers mean by "deaf" subjects,
2. the need for an operational definition of subjects who are "fluent in American Sign Language (ASL),"
3. the need for many more deaf researchers, and
4. methodological problems associated with sample sizes, statistical analyses, control groups, and a need for innovative procedures.

A survey of published literature on deafness shows that subjects who are termed "deaf" often differ greatly on a number of variables, including pure-tone losses, age-of-onset of deafness, differential hearing status of family members, and different communication methods to which individuals have been exposed. Researchers have an obligation to their readers to provide an operational definition of their criteria for subject selection, especially the defining variable "deaf."

The defining attributes of the subjects should always be related to the rationale of the study and to the population to whom the results can be generalized. These attributes also should be specified before data collection begins. The needed subjects may sometimes be difficult to locate, but once they are, there is then a sound basis for subject selection and for generalizing the results. These methodological changes will greatly enhance generalizability in the future.

A second problem that occurs in the literature on deafness research is that authors sometimes assert that their subjects were "fluent in ASL," but they often offer no real evidence for this claim. Sometimes it is reported that the subjects had deaf parents, as if this fact justified the assumption that the subjects were therefore fluent in ASL. But if their parents learned ASL in adolescence or adulthood, subjects may not qualify as "native" users. Linguists researching the properties of ASL are often careful to use only second- or even third-generation deaf children of deaf parents to safeguard their assumption that the subjects are native users of ASL. Some deaf parents also may have chosen to use a sign system based on English when communicating with their deaf child to enhance their child's English language skills. Clearly, "fluency in ASL" cannot be taken for granted, even when a deaf child has deaf parents. When the subject's language competence is an important consideration for a particular investigation, the researcher has a special responsibility for determining which language system(s) each subject can use and that person's fluency in each of them.

A recurring and troublesome question is, "Why are so few *deaf* people involved in research and in the publishing of research in deafness?" The group agreed that there are clear advantages to having deaf researchers as investigators or as members and leaders of a research team. For example, a deaf investigator is more likely than a hearing investigator to be able to establish rapport with a deaf subject, and a deaf investigator is more likely to have the practical understanding of deafness that may be needed to plan and execute a project involving deaf participants.

Barriers preventing deaf people from participating in research were said to include the need for intensive training and the need for mastery of English reading and writing skills. Some improvement in this situation is now visible in the field. More deaf people currently are involved in research activity than previously, and some deaf persons are now directors of their own research laboratories. Furthermore, more graduate schools are now admitting deaf individuals to degree programs that provide training in research. The participants strongly expressed the idea that deaf people should be actively encouraged to become involved in research, not only to study ASL but also to investigate all other aspects of deafness.

Another concern in any analysis of methodological issues is that the hearing status of the investigator does not automatically invalidate test results. No differences were found in deaf subjects' IQ scores when the scores were obtained by hearing psychometricians trained in administering batteries of tests to hearing-impaired students as compared to scores obtained by deaf psychometricians with such training. Investigators' prior training appears to be a more important factor than hearing status when assessing hearing-impaired students.

A final topic is the concern over specific methodological issues and problems. Four main issues were raised: problems associated with sample sizes and control groups, problems involving the proper use of statistics, the inclusion of control groups, and a need for innovative research methods.

The size of the samples needed for various investigations will always vary, depending on a number of factors associated with different problem areas. Some classic studies in the literature have been conducted with as few as three subjects and sometimes with one subject. There are acceptable research designs that do not require large n's to preserve rigor. These include (1) A B C designs (A: obtain a base rate; B: apply an intervention; and C: withdraw the intervention), (2) longitudinal observational research, (3) ethnographic analysis, and (4) studies with planned replications.

Many statistical methods are available to resolve issues of sample size and variability within a heterogeneous population. Nonparametric statistics some-times can deal with data that do not meet the assumptions required by parametric statistics. An analysis of covariance can be used to control for extraneous variables that affect the data but do not affect the question under study. Factor-analytic studies and multiple regression analyses also may prove useful and have been introduced in some projects.

The problem of obtaining appropriate control groups needs discussion. When comparing deaf and hearing groups, some researchers in the past have attempted to match groups on academic achievement or grade level, but in so doing have used hearing subjects who are several years younger than the deaf subjects. Such comparisons yield data that are difficult to interpret. Researchers should be aware that one can sometimes control statistically for sources of variance, and that this kind of control may be preferable to finding a suitable control group for that same purpose.

Innovative methods also need to be developed that will yield interpretable and reliable results. Procedures are needed to investigate specific aspects of deaf subjects' behavior or ability without resorting to large samples drawn randomly from all segments of the deaf population. Meanwhile, researchers must design studies that will reliably (if tentatively) answer a carefully considered question. Researchers should resist the temptation to try to answer all of their questions with a single study. A series of smaller studies with built-in replications of previous findings and controls for previous confounds is more likely to lead to a satisfactory (and more publishable) outcome.

The following seven actions are recommended to improve upon the present situation:

1. Time should be set aside at symposia and regional meetings for re-searchers to deal candidly with the issues and share with each other those strategies that have been most successful in improving their research methods.
2. Special interest groups should be formed within professional orga-nizations (e.g., the Deaf SIG in the American Educational Research Association) to establish the legitimacy of the problem area of deafness and to provide a forum for the best research currently being conducted in the field.
3. Deafness researchers should consult freely with colleagues in their own departments, colleges, or universities. These colleagues may not have a specific interest in deafness, but they may have constructive suggestions for dealing with problems in general research design or data analysis.
4. Research in troublesome areas facing many methodological problems should be programmatic and should continue over a long period. The

body of data that accumulates may eventually be impressive enough to be published.

5. Researchers should make preliminary contact with staff members of funding agencies to outline research objectives and to discover the agencies' funding priorities. Such preliminary consultation can produce constructive advice that may lead to successful grant proposals.

6. Editors of professional journals should be given information regarding the special methodological problems confronted by researchers in deafness.

7. Rather than attempting to bypass the existing system of peer review by creating specialty journals or in-house presses, researchers in deafness should apply their energies to conducting well-designed studies that advance knowledge. Thus, the clear commitment to quality will ultimately result in improved and more diverse research designs which will, in turn, significantly advance knowledge in this challenging field.

11

CURRENT RESEARCH IN COGNITION, EDUCATION, AND DEAFNESS

Some Observations from a Different Point of View

Howard R. Pollio
Marilyn R. Pollio

I n science as in politics, being an outsider has distinct advantages and disadvantages. There is a difference in perspective: Things that look ordinary, familiar, or unchangeable to insiders often have a certain freshness and possibility to the outsider. Also, however, the outsider is never sure that this new perspective is not simply the result of ignorance. When an outsider speaks it must be with caution so as not to present ignorance as wisdom. We will try to be careful.

It was with these cautions in mind that we approached the Second International Symposium on Cognition, Education, and Deafness. Within this context, we soon discovered a whole set of ideas, hypotheses, and maxims that seemed undeniably true both to the participants and to us. Among the most obvious of these shared "truths" were

1. ASL is a language.
2. Assessment should be tied to intervention.
3. Evaluations always should be carried out on the basis of a battery and not a single test.
4. Visual-spatial and verbal-sequential processes must be distinguished in language and cognition.

Each of these truths emerged many times during the conference, and after a while they were as undeniable for us as for the other members of the audience.

Other themes also emerged. Among these, the following three seemed most noteworthy:

1. Researchers on deafness are acutely sensitive to the ages of their subjects.
2. Researchers on deafness are ambivalent about which is more important: the deaf person or the situation in which the person is observed.
3. Researchers on deafness are uncomfortable, but not yet dissatisfied, with behavior as the major way to assess what is going on in a developmental or educational context.

Before we attempt to develop the specific implications of these themes for research on deafness, there is a prior question concerning each of the major terms describing what the symposium and the papers in this volume are about; that is *deafness*, *education*, and *cognition*. Linguistically, each of these terms is an abstract noun, and as Korzybski (1933) and Hayakawa (1949) warned long ago, all words are dangerous, nouns are more dangerous, and abstract nouns are the most dangerous of all. To protect against careless thinking, both Korzybski and Hayakawa suggested that it is necessary to break down our ordinary ways of evaluating what we say and understand by using cautionary techniques such as *indexing, dating, etcetering,* and *quotation-marking*. Indexing a particular individual, group, or concept (i.e., Republican$_1$ vs. Republican$_2$) is meant to remind us that differences among individuals or concepts are likely to be as significant as similarities: If we substitute Abraham Lincoln for Republican$_1$ and Ronald Reagan for Republican$_2$, the example seems less abstract. Dating, the second of these techniques, is meant to remind us that the socio-historical context of a word or concept profoundly affects its meaning, such as "feminist" in 1920 and in 1989. *Quotation marks* and *etc.* both are used to remind speakers and listeners that no symbol ever offers a perfect representation of its referent idea, object, or event. Quotation marks indicate that words such as "race," "justice," and "truth" are not to be trusted even though they are the only terms available in the language. The word *etc.* reminds us that words, considered as maps, are neither as complicated nor as complete as the territories they represent. The mistaken notion that maps are identical with their territories causes a great deal of semantic and conceptual trouble.

If we take these semantic cautions seriously, they suggest that deafness$_1$ is not deafness$_2$, and that neither says all there is to say about "deafness." Within the context of the present volume, everyone seems to be at pains to answer precise questions about what they mean by deafness in relation to their subjects: Was the person born deaf? Was he or she the child of deaf or hearing parents? Was the family attitude toward deafness accepting, rejecting, or neutral? Was there any residual hearing in one or both ears? Was the person taught ASL? At what age and under what circumstances? Each of these demonstrably significant factors only suggests the wisdom of Korzybski and Hayakawa's advice that deaf person$_1$ does not equal deaf person$_2$ and does not equal deaf person$_n$. These factors continue to remind us that we should always say a silent "etc." after the word *deafness* wherever and whenever we encounter it.

The situation with respect to "education" is no different. There are at least as many meanings for education as there are students, teachers, and educational institutions. If we add in the issue of deafness, the factors serving to differentiate deaf education₁ from deaf education₂ from deaf educationₙ must concern such obvious issues as Oralism vs. ASL vs. Total Communication; the attitude and training of teachers, school districts, and parents; the historical period in which the person was (is) educated; and so on. The map is not the territory, and we must be clear in letting everyone know what territory is being discussed.

Finally, we come to the issue of "cognition." Within the present volume, as in cognitive science more generally, the word *cognition* means anything from a single (cognitive) process to all of personal consciousness. In the former case, it encompasses such specific subprocesses as short- and long-term memory, mental representation, problem solving, concept formation, and so on. In the latter case, it encompasses such issues as metacognition, personal awareness, and mind. Although each of these terms raises its own unique issues (note, for example, that most are nouns), the one that seems most crucial concerns the use of "cognition" as synonymous with "mind." Although "mind" is a complex concept for all disciplines, it becomes especially significant for cognitive psychology where mind (and its adjective, mental) is often uncritically used to mean "person." Mental health, mental retardation, and mental block, for example, all characterize a style of personal existence (as healthy, retarded, or blocked); they do not characterize only a single aspect of the person. Other sentences, in which "mind" is equated with "person," easily come to mind:

> The mind shudders at what it does not know.
> There are things my mind will never understand.
> Conflicting thoughts confused my mind.

This use of "mind" as synonymous with "person" has a long and respectable history in western philosophy and psychology. Probably its most important proponent was Descartes, who coined the phrase "I think, therefore I am," suggesting that mind alone defines what it means to be human. Although this approach is extremely consequential for psychology, biology, medicine, and cognitive science, the important point in the present context is that we sometimes uncritically equate "mind" with "person" and forget that cognition is not all there is to a living, creating, changing, embodied, social human being. By itself, cognition does not define what it means to be a person.

Each of these semantic analyses of education, of deafness, and of cognition can be summarized by pointing out that nouns, but most especially abstract ones, provide a static and unchanging representation of our experiences and concepts. Concepts and experiences, rendered as abstract nouns, mislead us into considering the territory they name as a once-and-for-all event or achievement, not as an ongoing process. In English, as in other languages, nouns name relatively fixed and bounded territories. If we are to approach human life in a more open way, we would do well to replace abstract nouns with gerunds (deafness with being deaf; cognition with thinking and being; education with teaching and learning) to remind us continuously that we are dealing with ongoing processes and not with static objects. In this way it should be possible to reintroduce an element of time and change into our theories of education, cognition, and deafness.

THEMES OF THE SYMPOSIUM PAPERS

The major way in which we attempted to discern significant themes was to immerse ourselves fully in each session. Imagine a boiling cauldron with two cooks continuously circling around it. As they circle, each cook throws things into the pot. The things we threw in were the various sessions we attended, including the perspectives, the conversations, the arguments, and the discussions. We also threw in informal arguments and conversations among participants as well as conversations encompassing even larger groups of participants, and we let these ingredients simmer as one lets a winter soup simmer. When the soup had simmered long enough, three themes rose to the top of the pot.

Theme 1: Age and Stage Are Important

In almost every paper, the researcher is careful to locate the subjects in the appropriate segment of the life cycle, minimally in terms of chronological age. With few exceptions, the population was identified in the title—toddlers, infants, school children, adolescents, the elderly. We began to wonder about this concern with age. It seems to us that researchers in deafness are almost always interested in where in the life cycle their subjects fall: What can one understand about a person at this point in his or her life? How can one describe what deaf school children and adolescents are like, and how does this description affect what and how they learn? What can one do retrospectively in the case of infants and toddlers? There is an unmistakable emphasis on life cycle issues, and in locating subjects within the life cycle. Then we asked, "Is any stage missing from this array; is anything overlooked?" What is overlooked is *midlife*.

We are in midlife, and we might be particularly aware of that stage and so place an undue emphasis on it, but perhaps midlife was missing because this symposium emphasized education and the educational process. Sometimes we mistakenly assume that education ends with graduation from high school or college. A study of self-actualizing deaf adults might provide valuable insights for educating deaf children from infancy through college and beyond. Such a study would have to be conducted with its focus not on deficits, but on high-level achievements and functioning. It could include such questions as What do achieving deaf adults know? How do they do things? What are their patterns of skills, abilities, and familial relations? What are such adults like personally? Such research would serve to make Maslow as relevant as Myklebust to the study of deafness.

Why should people interested in educating deaf children and young adults be interested in learning about the skilled, achieving deaf adult? The major reason might be that such a study could provide a model toward which educational practices and processes could be oriented to educate deaf children and adolescents to become the next generation of fully functioning deaf adults. Our advice is: Focus on the best, on those who achieve and on those who attain, and let them serve to define educational objectives. We need to learn who these people are and how they function in their world, and then use that information to develop educational, social, and personal procedures for articulating a new definition of what deaf education ought to emphasize.

Perhaps because of our own experiences as college professors, one research program that seems to provide a near model of this type of approach is to be found in the work of Perry (1970, 1981) concerning gifted college students at Harvard University. This work began with a straightforward request by Perry and his coworkers to individual students to describe "What stood out for you during the college years?" Students were encouraged to talk freely, and from these conversations, Perry was able to chart the personal evolution of college students as they progressed through such significant stages of early adult life as Absolutism, Experiencing Multiple Perspectives, Experimenting with Relativism, and Evolving Commitments.

While these titles do not do justice to Perry's stages, they suggest that it is possible to ask people meaningful questions and to expect meaningful answers, and that such a program of research will yield an evolving pattern of what we (as teachers) must be sensitive to and what we might want to encourage in the way of student growth. Although Perry's work was mentioned as one example of research concerned with understanding the best and the brightest, we cannot help but wonder whether the Perry scheme and its attendant research methodology could not be adapted for the study of the deaf college student or, more pertinently, for the study of other competent deaf adults.

One study that attempted to deal with some of these issues was performed by Laurel Goodrich (1988) in her doctoral dissertation at the University of Tennessee. In this study, eighteen well-functioning and articulate deaf adults participated in open-ended interviews conducted in sign language about events at various times in their lives when "they were distinctly aware of being deaf." Data were analyzed by a procedure designed to capture meaningful changes in the world of deaf adults who talked to a sensitive interviewer about the events of their lives. Participants recounted the experience of being deaf by referring to a set of developmental phases during which they became aware of their deafness and came to terms with it. Goodrich's participants discussed the meaningful stages of their lives in terms such as Encountering, Knowing, Acknowledging the Facts of Deaf Life, Coping and Creating, and Accepting and Guiding.

During all the developmental phases, a single overarching theme kept recurring for Goodrich's participants: Deafness as difference. Participants described the changes that took place in their experience of difference and sameness over time. In the early phases (Encountering), before they could reflect on being deaf, difference impinged in painful ways. Over time, they came to know that the experience of being different had to do with being deaf (Knowing), and to recognize the limits and possibilities that deafness brings (Acknowledging the Facts of Deaf Life). Following this stage, the deaf person learned to act on these limits and possibilities (Coping and Creating). As they came to accept being deaf (Accepting) and to impart to others the knowledge and wisdom born of this acceptance (Guiding), difference *per se* was experienced as progressively less significant. Although their deafness was still fully acknowledged, being different from others by virtue of being deaf became less important than being the same as others by virtue of being human.

Goodrich discussed these themes in relation to minority group experiences as well as in terms of developmental theory. Particular attention was paid to the bearing of these findings on the development of self: Self-development for the deaf person involves coming to terms with being different and with the limits that these differences entail. Such constraints, however, are not unique to deaf persons. The deaf experience may be seen as a compelling and illuminating instance of the universal human task of facing limitations and acknowledging differences.

The overall suggestion that emerges from our cauldron-stirring on the issue of the life cycle is that it would be significant to describe what a self-actualized deaf adult is like and then to develop the implications that such a description could have for teachers. There is little research on this issue, and we feel it is necessary to start thinking about educating deaf students in terms of a self-actualizing model rather than solely in terms of an overcoming-deficiencies model. This change in focus might reinforce one of the major findings of Goodrich's work and might lead us to a view of deafness as difference, not deficiency.

Theme 2: People and Situations or People in Situations?

A second theme concerns a problem that might be captured in terms of the catch phrase *Person/World Interaction*. That is, some papers focus primarily on the (deaf) person and on issues such as abilities and disabilities, brain function, mathematical and reading skill, IQ level, memory ability, linguistic skill level, and so on. Each investigator takes a stand within the frame of an individual person. A second group of investigators focus more on the situation (i.e., the family, the school), and the role of individual properties, either biological or psychological, was deemphasized. For these investigators, it is not considered proper to talk about the individual without first looking at the larger contexts within which that person lives and functions.

From the late 1930s until the early 1950s, Kurt Lewin and his school of psychological research (Lewin 1935) discussed two types of errors in personality research: an organism error and a situation error. Lewin said that in order to understand any psychological process, personality included, we must always consider an organism in its world, not separate from its situation. Lewin ultimately summarized this insight in a significant little formula, Behavior equals some function of the Person and the Situation—$B = f(P,S)$—which was meant to serve as a general model for psychological theory and research.

In a more philosophical vein, this way of discussing personality research, suggests that all human existence is always situated, and we must worry about both who the human being is and what the situation is. For example, clinical psychologists (for the moment, let's pick on psychologists) who test children with "school problems" usually ask the child to come to their offices, where they administer the WRAT or the WISC-R. Then they proceed to give advice about the child without ever setting foot in the classroom or wondering about who the child's teacher might be, how the teacher teaches, or how he or she interacts with children. The child has been evaluated apart from the learning environment, and advice is offered on the basis of tests conducted and evaluated in a consulting office and not a classroom. At the other extreme is a different kind of psychologist, a behaviorist, who goes into the classroom and watches the way the teacher does things. The behaviorist does not consider the talents and abilities of the individual child, even if a baseline has been taken; what is crucial is the environment, and better and more orderly environments yield better and more orderly learning.

The philosopher Martin Heidegger has a nice phrase to cover both poles of this theme: *being-in-the-world*. It should be obvious that there are both near and far "worlds." In the case of education, near worlds include the classroom, the teacher, and the school. There also are far worlds, such as the cultural and historical milieu: Is there a Republican or Democratic president? What kind of Supreme Court do we have? The classroom always emerges from the larger socio-historical world. Often we do not need to consider the total complexity of the learner's world, but sometimes we must. The prototypical example of this situation is the case of a Jewish school child in Poland in 1939. Forces far removed from the classroom had a significant impact on everything that went on in the classroom for that child. While we do not want to say that we have to take every potential context into account each time we deal with a specific child, we do want to emphasize the situated nature of everything we (and they) do. In short, we are suggesting that our research and our pedagogy must always be historically and situationally located and must be multiperspectival.

Perhaps the clearest example of this issue in the present volume concerns the conversations, papers, questions, and arguments we see concerning language generally and ASL specifically. On one side—the person side—language is discussed as a system that is given life by an intrasubjective network of cognitive and biological processes. For this view, dialogue is the result of two language-producing devices that transfer and transform each other's input. On the other side—the situation side—language is discussed as intrasubjective both in its institutionalized form as a certain language (English, Chinese, ASL) and as a dialogue within which individual meanings emerge and change the person and the surrounding world. Both these views are represented in this volume. In the person-group, the major concerns deal with individual linguistic ability/disability; in the social-matrix group, the major concerns seem best captured by the Vygotskian view that the origins of all higher-order intellectual activities are experienced first in interactions among people and are used only later by single individuals. These considerations apply to the many discussions at the symposium: Some were concerned with specific capacities and properties of language users as well as with neurolinguistic substrates; others were concerned with the role of ASL in yielding a group identity and a shared reality among its users. ASL, like any language, is both social and personal. It must be situated both ways simultaneously. In any one case we may be more interested in the speaker or the situation; in no case are we allowed to forget that they form a union subsequent reflection may divide but can never separate in the living experiences of speakers and listeners.

Theme 3: What Should We Study?

In all of this volume, but most especially in the papers concerned with teaching, a peculiar issue occurs: How are we to determine that what the teacher (or student) says, the student (or teacher) understands? How do we determine how the world appears from the first-person perspective of the student, and how does that perspective agree with the third-person perspective of the instructor or the researcher? The student could ask the same question: Does my perception of the (third-person) instructor agree with the instructor's (first-person) perspective?

Because this issue of first-person/third-person perspective can be a bit tricky, let us describe some data we collected in a college classroom. The paper was called "What Students Think About and Do During College Lectures" (Pollio 1984)—a potentially daunting topic for college professors and for teachers generally. The procedure used in this study was simple: Students were interrupted at random times during a lecture and were asked to write down "What you were aware of just before the bell sounded." Although this procedure produced a great deal of educationally significant information (across a large number of undergraduate classes, only 61% of student protocols contained responses that were on target with respect to the instructor or the lecture content), the more significant results emerged from simultaneously sampling student awareness and student behavior. Self-reports from students were coded into two categories, on-target and off-target. At the same time, behavioral records were made of what students did during the 30-second period immediately preceding the self-report. These behavioral records were coded into the same two categories.

Table 1 presents the results of this two-way classification of self-reporting and behavioral observation. In the best of all possible worlds for researchers, the two diagonal cells—on/on and off/off—would sum to close to 100%, and the researcher could then use (as lecturers often do) student behavior as an index of student awareness (self-report). As may be seen, one of the four cells, Behavior-on/Self-Report-off, violates this simple pattern; in fact, about 29% of the cases fell into this cell. What these data reveal, at a minimum, is that *appearing* to be on-target does not always coincide with self-reports that *are* on-target.

One way to conceptualize these results is by defining *subjective* and *objective* within the context of the college classroom. Generally, "objective" means from the perspective of an outside observer, whereas "subjective" means private and inaccessible to observation from outside. Within the context of social science, what is objective is held to be more valuable and defensible; what is subjective, when not discredited altogether, is left to "softer," nonempirical disciplines such as literature.

Such an interpretation will not suffice in the present case. It seems better to

TABLE 1 Behavioral Reports and Self-Reports of Students' Awareness

Behavioral Record	Self-Report		Totals
	On-Target	*Off-Target*	
On-Target	.64	.29	.93
Off-Target	.03	.04	.07
Totals	.67	.33	1.00

describe self-reports not as subjective, but as a first-person perspective on the situation. Similarly, it seems better to describe behavior not as objective, but as a third-person perspective on the person in the situation. Behavior reports and self-reports provide different points of view on the same event or situation; they do not represent two separate and independent events, one scientifically more valuable than the other. We can, in fact, consider self-reports (or personal experience) as describing a "me-for-me" perspective and behavioral records as describing a "me-for-you" or, more generally, a "me-for-someone-else" perspective. Although social scientists try to produce objective data (i.e., behavior, carefully observed), it should be clear that such observations yield only a part of the real picture of human beings.

When approached with this problem, most social scientists and educational researchers probably would say that they take subjective (or objective) data into account to determine whether their objective (or subjective) measures give a valid picture of the person. But it seems wiser to say it is methodologically important to determine whether or not the two perspectives agree (i.e., if an on-target report is preceded by an on-target behavior) and not get stuck on the question of which perspective is "more correct." Only when the two agree almost completely would it seem reasonable to use just one measure, and we do not yet know whether or how often such circumstances occur.

The tendency to use behavior as the more significant measure for research has a long and understandable history. It also has the tendency to reduce the person being observed to an object or a thing considered solely from the outside. Such a restricted approach is potentially deleterious, not only to psychology and social science, but also to an understanding of education as a socio-personal event. Only if we accept the subject of our observations as a human being and accord him or her the possibility of both experiencing and doing in the classroom can we describe the nature of the classroom world as the student experiences it as well as how student behavior appears to the instructor.

This analysis suggests that there are two perspectives that researchers must take in describing the world of the classroom: The me-for-me view and the me-for-some-other-person view, whether this other person is the instructor, another student, or a researcher. Once we recognize these two perspectives, it seems clear that both have their own special histories and contemporary contexts—which sometimes overlap and sometimes do not. Whether we consider the 29% of items falling in the on/off cell to indicate politeness ("I'm bored but will try not to let you [the instructor] see it"), strategy ("I want a good grade and won't show I'm bored"), or consideration ("I don't want to hurt the instructor's feelings"), the general point must be that any description of the classroom world as the student lives it will have to take both perspectives into account.

Even if this analysis permits a clear exposition of the issue of first- and third-person perspectives, there is still the question of the range of methods that might be used in studying topics from both perspectives. One way this issue is raised here concerns the question of whether or not it is possible to do research that can recover rigorously what people are aware of in significant situations. The method used in the study just described is called the *Thought Sampling Method*. In this procedure, the experimenter interrupts people as they progress in their ordinary activities and asks them what they are aware of, or some similar question. The best studies of this genre are by Klinger (1981; Klinger, Bartoc & Mahoney 1976), who gave students beepers. Once they were accustomed to wearing the beepers, Klinger sent signals randomly that cued the students to write down what they were aware of at that moment. Since the researcher did not want the participants' lives disrupted by beeps, a certain number of hours a day were spent without the beeper. (No researcher wants his participants to have to say "Excuse me, dear, I have to write down what I'm thinking about now.") The major names in this area are Klinger (1981), Hurlburt (1980), and Hurlburt, Leach, and Saltman (1984).

A second method for assessing personal awareness, contributed by cognitive psychology, is called the *Think Aloud Procedure*. In this method, the participant talks aloud during an attempt to solve a problem or during some other type of activity. An examination of where the person gets stuck, ways of conceptualizing, ways that solutions are finally reached and so on can be assessed by this method. Here some of the major names are Ericsson and Simon (1984) and Aanstoos (1983). In this work, the goal is to describe the propositional structure underlying the activity in process.

A third procedure is known as *Cued Recall*. In this method, a videotape is made of a situation and is played back for participants (see, for example, the work of Shavelson & Stern 1981; Shavelson, Webb & Burstein, 1986; Clark & Peterson 1986; and Hector, Bradley, Daigle & Klukken 1989). For example a researcher might videotape a teacher teaching a class and then replay the tape, asking the teacher to stop the tape whenever he or she "remembers what he or she was aware of at that moment in the classroom." The researcher also may stop the tape and ask for a report whenever significant events (e.g., a question, a smile, excited discussion) occur on the tape, or whenever the researcher notes that the teacher changes behavior during the recall session (e.g., smiling, wincing, becoming more excited). Whenever the tape is stopped, the researcher asks questions such as "What were you aware of at that point?" "Can you tell more about that moment in the class?" Notice that a cued recall can be done for all participants in the setting.

The final method, and the method we prefer to use with adults, is called the *Phenomenological Interview*. This interview begins with a very simple question. If the topic under discussion is time, for example, the researcher might ask, "Can you think of some situations when you are aware of time?" When Dapkus (1985) did just this, she got answers such as "When I'm stuck in a traffic jam"; "When it's 11:10 and I'm supposed to have stopped speaking a few minutes ago"; "When I see people looking at their airplane tickets and saying, 'Oh my God, we have to get out of here'"; "When I see the leaves change in the fall"; and "When I look at my child who is now an adult."

After the person provides a list of crucial situations, the next step is to ask, "Which one of these situations would you like to talk about?" When the participant picks one to discuss, the interviewer then asks, "What are you aware of in this situation?" and follows the participant in much the same way as is done in a clinical interview; that is, the researcher follows the person respectfully, recognizing that the participant is the expert, not the researcher.

Notice how this subtle alteration in attitude changes the locus of power in this type of study. In most experiments, the power lies with the experimenter. In a phenomenological interview, the locus of power is with the participant—it is his or her world that we want to know about, not our hypothesis about that world. This point means that respect and deference are accorded to the person, and the interviewer simply goes along. The interviewer wants to know what only the participant can relate, and it is the interviewer's job to see that the participant helps us understand his or her experience. We want people to feel understood, and we want to let them know that we have understood. From such a protocol the researcher gets a thematic analysis in which the units of analysis are themes of experience as described by the participant.

We have already presented the results of the study by Goodrich concerning the experience of being deaf. As a second example, consider the study by Dapkus (1985) concerning experiences of time. On the basis of her analysis of many different interviews, Dapkus was able to describe the human experience of time (in Western culture) in terms of three major themes: Change and Continuity, Limits and Choices, and Tempo. These themes, taken together, were considered to describe the adult experience of time, although any one, two, or three could stand out as significant for the person in any specific situation.

Both of these studies offer examples of ways it is possible to capture the first-person world by means of thematic analysis. Several other researchers have also discussed either how to do interviews or what types of results can come from this kind of analysis. Falling in the former category are volumes by Valle and King (1978), Valle and Halling (1989), and Georgi (1970), as well as articles by Kvale (1983) and Polkinghorne (1988). Empirical studies using this method can be found in many different fields; most recently within the field of marketing, Thompson, Locander, and Pollio (1989) provided an extensive description and rationale for one use of this type of research.

Finally, just to show that behavior *is* still relevant, we would like to suggest that it is possible to use behavior, clearly observed, to tell us something about the first-person world of the individual. The maxim here is Do not look at behavior as a mechanical, third-person process; instead, try to see what the person is doing (behavior) as revealing something about what the person's world is like. If one looks at behavior in this way, it should be possible to "read behavior backwards" and find out what the person was experiencing during the behavior.

Probably the clearest example of this procedure in contemporary social science concerns the difference between a phonetic analysis and a phonemic analysis of the sounds of a language. A phonetic description is free of person, of language, and of context; in short, it is an objective description of differences detectable in the stream of sound in any and all languages. As such, it is precisely correct for no language but minimally wrong for all languages. In our terms, it offers a third-person description of sound by an outside observer (the linguist). Phonemic descriptions, on the other hand, require the participation of a native speaker/listener and thereby yield a minimal set of sounds that make a difference to the informant. As such, they provide a behaviorally based, first-person definition depending upon interactions between an outside observer and the person whose language is of interest. Phonemes, therefore, provide a first-person description of the significant sounds as heard and produced by the speakers of a specific language.

It is possible to generalize this usage as cultural anthropology regularly does in its distinction between *etic* and *emic* descriptions of culture. The analogy, derived from the linguistic concepts of phon*etic* and phon*emic* description, is meant to suggest that the anthropological observer may describe the meaning of objects, words, and actions as they relate to individuals in the culture (or subculture) under consideration or from the point of view of some detached observer. In both the cultural and linguistic case, it should be clear that while inquiry always starts with *etic* description, *emic* description is a second and more significant moment in our understanding of the language or culture in question.

It is also possible to see a similar distinction at work in Skinnerian therapists who for years have used their own variation of this technique to discover not only reinforcers but discriminative stimuli as well. It is important to point out that in the Skinnerian paradigm, the therapist (or researcher) must always discover the reinforcer or relevant stimulus *for the organism in its current situation*, and this goal requires that events be defined from that organism's point of view. Although it may sound scandalous to turn Skinner into a behavioral phenomenologist, he has always taught that it is the animal's and not the researcher's reactions to the environment that are important. If Skinner did not have such peculiar notions about control and freedom, perhaps we could agree with Kvale and Grenniss (1966), who long ago pointed out similarities between the views of Sartre and Skinner in dealing with human action-in-the-world.

CONCLUSION

This attempt at synthesis by two outsiders has gone on long enough, and the time seems ripe to bring it to a conclusion. As a way of reaching this conclusion, we want to describe something special about our experiences in this symposium. More than any other we have ever attended, this conference was made up of people who truly listened and cared about the topic and who were truly interested in what other people were saying and doing. There were no adversaries—only dedicated researchers, clinicians, and educators seeking to understand a significant and complicated phenomenon of great personal concern. This state of affairs suggests that it may not be enough in research on deafness to go about our business as we have been taught and as we have continued. Rather, it seems important that research adapt the method to the phenomenon and not vice versa. Deafness is not just another topic one happens to be researching, but one that matters very much to the researcher. Some might say that, because the topic is so significant, research ought to be more, not less, concerned about being "scientific." Our position on this issue is that the researcher must be aware of all the pitfalls attendant on doing research concerning a personally significant topic but must not let methodology determine content. Thus, it seems reasonable to propose that research in cognition, education, and deafness must take a multiperspectival approach and not be bound to one or another methodological stricture. If laboratory research, field research, or dialogic research suits the researcher and the problem best, then the researcher should choose accordingly. There must be a vigorous and respectful dialogue among all perspectives, both quantitative and qualitative, third- and first-person, laboratory and field, among scientists, scholars, and practitioners, if meaningful facts, procedures, and conclusions are to emerge. The researcher must be self-critical and rigorous, but must let neither rigor nor analytic strictures interfere with the choice of significant topics because they may not be viewed as "respectable" in light of contemporary methodologies. Finally, researchers in deafness must never lose sight of their phenomenon: the world as lived and experienced by the deaf person.

REFERENCES

Aanstoos, C. 1983. The think aloud method in descriptive work. *Journal of Physiological Research* 14:243 – 266.

Clark, C.M., & Peterson, P. 1986. Teachers' thought processes. In *Handbook of research on teaching*, ed. M.C. Wittrock, 255 – 296. New York: MacMillan Publishing Co.

Dapkus, M. 1985. A thematic analysis of the experience of time. *Journal of Personality and Social Psychology* 49:408 – 419.

Ericsson, K.A., & Simon, H.A. 1980. *Protocol analysis.* Cambridge: MIT Press.

Giorgi, A. 1970. *Psychology as a human science.* New York: Harper and Row.

Goodrich, L. 1988. *Deafness as difference: A phenomenological study of coming to terms with being deaf.* Ph.D. diss., University of Tennessee, Knoxville.

Hayakawa, S.I. 1949. *Language and thought in action.* New York: Harcourt, Brace.

Hector, M., Bradley, K., Daigle, S., & Klukken, G. 1989. *A phenomenologist study of counseling processes using video assisted recall.* Paper presented at the American Educational Research Association, San Francisco, CA.

Hurlburt, R.T. 1980. Validation and correlation of thought sampling, with retrospective measures. *Cognitive Theory and Research* 4:235 – 238.

Hurlburt, R.T., Leach, B.C., & Saltman, S. 1984. Random sampling of thought and mind. *Cognitive Theory and Research* 8:263 – 275.

Klinger, E. 1981. Modes of normal conscious flow. In *The stream of consciousness*, ed. K.S. Pope & T.L. Singer, 226 – 258. New York: Plenum Publishing Corp.

Klinger, E., Bartoc, S.G., & Mahoney, T.W. 1976. Maturation, mood and mental events: Problems and implications for adaptive processes. In *Psychotherapy of human adaptiveness*, ed. G. Serben, 95 – 112. New York: Plenum Publishing Corp.

Korzybski, A.S. 1933. *Science and sanity.* Lancaster PA: Science Press.

Kvale, S. 1983. The qualitative research interview. *Journal of Physiological Psychology* 14:171 – 196.

Kvale, S., & Grenniss, C.E. 1967. Sartre and Skinner. *Review of Existential Psychology and Psychiatry* 7:128 – 150.

Lewin, K. 1935. *A dynamic theory of personality.* New York: McGraw-Hill.

Perry, W.G., Jr. 1970. *Forms of intellectual and ethical development in the college years: A schema.* New York: Holt, Rinehart & Winston.

———. 1981. Cognitive and ethical growth. In *The modern American college*, ed. A.W. Chuckering, 76 – 116. San Francisco, CA: Jossey-Bass.

Polkinghorne, D.E. 1989. Phenomenological research methods. In *Existential phenomenological perspectives in psychology*, ed. R. Valle & S. Halling, 41 – 60. New York: Plenum Publishing Corp.

Pollio, H.R. 1984. *What students think about and do during college lectures: Teaching-learning issues.* Knoxville, TN: Learning Research Center Reports.

Shavelson, R.J., & Stern, D. 1981. Research on teachers' pedagogical thoughts, judgments, decisions, and behaviors. *Review of Educational Research* 51:455 – 498.

Shavelson, R.J., Webb, N.M., & Burstein, L. 1986. Measurement of teaching. In *Handbook of research on teaching*, ed. M.C. Wittrock, 80 – 86. New York: MacMillan Publishing Co.

Thompson, C., Locander, W., & Pollio, H.R. 1989. Putting consumer experience back in consumer research: The philosophy and method of existential- phenomenology. *Journal of Consumer Research* 16:133 – 146.

Valle, R., & Halling, S. 1989. *Existential phenomenological perspectives in psychology.* New York: Plenum Publishing Corp.

Valle, R., & King, M. 1978. *Existential-phenomenological alternatives for psychology.* New York: Oxford Press.

INDEX